HUNGARY IN REVOLUTION, 1918-19

HUNGARY IN REVOLUTION, 1918-19

Nine Essays

Edited by

IVÁN VÖLGYES

UNIVERSITY OF NEBRASKA PRESS · LINCOLN

Thanks are due to the editors of the *East European Quarterly* for permission to include "Soviet Russia and Soviet Hungary" by Iván Völgyes, which originally appeared in the *Quarterly* in somewhat different form.

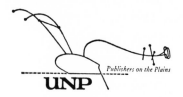

Publishers on the Plains

UNP

Manufactured in the United States of America

To Mary Rowena Völgyes

Contents

Preface

Revolutions, born out of man's disaffection with his environment, out of his impatience with intolerable conditions, and out of a conviction that the future possesses unexploited possibilities, are the proper study of all those concerned with man and his society. Historians have attempted to mark the course of revolutions, charting the great sweep of events leading up to them and recording the myriads of detail associated with them. Social scientists have developed theories about revolutions, have built models to explain how social change takes place, and have analyzed the revolutions of the past. This volume is another attempt at recording and analyzing a series of revolutionary changes. The events with which the essays are concerned took place after the end of World War I in Hungary, in a country where revolts and revolutions have occurred with relative frequency.

Hungary in Revolution, 1918-19 seeks a partial, probing answer to the questions posed by two of the revolutions of Hungary. Looking from the vantage point of well over fifty years, nine specialists on Hungarian history and politics dissect the series of events which occurred in Hungary during the second decade of the twentieth century. It is difficult to determine from a reading of these pages whether the contributors are historians, political scientists, or economists, for a deliberately broad range of expertise is represented by each of the authors. They were chosen for their expert knowledge; only scholars who had previously done research in the area were invited to write articles. It is hoped that the participation in this project by Zsuzsa L. Nagy of the Historical Institute of the Hungarian Academy of Science, whose essay was translated by the editor, will open the way for further joint efforts between American and Hungarian scholars.

These essays, the result of nearly three years of labor, reflect a wide variety of political belief. Their conclusions, tentative and sometimes hypothetical, are based on the best available information. While each essay is complete in itself, taken together they comprise the first comprehensive volume dealing with the subject of the two Hungarian revolutions of 1918 and 1919.

Focused on the history of the turbulent era prior to and immediately after World War I, *Hungary in Revolution* chronologically examines the background and causes of the upheaval. The first two articles by Held and Deák trace the development of the country and consider the contributions of modernization and defeat in the war to the rise of the revolutionary movements. The failure of the liberal bourgeois regime—the first of the revolutionary take-overs—to establish a democratic republic which in turn led to the nonviolent succession of the Communists to power is discussed by Vermes. The internal and external policies of the Hungarian Soviet Republic are treated in succeeding essays. Eckelt deals with the attempts of the Communist regime to accomplish too much too quickly in reforms on the domestic front: Balogh, with the special problem of integrating the many nationalities within the country into the soviet republic, in the face of these nationalities' desires for regional autonomy. The complex foreign problems confronting the regime's Revolutionary Governing Council are discussed by Nagy, while Low concentrates on the relations of the soviet regime with the Allied nations participating in the Paris Peace Conference. The minimal influence of Soviet Russia in the Hungarian Soviet Republic and the vast difference between the two Communist parties' accession to power, make-up, and policies are presented by Völgyes. The concluding essay by Tőkés supplies a biography of Béla Kun, the leader of the soviet republic, and offers a reassessment of his career as a revolutionary.

To assist readers who are unfamiliar with the Hungarian language, all Hungarian titles have been translated in the footnotes, which also in most cases give complete bibliographical information. In some instances it was impossible to ascertain the name of the publisher of a work.

My warmest thanks go to Joseph Held, Associate Professor of History, Rutgers University, who has corrected the page proofs of this volume and prepared the index.

HUNGARY IN REVOLUTION, 1918–19

The Heritage of the Past: Hungary before World War I

Joseph Held

February 13, 1896, was the day on which the mayor of the largest Hungarian city, Budapest, sponsored a ball to celebrate the one-thousandth anniversary of the establishment of the kingdom of the Hungarians. The ball opened at city hall where

> the halls were covered with drapery and flooded by bright lights. At the entrance, Hajdus of the city administration provided honor guards with drawn swords. Entering sponsors of the ball were received by the 86th Regiment Band, playing the Rákoczi-march, and a decorated tent was set up in the center of the main hall for them. . . . Every important person in the city felt compelled to crowd into the ballroom. Three hundred couples danced the opening number, and the celebrations lasted well into the early morning hours.[1]

Similar celebrations and a national exhibit were observed in other towns and cities, signifying a belief that everything was perfect in this best of all worlds.

It is, of course, easy for us to say that these celebrations, filled with a foreboding for the future of Hungary, were the last gasps of a decadent, dying society. In a way such a judgment is correct. Yet most Hungarians were not aware of the dangers threatening their way of life from within as well as from without their state. The tone of this society was set by the *Ausgleich* of 1867, a compromise between the ruling elite of Hungary and the Habsburg Dynasty. The contention of the Hungarian nobility that Hungary had regained her temporarily lost independence by the compromise was partly true. Gyula Szekfű, the most significant Hungarian historian of the interwar years, recognized that

> between 1526 and 1867, no integral Hungarian kingdom had existed. Parts of "Great Hungary," such as Transylvania, were independent; Central Hungary had been controlled by the Turks until the end of the 17th century; the border regions, including Croatia and Slavonia, had been under the control of foreign power during all this time. Hungary's affairs, on the other hand, had been handled by a foreign bureaucracy stationed in Vienna.[2]

1. Ferenc Harrer, *Egy magyar polgár élete* [Life of a Hungarian citizen] 2 vols. (Budapest: Gondolat, 1968), 1:59–60.
2. Gyula Szekfű, *Három nemzedék és ami utána következik* [Three generations and what follows them] (Budapest: Egyetemi Nyomda, 1934), pp. 185–98.

The continuity of Hungarian independence, therefore, was at best an illusion. The myth was strengthened by the brief period following the declaration of independence in 1848-49, which was then negated by the suppression of rebellious Hungary by the troops of Tsarist Russia.

The *Ausgleich* of 1867, therefore, provided for an entirely new situation. With the compromise, the Hungarian ruling elite had finally gained a degree of autonomy to deal with the internal affairs of the state that it had not possessed for hundreds of years. In turn, this elite used its new autonomy to suppress other nations and nationalities, as well as the lower classes of Hungarians. But this elite, despite the outward trappings of dress and style, was not Hungarian in spirit.

The magnates who composed the most important and narrow upper crust of the elite in Hungary, spent a great part of the national wealth in foreign countries. In turn, they performed almost no socially productive work within Hungary proper. Members of this group did have the time, leisure, and money to introduce Wagnerian music and impressionistic painting into Hungary, but their attitude toward the lesser nobles, as well as to other lower classes, was one of a deep contempt. They spent most of their lives in their castles and houses in Vienna, Paris, or Rome, returning to Hungary only at times of important state occasions or at the opening of the hunting season. Naturally, it would be grossly unfair not to mention the fact that there were exceptions to this rule. There were individual members of the Hungarian aristocracy who led highly successful and socially useful lives. To support this contention, one has only to mention Mihály Károlyi, later the first president of the Hungarian republic; Gyula Andrássy, the foreign secretary of the Habsburg monarchy; József Eötvös, liberal and enlightened politician and writer who was the main force behind a humane nationality law enacted in 1868, and Ferenc Deák, a moderate and excellent statesman. These were men of high moral character and of great personal integrity whose participation in the social and political life of Hungary contributed to raising its standards. However, as a class, the Hungarian aristocracy were truly parasites of society.

By the end of the nineteenth century, many of these magnates managed to have themselves elected to the boards of directors of important corporations where they did not have to perform any work and were paid enormous salaries. Many more considered participation in any sort of public activity as being beneath their dignity. In the nineteenth century they lived the lives similar to the great feudal lords of the Middle Ages.

Another part of the ruling elite was made up of the Hungarian gentry. The members of this group were descendants of the lower strata of the ancient nobility. They had considered themselves to be the real nation since the early sixteenth century, when their leader, János Szapolyai (himself already a member of the magnate class), suppressed the great peasant uprising of György Dózsa. István Werbőczi, the author of a Hungarian code of laws, provided this stratum with a philosophy according to which the lower nobility were the true state-creating elements in Hungarian history. It held that they were equal in every respect to the magnates and that they were entitled to the same rights and privileges.3 For almost four hundred years this ideology provided the lower nobility with a false sense of importance in affairs of state.

The reality was, however, that with the passage of time the gentry lost not only its political influence—a great deal of this fell to the Habsburg bureaucracy located in Vienna—but most of its wealth as well. As a result, they retired to their strongholds in the counties, whose administrations they controlled. They exerted every effort to maintain the *status quo* in these institutions. In time, their rule exerted a strangle hold over the counties, dominating every phase of the peasantry's life regardless of their national origin. Often the gentry sabotaged nationwide legislation which they judged dangerous to their interests. Their activities often assumed a patriotic garb, as resistance to the encroachment of foreign ideas and customs on Hungarian national life. Their resistance was especially effective in the case of the legislation of Joseph II during the 1780s, when the Habsburg ruler wanted to reform the monarchy and to transform it into a modern state.4

In the course of the late nineteenth century, many members of the gentry moved to urban areas where they soon occupied positions in the armed forces, in city and town administrations, and in bureaucracies. But moving into the cities did not basically change their ideology; they remained extremely proud of their provincialism and regarded the cities—especially Budapest—as sinful, alien territory grafted onto the body of the true Hungarian nation, i.e., the gentry.5 Any attempts at social reform and any moves toward a more democratic society were regarded by the gentry as a mortal danger to their way of life, and they resisted them accordingly. Social reformers, regardless of their class, were regarded by the gentry as aliens, or at least the carriers of alien ideologies. They especially objected to suggestions of reform in the outdated Hungarian land system.

There is a large and continuously growing literature dealing with Hungary's pre-World War I social and economic problems and its questions of nationality.6 Most writers seem to agree that an extremely uneven distribution of land was one of the major sources of discontent in the country. The origins of this problem may be found in the legislation of the Hungarian revolutionary government of 1848–49. In 1848 serfdom as an economic and political institution had been abolished in Hungary by

3. The original *Tripartitum* was published by Werbőczi in 1517, and it had never formally been accepted as the code of Hungarian laws by the Hungarian diets. Yet it was published in over thirty editions and it gradually became the law of the land.

4. See Bálint Hóman and Gyula Szekfű, *Magyar történet* [Hungarian history] 5 vols. (Budapest: Egyetemi Nyomda, 1936), 5: 9–52; Erik Molnár et al., *Magyarország története* [History of Hungary] 2 vols. (Budapest: Gondolat, 1964), 1: 372–407.

5. Characteristic was the speech delivered by Nicholas Horthy at his entrance to Budapest in 1919; see Admiral Nicholas Horthy, *Memoirs* (New York: Robert Speller, 1957), pp. 104–5.

6. Of this literature several works must be mentioned as most important for the understanding of Hungarian conditions; Gusztáv Gratz, *A dualizmus kora. Magyarország története, 1867–1918* [The age of dualism: History of Hungary, 1867–1918] 2 vols. (Budapest: Magyar Szemle, 1934); Gyula Szekfű, *Három nemzedék* [Three generations] (Budapest: Egyetemi Nyomda, 1920); Robert A. Kann, *The Multilingual Empire: Nationalism and National Reform in the Habsburg Monarchy* (New York: Columbia University Press, 1950), 2 vols., etc.

the government, but the liberated serfs were not given land. Although this legislation was not rescinded after the suppression of the revolution, the peasants were not provided with the basis for a livelihood. The consequence was the emergence of a large mass of agrarian proletarians dependent on their former masters for their living.

The official abolition of serfdom did not solve all of the problems that were characteristic of that institution. Although the privileges of the nobility were somewhat trimmed, they remained the ruling elites of the state. Social habits and customs, in existence for centuries, cannot be changed by fiat. The peasants of Hungary retained not only an inferior status, but also an actual feeling of inferiority in relation to the upper strata of society. Moreover, their economic situation was becoming gradually worse as the century progressed. The world wheat markets slowly became dominated by cheap American grain. The low grain prices, in turn, forced many of the smaller Hungarian landowners—the gentry—into bankruptcy, while the larger landowners gradually absorbed their landholdings. At the same time, the larger landowners began modernizing their production methods, trimming the number of jobs needed to produce larger and larger amounts of grain, and reducing job opportunities for the landless agrarian proletariat. Large numbers of Hungarian peasants, as well as peasants of the non-Magyar nationalities, had no choice except to leave the country in search of a living. Between 1871 and 1898, emigration increased from 119 to 270,000 yearly. Most of the peasants went to the United States, but there were a good number who left for Rumania and other areas of the Balkans.[7]

Among the peasants who could not promise to pay the exorbitant fees that some of the shipping companies demanded of them for their transatlantic trip were those who tried to change social conditions in Hungary proper. The Hungarian Social Democratic party, founded in 1890, began propaganda work in the countryside to support peasant demands. Soon there were disturbances in eastern Hungary, culminating in the peasant uprising at the town of Battonya in 1891, where the gendarmery opened fire on the crowd. Troops had to be moved into the area and the government was forced to use severe repressive measures to calm the countryside.[8] But these measures, coupled with an increasing vigilance against socialist agitators in the villages, were means which treated the consequences rather than the causes of peasant dissatisfaction. The cure would have been the introduction of a thoroughgoing land reform, social insurance for the peasants, and greater government investment in small peasant holdings. Hungarian society as a whole, however, was not ready to accept such reforms. The fact was that this society was basically conservative; the forces of change existed but they were not yet strong enough to make their influence felt. It was not until the beginning of the twentieth century that social reformers were to be heard with greater frequency because by then, the Hungarian middle class had acquired a certain weight in an increasingly restive society.

It seems that one can hardly speak of the existence of a Hungarian middle class, in the usual sense of the term, until about the middle of the nineteenth century. The

7. Hóman and Szekfű, *Magyar történet*, 5:546-47.

8. See István Szabó, *A parasztság Magyarországon a kapitalizmus korában* [The peasantry in Hungary in the age of capitalism] 2 vols. (Budapest: Akadémiai Kiadó, 1965), 2:345-46.

emerging middle class then consisted mainly of German and Jewish merchants with a sprinkling of small industrialists employing a few craftsmen in their shops. By the beginning of the twentieth century, however, this situation had completely changed. Second and third generations of foreigners became assimilated Hungarians. As is usually the case, they often became more zealously nationalistic Hungarians than their native counterparts. The main effort of this stratum of society was directed at freeing itself of the burdens they were forced to carry in a society whose values were still those of the feudal age. The first target for them was the county-system, dominated and ruled over by the gentry,[9] but instead of overthrowing the system, the new middle class eventually joined it. Through intermarriage and assimilation, members of this class gradually accepted the values and mores of the gentry. By the end of the nineteenth century they became ardent supporters of the *status quo* in political, economic, and social life.

Some middle-class members came to occupy important positions in the administration of cities and towns alongside the gentry. Others turned to banking or the wholesale trade. Still others remained as small businessmen, especially in the service industries. Their political and economic interests thus became divergent, and yet, the middle class as a whole was less interested in social reform than in an orderly transaction of business. Consequently, members of this class often sided with the gentry and the magnates in political matters, especially in cases when the question of nationality was involved. In one area the *bourgeoisie* was progressive—the field of education. Most sons of middle-class families were sent to the Gymnasia in Hungary and later attended the universities. Eventually, it was from this stratum that a group of social reformers emerged.

The Hungarian proletariat was basically different from similar social strata in Western societies. It began to emerge and acquire a sense of common identity during the second half of the nineteenth century. By the beginning of the twentieth it comprised about 600,000 members in a population of about 20 million.[10] As a class, the proletariat in Hungary was no more homogeneous than the middle class or the nobility. First of all, it consisted of a great number of transients who spent most of their time in the villages. These men were landless peasants who worked as sharecroppers on the large estates, turning to the towns and industry, particularly the construction trade, when work in the field was no longer possible. They spent the winters in barracks or in shacks on the edges of towns, returning to their homes once in a month and abandoning their jobs at the first signs of spring. Very few of them ever managed to acquire a trade or a skill, and the majority of them remained unskilled helpers. Some of these workers, when they were employed in machine shops and industry, were used to keep the wages of skilled workers at a low level. Such a situation often created tensions between skilled and unskilled labor.

In spite of such antagonisms, there soon emerged strong trade-unions, especially in the city of Budapest where industry became more and more concentrated.[11] The

9. Harrer, *Egy magyar*, 1:175.

10. Molnár, *Magyarország*, 1:165.

11. Samu Jászai, *A magyar szakszervezetek története* [A history of the Hungarian trade-unions] (Budapest: Szakszervezeti Tanács, 1925); Miklós Laczkó, *A magyar munkásosztály feiődésének fő*

Social Democratic party exerted most of its energy in organizing these unions since the workers were not enfranchised. The trade-unions often engaged in violent tactics in order to gain higher wages and better social insurance for workers. There can be little doubt about their success; by the end of the century living conditions were improving for the Hungarian proletariat. A system of medical institutions—small hospitals, pharmacies, etc.—were being extended into the countryside; the government introduced compulsory medical insurance for the workers—not yet for the peasants—and wages were improving. This was part of the general progress in the economic conditions of the lower strata of Hungarian society that was being slowly achieved. Yet, these improvements did not diminish social and political antagonisms between different classes in Hungary. Moreover, the cleavages often cut through class lines. Within the peasantry, for instance, there was much scorn for landless peasants on the part of the more well-to-do peasantry. Village peasants hated those who worked and lived on the large estates as servants. City residents and country people remained deeply suspicious of each other's intentions. These antagonisms were so deep that they were carried over well into the twentieth century.[12] The only clear break within this society appeared to have been between Hungarians as a whole on the one hand, and the non-Hungarian majority of their state on the other.

By the turn of the century the nationality question had reached an acute stage in both halves of the Habsburg monarchy. In the Hungarian half there was, if possible, greater antagonism between the nationalities and the ruling nation than in the Austrian half. Even in recent times, long after these antagonisms supposedly had been solved by the 1919 redistribution of territory among the nations of eastern Europe, they still linger on.[13]

The basic problem in Hungary was that less than half of the population were ethnically Hungarian. After the *Ausgleich* the Hungarians made at least one attempt to solve the cultural problem involved in the situation with the nationality law of 1868. The intent of this law was to arrange for a compromise between the non-Magyar nationalities and the Hungarians. The fact was, however, that the nationalities demanded more than cultural nationalism. They were in the process of establishing ties with their conationals—the Rumanians, Serbians, Czechs—living outside the monarchy or in the Austrian half, and were working for political independence. Moreover, the nationality law was seldom observed in Hungary; the rights of the nationalities were violated continuously by the Hungarian government. Their schools were closed and confiscated; their protests were suppressed by the police; their leaders were

vonásai a tőkés korszakban [The main lines of development of the Hungarian working class in the capitalist age] (Budapest: Kossuth, 1968).

12. See Joseph Held, "Notes on the Collapse of Hungarian Society in the 1930's," *East European Quarterly*, Sept.–Oct. 1968, pp. 303–13.

13. Two works produced in the West must be noted in this matter; Oscar Jászi's *The Dissolution of the Habsburg Monarchy* (Chicago: University of Chicago Press, 1929) and Robert A. Kann's *Multinational Empire*. Recent literature dealing with this problem in Hungary includes Endre Arató, *A nemzetiségi kérdés története Magyarországon* [History of the nationality problem in Hungary] 2 vols. (Budapest: Akadémiai Kiadó, 1960); and Erzsébet Andics, *1848–1849. Tanulmányok* [1848–1849: Studies] (Budapest: Kossuth, 1968).

jailed for long periods of time. Hungarian propagandists spoke of a country of thirty million Hungarians, and of the sacred right of Hungary to "Magyarize" its nationalities.

The Magyarizing efforts caused great indignation among the Rumanians, Croatians, Serbs, and Slovenes.[14] The few representatives who were permitted to enter the Hungarian Parliament found themselves in an alien environment and were continuously insulted by their legislative colleagues. They, in turn, replied to the insults with more insults, often causing fistfights among the representatives. Finally, they boycotted the sittings of Parliament conspiring, instead, to end their participation in Hungarian politics by becoming independent from Hungary.

What aggravated the situation was the connection between the nationality question and the struggle for political power among different social classes in Hungary. The representatives of the nobility—especially the two Tiszas—were fearful that the democratization of Hungarian political life would eventually result in the dominance of the other nationalities.[15] Keeping the non-Magyar nationalities disfranchised, as well as keeping the Hungarian peasants and workers off the voting rolls, seemed to be the only way to maintain the *status quo* and to secure the supremacy of the nobility. Hungarian nationalism was accustomed to frightening the populace about the danger of enfranchising the non-Hungarians; thus, the democratic progress of Hungary was retarded greatly by the unsolved problem of integrating the other nationalities.

The atmosphere between the non-Magyars and the Hungarians was becoming so poisonous by the end of the century, that the smallest insult often caused battles between the antagonists. By the time the celebrations of the Hungarian millennium were held, reconciliation between the two camps was an impossibility. It would be erroneous, however, to maintain that all Hungarians were "jingoistic," or that there was no opposition whatsoever to the oppressive policies of the ruling elites. There was a group of young Hungarian intellectuals, writers, publicists, poets, musicians, sometimes called the second generation of reformers in Hungary,[16] who set out at the beginning of the twentieth century to do battle with bigotry and prejudice in the hope of building a better country for themselves and their children. Their history is the story of the establishment of a radical party in Hungary, of teaching workers and students to fight for their rights, of the founding of the Galilei Circle for self-education, and, indeed, of the revolutionary era in Hungary after the end of World War I.

Today it is hardly possible to write a comprehensive history of this generation for the single reason that the biographies of the participants have not yet been written. Their activities created such opposition within the Hungarian ruling elites, that for more than two decades research on this problem was almost impossible. After World War II, Hungarian historians were too absorbed in problems of correcting the general

14. See Szekfű, *Három nemzedék és ami utána következik*, pp. 199–209; Grátz, *A dualizmus kora*, 2:147–70.

15. See István Tisza's speech in Parliament in *Képviselőházi Napló* [Minutes of the House of Representatives] 2 vols. (Budapest, 1914), 2:20.

16. Zoltán Horváth, *Magyar századforduló. A második reformgeneráció története* [Hungarian *fin de siécle:* History of the second reform generation] (Budapest: Gondolat, 1961).

misconceptions and eliminating the chauvinistic bias in Hungarian historiography to return to the subject of the second reform generation. Only after 1956 was attention turned to their activities, and it is only in very recent times that basic research is becoming possible on this subject.

The designation, "second generation of reformers" in Hungary, is a reflection on the fact that a first reform generation had operated on the Hungarian scene in the nineteenth century. This first generation began acting in Hungarian political life at about the middle of the third decade of that century. Its most outstanding members included Lajos Kossuth, István Széchenyi, József Eötvös, Ferenc Deák, Antal Csengery, László Szalay, and others. Their efforts were directed toward the reorganization of Hungarian economic and political life to correspond to the prevalent liberal ideology of progressive forces in Europe at the time. The labors of this generation came to an end abruptly with the revolutions of 1848-49; they shared the fate of many other European liberals whose ideas had been appropriated by conservative forces after 1850. The *Ausgleich* of 1867 incorporated many of their ideas without accepting the spirit in which these ideas had been formulated. The *egalitarianism* and rationalism of the first reform generation was replaced in the compromise by class consciousness and *Realpolitik*. The second reform generation largely shared the fate of the first. Their labors came to an end in another catastrophe—this time one of worldwide proportions—World War I. Their abrupt ends were the only similarity in the two groups' activities.

If the first reform generation failed mainly because they underestimated the power of conservatism and of the Habsburg Dynasty, the second generation fell because they overestimated conservative power. It is true that they faced overwhelming odds. Men such as Mihály Károlyi, Oszkár Jászi, Ernő Garami, Zsigmond Kunfi, Endre Ady, and Béla Bartók, never succeeded in becoming spokesmen for Hungarian public opinion before 1917. The Hungarian public was too absorbed in its own chauvinism, too selfishly negligent of other peoples' rights and interests, and too blind in recognizing the dangers of nationalism, to take notice of the warnings issued by this generation of reformers. Most of these men remained outside the main stream of Hungarian political and cultural life; most of them were subjected to humiliations and rejection when they advocated a humane and sensible policy toward the subject nationalities as well as toward the lower classes of Hungarians.

The strength of Hungarian conservatism, however, was largely an illusion. It is true that István Tisza ruled Hungary with an iron fist for a long time. It is also true that the police and gendarmery did succeed in quelling the movements of the peasants and workers for reform. But the men in power acted hesitantly, treating only the consequences, not the causes of dissatisfaction. The conservatives succeeded in remaining in power largely because of the lack of self-confidence on the part of the would-be reformers. When revolution finally came, the second reform generation was too fragmented, too enervated, to be able to act in a concerted way. They, too, were drifting with the events instead of giving them a new direction. Herein lies the tragedy of twentieth-century Hungary.

Thus, when World War I began, Hungarian society was utterly unprepared for this great trial of strength. Social tensions were dissolved for a short time in the euphoria of nationalism that followed the declaration of war, but were soon renewed. If the war had been won, it is likely that pressures for reform would have increased until the breaking point was reached. But since it was lost, the dissolution of the Habsburg monarchy became a foregone conclusion, and the nationalities of Hungary saw their opportunity to achieve self-determination. By 1918, as one observer remarked, "the muscles of the state-organism were still contracting and expanding, but such movements were those of a dead body's latent reflexes."[17]

17. Ibid., pp. 549–50.

The Decline and Fall of Habsburg Hungary, 1914-1918

István Deák

The outbreak of the Great War found Hungary the more dynamic and the more self-confident of the two partners in the Habsburg monarchy. With one thousand years of history but scarcely fifty as a fully autonomous state, she gave all the signs of youthful energy. Notwithstanding a recent setback, the Hungarian economy was generally sound; its industrial and agrarian growth rates had few parallels in Europe.[1] The population, despite an emigration of millions in the previous two decades, was on the increase. The cities were fast expanding and in the cities the process of Magyarization was making rapid headway. Following a grave crisis between 1903 and 1906, political stability had been almost completely re-established.

Within the monarchy itself, Hungary was moving toward independence, although a loose union with Austria through the person of the monarch was generally held desirable. Domestic political power was firmly in the hands of the aristocrats and the wealthier gentry who administered Hungary as they did their estates. The civil service, composed mainly of the poorer nobility, was dependable, fairly efficient and, for Central European conditions, remarkably honest. The Socialist Workers' movement, revolutionary in theory if not in practice, had exhausted itself in fruitless mass demonstrations for political emancipation. The wretched and often restive agrarian laborers were held safely in check by the landlords and by the gendarmes. Furthermore, when war broke out, the country had a leader who seemed well-suited to perpetuate that mixture of liberalism and authoritarianism which characterized Hungary's oligarchy. Prime Minister Count István Tisza was steadfast, cunning, intelligent, cautious, and tolerant if necessary, but just as often ruthless. A pessimist by temperament, he was nevertheless imbued with a fanatical belief in the divine mission of the nobility which, in his eyes, was identical with the nation. There was in Tisza and in his fellow politicians nothing of that exasperated resignation, coupled with sudden outbursts of near hysterical truculence, which characterized many of the monarchy's Austrian leaders.[2]

1. For detailed information on the Hungarian economic situation before World War I, see Iván Berend and György Ránki, *Magyarország gyáripara az imperializmus első világháború elötti korszakában, 1900-1914* [The industry of Hungary in the age of imperialism preceding the First World War] (Budapest: Szikra, 1955); József Szterényi and Jenő Ladányi, *A magyar ipar a világháborúban* [Hungarian industry in the world war] (Budapest: Franklin-Társulat, 1933), pp. 9-61.

2. There is no modern biography of Tisza. Gusztáv Erényi, *Graf Stefan Tisza* (Vienna: E. P. Tal and Co., 1935), is thorough but outdated and apologetic. *Tisza István összes munkái* [I. Tisza's complete

Only with the non-Magyar nationalities, and with the neighboring mother countries, did relations become worse in the years preceding the war. Not that the gendarmes were no longer able to keep order among Serbs, Croatians, Rumanians, or Slovaks, nor that the middle-class spokesmen of the nationalities had become less vulnerable to promises, bribes, and occasional persecution, the change had come in the tone of the quarrel. As the verbal militancy of the nationality leaders increased so did the impatience of the Hungarian statesmen. The Social Darwinist slogan of struggle for survival was freely invoked in the Budapest Parliament and the Council of Ministers, and there was a growing conviction that war over the nationality question was inevitable. A campaign against Serbia seemed as good as any. Unlike Rumania, Serbia was not a nominal ally; her people generally were held in contempt in Hungary, and chances were that even the rebellious Croats would rally to the Hungarian flag in a swift campaign against their schismatic and regicidal brothers. It was because of increasing Serbian and Rumanian political agitation that Hungary's political leadership greeted the outbreak of the war with visible relief and grim determination. Tisza himself opposed the idea of a military campaign against Serbia between July 1 and July 10, not because he believed that war could be indefinitely avoided, but because he found the timing inappropriate. He cast a watchful eye on the Balkan situation and feared that recently defeated Bulgaria would not dare side with the Central Powers, whereas Rumania might well attack them. Rumanian intervention would have meant the invasion of defenseless Transylvania and the threat of a native Rumanian uprising there. The German and Austrian solution of securing Rumanian neutrality with territorial concessions and with the granting of autonomy to the Rumanians in Transylvania was totally unacceptable to Tisza. When, at the Common Cabinet Council of July 14, he finally accepted the text and timing of the ultimatum to Serbia, it was because he had been persuaded by Austro-Hungarian diplomacy of Bulgaria's readiness to side with the Central Powers. Bulgarian troop concentrations on the Rumanian border would, Tisza now felt, guarantee the neutrality of Rumania. More importantly, by July 14, Tisza had become conscious of Germany's unalterable decision to wage war against the Entente powers. Consequently, there was nothing for Hungary to do, Tisza reasoned, but to fight on the side of the Germans, who were the ultimate guarantors of Hungarian territorial integrity and greatness. Once he had come to this conclusion, Tisza was as hawkish as his Austrian colleagues and pressed for speedy and decisive military action.[3]

The governing National Party of Work and its press faithfully mirrored Tisza's mental processes. Moderate at the start, the party came out strongly for war when Tisza so decided. The politicians and press of the "Patriotic Opposition," Hungary's

works], 6 vols. (Budapest: Franklin-Társulat, 1924–37) and Tisza's *Tanulmányok és értekezések* [Studies and essays], 4 vols. (Budapest, 1923–27), are of course valuable, as is the doctoral dissertation by Gábor Vermes, "The Political Biography of Count István Tisza" (Stanford University, 1966).

3. See especially, József Galántai, "István Tisza und der erste Weltkrieg," in *Budapest. Tudományegyetem. Annales. Sectio Historica*, vol. 5 (Budapest, 1963), pp. 185–205; and, by the same author, "Die Kriegszielpolitik der Tisza-Regierung, 1913–17," in *Nouvelles études historiques*, vol. 2 (Budapest: Akadémiai Kiadó, 1965), pp. 201–25.

other major parliamentary grouping, were interventionists from the start and later claimed, without any justification, that *they* had "boxed Tisza into the war."[4]

What there was of antiwar sentiment in Hungary during July, and there was a good deal of it in bourgeois democratic, pacifist, and Social Democratic circles, ended abruptly with the declaration of war. Now, suddenly, all embraced what *Népszava*, the daily paper of the Social Democratic party, termed the "Holy cause of the nation."[5] At least among the Magyars, there was no dissent in August, 1914. Nor did the leaders of the nationalities voice any opposition; only from the Serbian regions of Hungary did the police report some dissatisfaction. But since the discontent of the Serbs was taken for granted by the authorities, it is difficult to tell whether the police reports had any real meaning.

The nation went off to war in what all observers described as a mass delirium. "Beware, beware, you dog Serbia," the excited crowds shouted in the streets of Budapest, and also in the Croatian capital, Zagreb, on the day of mobilization. Admittedly, these observers concentrated their attention on the cities, while the few photographs and descriptions of village scenes testify to much less enthusiasm. Village youngsters were called up in the middle of the summer season, an event which no peasant can be expected to cherish. The monarchy was, however, an unsurpassed master in propaganda and popular entertainment; wherever the martial spirit was lagging, the proper atmosphere was promptly created. The assembled clergy blessed the guns and the soldiers; patriotic orators besieged the God of Hungarians to smite the enemy; church bells rang; school children waved tiny flags; and the magnificent Hussar squadrons paraded down the streets with drawn sabres gleaming.[6] Few people, and the realist Tisza was one of them, doubted that the war would be over before the autumn leaves had fallen.

How the Hungarian *ancien régime* declined within four years into complete dissolution, is the subject of this essay. When the front finally collapsed, the old political leadership and the old parties had long been discredited; the civil service was without authority in areas inhabited by non-Magyars, and the politically conscious Magyar population was anti-Habsburg and republican, if not outright socialist and revolutionary. Lamented virtually by no one, the demise of the kingdom in November, 1918, was celebrated as the inauguration of a better era.

Was it the war which swept away royal Hungary and its traditional institutions? Or did the war simply accelerate an earlier process of disintegration? The prewar premonitions of some politicians and of some poets like Endre Ady militate in favor of the latter argument. But there is no convincing evidence to support this thesis. Nor is there, on the other hand, an adequate explanation of the country's wartime deterioration. The collapse of the Dual Monarchy as a whole remains something of a mystery and the most apt interpretation is still Robert Musil's famous "*es ist passiert*" [it sort

4. See Mihály Károlyi, *Egy egész világ ellen* [Against the whole world] (Munich: Verlag für Kulturpolitik, 1923), p. 146.

5. *Népszava* [People's Voice], 3 Aug. 1914.

6. The great writer Zsigmond Móricz has left us a fine description of mobilization day in "Inter arma . . . ," *Nyugat* [West], 1 Aug. 1914.

of happened]. All that can be done, therefore, is to point out certain structural weaknesses and tactical errors which had emerged before the war and became more acute during the conflict. In the case of Hungary, the foremost weakness was that technological development was not accompanied by the necessary social and political changes: it failed to dethrone the landowning nobility. The nobles had been flexible enough to adopt a policy of industrialization, and to entrust Jews and Germans with the process, but they refused to relinquish political power. As the new *bourgeoisie* and, with them, the workers began to clamor for a modest share of this power, the old nobility—and the ennobled *bourgeoisie*—entrenched themselves even more rigidly, arguing cunningly that the inclusion of the disenfranchised Magyar population into the political arena would open the gates to the nationalities as well. Consequently, there was no political reform before the war, a situation tolerable only as long as the country was prosperous and peaceful. With war and its hardships, however, the traditional rigidity of Hungary's rulers became increasingly unbearable. Finally, the Magyar middle class and the workers made a revolution to gain political power.

Ironically, the soon-to-be embattled oligarchy did little to prepare itself for the test of war. As quickly became evident, the country was ill prepared for any kind of armed conflict, let alone what Raymond Aron has called "the first total war in history." Although legislative measures were taken in time to ready the government for a crisis, mobilization plans were inadequate, armaments insufficient and outmoded, and industry was not asked to shift quickly to the demands of war economy.

In 1912 with war already on the horizon, the Hungarian Parliament adopted Law No. 63—"Emergency Measures in Case of War." The law empowered the war cabinets to rule by decree with the single obligation that Parliament be informed of the measures taken. It also authorized the government to appoint district plenipotentiaries with authority over the gendarmery, police, and border guards; to transfer the notoriously harsh gendarmes into the cities; to annul the decisions of municipal councils; to control communications; to suspend associations; to forbid political meetings; to exercise precensorship; and to change the criminal code, imposing long-term prison sentences on strike agitators, etc. Another law, ratified shortly before the war, enabled the government to set up internment camps for undesirable elements. When war broke out, the cabinet immediately availed itself of its new authority, but few of the punitive or coercive measures had to be implemented. Domestic peace reigned and, while censorship was introduced, almost no newspapers were suspended.

The law of 1912 also provided for the introduction of wartime economic measures. The cabinet was authorized to fix price maximums; to draft all adult males up to the age of fifty into the labor force; to impose military control over a number of industrial enterprises; to oblige any industry to produce for the needs of the army; to extract forced deliveries from the agrarian producers; and to confiscate horses and wagons.[7]

7. For an analysis of the law of 1912, see József Galántai, *Magyarország az elsö világháborúban, 1914–1918* [Hungary in the First World War] (Budapest: Gondolat, 1964), pp. 142–43 and 145. Of the many general accounts of this period in modern Hungarian history, Péter Hanák's chapter on the years 1890–1918 in Erik Molnár, *Magyarország története* [History of Hungary] 2 vols. (Budapest: Gondolat, 1964), 2:131–279, is probably the best; other works dealing with the period include: Gusztáv Grátz, *A dualizmus kora. Magyarország története 1867–1918* [The age of dualism: History

Nevertheless, no sooner did war break out, than industry began to suffer from the lack of supplies. The economy, instead of accelerating, fell into a deep depression. Although some recovery followed a few months later, the economic situation remained unsatisfactory throughout the war. The reason for this lay not so much in prewar economic developments—they were generally positive—but in the fact that the economy, with all its progress, was still quite backward,[8] and that grave errors were committed during the war.

Despite all legislative preparations, the first weeks of the war were marked by confusion in the Hungarian economy. When war broke out, the government forbade all civilian transportation and decreed a moratorium on all debt payments.[9] The latter measure led to the disappearance of credit, and even of cash, to the point that banks refused to free currency for the payment of wages. Although a second moratorium, decreed on August 13, remedied this deficiency, no credit was freed for the purchase of raw materials and industrial products. A third moratorium, decreed on September 30, obliged contractors to pay their debts to the extent that they themselves had received payments. Meanwhile, many enterprises had reduced production and some stopped it altogether. The state itself stopped all construction work while orders for ammunition still went to the old armament factories exclusively. Civilian consumption dwindled and unemployment was so widespread that the minister of war had to

of Hungary, 1867-1918] 2 vols. (Budapest: Magyar Szemle Társaság, 1934), vol. 2; Arthur J. May, *The Passing of the Habsburg Monarchy, 1914-1918*, 2 vols. (Philadelphia: University of Pennsylvania Press, 1966); Z. A. B. Zeman, *The Break-up of the Habsburg Empire* (London: Oxford University Press, 1961); Oscar Jászi, *The Dissolution of the Habsburg Monarchy* (Chicago: University of Chicago Press, 1929); Robert A. Kann, *The Multinational Empire*, 2 vols. (New York: Columbia University Press, 1950); and C. A. Macartney and A. W. Palmer, *Independent Eastern Europe*, 2nd ed. (London: Macmillan, 1967). Julius Miskolczy, *Ungarn in der Habsburger Monarchie* (Vienna: Herold, 1959), devotes some attention to the period; and C. A. Macartney's recent, monumental *The Habsburg Empire, 1790-1918* (London: Weidenfels and Nicolson, 1968), presents some brilliant insights. The most comprehensive bibliographies are Walter Schinner, *Bibliographie zur Geschichte Österreich-Ungarns im Weltkrieg* (Stuttgart: Weltkriegsbücherei, 1934), and Karl Uhlirz and Mathilde Uhlirz, *Handbuch der Geschichte Österreichs und seine Nachbarländer Böhmen und Ungarn*, 4 vols. (Vienna: Leuschner & Lubensky, 1927-44), especially vol. 3. On Hungary specifically, see the bibliographical section in Molnár, *Magyarország*, vol. 2. An important source of documentation is Emma Iványi, ed., *Magyar minisztertanácsi jegyzőkönyvek az első világháború korából, 1914-1918* [The minutes of the Hungarian council of ministers during the First World War] (Budapest: Akadémiai Kiadó, 1960).

8. Almost two-thirds of the country's labor force was employed in agriculture and only 17 percent in industry and mining. More than four-fifths of the so-called industrial enterprises were family undertakings with no wage earner or only one wage earner. The total number of wage earners in industrial enterprises employing more than twenty workers barely exceeded 400,000 (out of a population of 20 million).

9. Szterényi and Ladányi, *A magyar ipar*, see also Gusztáv Gratz and Richard Schüller, *Der wirtschaftliche Zusammenbruch Österreich-Ungarns* (Vienna: Hölder, 1930), and by the same authors, *The Economic Policy of Austria-Hungary During the War in its External Relations* (New Haven, Conn.: Yale University Press, 1928). Furthermore, Leo Grebler and Wilhelm Winkler, *The Cost of the World War to Germany and Austria-Hungary* (New Haven, Conn.: Yale University Press, 1940); János Teleszky, *A magyar állam pénzügyei a háború alatt* [The financial affairs of the Hungarian state during the war] (Budapest: Magyar Tudományos Akadémia, 1927); and David Mitrany, *The Effect of the War in Southeastern Europe* (New Haven, Conn.: Yale University Press, 1936).

threaten with punitive measures all enterprises which continued to fire workers. In the middle of August, only thirteen of the two hundred major factories were willing to hire new workers. The supply of labor exceeded demand tenfold. In the construction and luxury industries only one-third of the labor force was engaged in production; fifty enterprises had simply ceased producing.

The moratorium of November 30 brought further relief to Hungarian industry: most payments were freed and firms could refuse deliveries to recipients insisting on the moratorium. But the mistake which lay at the bottom of the government's unwillingness to release credit had further repercussions. Not only was it calculating on a short war, but with the production and consumption levels of the past two depressed years. Government and business alike were afraid of overproduction. Thus, the iron and steel industry, which had experienced a market crisis in the depression year of 1912, decreased production in the second half of 1914. Steel consumption was simply not expected to exceed the prewar level. Yet by the following year, steel production had clearly proved itself inadequate, and the Hindenburg plan for the massive use of steel by the military caused the state to take over the industry in October, 1916.

By the end of 1914, instead of an unemployment problem there was a labor shortage, but by then serious damage had been done. Unemployed workers in essential industries and in mining had been inducted into the army. Now special commissions were sent to the front to search out skilled workers. But since the first months of the war had wiped out a great part of the army, most of the workers could no longer be found. These developments illustrate clearly the different roles assigned by the army high command to Austria and Hungary respectively. In Austria, most skilled workers were exempted from service at the front; in Hungary, thousands were drafted. On the other hand, the Hungarian (but not the Austrian) peasant soldiers were given generous furloughs in the first two years of the war to help bring in the harvest. Throughout the war, Austria was more successful in protecting her trained industrial workers than was Hungary.[10]

More serious than these initial errors was the monarchy's structural inability to recover from them. An efficient war economy was never established largely because the Dual Monarchy, instead of creating a single economic unit, tended to foster the perpetuation of two. For example, during the war Hungarian timber was exported to Austria as to a foreign state. Even though the survival of the monarchy required optimal division of labor, the Hungarian leaders favored Hungarian industry and did not defer to Austria's more efficient industry. As a result, there was no end to Austrian complaints that Hungary was not shouldering enough responsibility and to Hungarian insistence that any departure from constitutionally established proportions was an unfair burden on Hungary.

Because of the immediate and rapid reduction of manpower, draft animals, machine fuel, and the amount of land under cultivation, the 1914 grain harvest in Hungary fell from 60 million quintals to 44 million. At the same time, demand had risen

10. Of the exemptions from military service granted before the end of 1917, Hungarians made up only 26 percent—this despite the fact that the proportion of Hungarians in the armed forces was approximately 45 percent. See Szterényi and Ladányi, *A magyar ipar*, p. 83.

sharply, since every soldier had to be provisioned with a daily ratio of 500 grams of flour. Later the Entente blockade also caused people to substitute bread for rice, meat, potatoes, and other items once imported. Soil exhaustion and negligent farming compounded the already unfavorable situation. Although bread-grain production almost reached the 1913 level in the second year of the war, it fell to 70 percent of that level in the following year. Since Austrian production had also declined, this meant an early, permanent, and alarming deficit, and constant Austrian recriminations. It was true that the Hungarian government allowed a greater amount of grain to be withheld from the official market than did the Austrian government, and ultimately, both governments found it difficult to enforce deliveries. In Hungary, where county officials were often unduly friendly with the local producers, much grain was hidden. In Croatia the situation was even worse because the native administration helped to falsify production figures. By 1917 fear of peasant unrest prevented wholesale requisitioning anywhere in the monarchy. Only the inadequate imports from occupied Rumania and the Ukraine, plus German charity, postponed the collapse. Beginning in 1917 the people of Vienna were starving. The miserable condition of that city further aggravated the traditional Austrian distrust of the Hungarian peasant. As the former Hungarian Minister of Economics Gusztáv Grátz wrote, economic collapse came more quickly because each side sought to "pull over to itself a larger part of the all too small blanket."[11] The whole organism was, indeed, only as strong as its weakest part.

The Hungarian industrial picture during the war was not unlike the pattern which the whole monarchy experienced: after a bad start due to errors and lack of preparation, the mobilizing of all efforts gave rise to a feverish upturn in 1915–16. Then rapid decline followed in 1917, leading to utter exhaustion in 1918. Nevertheless, to the extent that the Hungarian government succeeded in holding on to what it considered its share of the blanket, Hungary's decline and exhaustion were not as great as Austria's, and her recovery in peacetime somewhat less problematic.

Orders for military supplies—of which Hungary assured herself 36.4 percent according to constitutionally established proportions—began to come in after the first few months of the war. Fierce competition for contracts ensued and industry pulled out of its slump in the winter of 1914. Measures to insure industrial labor supply (the law on universal labor service) and the inflationary policy of the government produced a sharp upturn in 1915–16, which meant surpassing 1913 levels for certain commodities. Hungarian coal production, to give one example, suffered no crisis until late in the war. Hungary, which continued to receive the bulk of the monarchy's coal imports throughout the war, managed to cover over half of the needs of the Austro-Hungarian war industry as late as 1917–18. Austria, on the other hand, which had always produced four times as much coal as Hungary, could cover only less than half. When the lack of coal shut down many flour mills in Hungary early in 1917, it was due more to bad transportation than to an actual shortage of coal.

Similarly, iron and steel production, after the initial faltering, revived in 1916 to

11. Gratz and Schüller, *Der wirtschaftliche Zusammenbruch Österreich-Ungarns*, p. 140.

optimum prewar levels. Only by the end of the war did it decline to two-thirds of that level because of transporting difficulties and weakened labor. In an average machine plant, the labor hours necessary to complete one machine increased to more than fourfold of the requirement in 1913. All in all, the decline in iron and steel was less critical in Hungary than in Austria.

The manpower shortage was somewhat compensated for by the massive employment of women, youth, and prisoners of war. In a veritable population exchange the Dual Monarchy and Russia captured—and employed—about one and a half million prisoners each. The Russian prisoners, supplemented by a significant number of Rumanians, Italians, and Serbs, were put to work mainly in agriculture, half of them in Hungary. They were usually well-treated, especially on small farms where they often became virtual members of orphaned families. Still, their forced labor was only an inadequate stopgap.

The cost of the war was staggering, even when compared with the enormous expenses of other countries. According to specialists, Hungary's "direct" war cost (feeding, clothing, and providing living quarters for the armed forces, and equipping them with arms and ammunition) amounted to eighteen billion gold crowns, almost three times the country's gross national product in the last year before the war.[12] Losses due to railroads and roads not repaired, houses not built (in Budapest in 1916 only twenty-nine licenses were issued, mainly for the construction of one-story apartment houses),[13] soil exhaustion, forfeited increases in population, etc., remain almost incalculable. Surprisingly, all these sacrifices were but insufficiently translated into military power.

Few states glorified the military as much as did Austria-Hungary before the Great War. Because it was the ultimate guarantor of political unity, the army stood under the direct patronage of the monarch. The officer's position was most exalted; his uniform commanded unquestioning respect and he was duty-bound to take immediate bloody revenge for an insult suffered from a civilian. The aim of every educated youth was to acquire the coveted title of *Leutnant der Reserve*. And yet, mainly because of Hungary's opposition to the "common" army and her constant haggling over "common" expenses, the Dual Monarchy operated with proportionally the lowest defense budget of all the European great powers. In 1911, when military preparations began in earnest, the defense budget of the monarchy was less than one-fourth of that of Russia and a bit over one-fourth of that of Great Britain.[14] Even by 1914 the Austro-Hungarian army had not trained all able-bodied men of military age: following mobilization, four hundred thousand of them could not be inducted for lack of military training. At the same time, the army was unable to accommodate and equip all the trained reservists. The cadres of existing regiments (especially of the eighty-eight infantry regiments) became rapidly overstaffed, and thousands of men wasted

12. On the enormously complicated problem of Hungarian war costs, see Teleszky, *A magyar állam*, pp. 401, and passim, and Grebler and Winkler, *The Cost of the World War*, pp. 130, and passim.
13. Szterényi and Ladányi, *A magyar ipar*, p. 248.
14. Macartney, *Habsburg Empire*, p. 791.

precious weeks waiting to be reassigned. New units, in which neither officers nor men knew each other, had to be created in haste.[15]

The first months of the war were a disaster for Austria-Hungary, due partly to the old, bravura style of fighting insisted upon by the generals. The losses suffered in Galicia and Serbia were so enormous that the army would have dwindled by the end of 1914 had there been no replacements. It became necessary to send a monthly supplement of a "march battalion" to every infantry regiment in the front lines. Hungary, which had about 180,000 men under arms before the war, inducted 1.6 million reservists following mobilization, and a further 2 million during the four years of the war. This could be achieved only by mobilizing the previously untrained, by lowering physical requirements, by eliminating several categories of exemptions, and by extending military obligation from ages 21–42 to 18–50. Territorial regiments and other support units, originally intended for occupation and garrison duties, had to be incorporated into front-line regiments, a process which led to a catastrophic increase in casualty figures.

Austria-Hungary mobilized some 8.3 million men during the war. Of these, 3.8 million or 45 percent were Hungarian citizens. This is a relatively high figure if we consider that Hungary's share in the total population of the monarchy was only 41 percent. Although no two sources agree on casualty figures, all historians concur that Austro-Hungarian casualties were horrendous, proportionately perhaps the highest of all the warring powers. According to the most conservative estimates, close to two-thirds of the monarchy's soldiers were either killed, wounded, or taken prisoner during the war. To this must be added the unknown number of those who suffered from such various illnesses as malaria (in the Balkans); typhus, dysentery, cholera, and frostbite (in the East); or Spanish influenza (on all fronts in 1918). Of the Hungarian soldiers alone, at least 660,000 were killed or died during the war, 740,000 were wounded, and 730,000 were taken prisoner by the enemy. These casualty figures were higher than for the other half of the monarchy. Specifically, the heaviest casualties were suffered by the German-speaking soldiers of Austria and the Magyar- and German-speaking soldiers of Hungary. Casualties among the Croatian and Slovene soldiers of the monarchy were somewhat less severe, and among the other Slavs, the Rumanians, and the Italians even less so.[16]

The explanation for this lies not so much in the relative unreliability of Czech, Polish, Ukrainian, Serbian, Italian, and Rumanian soldiers and in their willingness to surrender, but in the enemy occupation of parts of Galicia, Bukovina, Ruthenia, and Istria early in the war, and the impossibility of recruiting soldiers from there. Furthermore, the Magyar and Austro-German population was generally of better health than the other nationalities and thus qualified more easily for military service. Finally,

15. For a scathing indictment of Austria-Hungary's lack of preparation for war, and of Hungarian responsibility for it, see General Alfred Krauss, *Die Ursachen unserer Niederlage*, 2nd ed. (Munich: J. F. Lehmann, 1921), pp. 28–29, 63–66, 90–108; Rudolf Kiszling, *Österreich-Ungarns Anteil am Ersten Weltkrieg* (Graz: Strasny, 1959); Colonel Ferenc Julier, *1914–1918: A világháború magyar szemmel* [The world war seen through Hungarian eyes] (Budapest: Magyar Szemle Társaság, 1933).

16. See Wilhelm Winkler, *Die Totenverluste der öst.-ung. Monarchie nach Nationalitäten* (Vienna: Seidel, 1919), pp. 6 and 8.

the army high command was so suspicious of certain nationalities that it soon acquired the habit of sending Austro-German and Magyar (as well as Croatian, Slovene, and Bosnian) troops to the more dangerous fronts. Rural areas generally yielded a greater proportion of soldiers than did the cities. Since these peasant soldiers served mainly in the highly exposed infantry regiments, the rural areas—thus most of Hungary— suffered the heaviest casualties.

According to agreements concluded between the monarchy and Hungary before the war, Hungarians served either in the so-called common army or in the much smaller Honvéd army, a semiautonomous military organization in which the language of command was Hungarian. But even in the common army, in which the language of command was uniformly German, there was little mixing of soldiers originating from the two parts of the monarchy. Careful distinction was made among Austrian, Hungarian, and Croatian troops; only in Bosnia-Herzegovina, a commonly acquired and administered colony, were there two "mixed" army corps.

Territorial divisions in the army did not mean linguistic uniformity within one unit. On the contrary, because of the multilingual character of each half of the monarchy, most army units exhibited bewildering linguistic multiplicity, and even in Hungary's own Honvéd regiments there was often a non-Hungarian-speaking majority. There were many companies in which officers, noncommissioned officers, and enlisted men spoke three or more different languages and in which almost no one understood German or Hungarian.[17]

It is one of the myths of Austro-Hungarian history that non-Germans were systematically excluded from command posts in the army. On the contrary, the officers' corps was open to all races (and to almost all social classes) and between 1907 and 1912 the proportion of Slavs increased quite significantly. By the end of the war, there were 166 German-speaking generals, many of them from Hungary, but also 94 Magyars, 64 Czechs and Slovaks, 25 South Slavs, and a number of others. Of the monarchy's 6 field marshals, 2 were Germans, 2 Magyars, and 2 South Slavs.[18]

The first few months of the war brought about the virtual elimination of junior professional officers and of trained, first-line soldiers. Thereafter, the army of the Dual Monarchy was led on the junior level by officers of the reserve. It was also manned to a large extent by soldiers who in peacetime would have been considered too old, too young, or too weak for military service. By 1918, a substantial section of the army consisted of former casualties: men who had been wounded previously or who had fallen prisoners to the Russians and were repatriated after the Bolshevik revolution.

Hungarian politics and politicians exercised a fair amount of influence on Austro-Hungarian military strategy. In the winter of 1914/15, for instance, Tisza's fear of a

17. In theory, every officer in a "common" regiment was obliged to know the language of command (German) and the language of the regiment (the majority language of the district in which the regiment was recruited). But language barriers became almost insurmountable because of the rapid promotion of reserve officers, the constant shifting of personnel, and reduced training period for all. Macartney, *Habsburg Empire*, p. 556.

18. Wilhelm Winkler, *Der Anteil der nichtdeutschen Volksstämme an der öst.-ung. Wehrmacht* (Vienna: Seidel, 1919), p. 3.

Russian invasion of Rumanian-inhabited areas of Hungary, and of subsequent intervention by Rumania, caused the army high command to mass inordinate forces in the Carpathians for an attack across the snow-covered mountains. The campaign was a total disaster with hundreds of thousands of casualties.[19] On the other hand, when in August, 1916, the Rumanian army penetrated defenseless Transylvania with relative ease, Tisza was fiercely criticized in the Budapest Parliament for having placed high strategy above Hungarian national interests.[20] The Hungarian government thereupon used all its persuasive power for an immediate campaign of revenge against Rumania, and the ensuing transfer of German troops from the western front seriously weakened German positions there.

Throughout the war, the production of armaments failed to keep pace with the needs of the army. Armament production increased significantly after an initial crisis in 1914, but by 1917 there was a new decline due to the lack of raw materials and the decreasing productivity of workers. The army went to war with 3,366 pieces of artillery produced by the Škoda works in Bohemia. By 1918, there were 9,585 cannons, a still pitiful figure.[21] There were also too few machine guns in 1914 and almost no barbed wire, indispensable for trench warfare. These deficiencies, as well as the shortage of rifles and ammunition, were never completely overcome. Toward the end of 1914 there was a serious shortage of leather and garments because the reserves of the army administration had been exhausted and the newly ordered products had not yet arrived. This situation was vastly improved by 1915, but in the following year things were again almost as bad as they had been in late 1914. Toward the end of the war, the majority of soldiers were dressed in rags, walked on paper soles, and received food rations which were barely enough to keep body and soul together.[22] This army was infinitely less well fed, equipped, clothed, and led than its German or Entente counterparts; miraculously, it managed to fight on until early in November, 1918. True, the soldiers of the Dual Monarchy were never very good at offensive warfare and on such occasions had to be bolstered with German assault troops. But on the defensive, the Austro-Hungarian army fought both bravely and efficiently. This can be explained only by the particular patience, stoicism, and steadfastness of the Central and East European peasantry, and by the phenomenon common to many warring countries that the loyalty to the state of the soldiers at the front lasted longer than that of the population at home.

While the Austrian Reichsrat did not meet until May, 1917, the Hungarian Parliament held regular sessions during the war.[23] As a consequence, much that was withheld from the population of the other half of the monarchy was fully debated by deputies in Budapest. Austrian journalists rapidly acquired the habit of scanning Hungarian parliamentary reports for bits of confidential information. It is true that

19. Julier, *1914-1918*, p. 90, and passim.

20. Galántai, "Die Kriegszielpolitik," p. 223.

21. Gratz and Schüller, *Der wirtschaftliche Zusammenbruch Österreich-Ungarns*, p. 110.

22. Macartney, *Habsburg Empire*, p. 830.

23. The Hungarian Parliament consisted of an upper and a lower house. By 1914 much of the former power of the upper house had passed to the lower house, also called the House of Representatives.

the wartime survival of the Hungarian Parliament was only possible because of its exclusive social and ethnic composition.[24] But then, Parliament gave strength to the government in the latter's dealing with other organs of the monarchy. It prevented the military take-over of Hungary (much of Austria fell under military jurisdiction soon after the outbreak of the war), and it assured the survival of a harsh but still legalistic civilian bureaucracy. Peacetime politics continued during the war, with a few months of truce being followed by almost four years of the traditional Hungarian parliamentary quarrel.

Arno J. Mayer writes in his *Wilson vs. Lenin* that in the major belligerent nations there was "a precarious equilibrium in domestic politics immediately preceding the outbreak of the war." This was followed by the re-establishment of the political equilibrium in favor of the forces of order, i.e., the old regimes, between August, 1914, and March, 1917. A period of "acceleration," which was to outlast the war, then set in, during which the "forces of movement"—pacifists, Socialists, and revolutionaries, as well as the traditional opposition parties—came to the fore, their ranks swelled by the discontented masses.[25] Mayer's contention is valid for Hungary—which he did not investigate—with the modification that the rapid growth of popular discontent should be dated from 1916 and not from 1917, while "acceleration" in higher political circles, and in the Parliament, did not really begin until the end of the war.

In 1914, the absolute majority of deputies belonged to Tisza's National Party of Work. The Patriotic Opposition consisted of a much divided Party of Independence, with a right wing led by Count Albert Apponyi and its far left by Count Mihály Károlyi. There was also a Constitutional party under the younger Count Gyula Andrássy; a Catholic People's party (which pressed for social legislation and was somewhat anti-Semitic) under Count Aladár Zichy, and a number of other small parties. The differences between Tisza's party and the opposition were mainly over "public law," that is Hungary's relations to the monarch and to Austria, with the National Party of Work insisting on the preservation of the Compromise of 1867, and the opposition on a reform of the compromise in favor of Hungary. Economic interests fairly well coincided with the two basic divisions in politics: in one camp were the "Agrarians" under the leadership of the enlightened landlord Count Sándor Károlyi, and Apponyi, Zichy, and Andrássy; and in the other, the "Mercantilists" under the leadership of Tisza. The Agrarians, who were supported by the conservative aristocracy, stood for landed interest and, at least in theory, for a loose union with the other half of the monarchy. The Mercantilists, who were supported by big (mainly Jewish) business, most of the high functionaries, and a few landowners, favored rapid industrialization and upheld the compromise agreement.[26] Mihály Károlyi and his small group of followers who favored domestic political equality and a "personal

24. One out of every four adult males had the right to vote. There were only a handful of deputies in the lower house representing the non-Magyar nationalities, and neither factory workers nor agrarian laborers had any representation.

25. Arno J. Mayer, *Wilson vs. Lenin : Political Origins of the New Diplomacy, 1917–1918* (Cleveland: Meridian, 1967), p. 9.

26. See Iványi, *Magyar*, p. 38.

union" with Austria were outside the political structure in 1914, even though they belonged to the Party of Independence and thus were formally members of the Patriotic Opposition. Their support came mainly from the urban, Jewish middle class and from among part of the gentry. Károlyi himself wielded some influence only because he was one of Hungary's foremost magnates.

Unlike the Károlyi group, the two main parliamentary camps were one in advocating unconditional alliance with Germany and harsh treatment to be meted out to the potentially traitorous nationalities, and in warning against the dangers of suffrage reform. There was, however, a good deal of personal animosity between politicians in the two camps and a tradition of verbal extremism which had caused a serious crisis in the Hungarian parliament some ten years before the war.

The first wartime parliament met in November, 1914. By then Mihály Károlyi was back from his visit in the United States and a brief internment in France. Overwhelmed by appeals to party discipline and Hungarian patriotism, he pledged full support to the war.[27] Since all the other politicians vied with each other in declarations of loyalty, there was no obstacle to Tisza's energetic conduct of the war effort. A series of laws followed, strengthening the emergency measures provided for by the law of 1912. Tisza's position was bolstered by the support of the Catholic church, until then an enemy of this economically liberal, philo-Semitic, and staunchly Calvinist statesman. Indeed, throughout the war the church leaders outdid themselves in asking for ever greater sacrifices and in formulating wild plans for Hungarian expansion into the Balkans and the Near East through the use of missionaries.

The horrifying losses suffered during the war, and the persistent rumor that the high command was using Magyar troops as cannon fodder, led to the first grumblings in Parliament and to the opposition's demand that the heroism of the soldiers be politically rewarded. In April, 1915, the Party of Independence suggested, rather vaguely, that suffrage be granted to veterans of the front. This demand was coupled with equally vague recommendations for economic independence and a separate Hungarian army. Thus began the long debates in Parliament on the extension of suffrage and on national independence, debates which seemed to obscure the more pressing social questions and problems of nationality, and the threatening military and economic disaster. In reality, the issues of suffrage and independence came to be closely tied to those of peace and fundamental social change; but while suffrage and independence could be openly discussed in Parliament, peace and social reform could not be mentioned without incurring the accusation of treason. In a show of spite, all the major opposition parties voted in May, 1915, against the budget. Such an event would have wrecked the German Reichstag; in Hungary, where Tisza had an absolute majority and where such dramatic political gestures were traditional, parliamentary life continued.

The year 1916 brought grave setbacks to the Central Powers: the failures at Verdun and in South Tirol, the Brusilov offensive on the eastern front, and the entry of Rumania into the war. Now Tisza himself began to worry. The armies of the monarchy

27. Galántai, "Die Kriegszielpolitik," Gratz, *A dualizmus kora;* Macartney, *Habsburg Empire;* Hanák's chapter in Molnár, *Magyarország;* and Iványi, *Magyar.*

had been saved only by German assistance; for this they were to submit to German military leadership. Tisza was particularly galled by what he considered unfavorable trade relations with both Austria and Germany. Hungarian currency began to deteriorate fast; the introduction of an income tax and a war gains tax failed to slow down the inflation. In the lower house the opposition continued to indulge in spectacular gestures. At one point it walked out of the chamber as a body. Károlyi made himself especially unpleasant by asking pointed questions. Now, finally, the extra-parliamentary opposition of Social Democrats and of democratic-pacifist intellectuals began to make itself heard. To quiet the Social Democratic workers, the government extended military control over thousands of factories, regulated overtime pay, and ordered the creation of joint factory grievance committees consisting of employers, trade-union delegates, and representatives of the civil and military authority.[28] The joint committees ruled almost invariably in favour of the worker-complainants. Demands for some kind of land reform arose from the most unlikely quarters, as for instance from among the landowning Catholic bishops. The government itself began to make plans for land expropriations after the war to reward highly decorated or mutilated soldiers.

The first major shift in political winds occurred in July, 1916, when Mihály Károlyi resigned from his nominal post as president of the Party of Independence and from membership in the party. A few days later he founded, together with some twenty other deputies, the "United Party of Independence and of 1848." This was an odd combination of democratic intellectuals and ultranationalist gentry. Still, they could agree on a program of peace without annexations; "personal union" with Austria; economic, financial, and military independence for Hungary; general, secret, and equal elections; land reform; and social welfare legislation. Only the nationality question was left unmentioned. For the first time, there existed a major oppositionary group outside the pale of the Patriotic Opposition. The Károlyi party, as it came to be known, was to form the nucleus of the revolutionary government which assumed power in Hungary at the end of October, 1918. In fact, the political alliances concluded after July, 1916, foreshadowed postwar developments; and most of the politicians who stepped into the limelight between 1916 and 1918 were later to become revolutionary or counterrevolutionary leaders.

The Rumanian intervention in August, 1916, precipitated a drive for the resignation of Tisza who had always been cordially hated by the opposition politicians for his alleged dictatorial ambitions. Securing his resignation required the tactical unity of the entire opposition. Consequently, the Patriotic Opposition, instead of disavowing the renegade Károlyi, concluded an alliance with him and used him as a spearhead for attacks against Tisza. In so doing, such superpatriots as Apponyi or Andrássy were led to voice Károlyi's views on peace without annexations, although they still categorically repudiated his criticism of Germany. But it needed the death of Francis Joseph in November, 1916, and the accession to the throne of the peace-minded Emperor Charles (King Charles IV of Hungary) for Tisza's dismissal to become a practical possibility. Even though Charles had no difficulty in replacing the common

28. See especially Szterényi and Ladányi, *A magyar ipar*, pp. 84 ff.

foreign minister, the Austrian prime minister, and the chief of the general staff, all of whom were in the way of Charles's search for peace, it took several months before he could rid himself of the Hungarian prime minister. Meanwhile Tisza had prevailed upon Charles to have himself crowned king of Hungary and to swear allegiance to the constitution. At the coronation in Budapest in December, 1916, the Protestant Tisza had the supreme satisfaction of helping to place the holy crown on the head of His Apostolic Majesty. Two months later, Tisza was again in trouble in the House of Representatives on the issue of suffrage for "heroes." Political antagonisms had now become exacerbated. All sides feared national disaster, but while Tisza hoped to save the old order by changing nothing, the moderate opposition opted for token adjustments, and the Károlyi party for sweeping reforms. This situation was like pre-March, 1848, resurrected, save that Károlyi did not have the eloquence and charisma of Kossuth, and the moderates had no one with the wisdom of Deák. There were also other differences: the nationalities argued from an infinitely stronger position than before 1848, and in 1917 the Great Powers were leaning in the direction of the dismemberment of Hungary.

The February revolution in Russia only confirmed the three political camps in their convictions: the spread of revolutionary ideas was to be countered with force, moderate change, or drastic reforms and a separate peace with the Entente, respectively. The king himself sided with the moderate opposition but he also began to make cautious openings toward Károlyi. The Social Democratic party and the trade-unions entered the picture again, concluding a silent alliance with the opposition for a campaign against the prime minister. Meanwhile there were hundreds of local strikes for better wages and better working conditions, most of which were modestly successful. The king now requested that Tisza make public a plan for substantial suffrage reform; the government instead campaigned against such a reform. On May 22, 1917, Charles ordered the prime minister's resignation.

Undoubtedly, Tisza's policy of no change was disastrous for the survival of "Great Hungary," but it is also true that he had no worthy successor. The two prime ministers who followed him, Móric Esterházy and Sándor Wekerle, were weaklings, and Károlyi, the only person who could have saved Hungary, was not appointed prime minister until October 31, 1918. Károlyi himself, a man of enormous good will and foresight (A. J. P. Taylor called him a "saint"), lacked the necessary strength in conception and execution of truly revolutionary politics.

Tisza's resignation was followed by Social Democratic mass demonstrations for general, equal, and secret suffrage. At the same time, and rather incongruously, the leaders of that party entered into a secret agreement with Andrássy, the most likely candidate for the prime ministership, on the limited extension of suffrage (voting rights to be granted to all literate males over 24 and to all war veterans, but with open ballots to be maintained in rural areas). In June, 1917, the Social Democrats entered into a "suffrage bloc" with the Károlyi party and other small democratic, radical, and Christian social groups.[29] This was the Social Democrats' first open political alliance

29. For the history of Hungarian bourgeois radicalism, or of the democratic parties of the period, see Gyula Mérei, *Polgári radikalizmus Magyarországon, 1900–1919* [Bourgeois radicalism in Hungary],

with bourgeois parties, and it proved lasting. At the war's end, the suffrage bloc was to transform itself into a revolutionary National Council. Thus, a month before the future Weimar coalition came into being in the Reichstag, the Hungarian Left created its own postwar coalition.

The sudden importance of the Social Democrats was all the more amazing as this party had numbered only fifty thousand adherents before the war[30] and had never been permitted by the government to send a delegate to Parliament. Apart from a few outstanding men, party leadership consisted of decent and dedicated mediocrities. Mostly they were Jews and typical city people who had no intention of recruiting followers from among the millions of agrarian laborers. Their orthodox Marxist creed, and the government's prohibition against agitation among the peasants, only reinforced this basic disinclination. In fact, they were content to lead their devoted and fairly well-indoctrinated flock of Budapest artisans and factory workers. Organized closely after the Austrian model, Hungarian social democracy engaged in customary revolutionary rhetoric and in reformist action, none of which brought substantial achievements. The strength and the weakness of the party lay in its close association with the trade-unions, of which it was the political arm. Despite rigorous discipline, the party was unable to prevent its intellectuals from dissenting; criticism came mainly from the Left, from the direction of revolutionary syndicalism. Conforming again to the Austrian, and the German model, the party violently denounced war preparations in July, 1914. A few weeks later it reversed itself to advocate a determined struggle against Russian despotism. Social Democratic and trade-union functionaries were thereupon entrusted with the task of helping to organize war production but they never achieved the importance of their wartime German colleagues. In 1915, workers' agitation forced the party to end its truce with the government and the Social Democratic press took up the issues of military control in the factories, low wages, high prices, and long working hours. It also resumed its time-honored campaign for universal suffrage. A year later, peace without annexation was added to the party's program. Meanwhile, the trade-unions had undergone a grave crisis and then engaged in a phenomenal career. Before the war, the trade-unions had 107,000 members. Following the outbreak of the war, membership declined rapidly because

(Budapest: Karpinszky ny., 1947), and György Fukász, *A magyarországi polgári radikalizmus történetéhez, 1900–1918* [On the history of Hungarian bourgeois radicalism. A critique of Oszkár Jászi's ideology] (Budapest: Gondolat, 1960). Also, Károlyi, *Egy egész világ ellen* [Against the whole world] (Budapest: Gondolat, 1965) and, by the same author, *Memoirs* (New York: E. P. Dutton, 1957); Oscar Jászi, *Revolution and Counter-Revolution in Hungary* (London: King and Son, 1924); Theodor (Tivadar) Batthyány, *Für Ungarn gegen Hohenzollern* (Zurich: Amalthea-Verlag, 1930).

30. See Zoltán Horváth, *Magyar századforduló. A második reformnemzedék története, 1896–1914* [Hungarian fin de siécle: The history of the second reform generation] (Budapest: Gondolat, 1961), p. 349. *A magyar munkásmozgalom történetének válogatott dokumentumai* [Selected documents from the history of the Hungarian labor movement], vol. 5, *November 7, 1917–March 21, 1919*, ed. Mrs. Sándor Gábor et al. (Budapest: Szikra, 1956). See also: Erzsébet Andics, "A magyar munkásmozgalom as 1914–18-as világháború alatt" [The Hungarian labor movement during the world war], *Századok* [Centuries] 82, nos. 1–4 (1949):24–78; Pál Pándi, "A szociáldemokrata irodalom magatartása az 1914–18-as világháborúban" [The attitude of Social Democratic literature in the world war], *Irodalomtörténet* 39, no. 3 (1951):290–315.

of mobilization, lockouts, and popular indifference to the ideological dictates of class struggle. At the end of 1915 there were only 43,000 dues-paying trade-unionists. Then membership began to climb, first slowly, then very quickly. At the end of the next year, there were still only half as many organized workers as on the eve of the war but at the end of 1917 more than twice as many, and at the end of 1918 more than seven times as many.[31] Workers were prompted to join mainly because of the efficiency of the factory grievance committees, but in 1917 business clerks also began to enter the movement and, in 1918, it drew engineers, city employees, railroad officials and, finally, civil servants. The reason for this increase lay not only in the gradual lifting of government restrictions, but also in the rapidly deteriorating condition of the white-collar workers. By the end of 1916, the real income of business clerks had dropped to less than half of its prewar level. In the following two years only the wages of skilled artisans and skilled factory workers kept up, to a degree, with the inflation. By December, 1918, the cost of living index rose to 858 in comparison with the prewar level of 100. At the same time, the wage index of skilled artisans stood at 810, of skilled factory workers at 458, and of unskilled factory workers at 397. But for private employees the index stood at 282, and for civil servants at 183.[32] The massive influx of politically untrained laborers, female workers, and employees drastically changed the nature of the trade-union movement and gave it an "immediatist," revolutionary direction.

On June 8, 1917, the king appointed Count Móric Esterházy as prime minister. Andrássy was not chosen because he was considered too pro-German. Nevertheless, he greatly influenced the choice of the cabinet ministers, who included several of his followers, as well as Apponyi of the Party of Independence, Zichy of the People's party, and Count Tivadar Batthyány and Vilmos Vázsonyi, both of the suffrage bloc. This was then a cabinet of the moderate opposition, enlarged by two representatives of the radical opposition. The acknowledged task of the cabinet was to bring about suffrage reform but the king also hoped that the government would support him in his secret peace negotiations. The Esterházy cabinet met with widespread enthusiasm and expressions of hope for peace and social progress. The young and modest prime minister earned further acclaim when he paid a personal visit to the editorial offices of the Budapest newspapers, among them the main Social Democratic newspaper.

Károlyi says justly in his memoirs that the summer of 1917 was the Dual Monarchy's last chance to emerge from the war relatively unscathed.[33] The situation at the front was very favorable: Russia was on the way out of the war; the Italians had been unable to break through (at year's end they would be almost annihilated); the armies of the monarchy still numbered three and a half million men. It is probable that the western Allies would have reneged on at least part of their promises to then occupied Serbia and Rumania, had the Habsburg monarchy sued for a separate peace. Charles wanted peace desperately but, as is well known, he was willing to make sacrifices

31. Szterényi and Ladányi, *A magyar ipar*, pp. 208 ff. On the sociological composition of the Hungarian working class, see also: Miklós Lackó, *Ipari munkásságunk összetételének alakulása, 1867-1949* [Changes in the composition of our industrial working class] (Budapest: Kossuth, 1961).

32. Szterényi and Ladányi, *A magyar ipar*, pp. 222 ff.

33. Károlyi, *Memoirs*, p. 88.

only at the expense of Germany. His secret peace feelers ended in abject humiliation. Could Hungary have seceded alone from the war? Undoubtedly a great part of public opinion was ready to support such a move; the suffrage bloc was especially willing. There would have been territorial losses: Croatia certainly, and perhaps parts of Transylvania and southern Hungary. Still, losses could not have been terrible with Russia, Serbia, and Rumania prostrate, and the minority nationalities at home relatively quiet. Indeed, the non-Magyars had patiently shouldered the sufferings of the war. Some Rumanian and Slovak soldiers (but not the Croats or the Ruthenes) had surrendered voluntarily to the enemy, but at home peace reigned and that not only because of the vigilance of the gendarmes: unlike the *émigré* politicians, the domestic leadership of the nationalities suspended judgment on the future of the Hungarian kingdom until the end of the war.34 The old order still had a chance in 1917 to assure its survival, at least temporarily.

The Esterházy government neither put out peace feelers, nor did it institute suffrage reforms. Tisza still held an absolute majority in the lower house and he would not hear of substantial change. The only way out was to dissolve Parliament and to govern dictatorially. This Esterházy did not even consider undertaking, while the most ardent advocate of general suffrage in the cabinet, the bourgeois democratic Vázsonyi, surrendered rapidly to the conservatives—and to the pleasures of office-holding. The miserable failure of this talented and popular Jewish politician put the seal on reform efforts within the old system. One reason for the lack of any progress was, as Károlyi noted in his memoirs, that the landowning aristocracy had profited substantially from the war and their representatives in Parliament were not willing to engage in experiments.

Esterházy soon tired of his job, and in August, 1917, ceded the prime ministership to Sándor Wekerle, an old and little respected political tactician. Although Wekerle took over Esterházy's entire cabinet, it was clear that the much touted era of reform had ended before it had even begun. The new prime minister, who was of German descent, was reputed to be staunchly pro-German. From the time of his appointment the old order would try to hold on to power while awaiting German victory. Opposition to the old order would pass into the streets, the factories, the military barracks, and the secret conclaves of revolutionary intellectuals.

The growth of radicalism inside and outside social democracy will be the subject of other essays; here it is enough to note that there were scores of such small radical groups whose influence among the workers was increasing. The bulk of the activists was made up of writers, poets, journalists, students, and, surprisingly, engineers, but even the more moderate literati had by 1917 embraced the cause of peace and universal fraternity.35 Considering that the political influence of men of letters had always

34. On the non-Magyar nationalities during the war, see Péter Hanák, ed., *Die nationale Frage in der Österreichisch-Ungarischen Monarchie, 1900–1918* (Budapest: Akadémiai Kiadó, 1966), and Constantin Daicoviciu, ed., *La désagrégation de la Monarchie Austro-Hongroise, 1900–1918* (Bucharest: Éditions de l'Académie de la République Socialiste de Roumanie, 1965).

35. On the Hungarian literati and the war, see Farkas József, "*Rohanunk a forradalomba.*" *A modern magyar irodalom útja, 1914–1919* ["We are rushing into the revolution." The path of modern Hungarian literature] (Budapest: Bibliotheca, 1957).

been very great in Hungary, their role in the radicalization of the masses cannot be overestimated.

The October revolution and peace negotiations in Brest Litovsk added fuel to radical agitation. Not only the extremists, but the Social Democratic leaders and the entire bourgeois press celebrated Lenin's assumption of power, if for no other reason than because it seemed to hasten the defeat of the Entente. Naturally, governmental measures were taken to prevent the spreading of Bolshevik propaganda in Hungary. The number of gendarmes was raised at the end of 1917; certain gendarme units were transferred to the capital; censorship was made more rigorous; and prisoners of war returning from Russia were kept in quarantine for weeks for the purpose of re-education. The latter endeavor, bravely attempted by the clergy, must have been quite ineffectual for no sooner were the former prisoners of war sent to the front, than Bolshevik cells made their appearance there.[36]

In January, 1918, a general strike broke out in Budapest, immediately spreading to the other industrial centers and embracing half a million workers. Although the strike wave followed upon those in Berlin and Vienna, the Hungarian strike had been long prepared by small radical groups. The demands were for better wages, a just peace with Soviet Russia, and an immediate end to the war. The Social Democratic leadership joined the strike only to put an end to it in a few days after Wekerle had promised sweeping reforms in the vaguest possible terms. Soon there were fresh disturbances. In all probability, the majority of organized workers had no desire for bolshevism and were, therefore, willing to obey the orders of their party, but the initiative had now passed into the hands of the previously unorganized workers, and of the soldiers. The first half of 1918 saw scores of wildcat strikes, and several revolts in the barracks. It became most difficult to ship recruits to the front; many escaped from sealed boxcars. The forests of Hungary, and especially of Croatia, teemed with deserters—the so-called Green Cadres—who engaged in banditry and/or partisan warfare, often with the connivance of the peasants.

Their customary conceit and self-satisfaction now blinded the old regime politicians to the real situation. Their numerous confidential statements testify to an acute premonition of national disaster, still they refused to believe that Hungary was threatened with dismemberment. Instead, they vigorously pursued territorial expansion. During peace negotiations with Rumania in March, 1918, they engaged in fierce arguments with the Austrians over annexations, finally securing parts of Rumania for their country. But at least they tried to settle accounts with their domestic enemies. Back in January Wekerle had transformed his cabinet, dropping Batthyány (of the suffrage bloc) and appointing two followers of Andrássy who were strongly pro-German. He then proceeded to create a new "government party," consisting of the old Patriotic Opposition, Vázsonyi's Democratic party, and a few members of Tisza's National Party of Work. Vázsonyi, as minister of justice, prepared rigorous measures against the revolutionaries. It is to the old regime's credit that only then, in

36. See Antal Józsa and József Gazsi, "A magyar hadifoglyok hazatérése Szovjetoroszországból" [The return of the Hungarian prisoners of war from Soviet Russia], *Hadtörténelmi Közlemények* [Military History] 8, no. 2 (1961):792–854.

the spring of 1918, were some radical leaders arrested and the revolutionary activist Galilei Circle dissolved.[37] The government party made vigorous overtures for a coalition with the Party of Work: this necessitated the dropping of all pretenses of substantial suffrage reform. In April, 1918, Wekerle again reshuffled his cabinet, dropping Apponyi and Andrássy, who had refused to make further concessions on suffrage reform, and appointing two of Tisza's followers. Finally, in July, 1918, a modest suffrage reform was adopted by the House of Representatives.

By that time the new Right was as dissatisfied with the government as was the Left. New personalities had come forward who were using extremist language against old-regime liberalism, the nationalities, the workers, and especially the Jews. Anti-Semitic propaganda was the specialty of the clerics, with Bishop Prohászka, István Milotay, Pater Béla Bangha, and other future ideologists of the "Christian-National" counterrevolution distinguished for their odious statements.

Undoubtedly anti-Semitism was on the rise in Hungary, especially among the middle class but also among the peasants. Jews were accused of war profiteering and revolutionary agitation; meanwhile it was conveniently forgotten that business, and the organization of the working-class movement, had once been gladly left to Jews; nor did it make much difference that Jews had contributed their share in men and casualties to the war. For the time being, the yearning for peace and hatred of the old regime prevented the massive spread of anti-Semitism. But it would erupt with particular fury following the experience with Jewish Democrats and Jewish Bolsheviks in 1918–19.

In June, 1918, there was another general strike with half a million participants. Now, finally, agitation spread to the nationalities who also began to act, not as dis-satisfied workers or peasants, but as members of soon-to-be sovereign nations. The Croatians had been consistently readying themselves for secession; now the Slovaks also began to move, forming a nationalist coalition at the end of May. Still, all eyes were turned toward the western front, where General Erich von Ludendorff had promised a breakthrough. The German offensive failed during the summer, as did the Piave offensive of Austria-Hungary. At the end of September, Bulgaria surren-dered. There were no troops left to stop the Entente armies moving north from the Balkans. On October 16, Emperor Charles issued his famous manifesto on the federalization of the Austrian half of the monarchy but not—because of the Hungarian veto—of the lands of the Crown of St. Stephen. Thus on that day Hungarian states-men still believed that they could preserve the territorial integrity of Hungary without even giving autonomy to the nationalities. On the following day, Tisza admitted in the House of Representatives that the war was lost. Still, a few days later the Hungarian government could confidently decide that, because of the federalization of Austria, the compromise agreement had become null and void and that Hungary had regained her full sovereignty. She would be bound to Austria only through the person of the

37. On this fascinating group of predominantly Jewish students, see Márta Tömöry, "*Uj vizeken járok.*" *A Galilei Kör története* ["I'm walking on fresh waters." The history of the Galilei Circle] (Budapest: Gondolat, 1960); also, Jolán Kelen, *Galilei-per a XX. században* [Galilei trial in the twentieth century] (Budapest: Kossuth, 1957); and Rudolf L. Tőkés, *Béla Kun and the Hungarian Soviet Republic* (New York: Praeger, 1967), p. 20, and passim.

monarch. On October 23, Wekerle resigned but was asked by the king to remain at his post. Feverish negotiations began for his succession, with Charles personally interviewing candidates in Hungary. By that time national committees had taken charge of Bohemia, the South Slav provinces, Galicia, parts of Transylvania, and even of German Austria. Finally, on October 25, the Hungarian suffrage bloc transformed itself into the Hungarian National Council under the leadership of Károlyi, the bourgeois radical sociologist Oszkár Jászi, and the Social Democrats Ernő Garami and Zsigmond Kunfi.

The manifesto of the National Council called for the independence of Hungary; an immediate end to the war; the dissolution of the House of Representatives; new elections based on general, secret, and equal suffrage which would include women; freedom of the press; amnesty to all political prisoners; emergency measures to prevent the spread of famine; land reform; partial expropriation of the "accumulated capital"; and the application of Wilsonian principles in regard to the nationalities. What the latter meant was not made clear, but it is certain that even the National Council upheld the territorial integrity of Hungary. That the Hungarian parliamentary Left was still far from throwing all legality to the wind is shown by the fact that Károlyi wanted the king to appoint him prime minister. He was not to have his way. Upon the advice of Andrássy and others, Charles appointed Count János Hadik prime minister on October 29. Hadik had a reputation as a strong man and troops were put at his disposal for the re-establishment of order. But Hadik was not to have his way either.

Already on October 28 there had been a mass demonstration in Budapest for a government to be formed by members of the National Council. Army units attempted to stop the demonstrators from marching on the royal castle in Buda; there were three killed and many wounded. On October 30, disturbances broke out again at the news of Hadik's appointment. Overnight, Budapest fell into the hands of revolutionaries with a soldiers' council assuming control in the name of the National Council. General Géza Lukachich, the commander of Budapest, tried to suppress the revolt but found himself without soldiers or policemen, all of whom either went over to the revolutionaries or returned to their barracks. During the night of October 30 and 31, members of the National Council were still certain they would be arrested by the police. On October 31, they were presented to the jubilant crowd as the new government of revolutionary Hungary. The king himself gave his belated approval of the popular appointment by telephone on the same day.

The delirious "October Days" marked a great triumph of the workers and soldiers who had formed the bulk of the Budapest demonstrators. But there were hundreds of thousands of other demonstrators from all social classes in the Magyar-inhabited areas of Hungary. The nation felt that it had good cause for celebration. The war was over and independence had been won; there would be political equality and social justice for all. What was hard to realize then, and would be for decades to come, was that with the old order two-thirds of Hungary would also disappear.

The October Revolution in Hungary: from Károlyi to Kun

Gábor Vermes

"Revolutions are born and not made.[1] . . . The Revolution arrived as a hurricane, no one prepared it and no one arranged it; it broke out by its own irresistible momentum."[2] These eyewitness accounts of the Hungarian October revolution of 1918 underscore the common denominator of most revolutions: an unbounded explosion of spontaneous forces.

"We had to face Fate! A victorious nation is able to endure a society in decay . . . but with such a society, defeat in a war becomes unbearable. The revolution had to come to usher in those virtues which enabled us to reconcile ourselves to a lost war."[3] These words of a Hungarian writer summarized the close connection between the actual circumstances of the late summer and early fall of 1918 in Hungary and the inevitability of a revolutionary upheaval.

The old order collapsed under the harrowing weight of a lost war, and under a sense of guilt, both self-inflicted and aroused by an embittered public. This collapse, therefore, was not only political but also spiritual. "In order that no one else should annihilate us we decided upon suicide. . . ,"[4] wrote Count Gyula Andrássy, in his latter-day recollections. The known symptom of revolutions was to occur: the ruling classes and parties lost their faith in themselves.

Nothing could indicate this moral prostration more than the example of Count István Tisza, the symbol and paragon of the old order, who was both the highly respected and the violently hated strong man of tradition-bound Hungary. After the proclamation of the October 16 manifesto, which transformed the Austrian part of the monarchy into a federal state, Tisza joined with most of the other Hungarian politicians in renouncing dualism and in welcoming a Hungary with an independent army and foreign service, tied to Austria only through the person of the emperor-king. On Tisza's part, this renunciation of dualism was the abandonment of a lifelong conviction which had previously guided all his thoughts and actions. On October 18,

1. Oscar Jászi, *Revolution and Counter-Revolution in Hungary* (London: King and Son, 1924), p. 18.

2. Ferenc Göndör, *Vallomások könyve* [The book of confessions] (Vienna, 1922), p. 19.

3. Farkas József, ed., *Mindenki ujakra készül* [Everyone is preparing for the new] 2 vols. (Budapest: Akadémiai Kiadó, 1962), 1:67.

4. Julius Andrássy, *Diplomacy and the War* (London: J. Bale, 1921), p. 225.

in the Parliament, he let slip the words "we lost the war," and according to an eye-witness "what he said and did after that were the movements of a half-dead sleep walker."[5] On October 31, he was assassinated by a group of soldiers who held him responsible for the war. Falling to the floor, mortally wounded, his last words were, "it had to happen this way."[6]

If such was the case with the statesman, known to be the firmest and the strongest among the old guard, then it may not come as a surprise that the emerging power vacuum was not filled by the weak and the hesitant, whose feverish, last-minute activities could not conceal their mounting sense of defeatism. During the second half of October, all speculations and machinations to save what could be preserved from the old order proved to be forlorn hopes. On October 23, the Wekerle government resigned and no other government was formed until October 29. King Charles negotiated with politicians of a broad spectrum, finally appointing Count János Hadik, a well-meaning but insignificant aristocrat, as prime minister. However, on October 25 a national council was established, composed of members of the Károlyi party, the Radical party, and the Social Democratic party. By the last week of October, civilian power and moral support were behind this National Council and behind its acknowledged leader, Count Mihály Károlyi.

Who was Mihály Károlyi and what was the character of his party and of the Radical and Social Democratic parties, the future ruling parties of the revolution? According to a popular joke in Hungary, it is even impossible to stage a revolution without a count. This joke reflects the extensive role played by Hungarian aristocrats in Hungarian political life. Count Mihály Károlyi, however, was no average aristocrat, and as the leader of a revolution he had to break with his class. Born into one of the richest and most influential aristocratic families of Hungary, he became the heir and beneficiary of an immense fortune. During his college years, his monthly pocket money equalled the monthly salary of the prime minister of Hungary. A strong determination helped him overcome the physical handicap of defective vocal cords, but he nevertheless appeared to squander his money, time, and energy for no useful purpose. Considering the frivolous and extravagant way of life of most Hungarian aristocrats, his behavior brought forth no censure, it was taken for granted.

Yet, the seeds of his future change of mind and heart were already sown by his heritage. The traditional outlook of his family was anti-Habsburg, based partly on trying to atone for the betrayal of Hungarian independence by a paternal ancestor, and also upon the still vivid memories of the 1848 revolution and war of independence in which the Károlyis took an active part.

One of his uncles, Count Sándor Károlyi, was the founder of the cooperative movement in Hungary. He was conservative, religious, and a firm believer in the leadership of his class, not for its own sake, but for the good of all, in the best tradition of *noblesse oblige*. Count Sándor Károlyi hated laissez-faire capitalism; he read Marx's criticism of capitalism with approval but without embracing Marxian socialism. Unlike its English counterpart, this altruistic Tory "socialism" did not flourish in Hungary, mainly because of differences between British and Hungarian aristocratic

5. József, *Mindenki*, p. 50.
6. Gusztáv Erényi, *Graf Stefan Tisza* (Vienna: E. P. Tal and Co., 1935), p. 378.

traditions and character. Yet, the uncle's influence upon his young and bright nephew, Mihály, was evident.

These potential elements of future change notwithstanding, Count Mihály Károlyi was still regarded as a fundamentally conservative magnate. In 1909, at the age of thirty-four, he was elected president of the OMGE (National Agricultural Society), the powerful organization of Hungary's landowning class. In 1910, he was elected member of Parliament on the platform of the Party of Independence, and, in 1912, he became the chairman of that party. The party was divided into several factions and Károlyi moved to occupy the leadership of the left wing in the wake of the aged and ailing Gyula Justh. The left wing of the Party of Independence advocated a policy for broadening the base of political participation by extension of the suffrage; it further concerned itself with basic social issues and the problem of national minorities. In addition, it was groping for a new orientation of Hungarian foreign policy, hoping to substitute for the German "clutch" an alliance with the Entente, and with France in particular.

In spite of the seemingly popular appeal of these points, this left-wing faction remained isolated. It found itself in the midst of a largely indifferent peasant population which lacked education, political sophistication, and the majority of which was not even included in the electoral register. A mere 5.8 percent of the total population in 1910 had the privilege to vote. Eligibility was based on relative wealth and social status, and the enfranchised class was, for the most part, lukewarm, if not outright hostile, to social progress, to granting more rights to non-Magyars, and to any unsettling turnabout in foreign policy. In short, they were opposed to any radical change of the *status quo*. Consequently, when, in 1916, Károlyi broke with the Party of Independence and founded his own party, only about twenty members of the Parliament followed him.

By 1916, the hardships of World War I led to the dissolution of the *"union sacré"* of all parties as heavy losses at the fronts and war weariness generated a growing desire for peace. A demand for peace was added to the newly formed Károlyi party's platform which was already concerned with independence and social progress. The Károlyi party, however, was particularly unsuited for meaningful leadership, because it lacked a social base and unity. Consequently, it lacked the necessary initiative to organize under the restrictive circumstances of the war. The moral and political quality of several of its members also was questionable. In Oszkár Jászi's opinion, "it was neither a true middle class nor a peasant party . . . there was little of the spirit of Justh and Károlyi in the leaders of the Party, and it included all sorts of political malcontents and adventurers." [7] The judgment of Károlyi himself was no less harsh: "many members of the Károlyi Party withdrew from the Party of Independence only because they could not succeed there for some personal reason. I cannot maintain that either an idea of revolutionary pacifism or of a social ideology bound them to me; part of them wished merely to assure a better position for themselves." [8]

7. Jászi, *Revolution*, p. 22.
8. Mihály Károlyi, *Egy egész világ ellen* [Against the whole world] (Budapest: Gondolat, 1965), p. 141.

The question is still open as to what were the precise reasons and motives for Károlyi's transformation from a rich, spoiled, playboy aristocrat to an advocate of democracy. His enemies stigmatize him with charges of demagoguery, personal vanity, and unbridled ambition. They also assume that due to the power of Count Tisza, Count Andrássy and Count Apponyi, who, respectively, were the leaders of the conservative right, the center, and the left of center, Károlyi could only take over the solitary commanding position remaining in the Hungarian political arena: the leadership of the Left. It seems likely that Károlyi was not entirely devoid of personal vanity and ambition. A certain degree of aristocratic nonchalance and lofty amateurism never quite disappeared from his character, not even when he became a "tribune of the people"; yet, one cannot deny his fundamental sincerity in his gradually evolving desire to understand and to help the average man, both in the cities and in the countryside.

In Hungary, the first two decades of the twentieth century witnessed the blooming of a left-radical intellectual activity which was both encouragingly vigorous and painfully pathetic. It was vigorous in its criticism of the establishment and in its hopes for the future, but it was pathetic in its isolation from Hungarian society at large. The number of its outstanding exponents and the number of its adherents was relatively small. The same people clustered around the journals *Huszadik Század* [The twentieth century], the *Nyugat* [The west], and the newspaper *Világ* [The world]. The same people congregated in associations such as the Sociological Society and the Galileo Circle. These groups consisted of "a few intellectuals who by talking to each other and writing to each other made themselves believe—so far as they succeeded in doing so— that they had a camp and an echo in the country." [9] In fact, they did not. The only social class the radicals could have relied on was the Hungarian middle class. This class was timid and philistine, loyal and subservient to the establishment, and was much more prone to imitate the gentry or to embrace the "coffee-house liberalism" of a Vilmos Vázsonyi than to embark upon radical adventures. When the Radical party was established in 1914, one of the founders wrote, "The platform of the Radical Party is a platform of the opposition; it demands something different from what the government wants. [The only problem is] that the country does not agree with that platform. Not even the middle class [supports it] . . . anyone who has anything to lose, even a penny, supports the government." [10]

The leaders of the party, Oszkár Jászi, Pál Szende, and others, were of the highest intellectual caliber, but they were accused by the Hungarian Right of being pedants whose doctrines and political schemes were far removed from Hungarian reality. The accusers were correct if one understands reality as the ground for immediate action and accomplishment. The criticism was rather superficial, however, because social justice and equal rights to all national minorities, the major components of the party's platform, were conceived of as long-range goals, based on a profound and

9. Zoltán Horváth, *Magyar századforduló. A második reformnemzedék története, 1896-1914* [Hungarian *fin de siécle*. The history of the second reform generation, 1896-1914] (Budapest: Gondolat, 1961), p. 387.

10. Ibid., p. 532.

perceptive scrutiny of Hungarian reality. Yet, even if one accepts the relevance of their platform to the distant future, the party catapulted itself to the top of academic respectability by its intellectual and moral excellence and thereby lost its opportunity to exert a vital influence over the instantaneous and imminent course of Hungarian history.

The Social Democratic party was the only party which, at that time, had a popular program and a tight organization as well. The Hungarian party followed the orthodox Marxist line of the German and Austrian parties, but specific conditions in Hungary accounted for several dissimilarities. The Hungarian Socialists shared their German and Austrian comrades' disdain of the peasants who were looked upon by them as a conservative force eager only to preserve their private property or to gain some. The Hungarian Socialists added—if only in a concealed way—the national minorities to their list of mistrust. In Austria, Socialist theoreticians Otto Bauer and Karl Renner designed grandiose plans in an attempt to solve the nationality problems of the empire, but they had contact with the better educated and more prosperous minorities, the Czechs, Slovenes, and Poles. In Hungary, on the contrary, most of the Slovaks, Rumanians, Serbs, and Ruthenians belonged to the peasant class, held in contempt by the Socialists. Also, the intense indoctrination of all Magyars with the idea of Magyar superiority affected the attitudes of the Hungarian blue-collar workers. Furthermore, the German and Austrian parties were compelled to deal with questions of national importance from a broader point of view as soon as they became respectable parliamentary parties. In Hungary, the Social Democratic party never reached this stage. The party was not driven underground, but it was an object of incessant harassment from the authorities.

During the prewar period, the entire activity of the Hungarian Socialists was absorbed in a struggle for survival, for universal suffrage, and for reaching immediate economic gains for the working class. The bulk of the leadership consisted of trade-union officials, most of whom were former workers. They were honest but not out-standing; indeed, none of them possessed the qualities of a great leader. The party itself, its lip service to orthodox Marxism notwithstanding, did not develop a revolutionary character, since it felt obliged to concentrate on seeking instant results in a forceful but nonrevolutionary way. The outward strength and cohesion of the party was misleading, precisely because of the discrepancy between its doctrinaire adherence to a professed revolutionary ideology and its actual performance. In the case of the Hungarian Socialists, this predicament was aggravated by their semioutlawed status which deprived them of experience in handling national affairs on a higher level.

At the outbreak of World War I, the Hungarian Social Democratic party was not represented in the Parliament as a result of an unfair franchise system, and, thus, it derived the advantage of not having to vote for the war and assume partial responsibility for it. From about 1916 on, as disillusionment and war weariness began to affect the national morale, the party moved toward a definite antiwar policy, and in the course of 1917 and 1918 it launched trenchant assaults for achieving universal suffrage.

During the summer of 1918, workers' councils were formed in Budapest, but these councils failed to catch up with the fast-moving events of the times. A few days before the outbreak of the revolution, János Vanczák, the representative of the ironworkers, proposed arming the workers of Budapest. The proposal was received with complete indifference.[11] This stand of the workers' councils reflected the mentality of the party leadership which was in full control of the councils.

This leadership was rather confounded by the unexpected events of October, 1918. Suddenly, the near schizophrenic ambiguity of their policy came to the fore. A never expected opportunity for revolution arose. An old dream seemed to come true; yet the leadership responded to this challenge more with a sense of shock than with an exhilarating welcome. One of the Socialist leaders, Ernő Garami, expressed his doubts, "Are the masses of Hungarian workers mature enough to let the party jump from the street straight into the ministers' armchairs in the Parliament?"[12] The question was posed, but no Socialist leader returned a definite answer.

The Social Democratic party, the Radical party, and the Károlyi party, then, were the forces represented in the National Council. They were prepared to act, without quite knowing how. The obstacles in Károlyi's path to power were melting away rapidly. "Even the greatest enemies of Károlyi wished him to take power. Tisza himself advised the nomination of Károlyi."[13] The motives behind this strange support was not a sudden recognition of Károlyi's abilities as a leader, but rather a shrewd move to leave the steering of the ship in stormy weather in the hands of those who, with considerable reluctance, had declared their readiness to step on the deck and seize the rudder. It was also generally assumed that the victors in the war would be more lenient to Károlyi, whose pro-Entente sentiments were well known, than to any other politician.[14] The general concensus also held that only Károlyi could establish friendly relations with the neighboring countries and conclude an honorable peace; in short, only he could save the country.

Károlyi and his supporters were in a precarious position. They did not want a revolution and wished to avert one if at all possible. "The crowd was expecting and demanding deeds while upstairs we were trying to find a peaceful solution."[15] The demands upon the National Council grew daily by leaps and bounds as the mechanism of the state ceased to function. Associations, parties, clubs, and distinguished public figures rushed to join the council, and even the Budapest police force declared its allegiance to the council on October 29, only a day after firing at demonstrators.

The big question mark in Budapest was the loyalty of the army. The local garrison was composed of several Magyar and non-Magyar regiments (including mostly Bosnian Serbs). No one could be certain about the loyalty of these troops. As a further complication, the military commander in Budapest, General Géza Lukachich, was known to be a tough soldier and a staunch supporter of the dynasty. The atmosphere in the city was extremely tense. On the night of October 30/31, the outbreak

11. Manó Buchinger, *Küzdelem a szocializmusért* [Struggle for socialism] (Budapest: Népszava, 1947), pp. 11, 23.

12. Ernő Garami, *Forrongó Magyarország* [Revolutionary Hungary] (Vienna: Pegazus, 1922), p. 21.

13. Andrássy, *Diplomacy and the War*, p. 284.

14. Ibid., p. 261.

15. Károlyi, *Egy egész világ ellen*, p. 379.

of revolution was triggered by soldiers, acting upon the orders of the Soldiers' Council, an organization independent from the National Council. Soldiers occupied the Central Post Office, the central telephone switchboard, the banks, and various other public buildings. During the same night, in the Hotel Astoria, which served as the headquarters of the National Council, the leaders of the council expected at any moment an attack by Lukachich's troops. "When we found that the explosion had come, that a few hot-headed and impatient officers had commenced action on their own responsibility ... we were dismayed at the news," wrote Oszkár Jászi, the leader of the Radical party. Jászi at one time during the night turned to the Socialist Zsigmond Kunfi, saying "we shall probably hang at dawn." "I expect so" was the reply.[16]

The troops of Lukachich, however, stayed in their barracks. Their martial spirit was already undermined by the fact that the war was lost and by the constant anti-military agitation among their ranks, but the major factor in this inactivity was the king's order to General Lukachich to refrain from bloodshed, and thus to avoid a civil war. On the following day, October 31, the king appointed a coalition government with Károlyi at its head. Represented in it were the parties which had constituted the National Council—the Radicals, the Socialists, and the followers of Károlyi. The revolution had won its first major battle.

The crowds in Budapest were ecstatic. Every able-bodied person, old and young, was on the streets waving a chrysanthemum which became the symbol of the revolution. Trucks, loaded with soldiers and workers, were cheered by jubilant onlookers. A sense of instant triumph seemed to blend with the expectation of a bright future.

This revolution, no doubt, was the revolution of the people of Budapest. In the somewhat cocky words of an observer, "Who was the Brutus, the Robespierre, the Trotsky of the Hungarian Revolution? ... The people of Budapest, the marketplace of Budapest, the soldier from the Józsefváros, the sailor from Óbuda, and the students from the Galileo Circle ... the victory was quite easy, it was a joke.... We put an end to the war with a flip and shook off that monster as if it were an odious nothing."[17]

The news of the revolution spread to the countryside with alacrity but the revolutionary spirit did not spread. The enthusiasm of the Hungarian peasants and small-town burghers was tempered by their perennial and deep-rooted suspicion of Budapest. The city was an island within the land—huge, fascinating, but strange. The city was proudly, even ostentatiously, Hungarian, but it also claimed its rightful place along with Vienna, Berlin, perhaps even Paris and London. The city life, in the peasants' view, was to be admired, but also to be feared and avoided. Eventually, certain measures, such as a successful land reform, could have somewhat eased the tension between Budapest and the provinces, but the basic elements of conflict did not disappear because of the abrupt explosion of the revolution.

One should also be careful not to overestimate the significance of the joy the people of Budapest manifested in those October days. That joy was a rational and somewhat limited endorsement of the revolution. In part, this endorsement was an emotional

16. Jászi, *Revolution*, p. 32.
17. József, *Mindenki*, 1:194.

release from the strain and suspense of the preceding war years. Soon, the revolutionary fervor was channeled into an agitation for a republic. This development was surprising because Hungary had no republican tradition except for the short-lived Republic of Kossuth in 1849. Opposition to the Habsburgs rested on a hostility to an alien dynasty rather than to a royal form of government. However, an overwhelming desire for immediate results is a cardinal part of revolutionary outlook, and it is much easier to vary form than to alter substance. Also, the fall of the Hohenzollerns in Germany, the Romanovs in Russia, and most significantly, the Habsburgs in Austria, impressed people as a mark of a universal cataclysm for crowned monarchs everywhere. The republican bandwagon started to roll with an increasing number of adherents on board, including even the king's representative in Hungary, Archduke Joseph. The archduke, in fact, carried a major responsibility for exerting pressure on the king to release the Károlyi government from its oath to the crown and for persuading the king to withdraw from the affairs of the Hungarian state. The motive behind the archduke's position was hardly a sign of sincere republicanism; rather it was fear of the possible further spread of revolutionary activity, even perhaps violence, should the king resist the public's compulsive demands.

King Charles yielded reluctantly, and on November 1 he freed the Károlyi government from its oath. On November 16 the founding of the Republic of Hungary was proclaimed in front of the Houses of the Parliament. The Socialist leaders, Kunfi and Garami, were the principal speakers. The emotional Kunfi made a fiery and exuberant speech, whereas the sober Garami spoke very briefly, "we have talked a great deal, let us now start to work!"[18] The city was in no mood to follow Garami's advice. People were still in a state of joyful frenzy as "everyone, from the archbishops down to the chimney sweepers, swore allegiance to the Republic."[19] Alas, before long, the harsh facts of reality brought forth a bitter awakening from the "honeymoon" spirit of the revolution's early days and weeks.

As a result of devastating defeats and chaos at the front, train after train arrived in Budapest, and each coach was overcrowded with Hungarian soldiers. Their surge was spontaneous for the most part, but it was legalized by the new revolutionary government's order, which on November 1 called for their return. The regime thus incurred the charge of disrupting the unity and fitness for fighting of a still-intact front.[20] In fact, however, by the time the Hungarian government's order was issued, the disintegration of the front had advanced into an irreversible stage, and General Victor Weber was already on his way to Padua to conclude an armistice for the entire Austro-Hungarian army.[21]

Had revolutionary propaganda caused and expedited the rout of this army, or did the state of demoralization at the front originate in the war-weariness of the soldiers?

18. Garami, *Forrongó Magyarország*, p. 53.

19. Katalin Károlyi, *Együtt a forradalomban* [Together in the revolution] (Budapest: Gondolat, 1967), p. 446.

20. Gusztáv Grátz, *A forradalmak kora* [The age of revolutions] (Budapest: Magyar Szemle, 1935), p. 40.

21. Sándor Juhász-Nagy, *A magyar októberi forradalom története* [The history of the Hungarian October revolution] (Budapest, 1945), p. 248.

The "stab-in-the-back" theory, of course, always appealed to people who wished to explain defeat as the final outcome of a conspiracy. Among the ranks of the military, a modicum of political radicalism certainly was manifest, especially after the soldiers, who had experienced the Russian revolutions as prisoners of war, were released, transported home, and sent again to the front. The average peasant soldier, however, was immune to any kind of political propaganda, and a less intricate but more plausible interpretation would simply assume a sincere and compelling desire for peace after four years of carnage and misery. Therefore, the words of Béla Linder, the minister of defense in the new revolutionary government, "I do not want to see soldiers any-more," although quite unfortunate in the light of Hungary's still pressing defense needs, were probably of no great importance in influencing the average soldier.

The yearning for a tranquil life was universal and was expressed by a Hungarian poet with touching force:

To a Returning Veteran

On the road of the Army's march
Fallen leaves cover the path

Please come, the old home waits
The sorrowful, gentle, with open gates

Wipe out from your heart four years of hell
As children awakening from a dreadful spell

The gun is dropped under a happy sky
The churchbell is ringing and spirits run high

Into shovel and spade is the bayonet cast
As the tired old veteran sheds his past

From the filthy trench of Death, full of tears
Emerges the wonder of golden wheat sheaves

The hobnailed boots, torn to rag and shred,
Will lead you home to your nuptial bed

Throw all evil out with your cartridge case
All the ghastly burdens of an ungodly chase

Be off to a future better and bright
With exultant joy, hope and delight.[22]

Surely, there were soldiers who, motivated by patriotism, intended to keep on fighting; but, in all likelihood, the majority in the army thought solely of a swift return home. Most soldiers stayed together in compact units in order to secure easy transportation home.[23]

22. József, *Mindenki*, 1:71–72. Poem by Gyula Juhász. Free translation by Gábor Vermes.
23. László Fényes, *Védőbeszéd a Tisza-perben* [Speech for the defense in the Tisza-trial] (Budapest, 1922), p. 132.

The trials and tribulations of war, usually do not improve upon human nature, and the civilian population, as much as it welcomed the soldiers' homecoming, was also concerned for its own safety, in case some of the returning soldiers turn into brigands. An observer's remark reveals genuine alarm, "On November 1 and 2 of 1918, the entire country was most anxiously thinking how to take the weapons away from the soldiers."[24] The police chief of Budapest was more than anxious to see the speedy demobilization of the army for the sake of public safety.[25]

Although the Socialist Deputy Minister of Defense Vilmos Böhm referred to disciplined units who were enthusiastic in their collective support of the revolution,[26] the discipline was rather lax among those troops which did not vanish after their return from the front. Their ranks were augmented by new recruits of extremely dubious military value.

Admittedly, the leaders of the revolution were influenced by pacifist emotions and thus sacrificed effective military organization. The situation was aggravated by administrative chaos and the destructive influence of the soldiers' councils, those unruly, *ad hoc* products of the revolution. Unprincipled opportunists of the first caliber seemed to have their eyes set on the golden advantages they could exploit in a disarrayed military establishment. One example would be István Friedrich, a most enthusiastic devotee of Károlyi in the October days, and later prime minister of the counterrevolution, who appointed himself deputy minister of defense. Károlyi was sure that the minister of defense, Béla Linder, nominated him, while Linder was convinced that Károlyi did so. Characteristically, after the confusion was cleared and Friedrich's "mischief" was revealed, he still retained his position for another two months.

However, it was a Socialist journalist, József Pogány, who emerged as the chief "culprit," at the head of the Budapest Soldiers' Council, with no military background other than war reporting for the Socialist newspaper *Népszava*. His intelligence was not questioned but a vaulting ambition and an intense drive for popularity seemed to have impelled him above all. His major concern was to promote and encourage the often impossible demands of the soldiers. Under his leadership the soldiers' councils had become the hotbeds of reckless insubordination. It was an ominous sign for the future that even the Social Democratic party, the only truly organized force in the country, proved to be unable to control the activities of its own representative, who held a most crucial position.

In Padua on November 3, 1918, an armistice was signed by General Armando Diaz of the Entente, and General Weber, representing the Austro-Hungarian monarchy. The Hungarian Council of Ministers, and Minister of Defense Béla Linder in particular, insisted on concluding a separate armistice in the name of Hungary alone, in order to impress Hungary's newly gained full independence and sovereignty. Károlyi

24. László Szabó, *Mi okozta az összeomlást?* [What was the cause of the collapse?] (Budapest, 1922), p. 157.

25. Károly Dietz, *Októbertől Augusztusig. Emlékirataim.* [From October until August. My memoirs.] (Budapest, 1920), p. 65.

26. Vilmos Böhm, *Két forradalom tüzében* [In the cross fire of two revolutions] (Vienna: Bécsi Magyar Kiadó, 1923), pp. 81-85.

protested; in his opinion those who were responsible for the war in the first place should terminate it. They should bear the responsibility for the terms of the settlement.[27] Károlyi's objection was overruled and a Hungarian delegation arrived in Belgrade on November 7 to enter into negotiation with General Franchet d'Esperey, the commander in chief of all Entente forces in the Balkans. There was a definite urgency for the Hungarian delegation in rushing to Belgrade. Serbian troops, under Franchet d'Esperey's supreme command, crossed the Száva River and were advancing into Hungarian territory. Károlyi, who headed the Hungarian delegation, asked the French general whether the army under his command was bound by the Diaz–Weber armistice or not. Franchet d'Esperey's answer was: No![28] During the subsequent time of the parley, the general displayed utter rudeness and contempt toward the Hungarian delegation. His behavior was described by Oszkár Jászi, who was present as follows: "The little general put on the airs of a Napoleon and showed an ignorance and a narrowness which would have disgraced a Breton village dominie."[29]

The terms of the Belgrade armistice were much harsher than the ones imposed on Weber by Diaz. The Hungarian government was compelled to withdraw its troops behind the line of Besztercze, Maros, Szabadka, Baja, Pécs, Dráva; it had to comply with a demand for an almost total demobilization, leaving only eight divisions for the maintenance of internal public order; and it had to acknowledge the right of the Allies to occupy any part of Hungary they deemed strategically important. The Hungarian delegation returned to Budapest but sent Linder back to Belgrade to sign the armistice. There seemed to be no realistic alternative to a compliance with the stringent conditions of the armistice. Military resistance would have resulted in national suicide. On the southern border of Hungary, twelve Hungarian divisions stood against the Entente's forty-nine.[30] The country's defense was also handicapped by a severe shortage of war materials, food, and coal.

Immediate blame for the acceptance of harsh terms, however, has always been placed on the signatories who sit on the wrong side of the negotiating table. By the mere fact of having signed the Belgrade armistice, the Károlyi government suffered its first humiliating defeat; it lost prestige both at home and abroad. The Hungarian public had faith in Károlyi. He was regarded by this public as the only statesman who could possibly accomplish an understanding with the Entente. The unfairness of the armistice was seen by many as a sign of Károlyi's failure and not as a symptom of the Entente's shortsighted policy, which treated friends as reincarnations of old enemies. In Belgrade, General Franchet d'Esperey was quite explicit, "Vous avez marché avec eux, vous sevez punis avec eux. . . . Vous avez comme ennemis les checques les slovaques, les roumains et les yugoslaves. Je n'ai qu'un signe à faire, et vous serez détruits." [You marched with them, now you will be punished with them. . . . The Czechs, Slovaks, Rumanians and Yugoslavs are your enemies. I have only to give a signal and you will be destroyed.][31]

27. Mihály Károlyi, *Az uj Magyarországért* [For the new Hungary] (Budapest: Gondolat, 1968), p. 414.
28. Jászi, *Revolution*, p. 54.
29. Ibid., p. 53.
30. Tivadar Battyhány, *Beszámolóm* [My accounts] 2 vols. (Budapest, n.d.), 2:12.
31. Juhász-Nagy, *A magyar*, p. 263. My translation.

Károlyi was also accused of betraying Hungary's interest by hurrying to Belgrade in panic. According to adherents of this view, the Diaz–Weber armistice was applicable to all the theaters of war, and the comparatively milder terms of the Diaz–Weber armistice were needlessly exchanged by the imperious dictates of Franchet d'Esperey.[32] It is a fact that the Diaz–Weber armistice was concluded between the Entente and Austria-Hungary. Also, the insistence on following a separate Hungarian course of action, primarily for reasons of prestige, might have been an error. Nevertheless, the academic nature of these considerations becomes evident in light of the Entente's actual policy. On the Balkans front, General d'Esperey considered himself and not General Diaz empowered to negotiate an armistice with Hungary. He made this state of affairs clear in Belgrade, and in October, 1924, he reiterated it in an interview with Géza Supka, a Hungarian journalist, "Foch in France, Diaz in Italy, and I in the Balkans were commanders with full power, independent from each other. . . . My plan was to advance towards Berlin through Budapest, Vienna, Prague and Dresden. Therefore, it was in my interest to sign an armistice with Hungary, in order to gain control over its water and railway routes for a quick transportation of my troops. On November 6 no one could foresee that an armistice with Germany was imminent."[33]

After the conclusion of the armistice, a continuous punishment of Hungary gradually wore out whatever power of resistance was still left in the country, and it further undermined the Hungarian government's already tarnished reputation. During the following months, Czech, Rumanian, and Yugoslav troops with the approval of the Entente high command persevered in their incessant violation of both the Diaz–Weber and the Belgrade armistices. However, these actions were not sporadic and whimsical military forays, but were politically motivated, and should be seen and discussed as the final acts of Austria-Hungary's fiasco in solving its problems of nationality.

The Austro-Hungarian monarchy had been a conglomerate of various nations. From any logical and pragmatic point of view, some form of federalism should have been accomplished. However, the two ruling nations, the Germans in Austria and the Magyars in Hungary, clung stubbornly to the maintenance of "dualism" which was based on a joint rule of Germans and Magyars. The resentment of the other nations was boiling beneath the surface, and the monarchy's defeat in World War I brought to the fore their bitterness, and by 1918, their wish to secede. Croats, Serbians, Slovaks, and Rumanians harbored a long list of grievances against the Magyars, and the chaotic conditions of 1918—disintegrating armies, fluctuating demarcation lines, ambiguous armistice terms—only intensified them. Above all, active Entente support played into their hands. It would be futile to argue the issues from a legal viewpoint, or even from an ideological viewpoint, because in 1918, the military and political atmosphere was charged with emotions, and conflict between the onetime rulers and onetime subjects was not to be solved in a rational and sensible way.

No one expressed this sense of futility better than Oszkár Jászi, the Hungarian minister in charge of nationality affairs: "A considerable section of Hungarian public

32. Gratz, A forradalmak Kora, p. 48.
33. Tivadar Batthyány, Fuer Ungarn gegen Hohenzollern (Zurich: Amalthea Verlag, 1930), pp. 183–84.

opinion hoped that my policy would provide a solution for the nationality problem, which had become acutely inflamed during the War. I myself never shared this illusion. The moment we lost the war, I realized that the political integrity of Hungary was lost."[34] Jászi proposed an "Eastern Switzerland," a federalist Hungary, where all nations would enjoy complete autonomy. "I aimed at defeating the Entente with their own weapons by means of argument based on the principles they had announced."[35]

The Károlyi regime, and Jászi in particular, again bore the brunt of accusations which stressed the unreal naïveté and abortive idealism of an "Eastern Switzerland" solution in face of the iron intransigence of Czechoslovaks, Yugoslavs, and Rumanians.[36] Perhaps rightly so. Jászi himself admitted that "my policy was directed to the future rather than to the present."[37] One alternative to his proposal could have been a full acceptance of the non-Magyar nations' desire to secede from Hungary and the acknowledgment of their territorial claims. Another alternative could have been to leave the negotiating table and resort to arms.

None of these alternatives appealed to Jászi and, through him, to the Hungarian government. A "splintering" of the natural political and economic unity of the Danube basin seemed unwise and likely to perpetuate national hatred. The only change would have been the shifting of the frontiers, and within these frontiers, the role of masters and subjects would be reversed. The alternative of an armed resistance was beyond reality for lack of a well-organized Hungarian army. During the November negotiations with the Rumanian leaders in Arad, Jászi felt that he could solve this dilemma only by asserting the principles of national self-determination, and he hoped to achieve no more than a moral victory.[38]

To place the blame for Hungary's losses on Jászi's assumed naïveté would be highly unfair. Sándor Belitska, minister of defense under the Horthy regime, admitted in 1922 that "the disintegration of Hungary was already decided in the process of the war."[39] In confronting Jászi, the leaders of the non-Magyar nations committed the same error of judgment as General d'Esperey. These leaders did not distinguish their onetime oppressors from their onetime allies against oppression, notably Oszkár Jászi himself. In their view, no difference existed in substance between the Tisza and the Károlyi regimes, since both wished to preserve Hungary's territorial integrity.[40] That charge was literally true as far as the preservation of Hungary's territorial integrity was concerned. But the Károlyi government wished to transform this territorial integrity from a revered but obsolete fetish into an ideal of progress. Simultaneously, the principle of national self-determination was to be upheld. These two concepts, however, are incongruous. What would have happened to Hungary's territorial integrity had any or all non-Magyar groups chosen the path of secession,

34. Jászi, *Revolution*, p. 57.
35. Ibid., p. 58.
36. Sándor Pethő and Ferenc Fodor, *Világostól Trianonig* [From Világos to Trianon] (Budapest: Encyklopedia, Rt., 1925), p. 205.
37. Jászi, *Revolution*, p. 58.
38. Ibid., p. 58.
39. Dezső Rubint, *Az összeomlás* [The collapse] (Budapest, 1918), p. 7.
40. Ludwig Hatvany, *Das Verwundete Land* (Vienna, 1921), p. 44.

not by the use of force, but through plebiscites, as proposed by the Károlyi government? This contradiction notwithstanding, Tisza's idea of Magyar superiority bore no resemblance to Jászi's plan of a Danubian federation.

The Sabor, the assembly of the Croats, declared Croatia's secession from Hungary on October 29. The Slovaks followed suit on the following day, and Czech troops invaded Hungary on November 8. In a statement made on November 14, Karel Kramář, the prime minister of the new state of Czechoslovakia, justified the intervention of the Czech troops on the ground that the Hungarian officials had left their places and the Czechs had been invited by the Slovaks to replace them in order to avert anarchy.[41] In the same statement Kramář maintained that the Czechs, too, were expecting the final solution at the peace conference. In fact, the Slovak question was already settled; the Republic of Czechoslovakia had been recognized by the Allies prior to the peace negotiations. When the representative of the Entente in Budapest, the French Lieutenant Colonel Vyx, insisted on the evacuation of Hungarian troops from Slovakia, he justified his demand on the basis of that recognition. The Hungarian government protested, citing the terms of the Belgrade armistice, which assured Hungarian public administration even in occupied territories. The final answer came from General d'Esperey on January 10, 1919:

> The armistice upon which the Hungarian government relied had reference exclusively to the front of the Eastern Allied Armies, that is, to the demarcation line to the south and east of Hungary, facing the Serbs and the Rumanians, and in no way prejudiced Allied decisions respecting other fronts. In consequence the Czechoslovak state which has been recognized by the Allies possesses absolute sovereign authority over the reoccupied territories within the provisional boundaries.[42]

By November 14, Jászi's negotiations with the Rumanian leaders of Transylvania in Arad ended in failure. About the same time, Rumanian troops penetrated into Transylvania. They were authorized to go as far as the Maros River, the demarcation line fixed by the Belgrade armistice. The territory promised to them in 1916 by the secret Treaty of Bucharest, extended beyond the Maros, and the Rumanian army was prepared to cross the river. This apparent incongruity between the armistice and the secret treaty became the principal source of misunderstanding between Hungarians and Rumanians. On December 1, 1918, the National Assembly of Transylvanian Rumanians proclaimed the union of Transylvania with Rumania. Soon, Rumanian troops crossed the Maros. The Hungarian government protested, but to no avail. On December 23, Lieutenant Colonel Vyx informed the Hungarian government that the Entente had decided to authorize the Rumanians to occupy the disputed territories.

The Hungarian government also protested against the penetration of Yugoslav troops beyond the line of demarcation. In all territories occupied by Czechs, Yugo-

---

41. *Pesti Hirlap* [Pest Newspaper], 21 Nov. 1918, p. 4.

42. Francis Deák, *Hungary at the Paris Peace Conference* (New York: Columbia University Press, 1942), p. 13.

slavs, and Rumanians, the functions of government and public administration slipped into the hands of the occupying powers, although according to an appendix attached to the armistice on January 28, 1919, the demarcation line was to be of a strictly military and not of a political nature.[43]

The Károlyi government was able to come to terms only with the Germans and Ruthenians. The combined numerical strength and political significance of these two groups, however, were slight in comparison to the number and importance of Slovaks, Yugoslavs, and Rumanians, who, already had decided to secede.

Changes brought about by the reshuffling of the government had not resulted in any substantial improvements as far as the military resistance against the raiding armies of Czechs, Rumanians, and Yugoslavs was concerned. After Béla Linder's resignation on November 8, the new minister of defense, Albert Bartha, became engaged in an unfortunate struggle with József Pogány. On November 13, Bartha declared, "I will not tolerate Soldiers' Councils."[44] By December 4, he was forced to acknowledge the councils and the transfer of the officers' disciplinary power to popularly elected military tribunals. Bartha attempted to offset these measures by the organization of flying squads, but the Socialists regarded this move as counterrevolutionary and forced his resignation on December 11. Before this resignation became public, Pogány, without the endorsement of the Social Democratic party, led a soldiers' demonstration to the Ministry of Defense to demand Bartha's dismissal. On December 12, Bartha's resignation was publicly announced and it appeared to be the direct result of the soldiers' action. This incident damaged the government's prestige and corrupted the army's morale even further. Count Sándor Festetich, the new minister of defense, approved of the soldiers' councils and promised a variety of benefits to the soldiers, yet he too came under the relentless attacks of Pogány. The officers' corps was another favorite target of Pogány. No doubt, the bulk of the officers' corps was hostile to the revolution, but it was irreplaceable for the time being and its influence could have been neutralized or at least blunted by a strong peasant army. The Socialists, however, always suspicious of the peasantry as potentially counterrevolutionary, were opposed to any such solution, though as Jászi could see, "it depended entirely on us whether the peasantry was revolutionary or not."[45]

In Hungary, about 4,000 families owned one-third of all agricultural land, while about one-seventh of this land was in the possession of approximately 1.7 million smallholders.[46] In addition, there were millions of peasants without any land whatsoever, eking out a livelihood as agricultural laborers. All three major parties were pledged to a program of land reform. At the beginning the task seemed quite easy, for the big landowners were terrified by the threat of violence. On November 14, a spokesman for their association, the OMGE, camouflaged this fear with flowery and manifestly insincere words, "The Hungarian landlords understand the voice of the times;

43. Juhász-Nagy, *A magyar*, p. 361.
44. Ibid., p. 340.
45. Jászi, *Revolution*, p. 47.
46. Vince Nagy, ed., *Öt év multán. Résztvevők visszaemlékezései a forradalomra* [After five years. Reminiscences of participants of the revolution] (Budapest, 1923), p. 36.

they realize the necessity of a land reform and for that purpose they offer a share of their holdings to the peasants voluntarily, they offer the part they can do without."[47]

The ambiguity of the statement's very last portion notwithstanding, these words sounded encouraging. The real opposition to a land reform came from another source. The Socialists were not particularly eager to increase the number of smallholders; an action which, from an orthodox Marxist viewpoint, could be characterized as the proliferation of capitalism on land. The Socialists also feared a considerable drop in productivity and an ensuing starvation of the townspeople. At an agrarian conference held in November, all the Socialist representatives—Sándor Csizmadia, Zsigmond Kunfi, and Jenő Varga—took a stand against the redistribution of land. Gradually, the Socialist attitude changed, and the same Sándor Csizmadia who was so opposed to the carving up of the big estates in November, struck a quite different note at the agrarian conference held in December. At that conference he discarded the socialist idea of collective farming, at least for the time being.[48] On December 20, the Workers' Council of Budapest accepted a proposal of the Social Democratic party which, in fact, acknowledge private property. The reason for their change of heart lay in the realization of the peasantry's most exigent land hunger. Most of them, however, could never consent wholeheartedly to the idea of a boldly and resolutely executed redistribution of the land and their support of such redistribution remained lukewarm at best.

As far as the other parties were concerned, the radicals favored the extension of marketing and agricultural cooperatives, combined with the private ownership of the smallholders. The Károlyi party was divided; the left wing standing by the Radicals and the right wing advocating a cautious, go-slow policy.[49] By December, 1918, and January, 1919, the big landowners woke up from their "Sleeping Beauty's" dream and opened hostilities against a land reform.[50] About the same time, the Communist party was pressing for the immediate socialization of the land. The result has been vividly described by Jászi: "The concentrated attack from all sides perplexed the well-intentioned Barna Buza, the Minister of Agriculture. Instead of doing something he began to set up committees of inquiry, thus placing himself at the mercy of obstruction from all sides."[51] Jászi believed that land reform was connected not only with the military problem but also with the question of territorial integrity, for a drastic land reform might have persuaded a large number of peasants from various national groups to cast their votes in favor of staying with Hungary. The failure to carry out a land reform was fatal. The Hungarian peasant, called by Jászi "the Archimedes lever of the Revolution,"[52] remained neutral, if not hostile, toward the chaos emanating from Budapest.

Other issues of an economic nature, with significant political implications, aroused similar storms. Pál Szende, deputy then later minister of finance, a left-wing radical, planned to introduce a drastic income tax reform. His project met with the furious

47. Ibid., p. 32.
48. *Pesti Hirlap*, 27 Dec. 1918, p. 3.
49. Battyhány, *Fuer Ungarn gegen Hohenzollern*, p. 211.
50. Nagy, *Öt év multán*, p. 48.
51. Jászi, *Revolution*, p. 83.
52. Ibid., p. 84.

antagonism of the propertied classes and it also divided both the Radical and the Károlyi parties, their members on the right opposing and their members on the left favoring the plan. Industry created another problem. Socialization had been one of the primary goals of the Socialist platform. In view of the national economy's impoverished state, it was obvious to the moderates of the party that socialization would end in anarchy and lead to a further decline in production. The party, as a whole, however, did not comprehend the dangers involved in socialization and kept the issue alive. In several factories so-called "wild socializations" occurred, that is, the workers drove the managers away and started to run the factories on their own.

The country's economy was also seriously handicapped by the loss of territories. A considerable part of Hungary's industries and mines were under foreign occupation, and there was a shortage in raw materials, food, and consumer goods. At one of the first cabinet meetings, Commissioner Jenő Vázsonyi reported that the coal reserves of the state railways were sufficient to guarantee the regular operation of the railways only for another day and a half.[53] A lack of incentive to work aggravated the economic situation even more.

If formerly there were ten or fifty thousand potentates who loafed and waited for the plums to fall into their mouth, now we have ten million doing the same. Everybody wants to live better and nobody wants to work. Commissioner Vázsonyi says that the engineers have to shovel the coal at the railway stations because there are no workers who would do the job even at a high daily wage.[54]

The government received an incessant flow of demands. Soldiers, civil servants, and workers claimed higher wages and every kind of benefits. There was no question of requests; everyone came forward with arbitrary demands.

This rather universal disposition of the masses was skillfully exploited by the Communists. The Communist party of Hungary was founded on November 20, 1918, in part by former prisoners of war who had returned from Soviet Russia, and partly by leftist Socialists who had been disappointed with the policy of the Social Democratic party. Béla Kun, who belonged to the first group, emerged as their leader. Before the war, he was a minor trade-union official with the ambition of becoming a journalist, but his efforts, for the most part, ended in frustrating failures. In Russia, he joined the Bolsheviks and rose to some prominence among their ranks, though his role under the new Soviet regime was unduly exaggerated by the yellow journalist press of Budapest.[55] He was a successful organizer but by no means an original thinker or great leader. He acquired a rather superficial knowledge of Bolshevik principles, strategy, and tactics, but under his leadership, the Communist party never attained the cohesion and firm direction of its Russian counterpart. This phenomenon has been acknowledged even by Communist commentators; "the Communist Party of Hungary

53. Battyhány, *Beszámolóm*, 11:10.
54. *Pesti Hírlap*, 6 Dec. 1918, p. 1.
55. Rudolf Tőkés, *Béla Kun and the Hungarian Soviet Republic* (New York: Praeger, 1967), p. 92.

did not reach the maturity of the Russian Bolshevik Party and it was not a party of a new type in the fullest sense of the word."[56]

In revolutionary situations, motives for certain actions and behavior are much more individualized than under normal conditions, and it would not be fair to cast the reasons for joining the new party into a narrow mold. Among the founders, there were onetime members of the so-called socialist-opposition, a leftist faction within the Social Democratic party, with long-established grudges against that party's leadership. Some other founders were veterans of syndicalist and antimilitary groups. Certain individuals joined the party out of personal frustration, and others were attracted by the messianic character of the movement. What united them all was an impatient urge for a violent change: a wish to overthrow the Károlyi regime and transform it into a soviet republic, following Russia's example and Lenin's call for a world revolution.

Communist influence spread swiftly because the Communist party could take advantage of the country's difficult political and economic situation. In its propaganda, it could also exploit the government's rather inefficient and rudderless handling of the difficulties. The Communists drew their mass support from the unemployed and the disabled veterans, in short, from those who were in a deplorable state as a consequence of the war and the country's condition. Although these groups received the highest benefits the government could afford to pay, the Communists demanded even more. Their platform was simple and stirring. It called for the dictatorship of the proletariat; the socialization of houses, lands, and factories without compensation; for all power to the workers' councils; and for an imminent world revolution.

Apologists for the Károlyi regime have been inclined to chide the Communists for their demagogy, lack of constructive criticism, and smear-campaigns.[57] These apologists, however, have overlooked the fact that the Communists were not to play the game according to the rules; they had no intention of being the loyal opposition. In their propaganda, they did not hide their primary goal: the overthrow of the Károlyi government, which they viewed as the Hungarian version of Kerensky's regime.[58]

On the other side of the political spectrum, the extreme right had raised its head, gaining its main support from politicians of the old order, officers, refugees from the occupied territories, and college students. Associations were formed, such as the MOVE (Hungarian National Defense Association) and the Ébredő Magyarok (Awakening Hungarians), with only thinly disguised counterrevolutionary programs. The erosion of Hungary's defense, in face of external threats, provided the most inflammatory and effective point on their platform: the restoration of old Hungary, both in spirit and in square miles. The large number of Jews among the Socialist and Communist leadership added a further inciting component to their frame of mind, already prejudiced against Jews in general.

56. Heinz Lindner, *Revolution und Konterrevolution in Ungarn in den Jahren 1918/1919.* (Berlin: Dietz, 1958), p. 63.

57. Nagy, *Öt év multán*, p. 100.

58. Tőkés, *Béla Kun*, p. 94.

The governing parties were haplessly caught between the two extremes. The Radical party, never noted for its expertise in the rough and tumble of everyday politics, was gradually disintegrating. Its left wing intellectuals, with Oszkár Jászi and Pál Szende, were drawing closer to the Socialists and were willing to make concessions at the expense of private enterprise. The party's right wing, which represented business interests, was opposed to any such trend. The Károlyi party, in spite of its limited social base, had political experience, for all of its leaders had been members of the Parliament before 1918. This fact, however, proved to be more of a liability than an asset under the new revolutionary circumstances. Their democratic and progressive principles notwithstanding, the leaders and the membership of the Károlyi party were very much part of traditional Hungary. Most of them belonged to the gentry or aristocracy and they were accustomed to a certain set way of political maneuvering. In this sense, they had more in common with their onetime opponents, the conservative following of István Tisza, than with their recent plebeian socialist and intellectual radical allies. Most leaders of the party were at a loss in coping with the growing troubles and chaos and dropped out from the political scene one by one. On December 12, Count Tivadar Battyhány resigned as minister of interior, and on December 23, Márton Lovászy, the minister of education, followed suit. Lovászy then attempted to organize an anti-Socialist alliance of all moderate elements. His attempt met with failure because these moderate elements were either in a state of frightened passivity or they were drifting more and more toward one or the other extreme under the strongly polarizing influence of current events. Among the leaders of the party, Károlyi himself, though with only a small and rather obscure following, moved toward the Left and stressed the necessity of further social reforms. Although he did not abandon the principle of private ownership, he concluded that the capitalist system could not be maintained in its old form.[59] Yet, his sincere intention to live up to the idea of a democratic fair play resulted in a catastrophic state of ambiguity, because on the one hand he did not condemn Lovászy's plan for a bourgeois alliance, while on the other, he declared his determination to go along with trends of social, political, and economic radicalism.[60] Noble as his attitude was in principle, in fact, this ambiguity yielded a lacuna in leadership. This power vacuum, in turn, led to a state of chronic indecision on all levels of the administration, for Károlyi was not only the leader of his party, but the head of the government as well. Baron Lajos Hatvany, a rich patron of the arts and literature and a well-known writer himself, commented on the Károlyi government as follows, "From the discussions no decisions arose and from the decisions no actions. A cabinet? No, it was a debating club."[61]

With the extreme right in sullen defiance, the moderate middle in flustered bewilderment, and the extreme left in angry frustration, the Social Democratic party was the only viable force in the country. This political panorama was a typical phenomenon immediately following the war in several of the defeated countries. In their response to the unwanted challenge, the socialist parties of the respective countries

59. *Népszava* [People's Voice] (Budapest), 24 Dec. 1918.
60. Károlyi, *Az uj Magyarországért*, pp. 279–88.
61. Hatvany, *Das Verwundete Land*, p. 45.

reacted in different ways. In Germany and Austria, the socialist parties, for better or for worse, had saved bourgeois democracy and the bourgeois state. They were not merely able but willing to do so, because as part of the German and Austrian political establishment they, in fact, were revisionists and only paid lip service to revolutionary Marxism. In short, they knew what was at stake as they confronted the "threat" of a Communist revolution.

In Hungary, the Social Democratic party was thrust into power as well. In taking over the responsibility of governing, however, it carried over the burdens of its past inconsistencies. In the Hungarian party's case, beyond the major contrast between noisy, revolutionary slogans and firm actions in defense of the *status quo*, half-hearted attempts at actually joining the revolutionary bandwagon conflicted with half-hearted attempts at blowing it up. Most of its leaders abhorred the methods of Gustav Noske.[62]

The reason for the Hungarian party's uniqueness lay in its pre-1918 tradition as an oppositional party of a semilegal character. As such, it lacked the respectability and political experience of the German and Austrian parties without ever acquiring the toughness of an openly persecuted revolutionary underground. The Hungarian party shared enough of the general characteristics of social democracy not to follow the Bolshevik example, but it failed in its determination to combat it effectively. The inconsistency plaguing the party, therefore, was more than just ideological; it perpetuated and transformed into often contradictory actions a mentality which was torn between the equally unappealing alternatives of a communist revolution and an alliance with the *bourgeoisie*. Zsigmond Kunfi, in an interview with the United Press, said, "As a socialist I appreciate the aims of Bolshevism, but I disapprove of its terroristic, antidemocratic methods."[63] The December 15 issue of the Socialist newspaper *Népszava* outlined the main objections of the Socialists to the realization of communism in Hungary. First, the internal relation of forces and the lack of a politically educated proletariat would not make it possible to establish communism. Secondly, as the article pointed out, the position of Hungary was precarious; the Entente would not tolerate a Bolshevik revolution, and "we do not want to lead the Hungarian proletariat to destruction, nor to starvation, nor to anarchy."[64] Yet only a week later, the *Népszava* struck a different note, "We are much closer to the bolsheviks than to the most extreme and radical bourgeois party."[65] In fact, by January, 1919, some left-wing members of the party began to waver in their opposition to the Communists, although on the surface the front against them remained united for the time being.

The power monopoly of the Social Democratic party was generally recognized by contemporary observers. The conclusion drawn by some of the bourgeois journalists, however, went beyond the mere registration of the indisputable fact, "if fate threw power into the socialists' hands, then the bourgeois parties have to withdraw and let the socialists do the job alone."[66] This solution clearly would have been an easy way

62. Garami, *Forrongó Magyarország*, p. 105.

63. *Pesti Hirlap*, 6 Dec. 1918, p. 2.

64. *Népszava*, 15 Dec. 1918, p. 3.

65. Ibid., 22 Dec. 1918.

66. István Milotay, *Tíz esztendő* [Ten years] (Budapest, 1924), p. 150.

out for the bourgeois parties. To maintain the coalition was a farce, after all, for if one side held the actual power the other side had virtually none. By the same token, prospects for a purely bourgeois government were rather slim.

On January 8, under Socialist pressure, the Károlyi government resigned. On the same day, the Workers' Council of Budapest held a meeting, where a decision had to be made. Ernő Garami voiced the opinion that the Social Democratic party should leave the cabinet and allow the formation of a bourgeois government. He pointed out that the power monopoly of the Social Democratic party was an illusion. The government was attacked because, in spite of Socialist participation, it did not accomplish much. It did not because it could not. Should the party assume full responsibility of governing, it would either have to yield to the pressure of the masses and carry out certain economic measures that might lead to catastrophe, or it would have to follow the moderate policy of the former coalition government, thereby arousing even greater opposition by the disgruntled masses, incited by Communist propaganda. Garami asserted that the only sound course to follow was to realize the weakness of the party, to withdraw, and to preserve freedom of action by not taking any responsibility for the ruling of the country at all. The leaders of the party would then be relieved of the burden of governing and would be able to devote their time and energy to the reorganization and strengthening of the party and the trade-unions.

Sándor Garbai, another leader of the party, represented the opposite view. According to him, the Social Democratic party should not stop on the road to the attainment of full power and responsibility. The rank and file of the army had been won over to the side of the party, but the bureaucracy was still hostile and could be broken only by a purely Socialist administration. This step would also be a necessary prerequisite to the nationalization of large factories and mines. A wholly Socialist government could oppose the Communists more effectively, since any subversive Communist propaganda could then be considered as the intrigue of traitors to the cause of the proletariat and dealt with accordingly.

Zsigmond Kunfi proposed a compromise solution. In his opinion, a withdrawal would strengthen the counterrevolutionary forces, and also, from a moral point of view, it would be deplorable to step aside when times were hard. A wholly Socialist government would lead to the dictatorship of the proletariat antagonizing both the peasantry and the Entente, therefore, it would have little chance of survival. The only solution was to form a new coalition government in which Socialist influence and control should be increased.

The Worker's Council voted in favor of Garbai's proposal by 169 to 101. Garami left the hall in despair but suddenly he was recalled. Garbai decided that without a decisive majority he should not press for the acceptance of his proposal. A new ballot gave almost unanimous support—with only five Communists voting against it—to Kunfi's compromise proposition: the endorsement of further Socialist participation in a coalition government. A momentous decision had been made as subsequent events were soon to prove.

After his resignation as prime minister, Károlyi took upon himself the equally onerous task of the president of the republic; the position had remained vacant during the time of his premiership. This shift in office proceeded without the customary flourish of trumpets. On the contrary, voices of sympathy rather than voices of cheer were heard; "Károlyi became the President of the Hungarian Republic. The poor Hungarian Republic has offered its supreme post to him not as a holiday present but as a crown of thorns . . . carry it until you will collapse from its deadly grip."[67]

On January 18, 1919, Károlyi appointed Dénes Berinkey as the head of the new government. Although Berinkey was a member of the Károlyi party, he was not a politician, but a well-known expert in international law. His appointment did not indicate the emergence of a new leader; rather it represented the ascendancy of an apolitical third force trying to hold the heterogeneous elements of the coalition together. In the new cabinet the Károlyi party was represented by five members; the Radical and a newly formed peasant organization, the Smallholder party, by one member each. The Socialists, in addition to the two posts they held in the previous government, gained two more, the Ministry of Defense and the Ministry of Public Welfare. The twofold increase in the number of Socialist ministers and the fact that all five representatives of the Károlyi party in the government belonged to the left wing of their party, reflected a definite trend toward the Left.

In spite of the greater homogeneity of the coalition, the prospects for the new government were not bright. The unchanged outside pressure on Hungary was mainly responsible for the lack of improvement. By the middle of January, 1919, the Czechs had completed the occupation of northern Hungary. The advance of the Rumanians had slowed down, but they were still firmly in the possession of the previously occupied territories. The insistence of the Berinkey administration on holding plebiscites and its protests to the Entente were as ineffective as those of the Károlyi government.

Disillusionment and bitterness led to the use of strong words. On March 2, in Szatmár County, President Károlyi emphasized the possibility of liberating the country by force should the Wilsonian principles fail at the Paris Peace Conference.[68] In view of the internal situation of Hungary, these strong words seemed rather self-deceptive. If the external pressure impeded Hungary's consolidation, the centrifugal forces within the country worked in the same direction. The greater homogeneity within the cabinet by no means implied a truly united support of the government, and all the factors which had led to the Károlyi government's fall remained essentially the same.

The Land Reform Bill of February 16 appeared to be a legislative act of considerable importance. Its principal point called for the division of all properties larger than 700 acres. In fact, however, the written words were not followed by prompt action. President Károlyi, in a noble gesture, divided his own land on February 23, but the general application of the bill did not take place. Opposition to the land reform had grown both in size and in influence. The conservative attack was not an open one, for the political situation hardly lent itself to a frank defense of the *latifundia*. In addition, it seemed totally impossible to preserve the old system unaltered. However, by

67. József, *Mindenki*, 2:288.
68. *Pesti Hirlap*, 4 March 1919, p. 1.

urging the importance of assuring the food supply for the cities, which was allegedly better secured by keeping the large estates intact, the conservatives hoped to save as much as possible.

On the extreme left, the Communists were adamant in their opposition to the reform. They spoke scornfully of the bill, which would increase the class of small-holders, who, according to the Communists, were eager to serve the cause of a counter-revolution.[69] The views of a great number of Socialists did not differ much from the Communist position. As already stated, the support of the land reform by the Social Democratic party as a whole had always been ambiguous. This fact became increasingly evident during the early months of 1919. On March 13, the *Népszava* maintained that "although we can prove that collective farming is far superior, we are not going to stand in the way of the distribution of land."[70] Yet, only a few days before, on March 4, the same paper asserted that "it would be a fatal mistake if the land reform would divide all of the available land."[71]

The practical outcome of this situation was discord, confusion, red tape, and inefficiency. The violent actions of certain Socialist groups accelerated the collapse of internal order. Most of these actions took place during the latter part of February and in March. In February, large estates were expropriated and collectives were formed in the county of Somogy. A Socialist directorate also took over the administration of the county. The Socialist ministers protested, but the Socialists of Somogy had the backing of the *Népszava* and of some of the leaders of the party, including the principal party secretary, Jenő Hamburger, himself. In March, the events of Somogy were repeated on a smaller scale in other country towns and villages. In all of these places, the peasants' satisfaction was only temporary. They rejoiced in the loss which the landowners had suffered but the formation of the collectives did not gratify their land hunger.

In the meantime, the Communists continued to exploit the country's deteriorating conditions and their opponents' weakness. Demonstration followed demonstration and the inflammatory speeches of Communist agitators combined with the stirring articles of the *Vörös Ujság* in sowing the seeds of discontent. On February 20, in Budapest, a crowd, incited by the speeches of Communist agitators, proceeded to the editorial office of the *Népszava*, in order to destroy it. In the fight between demonstrators and the police, six policemen were killed and several others were wounded. The government acted with unexpected swiftness and resolve. Forty-two Communist leaders were arrested. A few of them, Béla Kun in particular, were severely beaten by the colleagues of the policemen who had lost their lives in the fight. As a result of the shocked reaction to this incident, the Communist leaders were granted preferential treatment, and they were able to enjoy the greatest possible freedom within the limits of their confinement. Also, their "martyrdom" was exploited by the Communists at large and, together with other inflammatory slogans, it proved to be another effective propaganda weapon. The beating was a fact, but some reports in the sensationalist

69. *Vörös Ujság* (Red Newspaper), 15 Feb. 1919, p. 1.
70. *Népszava*, 13 March 1919, p. 2.
71. Ibid., 4 March 1919, p. 1.

press magnified and embroidered this incident, and, therefore, blunted the public indignation over the Communist attack. Nevertheless, on February 22, in a mass meeting called by the Social Democratic party, a hundred thousand workers demonstrated against the Communists. The slogan of this meeting was: "Down with the leftist and rightist counterrevolutions!" Under Socialist pressure the government arrested a few rightist politicians as well. At that time still, the danger from both extremes looked real enough to most Socialists, for the extreme right and the extreme left appeared to thrive on each other, creating an atmosphere filled with real and imagined dangers, suspicion and hysteria.

The situation was critical in the case of the army as well. In his memoirs, Vilmos Böhm, the Socialist minister of defense, called the army "the sickest organization of the revolution."[72] Even his energy and devotion and the superb work of some of his associates, such as the Colonels Aurél Stromfeld and Ujváry, could not halt the process of disintegration. The Soldiers' Council, which Böhm labelled the "avant-garde of pseudo-radicalism,"[73] was still under József Pogány's leadership.

Böhm tried to reorganize the army on a voluntary basis. The results were disappointing. During the five-week recruiting campaign the number of volunteers rose only to five thousand instead of the expected seventy thousand.[74] On February 25, Colonels Stromfeld and Ujváry resigned their commissions. The next day, Stromfeld declared in a Socialist meeting that if the Soldiers' Council was not going to change its course of action, the army's disruption and consequently the revolution's failure were inevitable.[75] At this meeting even Pogány felt that he had overreached himself, but it was too late. He was no longer the master but the servant of the anarchical forces he had helped to call into existence and foster since the beginning of the revolution.

On January 25, the long expected split in the Károlyi party took place. The minority left wing, under Károlyi's leadership, walked out. The remaining right wing was organized by Márton Lovászy into a new party, and he again attempted the formation of an alliance of all moderate elements. However, this bloc included certain groups which, on a whole, were definitely to the right of the former Károlyi party. The major and perhaps the only bond which held this heterogeneous bloc together was its opposition to the Socialists and Communists, and soon it became the rallying point for conservatives of all shades. Lovászy was an honest democrat but Count István Bethlen and a few others who joined this block were counterrevolutionaries. Nevertheless, Socialist charges that this entire group was the prime mover behind a counterrevolutionary plot were, on the whole, exaggerated and unfounded. Moreover, these charges hindered the development of a responsible, democratic opposition. The unimpeded growth of a legal opposition would have been important, since by the end of February, the government had decided to hold a general election in April.

The Electoral Law of March 5 realized the most cherished dream of all Hungarian liberals by preparing the way for universal suffrage and election by secret ballot. In

72. Böhm, *Két forradalom tüzében*, p. 200.
73. Ibid., p. 208.
74. Juhász-Nagy, *A magyar*, p. 453.
75. Böhm, *Két forradalom tüzében*, p. 212.

addition, an election would have put an end to the provisional nature of the government which was both a source of vacillation and inertia, and an excuse for the same.

A clue to the situation and to a possible solution lay again in the hands of the Social Democratic party. However, ambiguous Socialist policy again reduced to nothing the beautiful designs of the election reform. A few moderates, such as Garami and Manó Buchinger, insisted on placing equal emphasis on the "democratic" half of the party's title. These moderates also alluded to the past history of the party, which, for decades, was centered around the demand for universal suffrage. With the elevation of the party to power, this demand, which was to be exacted from the ruling classes before 1918, turned into a promise to the people. In the moderates' mind the honor and integrity of the Social Democratic party would have been debased by not fulfilling this promise.

The Socialist left wing, however, cared less and less about ethics, whether Socialist or not. They were afraid of losing their power at the polls. Also, Communist propaganda gradually undermined their never-too-firm faith in the democratic tradition of their party. Most leaders of the left wing, Jenő Hamburger, Jenő Landler, Pogány, and Jenő Varga were renegade intellectuals who were carried away by their own revolutionary rhetoric and by their intense hatred of their own class, the *bourgeoisie*. Step by step, these left-wing leaders had come to accept bolshevism which soon appeared to them as a congenial ally rather than a mortal foe.

These left-wing leaders were the most active elements in the party, occupying the positions of real power. They were especially strong in the secretariat, the executive organ of the party. The moderates, Garami and Buchinger, and others, were outnumbered and outshouted by the left wing. This faction was soon in almost full control of what really counted in Socialist power: the thousands of local committees and councils, and even of a few trade-unions, the embodiments of sedate and cautious socialist conservatism under normal conditions.

Socialist ambiguity became most manifest in their handling of the election. The bourgeois parties in the Berinkey government repeatedly declared their loyalty to the revolution, and asserted—to the point of servility—their wish to maintain the alliance with the Socialists. Yet, when the election campaign began, the political rights of even these political allies were not respected by the Socialists. Sometimes the impatience of the Socialists manifested itself in physical violence, not sparing members of the cabinet, as was the case with Minister János Vas, a member of the Károlyi party, who was openly assaulted in an election meeting.

The Radical party became so discouraged that on March 19 it declared its intention to abstain from the elections. According to this declaration the country was "in the state of latent civil war which makes the application of parliamentary methods illusory . . . in the present situation only a purely socialist government could solve the problem of society and save the country from a fatal disorder."[76] If this was the way the so-called allies were treated by their Socialist partners, the situation was much worse with the opposition, namely Lovászy's bloc, which was ceaselessly threatened and intimidated.

76. *Népszava*, 20 March 1919, p. 1.

The major reason for the impatience and nervousness of the Socialist left wing rested in their growing realization of the fact that the Social Democratic party had a narrower popular base than it hoped and claimed to have. Sooner or later, the party had to become aware of the risks involved in a free election. On March 1, the *Népszava* solemnly promised its respect for the preservation of political and human rights,[77] but in several other issues it threatened civil war should the election fail to assure a Socialist majority.[78] In the words of Sándor Juhász-Nagy, who was the minister of justice at that time, "every difference between the communist and the socialist masses became obliterated."[79] To be sure, in spite of the striking similarities, the antagonism between the Communists and Socialists, including the left wing of the latter, did not entirely disappear even during that period. On March 13, the *Népszava* still referred to the Communists as "red counterrevolutionaries,"[80] and the Communists were even more vocal in their name-calling. The shallowness of this antagonism, however, became evident from the fateful events of March 21.

On March 20, the representative of the Entente in Budapest, Lieutenant Colonel Vyx, presented a note to Károlyi. This note demanded the withdrawal of Hungarian troops behind a newly established line, running from Arad through Nagyszalonta, Nagyvárad up to Szatmár-Németi. The Hungarian and Rumanian troops were to be separated by a neutral zone. This neutral zone was to include such thoroughly Hungarian towns as Debrecen and Szeged. The note, in fact, was an ultimatum, for it demanded a reply within eighteen hours. Yet it was not the result of a sudden decision on the Entente's part. At the Paris Peace Conference, the Committee on Rumanian Affairs held a meeting on February 21, 1919, and expressed its concern over the possibility of an armed conflict between the Hungarians and Rumanians. As a result of this meeting the committee submitted the following proposals to the Supreme War Council:

1. The fixing of two lines at a certain distance from each other beyond which the Hungarian and Rumanian troops should not be permitted to advance.

2. The establishment of a neutral zone between the two proposed lines to be occupied by Allied troops with a view of preventing the spread of bolshevism which was prevalent in Hungary.[81]

The line drawn on the Rumanian side of the neutral zone extended five kilometers west of the line fixed by the secret treaty of 1916, which was concluded between Rumania and the Allies. On February 26, 1919, the Supreme War Council adopted the proposal of the Committee on Rumanian Affairs. The only objection was made by Arthur Balfour, the British foreign secretary. He said that since there had been much discussion about the validity of the secret treaty of 1916, it would be better not to

77. Ibid., 1 March 1919, p. 1.
78. Ibid., 5 March 1919, p. 1; 12 March 1919, p. 1; 19 March 1919, p. 1.
79. Juhász-Nagy, *A magyar*, p. 475.
80. *Népszava*, 13 March 1919, p. 1.
81. U.S. Department of State, *Papers Relating to the Foreign Relations of the United States: The Paris Peace Conference*, 13 vols. (Washington, D.C.: Government Printing Office, 1943), 4:22.

mention it openly in the note and to define the new lines in geographical terms only.[82] This modification was small and insignificant but it was characteristic of the cynical approach to the question.

The Entente's most obvious reason for fixing these lines of demarcation was to procure advantageous new frontiers for the Rumanians. Also, the Entente intended to use Rumanian troops against the Bolsheviks in Russia, and the establishment of a neutral zone was meant to secure the rear guard of the Rumanians. There had been much debate as to whether Lieutenant Colonel Vyx specified these new lines as temporary political frontiers or merely as military demarcation lines. Károlyi, Böhm, and Garami unanimously maintained that Lieutenant Colonel Vyx talked of political frontiers, but Vyx denied it. This discussion was rather academic, since the truly important matter was that Hungary faced a further loss of territory, population, and prestige.

Only a week after the Entente note was handed over to the Hungarian government, General Tasker Bliss, one of the American delegates at the peace conference, made the following objections in a memorandum prepared for President Woodrow Wilson:

1. The entire neutral zone lies within territory that is ethnically Hungarian.

2. Through sanctioning a further and extended advance of Rumanian troops beyond the demarcation line laid down in the Belgrade Armistice, it subjects the Associated Powers to a charge of breach of faith.

3. It has been interpreted by the Hungarians as a recognition by the Supreme War Council of the secret treaty of 1916.

Consequently, General Bliss strongly advised President Wilson not to participate in any armed intervention to enforce the committee's resolution.[83] The memorandum of General Bliss came too late. The Hungarian government was compelled to make a decision by 6:00 P.M. of March 21.

In the afternoon of March 20, the atmosphere at the cabinet meeting was desperate. It was clear that the government could neither accept the ultimatum nor resist the Entente. Acceptance would have outraged public opinion and swept away the government; resistance was out of the question because the government lacked the power to resist. The only recourse for the government was to resign and hand over the power to the Socialists. Resignation had the additional advantage of allowing the bourgeois ministers to rid themselves of their responsibilities, which they were no longer able to combine with real authority. President Károlyi began to consider the appointment of a purely Socialist government, but the decision again lay with the Socialists and not with him.

The situation resembled the one of January 8 in that the fate of the country again depended on the decision the Social Democratic party was to make. There were, however, important differences. In January, the Socialists had a free choice, a genuine

82. Ibid., 5:11.
83. Deák, *Hungary*, p. 60.

opportunity. In March, they had to choose between "two methods of suicide,"[84] one being the acceptance of the Entente's ultimatum, and the other, consolidation with the Communists. Yet, the idea of suicide was not merely an emotional reaction to the blow the Entente had inflicted upon Hungary; it also reflected the spirit of the Social Democratic party. By March, the party had lost much of its former courage. In this sense the Vyx note merely touched off a process of decline which under the circumstances ran its full course in a matter of hours.

The party executive committee met on March 21. Garami again proposed the withdrawal of the party, implying that the Communists be left to ruin the country without the participation of the Socialists. This proposal was rejected by an overwhelming majority. Most leaders felt that the party should not betray Hungary and abandon the working class in time of danger.[85] The only realistic alternative appeared to be the establishment of a Socialist-Communist government. Böhm stated in his memoirs that no one in the meeting proposed the formation of a Socialist government without Communist support. The committee felt that in the face of the outside threat there should be unity both in the country and among the working class. The committee also understood that a Socialist government opposed by the Communists would have had no chance of survival. The power of the Communist party was growing day by day, even though most of the Communist leaders were still in jail. On March 20, a Communist-organized printers' strike paralyzed the press in Budapest. On the same day, several thousand ironworkers joined the Communist party. There were rumors that soldiers and armed workers were plotting to set the Communist leaders free. Moreover, there was a general resentment against the Entente and the West. Even people of middle-class background seemed to assume a defiant attitude, which was ready to embrace bolshevism merely for the purpose of annoying the Entente.[86] The spreading news of Bolshevik military victories in Russia encouraged this mood. The general feeling was best expressed by the Socialist leader Garbai in a meeting of the Workers' Council on March 21, "The meaning of the new trend is that what we did not get from the West we want to obtain now from the East."[87]

The way the Socialist-Communist pact was concluded sadly characterized the weakness, defeatism, and lost spirit of the Social Democratic party. Kunfi, Landler, Pogány, and Jakab Weltner rushed to the jail to negotiate with the Communists. Béla Kun, the imprisoned Communist leader, was pleasantly surprised to find out that he was about to receive his maximum terms, which he had demanded but had never expected to obtain so smoothly. Power virtually fell into his lap.[88] The joint manifesto resulting from these negotiations declared the union of the two parties, the dictatorship of the proletariat, the organization of a proletarian Red Army, and alliance with the Russian Bolsheviks.

84. Böhm, *Két forradalom tüzében*, p. 247.
85. Ibid., p. 276.
86. Jászi, *Revolution*, p. 88.
87. Jakab Weltner, *Forradalom, bolsevizmus, emigráció* [Revolution, bolshevism, exile] (Budapest: Weltner, 1929), p. 151.
88. Mihály Károlyi, *Memoirs* (New York: E. P. Dutton, 1957), p. 154.

Among the gravest charges leveled against Károlyi was the one which accused him of handing over the power to the Communists without any resistance, and moreover of giving them power without any sense of regret.[89] This charge is false, because it has been refuted not only by Károlyi himself,[90] but also by participants of the cabinet meeting held on March 21. At this late afternoon meeting only administrative matters were discussed. Károlyi was engaged in trying to forge a new government. He announced that on the next day, March 22, he was going to receive Lovászy and other bourgeois politicians in an audience, and he asked the Socialist ministers whether they had any objection to the meeting between him and the leaders of the Right.[91] The Socialist ministers concurred with this plan; moreover when Károlyi sounded Kunfi about the possibility of a government headed by the Socialist leader, Kunfi did not commit himself in either way.[92] "The socialist ministers made themselves conspicuous by their silence,"[93] wrote Károlyi in his memoirs, although the Social Democratic party had already decided for a Socialist-Communist alliance immediately preceding the cabinet meeting, on the early afternoon of the same day.

One can only guess the reasons for the Socialist ministers' reticence which amounted to duplicity. Most likely, all four of them, Böhm, Garami, Kunfi, and Gyula Peidl, being moderates or centrists, were too preoccupied with their own forebodings about the Socialist-Communist alliance and they did not wish to add to their predicament the extra burden of a presumably unpleasant discussion with Károlyi and the bourgeois ministers. Consequently, Károlyi was faced with a *fait accompli* when the news reached him through a journalist friend, Pál Kéri, on the evening of March 21.[94] Károlyi had no alternative to resignation. Even Károlyi's father-in-law, Count Gyula Andrássy, Jr., no great friend of Károlyi at that time, wrote of Károlyi's approval of the new regime as an "enforced blessing by Károlyi."[95] The October revolution changed into the expected or feared experiment of the dictatorship of the proletariat without a shot being fired.

"Consummatum est!... The October Revolution, full of hopes, collapsed."[96] With the gradual weakening of the Károlyi and the Radical parties, the key to the success or failure of the revolution lay in the hands of the Socialists. They began to dominate the Hungarian political scene in December, 1918. During their rule, despite their large membership, their growing power on all levels of the central and local administration, and their dynamic organization, the Socialists could not conceal the inner weakness of their party. By March, 1919, the continuous Communist challenge began to succeed, and contributed to the downfall of the October revolution on March 21.

89. Grátz, *A forradalmak kora*, pp. 92–93.
90. Jászi, *Revolution*, p. 95.
91. Juhász-Nagy, *A magyar*, p. 495.
92. Károlyi, *Memoirs*, p. 154.
93. Ibid., p. 154.
94. Tibor Hajdu, "Michael Károlyi and the Revolutions of 1918–19," *Acta Historica* 10 (1964):364.
95. Andrássy, *Diplomacy and the War*, p. 312.
96. Böhm, *Két forradalom tüzében*, p. 287.

The Social Democratic party's plight was due primarily to the disunity and confusion within its ranks. The leftists of the party had no training in the true art of a revolution, neither in an ideological nor in a tactical sense. They began to flirt with bolshevism, and before long, they were completely captivated by its promises. The "menshevik" right wing wanted to follow the orthodox Marxist blueprint. They did not want to take any decisive action until conditions ripened to a proper stage for a social transformation. The center vacillated and seldom took a consistent stand on any issue. Because of this chronic state of disunity and lack of direction, it was highly unlikely that a Socialist takeover would have or could have saved Hungarian democracy in 1918–19. The party's January, 1919, decision to reject one-party rule was momentous only in a short-run, tactical sense. In all likelihood, no alternative—total withdrawal, all-Socialist rule, or continued alliance with the bourgeois parties—could have forestalled the doom of the revolution and of the Social Democratic party.

There were, of course, other reasons for the revolution's fall: the Entente's abandonment of Károlyi; the social turmoil and economic hardships which the new regime inherited from a disowned, yet haunting past; and the dismal consequences of a lost war. These very same or similar factors were prevalent in Bolshevik Russia, but the Russian Bolsheviks were able to overcome the impasse by virtue of their unity and discipline. Also, in the crucial early period of the Bolshevik revolution, they executed a drastic land reform, thereby winning the peasants over to their side. In Hungary, the Socialists failed with the peasants because of the ambiguous socialist position on the land reform.

The Hungarian Socialists alienated the peasantry but also antagonized their bourgeois allies by not following the German Socialist hard line against the Communists. The Hungarian Social Democratic party since its inception had straddled the borderline between a reluctant revolutionary desire and a compelling urge for respectability. Consequently, when faced with a situation which demanded a clear choice between a socialist revolution or cooperation with the *bourgeoisie*, the party disintegrated.

Was the October revolution merely a futile incident with no hope for even a modicum of success? If success is judged by actual accomplishments, the answer to this question is affirmative. The October revolution's significance should not be measured by such a narrow scale. The October revolution did not initiate the idea of transforming Hungary into a democracy based on social justice, but it certainly reinforced and transmitted this idea to subsequent periods of Hungarian history. After March, 1919, the country, filled with bitterness and frustration, fell from one extreme to another. Ultimately, it consolidated into a replica of the old order, but without the old order's grandeur and deceptive stability. Under the new, semiauthoritarian regime, the democratic opposition continued to advocate the concept of a democratic Hungary. This goal formed the substance of the platforms of all democratic political parties between 1945 and 1948.

The Internal Policies of the
Hungarian Soviet Republic

Frank Eckelt

In no other aspect of its existence did the Hungarian Soviet Republic follow the straight path of Marxist ideology as rigidly as in the orders, proclamations, and directives which were issued by the Revolutionary Governing Council and the various commissariats and which shaped the internal affairs of Hungary. Conversely, since these policies attempted to change the set patterns of life and the internalized value system of the populace, in no other area did the government fail as abysmally as it did in this regard. The failure may also be attributed to the shortage of time, the lack of experienced personnel, organization, and, in some cases, the political and economic naïveté with which the government and its agencies attempted to turn feudal Hungary into the Marxian Utopia. The effort, the output, and the attention to detail were phenomenal. One is struck by the unreal atmosphere in which this government, encircled by hostile neighbors, strangled by an economic blockade, quarantined as a political disease, attempted to solve the social ills of society plaguing man for millenniums.

The master plan called for the cultural rejuvenation of the proletariat and the amelioration of its economic plight. The financial basis for this extremely expensive program was to be the socialization of the wealth of the nation, both the goods and the means of production, as well as an economic and fiscal policy based on Marxian dogma. The dichotomous nature of the plan makes objective criticism difficult. Its progressive and humanitarian purposes were obvious. However, so was its underlying and basic motivation: maintaining and perpetuating the dictatorship of the proletariat and its elite in power, and eliminating all social, economic, and cultural entities challenging it.

Nowhere is the dichotomy of the system so apparent as in the social and cultural policy of the regime. No progressive individual, then or now, could fail to admire the humanitarian and socially conscious concepts promulgated into law by the Revolutionary Governing Council and the Commissariat of Education. Believing alcoholism to be the major cause of human depravation, the Revolutionary Governing Council, in one of its first acts, forbade the consumption of alcoholic beverages.[1] Interestingly,

1. Jenő Pongrácz, ed., *A Forradalmi Kormányzótanács és a népbiztosok rendeletei* [The orders of the Revolutionary Governing Council and the commissars] 5 vols. (Budapest: Franklin, 1919), 1:13.

the order called for the punishment of the seller and the consumer as well. The confiscation of his store and a fine up to K50,000 was meted out to the seller; the consumer faced a year in jail and a fine up to K10,000 for breaking the law. No one could plead ignorance of the law, for according to a decision of the Press Directorate, every order of the Revolutionary Governing Council had to be listed on the front page of every newspaper, while orders of the commissariat had to be made public on the inside pages of the newspapers.[2]

But the orders were publicized and dramatized principally by the truly outstanding poster art developed during this time. The revolutionary placards were everywhere, on every wall of every street, in enormous quantities. Most were in color, with red dominant, and each had a simple and graphic message. Some of the outstanding artists and lithographers of Hungary, such as Marcell Vértes, Robert Berény, Bertalan Pór, and Mihály Biró, gave their talents to this art.[3] Although some excellent posters were produced during the Károlyi regime, the medium found its fullest expression during the 133 days. As an American admirer, Cyril Eastman, wrote of her trip to Hungary: "It seemed to me that Pór and the other Commissars of Propaganda . . . had put the National Security League, the American Defense Society and all the other patriotic poster designers of America wholly in the shade. . . ."[4] It was such a poster campaign which made alcoholism into the greatest of social evils. The posters usually linked prostitution to alcoholism calling them the "murderers" of mankind. Few opportunities were missed to link both to capitalism. Thus, one of the posters proclaimed that the most powerful weapon of capitalist exploitation was alcohol poisoning and the most dangerous kind of capitalism was that of the wine industry.[5] Similarly, newspaper articles describing raids to eliminate prostitution always managed, among some intelligent suggestions leading to the prevention of this social evil, to provide space to describe fourteen- and fifteen-year-old girls found in the company of old *bourgeoisie*.[6]

Prohibition drew heavy fire from the countryside for a number of reasons. Peasant delegates to the National Congress of Councils repeatedly criticized the order, insisting that it was unfairly administered. They described political trustees, sent to the villages from the capital, reeling and reeking from alcohol acquired on "doctor's orders." The delegates believed that after a hard day's work a peasant deserved and needed a half a liter of wine.[7] They also accused the government of allowing wine worth billions to turn into vinegar, thus contributing to the financial crisis of the

2. *P. I. Archivum, A.*, II, 15/43, Fond 24/2 (Minutes of the Meeting of the Press Directorate), 27 March 1919, p. 3.

3. Filmed copies of some of the outstanding posters are in my possession through the courtesy of the National Széchényi Library.

4. Cyril Eastman, "In Communist Hungary," *The Liberator* 2, no. 8 (August 1919):9.

5. *A Magyar Tanácsköztársaság plakátjai az Országos Széchényi Könyvtárban* [The placards of the Hungarian republic of councils in the National Széchényi: Library] (Budapest, 1919), p. 194.

6. "Erkölcsrendészeti razzia" [Raids for moral order], *Vörös Ujság*, 3 July 1919, p. 3.

7. *A Tanácsok Országos Gyűlésének Naplója* [Minutes of the National Congress of Councils], 14 June 1919, 23 June 1919 (Based on notes of the stenographer of the Workers' and Soldiers' Council) (Budapest, 1919), p. 64.

nation.[8] The government finally had to succumb to these pressures and the prohibition was partially lifted on July 23, 1919, allowing each worker over eighteen the consumption of half a liter of wine.[9]

The government's all out attempt to raise the cultural level of its adult population was conducted on a gigantic scale. First, it nationalized all theaters, making actors state employees.[10] The Commissariat of Education then ordered two-thirds of all tickets to be submitted, two days before each performance, to the central ticket office of the Trade Union Council for distribution to workers at lowered prices.[11] In a separate appeal it asked workers to buy tickets for no one but themselves so that only workers could benefit from the order. It permitted the remaining one-third of the tickets to be sold at the box office at regular prices. The appeal ended with "from now on the arts will not be for the special enjoyment of the idle rich. Culture is the just due of the working people."[12] The movie industry, including movie houses,[13] as well as museums[14] were socialized. Theaters in the capital proliferated. Newspapers abounded with theater and opera news, with special free nights for soldiers of the Red Army, trade-union groups, and special events. The agency in charge of communization made arrangements for brief talks by leading artists, during intermission, "to arouse and revolutionize the souls."[15]

Criticism was voiced against the cost of this program and the bureaucracy it created.[16] Experimental theaters, *avant-garde* plays, concerts, and lectures involved vast expenditures. Artists, writers, and composers were now on the state payroll in increasing numbers. Plans were made for the creation of a "College of the Theater," which was to train actors, singers, dancers, and directors.[17] Accusations of waste, of giving everyone a job, of hiring ten men to perform the task of one were vehemently denied by bureau chiefs, but the charges persisted.[18] The peasants also voiced a bitter complaint against the unemployed proletarian who "used to daily concerts, failed to lift a finger for fear that their golden wedding bands would fall off" if they would take the trolley to the outskirts of the city to grow vegetables.[19] Thus, despite the

8. Ibid., p. 83.

9. Mrs. Sándor Gabor et al., eds., *A magyar munkásmozgalom történetének válogatott dokumentai* [Selected documents from the history of the Hungarian labor movement], 6 vols. (Budapest: Kossuth, Szikra, 1956–64), 6/B:469 (hereafter cited as *MMTVD*).

10. *P. I. Archivum*, "A Forradalmi Kormányzótanács üléseinek jegyzőkönyve" [Minutes of the meetings of the Revolutionary Governing Council] 22 March 1919, p. 9.

11. *P. I. Archivum*, A, II, 7/4, p. 5.

12. *P.I. Archivum*, V/130/1919, Plakátgyüjtemény [Collection of Placards].

13. Pongrácz, *A Forradalmi*, 1:62.

14. Ibid., 5:26.

15. "Forradalmi előadások a szinházakban" [Revolutionary lectures in the theaters], *Az Ujság* (The News), 27 March 1919.

16. János Komáromi, *A nagy haboru anekdótái* [The anecdotes of the Great War] (Budapest, 1936), pp. 201–2.

17. "Közoktatásügyi Népbiztosság 42. K.N. sz. rendelete" [Order No. 42 of the Commissariat of Education], *Tanácsköztársaság* (Soviet Republic) 12 June 1919, p. 1.

18. "Kommunista kultura" [Communist culture], *Vörös Ujság*, 6 July 1919, p. 7.

19. *A Tanácsok*, p. 61.

enthusiasm and zeal with which the cultural program for adults was introduced, by mid-June it had become a liability both financially and politically. In a state torn by dissension between country and city, in the midst of a crippling inflation, with cries of corruption and recriminations filling the air, the ambitious cultural program of the regime became a powerful weapon of counterrevolutionary propaganda.

Although errors in policy were committed, no major critic of the regime ever criticized its program for children. The government's social and cultural programs for the young seem to have been drawn from the pages of *Huszadik Század* and the most advanced pedagogical journals.[20] Most of the executed and planned programs and directives had their roots in the ideological foundations of Marxism. One of the most significant laws passed by the regime removed the stigma of illegitimacy from children.[21] The law called for the insertion of the father's name on the birth certificate without the addition being made noticeable. If the paternity was contested, the courts were to decide the issue. All rights due to children of legally married couples were due to those born out of wedlock.

The physical and mental health of children became the primary concern of the state. Compulsory, free, medical examination was ordered for all children between six and fourteen years of age;[22] dentists, for a fee of K1,000 a month plus compensation for materials used, were to give two hours a day free care to school children recommended to them.[23] Cleanliness became the subject of many posters and pamphlets. All public baths and spas were nationalized,[24] but even before nationalization, orders were given in Budapest that twice a week, school children, accompanied by their teachers, were to go to public baths to be examined by a doctor, bathed and, if necessary, have their hair cut. Private individuals, possessing a bath tub, were ordered, once a week, all day Saturday, to allow children, with proper school certificates, to take a bath. The owners were to supply the necessary heat, light, towels, and soap, without compensation.[25] Countless newspaper articles relate the ecstasy of some of these children, many of whom were experiencing the first bath of their life.[26]

Fresh country air for underprivileged children of the cities was another target of the regime. Accordingly, a directive of the Commissariat of Labor and Welfare[27] ordered a monthly payment of K150 to any rural family who was willing to accept the

20. Professor György Lukács told me that the Commissariat of Education prevailed upon "left-wing" members of the profession to create a new leadership in education. They were allowed an amazing amount of freedom in their executive committees. It did not matter whether they were Communists or not, as long as they were dedicated men who knew their profession. Thus, he hired Bartók and Kodály, knowing full well that neither was a Communist.

21. Pongrácz, *A Forradalmi*, 1:17.

22. Katalin Petrák and György Milei, eds., *A Magyar Tanácsköztársaság szociálpolitikája ; Válogatott rendeletek documentok, cikkek* [The social politics of the Hungarian Soviet Republic; selected orders, documents, articles] (Budapest: Gondolat, 1959), pp. 137–38.

23. *Tanácsköztársaság*, 2 April 1919, p. 1.

24. Pongrácz, *A Forradalmi*, 2:31–32.

25. Petrák and Milei, *A Magyar Tanácsköztársaság*, p. 174.

26. "Fürdenek a proletárgyermekek" [The children of the proletariat are bathing], *Népszava*, 5 April 1919; similar articles appeared in *Vörös Ujság*.

27. Pongrácz, *A Forradalmi*, 3:122–23.

responsibility of, and supply food and board to, a child from the Budapest area. The local workers', soldiers', and peasants' councils were to investigate each family, to see whether or not the surroundings were conducive to the physical and moral health of the child.

Sick and troubled children were dealt with in a series of ordinances. Trained guardians or tutors (*gyámok*), usually teachers with special training, were appointed in schools, with wide discretionary powers in both the home and the school, to watch over the physical and mental health of the children.[28] A most progressive directive[29] dealt with the setting up of institutions for the disturbed, feeble-minded, socially maladjusted, and psychotic child.

Specialists were to deal with children exposed to moral degeneration and committees were to expose parents, guardians, and all others who contributed to the delinquency of minors. Antisocial children were to be placed in special institutions to turn them, again, into useful members of society. Only pedagogically approved punishments (scolding, extra work as punishment, and withdrawal of privileges) were allowed. The program was placed under the auspices of the Hungarian Teachers' Union, the Friends of Children, Society of the Hungarian Workers, and the trustees for the children.

Hopelessly psychotic children were to be placed in special institutions of eighty to one hundred each, with necessary staff and equipment.[30] The government also planned to set up a "Child's Protective Office" to deal with delinquent and morally depraved minors under eighteen, with homes, sanitariums, and dispensaries, as well as special restrictive institutions under its jurisdictions, but it was overthrown before these plans could be realized.[31]

The educational entertainment of children was another task which the government took very seriously. Kindergartens were renamed "play schools," for it was here that the child was to be indoctrinated by means of fairy tales, poems, physical exercise, and directed handicraft to be a member of the group.[32] All poems glorifying war were to be eliminated and tales were to be carefully chosen to introduce into the pure soul of the child the concepts of peace, brotherly love, and equality.[33] A great deal of emphasis was placed on the fairy tale approach to cultural indoctrination. Specialists were to be sent from school to school to give "fairy tale recitals" accompanied by drawings or animated cartoons, when possible, or available.[34]

A special theater was set aside for children. Movie houses, exclusively for children, with appropriate names such as, Andersen, Cinderella, and Gulliver, gave two performances a day, with films tailored to the age groups five to nine and ten to fourteen

28. Ibid., 2:40–41.
29. Ibid., pp. 42–47.
30. *Tanácsköztársaság*, 11 May 1919, p. 2.
31. *P. I. Archivum*, A, II, 5/10.
32. Petrák and Milei, *A Magyar Tanácsköztársaság*, p. 47.
33. Hilda Neumann, "Az óvodai foglalkozások átreformálása" [The transformation of kindergarten employment], *Kisdednevelés* [Baby care], 1 April 1919.
34. "Mesét a proletárgyermekeknek" [Tales for the children of the proletariat], *Pesti Napló* [Pest Diary], 5 April 1919.

respectively.[35] A description of such a performance (at the Cinderella) indicates the dual purpose of these events. One of the colored shorts, entitled "Porcupine," was scientific; the other, "The Golden Spider," served the purpose of indoctrination, showing the evils of capitalism and its resultant punishment.[36] The government took a puritanical viewpoint of movie attendance, strictly enforcing its edict that children under fourteen could attend movies only when children's performances were given.[37]

The regime was most thorough in its consideration of the educational institutions and programs, and the people who administered them. On March 29, 1919, all non-governmental educational and training institutions were nationalized.[38] The edict expressed the hope that all those who could adjust to the new social order would stay at their teaching and administrative posts on a temporary basis. Religious personnel (nuns and priests) were included only if they left their orders. Within three months the commissar of education promised to administer an examination, testing the social understanding and knowledge of all those connected with education.

Education became centralized in order to utilize, to the fullest, the existing plants and teachers by means of planned distribution of available resources.[39] One of the first successes of this planned program was the elimination of the gradeless schools in the villages and smaller cities. Some of these schools had one teacher for grades one through six in a single large room. The order called for consolidation of one or more of these schools for grade distribution and the better utilization of teachers. Ingenious combinations of classes were worked out depending on the age distribution of the children. The order also called for homogeneous grouping according to ability; reduction of class size; coeducational classes and schools; common utilization of gyms and play areas of the district by all the schools in it. Curriculum was also a prime target of the new order. Mathematics and physics studies were to be left unchanged, but the instruction of Latin and Greek was to cease, to be replaced by an expanded study of the Hungarian language and world literature. Special emphasis was placed on the reading of good books without hair splitting debates as to their literary merit preceding the reading. Courses in composition, modern languages, the natural sciences, as well as physical exercise were to be enlarged.[40]

History was to be the only subject radically changed, for it was in this field that the students, as well as the teachers, were to undergo a radical reorientation in order to prepare themselves for the new society. Realizing the inadequate preparation of its teachers in the Marxian interpretation of history, the commissar of education improvised. The order in May for history instructions called for a broad understanding of the concepts of wage-labor and capitalist production, the different classes, the laws

35. "A proletárgyerekek . . ." [The proletar children], Népszava, 17 April 1919, p. 5.

36. "Budapesti gyermekmozik" [Children's movies in Budapest], Vörös Film [Red Film], 7 June 1919.

37. Pongrácz, A Forradalmi, 4:57.

38. Tanácsköztársaság, 1 April 1919, p. 1.

39. Tanácsköztársaság, 20 April 1919, p. 2.

40. Petrák and Milei, A Magyar Tanácsköztársaság, pp. 31–33. ("Instruction to Insure the Undisturbed Continuance of Instruction," May 5; Order No. 87039 of the Commissar of Education.)

protecting class interest in a bourgeois capitalist state, and the imperialist internationalist competition growing out of capitalist production. The students were also to know about the sufferings of the proletariat in the world war, and their prescribed role in the world revolution. The basic lessons of these instructions for the lower grades appeared in the professional journals of the teachers. In the upper grades, available copies of the *Communist Manifesto* and Nikolai Bukharin's *The Program of the Communist Party* were to be read and studied.[41]

The official paper of the Commissariat of Education, *Fáklya* [The Torch], stated that history could no longer remain the culture of individuals, the reiteration of worn-out slogans, and the overemphasis on the influence of ideologies. The past was to be seen through a sociological and economic viewpoint. Future Hungarians would have no use for the slogan "Extra Hungariam non est vita." They were to be more concerned with the history of the development of production, trade, the arts and sciences.[42]

Grading also was to undergo radical changes. In the lower grades, year-end marks were abolished with only "satisfactory" and "nonsatisfactory" appearing on the report card. Since every child had to finish six grades, "nonsatisfactory" was given only in the rare cases in which the child failed to succeed in most of his lessons. This system of grading did not apply to the middle schools (high school). No incompetent was to ascend to the higher branches of learning. Only those who showed great hope for future success were to be passed.[43]

A great deal of money, effort, and planning was used to realize these plans. Up to June, 1919, 3,783,000 copies of pamphlets and books were printed in Hungarian and German and 5,951,000 copies in Rumanian, Serb, Croat, Slovak, Czech, and Hebrew.[44] Some of the pamphlets appeared in editions of 100,000 copies, such as: *Szózat az ifjakhoz* [A call to the young]; *Mi a bolsevizmus?* [What is bolshevism?]; *Jön az orosz testvér* [The Russian brother is coming]; *Az Ellenforradalmi kalózok* [The counterrevolutionary pirates]; *Die Lüge von der Kirchensendung.*[45]

But most of the effort and money was channeled into the task of gaining the cooperation of the teachers. They were acknowledged as better paid specialists. Their pay,[46] based on years of service, was indeed most generous:

Up to two years	K300 per week
3–5 years	K350 per week
6–7 years	K400 per week
8–10 years	K430 per week

41. Ibid., pp. 61–62. ("Instruction for New Directions in the Teaching of History," May 13; Order No. 91609 of the Commissar of Education.)

42. Vilma Bresztovszky, "A történelem az uj iskolában" [History in the new school], *Fáklya*, 29 April 1919.

43. Pongrácz, *A Forradalmi*, 3:104–5. (May 12, Order No. 28 of the Commissar of Education.)

44. *P. I. Archivum*, A, II, 7/12, pp. 97–100.

45. *P. I. Archivum*, A, II, 7/12, p. 96.

46. Pongrácz, *A Forradalmi*, 3:21–23.

11–13 years	K460 per week
14–16 years	K490 per week
17–20 years	K520 per week
20 years and above	K550 per week

Special preparation increased the wages, military service increased seniority. When one considers that the best paid skilled worker was paid K500, and directors of large plants K650, after fifteen years of service,[47] with the average income of a worker at K372.42 in July, 1919,[48] the teachers' salaries, which continued throughout the summer vacation, were impressive indeed. It is true that teachers were obligated for these wages to work above and beyond the hourly work prescribed in order to enlighten the public, to teach the illiterates, and to teach agricultural technology, all without additional compensation. During the summer of 1919, they were faced with the additional task of transforming themselves into individuals who understood and were able to teach about the organization, the tasks, and the principles of the Communist society. For this purpose each teacher had to read and understand the materials contained in the following works: (1) Karl Marx and Friederich Engels, *The Communist Manifesto;* (2) Marx, *The Civil War in France;* (3) Engels, *Utopian and Scientific Socialism;* and (4) Bukharin, *The Program of the Communists (Bolshevism).*

An examination, testing their understanding, was to be given in the second half of August. Teachers also had to study Ervin Szabó's *The Selected Works of Marx and Engels* and were to be tested on this work by school inspectors in the fall semester.[49] All teachers, up to the high school level, also had to attend lectures dealing with the history of socialism and the Communist program, with special emphasis on its cultural and economic aspects. Seminar-type discussions of the works above were also in progress.[50] The teacher was to be the key to the future. Kunfi, commissar of education, summarized all of the speeches of all the leaders when he said: "The schools from now on will become, through the efforts of the teachers, the most important institution for the training of socialism."[51]

Despite preferential treatment, despite relatively high salaries, the bulk of the teachers were either hostile or passive to the new order for a number of reasons. In the first place, the transition was too rapid and, coming at the virtual end of the school year, the numerous orders of the government, enforced by a most active Commissariat of Education, had to be telescoped into the three months available before the dispersal of teachers and students. Cultural reorientation takes time, and ninety days were obviously not enough to bring about the desired change. Most teachers felt a loyalty to the old order, for it was they who had indoctrinated the children in the love of God, king and country. Even the more liberal-minded, who applauded the

47. *Tanácsköztársaság*, 31 May 1919 (May 30, Order No. 106).
48. Petrák and Milei, *A Magyar Tanácsköztársaság*, p. xv.
49. Pongrácz, *A Forradalmi*, 5:87–88.
50. "A tanítók átképzése" [The re-education of teachers], *Népszava*, 1 July 1919, p. 1.
51. "A tanítók forradalmasítása" [The revolutionizing of the teachers], *Népszava*, 21 June 1919, p. 6.

progressive nature of the new program, were oriented toward a liberal viewpoint respecting the rights of freedom of the individual.

These liberal viewpoints and sensitivities of the teachers were put to a severe test in the revolutionary atmosphere permeating the school and society. Errors committed in the revolutionary fervor of the first few days remained to plague the government. Thus "student directories," appointed by student representatives, who were nominated to watch over the loyalty of the teachers and the orthodoxy of the curriculum, cleansed school libraries of reactionary, chauvinistic books and replaced them with "progressive works of Marxist literature."[52] The resultant clash between teachers and students was finally ended by an order of the commissar of education, abolishing student trustees in schools, admitting the harm they caused to discipline and to the serious pursuit of learning.[53]

Sex education in the schools was another revolutionary innovation which had to be abolished due to unprepared, and consequently, embarrassing presentation, of a too hasty introduction of the subject in the curriculum.[54] The initial harm, enlarged by growing dissatisfaction, could not be reversed. Nor was it helpful for a professional journal to ask teachers specifically to act as informers in reporting anyone to the police who evidenced any opposition to the dictatorship of the proletariat.[55]

Another point of friction was religion. The lay teaching staffs of parochial and private schools (they constituted nearly 70 percent of the schools in Hungary) were permitted to retain their positions, at least temporarily. After nationalization their problems were compounded by their natural antipathy to the new system. Thus, when prayer was forbidden in the schools of Budapest;[56] when orders were given for the removal of crucifixes in all schools;[57] when in the National Congress of Councils accusations were made of desecration of the host by young revolutionary and political trustees who were sent to the villages advocating turning the churches into movie houses,[58] the enemies of the regime received ready-made weapons for their arsenal, used them, and enlarged upon them most effectively. It was to no avail that the government guaranteed freedom of religion, declaring it to be a private affair, and considered everyone who either stopped or disturbed any individual in the free exercise of his religion a counterrevolutionary.[59] The fact that even an avowed enemy of

52. Gellért László, "Szociálista középiskolai diákmozgalom, 1918–1919" [Student movements in the middle schools, 1918–1919], *Pedagógiai Szemle* [Pedagogical Review], 9, no. 3 (March 1959):313.

53. *Tanácskötársaság*, 10 July 1919 (Order No. 55 of the Commissariat of Education).

54. *Tanácsköztársaság*, 10 July 1919 (Order No. 56 of the Commissariat of Education).

55. Sándor Köte, "A pedagógusok helyzete és szerepe a Tanácskötársaság idején" [The position and role of the teachers during the time of the soviet republic], *Köznevelés* [Public Education], no. 5 (March 1959):99–100.

56. Katalin Petrák and György Milei, eds., *A Magyar Tanácsköztársaság művelődéspolitikája* [The cultural policy of the Hungarian Soviet Republic] (Budapest: Gondolat, 1959), p. 12.

57. "Szombathelyi sajtónk jelenti" [Our correspondent reports from Szombathely), 11 April 1919, in *P. I. Archivum*, A, II, 15/21, Fond 24/21.

58. *A Tanácsok*, p. 216.

59. Zsigmond Kunfi, "A vallás szabad gyakorlása" [The free exercise of religion],*Népszava*, 18 April 1919, p. 1.

the state, who saw in the new regime nothing but Jewish desecration and disrespect for the church, described the scrupulous observance of the proviso (Paragraph 2) in the law respecting the inviolatibility of church property used for religious purposes (in this case wine) did not change public opinion.[60] Only the stories of the excesses were remembered and repeated.

Much more justifiable was the dissatisfaction of the teachers with the policy of the government in regard to the freedom of the press. In a lecture, Béla Kőhalmi, director of the capital's library and an intrepid Communist, warned his listeners against all bourgeois and Social Democratic literature. After absorbing the technical knowledge, especially from the bourgeois works, the rest of the literature was to be viewed with precaution and distrust. In answering the question what a good Communist should read, he suggested repeated readings of the *Communist Manifesto*, until it was memorized and could be repeated by heart. For entertainment he suggested the reading of Edward Bellamy's *Looking Backward*, H. G. Wells's *New World in Its Old Place*, and Anatole France's *White Stone*.[61] Future plans of the Commissariat of Education, announced by Béla Balázs, were to include censorship. At a meeting of the Research Workers' Association he said that the state would exercise censorship over literature, justifying this action by stating that censorship existed previously. The state was ready to appoint and pay boards of censors made up of writers and officials of the government.[62]

However, the greatest blow to the freedom to read and write came in the field of journalism. The government appointed a Press Directorate on March 25, 1919, and suspended the publication of ten dailies in Budapest;[63] on April 7 it closed 225 newspapers (union, technical, professional, religious, and school publications) some on direct orders from commissars.[64] Although paper shortages could be claimed justifiably by May, these earlier closings were based on political reasons, especially the desire to eliminate the bourgeois press. For instance, plans were made by the Press Directorate on April 1, 1919, to close all the remaining bourgeois dailies and to turn their plants and personnel over to individual commissariats. On April 20 the newspaper *Világ* was actually turned over to the Commissariat of Education, under the name of *Fáklya*. However, on May 24, 1919, all newspapers in Budapest, except five, were closed due to drastic shortages of paper. The only remaining newspapers were *Népszava*, *Vörös Ujság*, *Világszabadság*, *Volksstimme*, and *Pester Lloyd*, whose duty it was to keep the world informed of events occurring in Hungary.[65]

60. Zsigmond Bernhard, S.J., *Egy jezsuita emlékei a kommunizmus idejéből* [A Jesuit's recollection of the time of communism] (Budapest, 1919), p. 33.

61. Béla Kőhalmi, *Mit olvassunk a szociálista irodalomból* [What we should read from Socialist literature] (Budapest, 1919), pp. 11–15.

62. "A jövő irodalma" [The literature of the future], *Pesti Hirlap*, 18 April 1919.

63. *P. I. Archivum*, A, II, 15/43, Fond 24/2 (Minutes of the Press Directorate), 25 March 1919, p. 1.

64. *P. I. Archivum*, A, II, 15/43, Fond 24/2 (Minutes), 7 April 1919, pp. 51–52.

65. András Siklós, *Az 1918–1919 évi magyarországi forradalmak* [The 1918–1919 Hungarian revolution] (Budapest: Tankönyvkiadó, 1964), p. 62.

That political considerations were paramount in the closing of the papers became obvious when, at a meeting of a nine-man commission of the Press Directorate on April 15, 1919, Béla Vágó, commissar of interior, condemned the weekly *Az Ember* for attacking a "valuable member" of the Revolutionary Governing Council. Influenced by this attack, the members of the Revolutionary Governing Council decided to take the strongest steps to destroy the bourgeois press. There was a shocked, but guarded, reaction from the men representing the working members of the press. Ignác Bogár, speaking for the printers, although agreeing with Vágó, uttered a veiled threat by saying that printers who were making K300–400 a week, and living accordingly, would find it difficult to adjust to the K105 unemployment insurance. Bogár felt that reassurance by Vágó was called for since it would be sad "if unrest were to start in the ranks of the printers."

Vágó in his reply stated that every sacrifice had to be made when one considered what the closing of the bourgeois press meant to the dictatorship of the proletariat. But, recognizing the strength of organized labor, he gave assurances that nothing would be done without consultation with the printers.[66] The paper shortage made further debate academic. The government promised the printers, the office workers, and the reporters full pay, utilizing the confiscated wealth of the former owners[67] to meet these expenses. In return, it asked reporters to go to the country to teach illiterates to read and write. That this request, as well as the pressure of inflation, irregular compensation, and erratic administration was disliked and resented was well evidenced in a pejorative article about the trade-union of the reporters, in *Népszava*. For declaring against the dictatorship and demanding the restoration of the freedom of the press, the union was called a lackey of the *bourgeoisie* and its members referred to as traitors to their country. The leadership resigned and the union was dissolved.[68] Too much haste in fulfilling the Marxian blueprint and the insistence on rigid enforcement without the power, personnel, materials, and time led to the failure of the cultural policy of the regime.

The government's social welfare program was as radical, as detailed, as expensive and, in some areas, as visionary as its cultural program. In an overall evaluation of its successes and failures one should not lose sight of the fact that these plans were undertaken at the conclusion of a disastrous war of over four years' duration, and under Entente blockade and intervention. Also, due to the regime's short existence, many of these policies could not be carried out. It will be seen that under the severe test of reality, many of the social welfare programs that were implemented, had to be modified and, in some cases, completely changed. As in its cultural program, the government tried enthusiastically and unrealistically to correct the abuses of centuries. Again one is struck by the textbook recitation of the ills of society and their scientific (Marxian) remedy, regardless of cost, human weaknesses, and contradictions.

66. *P. I. Archivum*, A, II, 15/43, Fond 24/2 (Minutes of the nine-man Commission of the Press Directorate), 15 April 1919, pp. 59–62.
67. *P. I. Archivum*, A, II, 15/43, Fond 24/2 (Minutes of the Press Directorate), 25 March 1919.
68. "Fölbómlott az ujságirók szakszervezete" [The union of journalists was dissolved], *Népszava*, 9 July 1919, p. 5.

The new society eliminated all titles, including gradations of address (excellency, right honorable, etc.). Only titles denoting occupations were permitted, i.e., doctor, accountant, etc.[69] The interesting juxtaposition of those denied the right to vote was another indication of the new power structure of society.[70] Finally, when the government forced everyone to work and also assumed the duty of supporting all those unable to work, as well as those who wanted work but could not find jobs, it created a welfare state and, at the same time, sealed its own economic doom.[71]

All the problems associated with the right to work law were to plague the regime: the necessity of creating economically wasteful jobs; the impossibility of getting rid of dead wood; and the financial drain on the treasury. Nevertheless, the attempt to overcome unemployment, one of the greatest social evils of industrial society, had begun and despite the faults found in its cure, it was greeted with enthusiasm.

The social policy of the government toward children, prostitution, and alcoholism have already been discussed. The institution of marriage was somewhat weakened by the ease with which divorces were obtainable. If both parties desired a divorce, all they had to do was to register their desire, sign a record of it, and the divorce was legal and final. In case of dispute, the court decided the matter, after hearing evidence from both parties. Alimony was decided in a separate decision by the court, depending on the need and guilt of the party seeking it. There was no appeal.[72] Women were now the equals of men. There was a great deal of literature and discussion as to how the exploited women of capitalism, the "kitchen slaves, who from morning to night see nothing but dishes, dish cloths, scrubbing brushes and garbage," were to be liberated under communism. Almost tongue in cheek, was the statement of an official of the Commissariat of Education who stated: "The fulfillment of the task of motherhood is such a serious undertaking . . . consumes so much energy and physical strength that the Communist order recognizes its fulfillment as much as it does productive labor."[73] The "communization of women," a charge made by counterrevolutionaries with great effect in the villages, was scornfully and justifiably refuted.

The medical program of the government was progressive and thorough. It was carried out, in most cases, by physicians who were impressed by the humanitarian aspects of the program. Physicians may also have been cooperative as a result of the preferential treatment given them by the government. Thus, until the end of its reign, the Hungarian Soviet Republic did not put a ceiling on physicians' pay, except in cases of interns and residents, whose wages were raised.[74]

69. Pongrácz, A Forradalmi, 1:16 (March 25; Order No. 6).

70. "Ineligible to vote a) those who employ others for profit, b) those living on incomes not derived from work, c) businessmen, d) priests and canons, e) those insane, f) common criminals whose voting rights have been abrogated, for the duration of their prison term." Ibid., 1:46 (April 12; Order No. 26).

71. Tanácsköztársaság, 27 March 1919, p. 1 (Order No. 9).

72. Tanácsköztársaság, 20 May 1919, p. 1 (Order No. 99).

73. Zsófia Dénes, A nő a kommunista társadalomban [Women in the communist society] (Budapest, 1919), p. 17. (The charge of "kitchen slaves" is made by Bukharin in his "The Program of the Communists." His solution: communal kitchens.)

74. Petrák and Milei, A Magyar Tanácsköztársaság, Szociálpolitikája, p. 285.

Professional men also retained their authority to run hospitals despite nationalization. The government was most definite in abolishing the practice of political trustees running hospitals, calling this a misinterpretation of Order No. 9 of the Revolutionary Governing Council (dealing with the nationalization of industry and mines) and an infringement on the medical director's authority.[75] Another act, no doubt pleasing to the profession, was the order prohibiting advertising, calling it "unethical and below the dignity of the profession."[76]

The basic medical program of the government, however, was the nationalization of all private hospitals and sanitariums. The different classes of care, food, and rooms were abolished and free and identical care and food for all patients was substituted. Private rooms were reserved for the very ill.[77] Care for the insane, their admission and discharge, was taken care of by a progressive and detailed order, providing for plenty of supervision and control.[78] All drug manufacturing firms, wholesale and retail stores selling drugs and medical equipment were nationalized.[79] The regime's predilection for detail extended even to the prescription of the type of scissors that were to be used in first aid kits in factories.[80]

Even in death, the regime followed its policy of absolute equality. In Budapest, all graves were to be identical; the further sale of double plots and crypts was forbidden; the deceased was to be buried in the grave which numerically followed the previous burial; all adult plots were to cost K100 and children's plots K50 each.[81]

No policy of the government caused as many problems, led to as much dissatisfaction and corruption, as the socialization of apartments and houses. Considering the deplorable housing conditions, the totally inadequate space available (practically no new houses were built during the war years), the program should have been popular. But the avariciousness of many people and the methods of the administration, which ignored the basic human emotion of defending one's private personal property, brought about corruption and engendered a growing hatred against the regime. As with all its social and welfare laws, the government tried to do too much in too short a time, thus satisfying no one. The basic law affecting this subject declared all apartments, their attachments and belongings, the property of the Hungarian government. Rent was to be collected by the house inspector and the trustees of the tenants, jointly. Private house owners, who previously paid no rent, had their rent determined by the Commissariat of Socialist Production. Those houses built by wage earners (workers, both white- and blue-collar) and used by the same were exempt from the law.[82]

---

75. Ibid., p. 86.

76. *Tanácsköztársaság*, 17 April 1919, p. 1 (Order No. 8 of the Commissariat of Labor and Welfare).

77. Pongrácz, *A Forradalmi*, 2:37–38 (April 24; Order No. 70).

78. Ibid., 5:25 (June 15; Order No. 117).

79. *Tanácsköztársaság*, 9 April 1919, p. 1 (Order No. 117).

80. Pongrácz, *A Forradalmi*, 5:107 (June 25; General Order of the Commissariat of Labor and Welfare).

81. Petrák and Milei, *A Magyar Tanácsköztársaság Szociálpolitikja*, pp. 60–61.

82. Ibid., 1:19 (March 26; Order No. 10).

The essence of the program, however, was stated in Order No. 15 which spelled out the principles which were to govern the requisitioning and the distribution of the rooms and furniture.[83] The edict established in Budapest and its environs a central Housing Commission with broad confiscatory powers. In rather loose terminology it called for the "confiscation of all superfluous furniture needed for everyday life" and, although limiting the maximum living space of one family to three rooms, it contradicted this by stating that the commission had to consider the number of children, their sex, age, and occupation, when issuing the order of confiscation. Confusion, and the possibility of circumvention of the law, was further compounded by exempting all foyers, closets, servants' rooms, and rooms utilized in a professional capacity, thus creating the possibility of evasion. Severe penalties for hoarding rooms or furniture— ten years in prison and a fine of K50,000 plus the loss of the whole apartment—were imposed in an attempt to eliminate cheating.

Armed with these basic and loosely defined orders the commission set to work. Its failures must have been catastrophic, for on April 10, 1919, the Revolutionary Governing Council appointed its most dedicated member and servant, Tibor Szamuely, a convinced believer of draconic measures, to head the Housing Commission. Although Béla Vágó shared this post with him, the sentiment and words of consequent statements and edicts had the "Szamuely touch." In his acceptance "speech" he declared the commission the "garbage dump" of the exploitation of labor, dismissed three-fourths of its employees (300 people), and stated that the majority of the apartment hunters were useless rabble, seeking only self-gain and profit. His methods of attacking the problem were equally direct. He deported 200,000 idlers, who had arrived in Budapest, principally from Galicia, and took an exact and thorough census utilizing new questionnaires (the death penalty was threatened for falsification). He decreed that any man coming to the Housing Office with a letter of recommendation was to be immediately arrested, and he confiscated all superfluous apartments. In distribution of property trade-union members were to be taken care of first, while the best place for the others (shirkers and speculators) was, in his opinion, the Red Army barracks.[84] Five days later, even Szamuely admitted his defeat and his inability to clear the Augean stables of the Housing Commission and to cope with the avarice of the majority of the applicants who repeatedly applied for new quarters, trafficking in apartments and reaping huge profits.[85] A series of directives aimed at stopping the abuses and liberally sprinkled with threats of death penalties were obviously ineffective. After the short tenure of Szamuely (on April 21 he was appointed president of the Extraordinary Commission Behind the Front, to deal with desertion, cowardice, and treason), the cheating, the speculation, and the subversion continued. Debates in the National Congress of Councils repeatedly pointed to corruption, nepotism, and protectionism.[86] Commissar Varga admitted to corruption in various bureaus and even

83. *Tanácsköztársaság*, 30 March 1919, p. 1.
84. *Vörös Ujság*, 10 April 1919 (A Proclamation), p. 1.
85. Tibor Szamuely, "Lakáskeresők" [Apartment seekers], *Vörös Ujság*, 15 April 1919, p. 1.
86. *A Tanácsok*, pp. 98-99.

among the workers;[87] as late as July 12 he made charges of nepotism and corruption in both apartment and furniture distribution.[88]

What then was accomplished by the housing laws? On July 4, a general statistical summary claimed that about 70,000 individuals in Budapest had received new quarters, with about 24,000 apartments requisitioned up to June 12, but about 200,000 persons still were in need of decent living quarters.[89] The same report points out the tremendous cost of this service—K1,314,000 in May alone. It also touches on the cost of necessary repairs: K30,000,000 of initial investment.[90] The astronomical cost of maintaining and running the nationalized houses was compounded by the order which reduced all annual rents under K2,000 by 20 percent[91] and another which cancelled all accrued nonpaid rents for veterans and their families.[92] Because of inflation and the consequent disproportion between rents and general prices, the government was contemplating a rise of twenty to fifty percent in rents when it was overthrown.[93]

The distribution of furniture was conducted in a more businesslike fashion. The confiscated furniture was sold to the workers, at cost, in forty monthly installments, payable to the state by payroll deductions. On the death of the purchaser his heir or family could keep the furniture if they assumed the debt.[94] In most other cities of Hungary neither nationalization of apartments nor furniture was as rapid and extensive as in Budapest.[95]

The wage and price policy of the government reflected the usual economic and social maladjustment of revolutionary change, telescoped into a brief period of time. The transition, from the first wage law to the last, demonstrates the metamorphosis from the fulfillment of cherished union goals to the stark realities of a dictatorship facing declining production and a labor force totally lacking in incentive. All of the average worker's cherished goals were fulfilled: piece work was abolished, a forty-eight-hour week was instituted, salaries increased, insurances were made compulsory, and the government was obligated to supply the worker with a job. The psychological and social consequences of these policies were detrimental to production which, in turn, was the key to all other problems. Since he could not be fired, since he was told that he was a member of the class that ruled, since his wages were now based on the hour or week, and not on the quantity he produced, the worker no longer saw the necessity of working to capacity. He no longer considered himself a wage slave.

87. Ibid., pp. 28–30.
88. "Befejezték a lakásügyről szoló vitát" [The debates about apartments are finished], Népszava, 12 July 1919, p. 4.
89. "Budapest számokban. Lakók és lakások, 1919 Junius 4" [Budapest in numbers. Dwellers and dwellings], MMTVD, 6/B:238–39.
90. Ibid.
91. Pongrácz, A Forradalmi, 1:31 (March 28; Order 17).
92. Tanácskztársaság, 16 April 1919 (Order 59).
93. MMTVD, 6/B:241.
94. Tanácskötársaság, 27 April 1919 (Order No. 24 of the Commissariat of the Treasury).
95. Petrák and Milei, A Magyar Tanácsköztársaság, Szociálpolitikája, p. xxxiii.

TABLE 1

Category	Weekly Wages*
I Skilled workers and workers with practical experience of over ten years	K192 to K508
II Practical experience of less than ten years and unskilled workers of more than ten years' experience	K144 to K311
III Unskilled workers with less than ten years of experience	K120 to K264
IV Apprentices	K72 to K120

SOURCE: Pongrácz, *A Forradalmi*, 2:32–33 (Order No. 64; April 17, 1919).
* Although the law quoted hourly wages, they are given on a weekly basis for purposes of comparison.

When—despite all the promises and all the propaganda—inflation destroyed his gain in wages, shortages removed most goods from his reach, and a desperate government tried to restore piece work, pay differentials, and labor discipline, the average individual gave vent to his anger and frustration by passive resistance and by petty acts of corruption.

An examination of the wage laws will demonstrate the difficulties faced by a regime attempting to institute uniform wages. The first general directive for industrial workers set up four categories of wages (see table 1), based on a forty-eight-hour week, overtime pay up to 100 percent (to be given only under extremely rare circumstances), and a 20 percent extra compensation for night work. Outdoor workers were to get full pay during work stoppages caused by inclement weather and workers having to travel to provinces were to receive up to 70 percent extra pay.

The following two orders were more specific in an attempt to clarify the pay scale each individual belonged in. On May 3, 1919, three wage categories were created,

TABLE 2

Experience of Worker	Category		
	I	II	III
Under 18	160	160	. . .
Above 18, up to two years	180	200	. . .
Three to four years	200	250	. . .
Five to eight years	250	300	. . .
Nine to twelve years	300	400	450
Thirteen to fifteen years	325	450	500
Sixteen to twenty years	350	500	600
More than twenty years	400	500	650

SOURCE: Pongrácz, *A Forradalmi*, 3:14–15 (Order No. 83).

TABLE 3

Experience of Worker	Category				
	I	II	III	IV	V
Under 17 years, without experience	120	...	...	...	...
Under 17 years, with experience	150	...	...	...	...
Over 17 years, with zero to two years	170	...	...	...	...
Two to five years	230	270	320	...	...
Five to ten years	270	320	380	430	520
Ten to fifteen years	300	370	450	520	600
Fifteen years and over	320	400	500	600	650

SOURCE: Pongrácz, *A Forradalmi*, 5:13–16 (Order No. 106).

placing the responsibility of interpretation and execution under the jurisdiction of the Commissariat of Socialist Production (see table 2). On May 7, 1919, the Commissariat of Socialist Production supplemented and clarified the question of classification. In the first category it placed all those without technical skill, i.e., salesmen, clerks, and supervisors without technical skill; in the second category those having technical skills, including engineers, college graduates, or those who had similar positions although lacking college degrees; in the third category, responsible heads of departments, factories, and other large concerns. Those not fitting into any category (inventors, philosophers, explorers, researchers) were to have their salaries determined by the commissariat. Overtime pay was set at 25 percent extra and miners working underground received an additional 20 percent.[96]

The last industrial wage law, passed on May 30, 1919, set up five categories for workers in shops, factories, commerce, transportation, and other occupations, including office workers (see table 3). The first category included all the unskilled workers; the second, skilled office, business, and technical employees; the third, skilled self-employed workers and group and section foremen; the fourth, leaders of small firms,

TABLE 4

	Budapest and Surroundings	Other Parts of the Country
Men's daily wages	K40	K35
Women's daily wages	K35	K30
Boys and girls (16–18)	K25	K20
Boys and girls (14–16)	K16	K14
Wages of those younger than 14	K12	K10

SOURCE: *Tanácsköztársaság*, 18 June 1919 (Order No. 47, Public Economic Council). The order was effective between June 15 and September 1, 1919.

96. Pongrácz, *A Forradalmi*, 3:173–76 (Order No. 71 of the Commissariat of Socialist Production).

section directors of large firms, and specialists; and the fifth, directors of plants and highly specialized individuals.[97]

As nebulous in detail as proper wage classification of industrial workers seemed to be, the orders affecting agricultural wages were much more direct, brief, and even curt. After a tentative attempt to set the hours for agricultural work,[98] a wage law was issued setting a single salary scale which called for an hourly wage of K30 for men and K25 for women with a decreasing scale for children under fifteen years of age (see table 4). Farmers near Budapest were to receive K5 more than farmers in the other areas of the country, with reapers receiving 10 percent more in all areas. Strict work rules were set up. Supervisors were to determine the hours of work and their orders were to be strictly obeyed.[99] The last wage law affecting farmers was passed June 17, 1919, and called for the average work day to be from sunup to sundown, interspaced with rest periods amounting to three and one-half hours. Harvesters were to receive 10 percent more in salary, but otherwise the wages could not be lowered nor could the farmers demand more.

A comparison of the weekly wages of the best paid farm worker with that of the industrial worker, demonstrated his inferior position. A harvester, with his weekly salary set at K264, working from sunup to sundown (compared to the forty-eight hours of the industrial worker) was on the lowest rung of the industrial worker's wage scale. Although complaints were repeatedly voiced concerning this inequality, the major problem was the farmer's inability to purchase merchandise, due to shortages of consumer goods and the crippling inflation. At the National Congress of Councils, farm representatives, after admitting that farmers made more money than ever before, pointed out that they were able to buy less than previously. Thus, an ordinary shirt (if available) cost K200; a scythe, which the harvester had to purchase for himself, cost K300.[100]

If wages differentiated between industrial and farm laborers, the comprehensive insurance policy of the government did not. Both benefited by the accident and health insurance which compensated the worker a full year, commencing with the first day of his illness. For the first four weeks he received 60 percent and after that 75 percent of his wages; a family man, after twenty-six weeks, received 100 percent of his salary for up to a year. Pregnant women received full salary in the last four weeks of their pregnancy. The contribution of each worker to his insurance was 6 percent of his daily wage.[101] Major discrepancies existed between this order of the Revolutionary Governing Council and that of Order No. 3 of the Commissariat of Labor and Public Welfare, issued on April 5, 1919.[102] Contributions were lower than 6 percent, but the highest benefit paid to a worker with a family, based on his wage-scale category, amounted to K120, the lowest K30 weekly, nowhere near 60 percent or 75 percent of the salary spoken of in the previous order.

97. Ibid., 5:13–16 (Order No. 106).
98. Ibid., 2:62–63 (April; Order No. 22 of the Commissariat of Agriculture).
99. Ibid., 3:48–50 (May 10; Order No. 41 of the Commissariat of Agriculture).
100. A Tanácsok, p. 97 and p. 61. The prices are quoted as of May, 1919.
101. Pongrácz, A Forradalmi, 1:34–36 (March 29; Order No. 21).
102. Tanácsköztársaság, 5 April 1919 (Order No. 10).

There were obvious shortcomings in the execution of the government's insurance policies. Numerous newspaper articles and speeches at various meetings deal with this topic. Typical of the confusion and the ineffectiveness is the case of totally disabled veterans. On April 18, 1919, Szamuely, as head of the disabled veterans' affairs, issued his Order No. 1 in which he raised the yearly benefits of the totally disabled veterans by 100 percent to K4,800.[103] However, on May 21, 1919, all affairs concerning disabled veterans were placed under the jurisdiction of the Commissariat of Welfare and Health,[104] thus all orders of Szamuely dealing with the subject became null and void. On June 14, 1919, one of the officials of this commissariat admitted that it was useless to set down permanent rules.[105] Changes occurred practically daily[106] until the very last day of the regime when the Revolutionary Governing Council reiterated the instructions of May 21, 1919.[107]

The administration's price policy, although detailed enough to prescribe the price, as well as the exact composition of a lemonade sold at theaters and movies,[108] was unrealistic and impossible to enforce, due to decreased production, the black market, and shortages of raw materials which were caused by the blockade of the Entente. The price of goods was to include not only the cost of production but the price tag for the "services" of the Communist state. As Jenő Varga stated, "all the goods produced in our factories will be sold, not at production cost, but social production cost, with an increase in prices which will include the share needed for the livelihood of teachers, Red soldiers and office workers."[109] Instead of income taxes, taxation of goods was to supply the necessary revenue to pay for the social services supplied by the state.

A composite list of some official prices[110] in June and July demonstrated their divorce from reality:

Men's shoes	K95–290
Men's shirts	K200
Men's suits	K4,000
Three-course meal	K11.70–16.40 (depending on the class of restaurant)

103. "A teljesen megrokkant proletárok évi járuléka ezentul évi 4,800 korona" [The yearly compensation of those totally disabled is 4,800 crowns from the present time], *Világ* [World], 19 April 1919, p. 3.

104. *Tanácsköztársaság*, 22 May 1919 (Order No. 103).

105. Dr. István Nagy, "A Munkaügyi és Népjóléti Népbiztosság Rokkantügyi Föcsoportja" [The main division for the disabled in the Commissariat of Labor and Public Welfare], *A Bajtárs* [The Comrade], 14 June 1919 (Order No. 13).

106. *A Tanácsok*, pp. 100–101.

107. *Tanácsköztársaság*, 31 July 1919 (Order No. 134).

108. Pongrácz, *A Forradalmi*, 5:167–69 (6.910/1919 O.K.A.B.).

109. *A Tanácsok*, pp. 32–33.

110. Pongrácz, *A Forradalmi*, 4:201–2 (6870/1919; 7.250/1919; 7620/1919 O.K.A.B.); and "Megállapitottuk az uj husárakat" [We established the new meat prices], *Vörös Ujság*, 6 July 1919, pp. 6–7.

Men's haircuts	K3–5
Beef	K46 per kg.
Raw bacon	K24 per kg.
Pork	K32 per kg.

The many meatless weeks, proclaimed by the government, and newspaper articles, such as the one reporting a woman caught selling two geese for K2,590, present a more realistic picture of supply and demand and the resultant prices.[111] Gyula Lengyel pointed to still another shortcoming of the official price policy: the prices asked for, failed even to cover the cost of production, much less the social cost of the welfare state. For things costing three billion the government received one billion. The causes, according to Lengyel, were shortages of goods, lack of organization, and an incorrect price policy.[112]

All industry, mines, and transportation facilities whose working force exceeded twenty became the property of the state, retroactive to March 20, 1919, and were to be administered jointly by production commissars appointed by the state and workers' councils.[113] Apartments were socialized on March 26, 1919.[114] Banks became state property on the same date, with a proviso that no one could withdraw more than K2,000 of his savings and that directors were to stay on their jobs (at a maximum salary of K3,000 a month), instructing others who would take over at a later date.[115] Safe-deposit boxes were opened; gold coins and foreign coins were to be turned over to the government.[116] All wholesale and retail stores (those having more than ten employees) became state property as of March 22, 1919.[117] All hotels and spas were socialized,[118] as was the film industry and the movies. Gold pieces, jewelry, diamonds (in the possession of individuals), whose value exceeded K2,000, were confiscated by the state without compensation.[119] Life insurance companies were socialized with the order that no claim exceeding K2,000 was to be paid out (unless the beneficiary was the government).[120] In rapid succession, most trades and businesses (photographers, employment agencies, exterminators, etc.) and private possessions (stamp and coin collections, horses, carriages, fodder) were either socialized or confiscated by the government.

Huge sums thus fell into the hands of the government, including about K16 billion in deposits, securities, bonds, and stocks, due to the socialization of 800 banks and their branches. However, as Varga pointed out, although this vast sum deprived the

111. "Drága libák" [Expensive geese], *Vörös Ujság*, 27 July 1919, p. 5.
112. "A Tanácsköztársaság gazdasági helyzete" [The economic situation of the government], *Népszava*, 12 June 1919, p. 4.
113. Pongrácz, *A Forradalmi*, 1:18–19 (Order No. 9).
114. Ibid., 1:19 (Order No. 10).
115. Ibid., 1:22–23 (Order No. 12).
116. Ibid., 1:23–25 (Orders No. 13 and No. 14).
117. Ibid., 1:50–51 (12 April 1919; Order No. 31).
118. Ibid., 1:53 (Order No. 33).
119. *Tanácsköztársaság*, 13 April 1919, p. 1.
120. Pongrácz, *A Forradalmi*, 1:41 (March 30; Order No. 25).

bourgeoisie of the concentrated fiscal power to strike back, it did not add a single positive contribution to the economic salvation of the nation.[121]

A vast bureaucracy was created to transform this fiscal wealth into productive power. The People's Economic Council, through its nine major departments, created on June 29, 1919, was to perform this task, but due to the fall of the regime on August 1, 1919, it was unable to carry out its planned program.[122] The lack of time was not the only reason for its failure. There were three major reasons: (1) the inability of the government to solve the monetary problems of the nation; (2) the mistakes the government made in its agricultural policies; (3) the corruption permeating the whole social and economic fabric of a political system rapidly approaching dissolution.

The monetary problem of the government was directly traceable to the fiscal dislocation caused by the war years. Expressed in its simplest terms, at the time of the founding of the soviet republic, most of the available cash was in the hands of the peasantry, who hoarded it, while most of the savings bank deposits belonged to the *bourgeoisie*. We have seen how the funds which were institutionalized were confiscated by the state (deposits, stocks, bonds, and insurances). However, when it came to jewelry, gold, stamp collections, securities, and valuables, there was an excellently functioning and almost professionally efficient sabotage, so that utilization of this wealth never even came into the question. The jewels and stamp collections remained, by and large, intact in private hands and only a few foreign securities could be converted into money.[123]

Compounding this problem of the government was the fact that there were two kinds of paper money in circulation when it assumed power. This situation was caused by the Károlyi regime, which, in order to enhance the printing of money, ordered it printed in Vienna, using plates brought from Budapest. This money had no printing on one side and, therefore, was dubbed *white money* (first issue) in comparison to the old bank notes, which were called *blue money*. On March 21, 1919, the Austro-Hungarian Bank in Budapest had 706 million korona in blue money, and 1,207 billion in white money; with the socialized banks shortly delivering another 1.08 billion in blue money.

When the monetary experts of the soviet republic saw that further printing of money was necessary, they ordered the printing of K25 and K200 notes (using plates left in Budapest, with different serial numbers). The K25 notes appeared at the end of April, the K200 notes in the middle of May. The total issue amounted to 3.7 billion. This new money was dubbed the *new white money*.[124] The public already disliked the

121. *A Tanácsok*, p. 24.

122. *Tanácsköztársaság*, 29 June 1919, p. 1. The nine departments and their leaders were: I. General Economy, Jenő Varga; II. Agricultural Affairs, Jenő Hamburger and Károly Vántus; III. Industrial Production, Antal Dovcsák; IV. Monetary Affairs, Béla Székely; V. Food Office, István Kulcsár; VI. Transportation, Richárd Bodó; VII. Economic Organization, Gyula Lengyel; VIII. Public Building, Sándor Garbai; IX. Labor Affairs, Ferenc Bojáki.

123. Ádám Schmidt, "A Tanácsköztársaság néhany pénzügyi kérdése" [A few fiscal questions of the soviet republic], *Közgazdasági Szemle* [Economic Review], 4, no. 3 (March 1959):271.

124. Ibid., p. 278.

old issue of K200 and K25 notes. This mistrust was caused by their different appearance (one side was blank) and the unfortunate text on the note, which created the impression that it would become invalid, as legal tender, as of June 30, 1919.

The government was remiss in failing to clarify and correct this impression.[125] Attempts were made to make the white money accepted,[126] but they were to no avail. There then developed a serious shortage of small change; everyone was reluctant to give up his blue money (small denominations) for white money (large denominations).[127]

To alleviate this situation the Revolutionary Governing Council ordered a printing of postal savings notes, in denominations of K5, 10, 15, and 20.[128] This eased the problem of small change somewhat, but the amount of blue notes in circulation took another drop. The peasantry, especially, refused to accept the white money for payment and would release its produce only for blue money, which they then hoarded. To compound this problem, the blue money was accepted as legal tender in Austria and the succession states, while the new white money was not. White money, therefore, became the means of exchange in governmental circles and the cities, while blue money served this function in the country. Hoarding and speculation created a great discrepancy between their relative values, contributing to embittered relations between the urban and rural population.

The government's order of June 5, 1919, calling for the gradual withdrawal of blue money from circulation, was totally ineffectual.[129] The continued deterioration of the korona and the consequent inflation put an end to all hopes for a sound fiscal program. Pressed by the economic blockade and warfare of its neighbors as well as by the cost of its own overambitious domestic programs, all of the soviet republic's efforts to solve its monetary problems were doomed.

The government was even more unsuccessful in its agricultural policy. It faced a curious dilemma in its approach to this crucial problem. If land were parcelled out among small, individual owners, the regime was assured of the support of the great majority of the landless peasants. However, with the fragmentation of the land, and the resultant inefficient production, food supplies to the cities would have dropped, causing dissatisfaction and hunger among the industrial workers who were essential to the dictatorship of the proletariat. As was pointed out repeatedly, the revolution was won by the industrial proletariat of the cities and they had to be fed.[130]

After some procrastination the government finally decided in favor of the maintenance of large socialized estates in the form of agricultural cooperatives. Accordingly, the Revolutionary Governing Council, in its order to socialize all medium and large holdings, gave strict orders to the effect that confiscated land, its equipment and

125. *A Tanácsok*, p. 57.

126. Pongrácz, *A Forradalmi*, 3:16 (May 7; Order No. 85).

127. *P. I. Archivum Fol. Hung.*, 2191/V, pp. 24-25.

128. Pongrácz, *A Forradalmi*, 3:24 (May 15; Order No. 92).

129. Ibid., 4:35-36 (Order No. 109); after the fall of the soviet republic white money could be redeemed at one-fifth of its value.

130. "Országos földmüves-kongresszus" [National agricultural Congress], *Vörös Ujság*, 3 June 1919, p. 2.

possessions, should not be distributed among individuals and groups. State land was to be given to the agricultural proletariat who were to work it as agricultural co-operatives. All men and women over sixteen who worked the prescribed number of working days (120) could be members, with each person sharing in the income according to the percentage of the work contributed. Small and dwarf holdings, with all their possessions, were to remain in private hands.[131] The question of what constituted small holdings was left unclear for some time, but was finally settled by indirect legislation putting the upper limit of a "small" estate at 100 holds (1 hold = 1.42 acres).[132]

This "solution" satisfied no one in the country. The wealthy peasant who acquired a great deal of paper money during the war was now anxious to buy more land. The government's commitment to cooperatives deprived him of this opportunity, causing resentment and the hoarding of money as well as goods for the day when the regime was overthrown. The landless peasants, on the other hand, found themselves to be employees of the state, earning higher wages but being unable to utilize their new wealth, due to the scarcity of the industrial goods and the inflationary erosion of the money. Compounding this fiscal difficulty was the refusal, on the part of the peasant, to accept anything but blue money. The government tried, for a brief period of time, to overcome this difficulty with its so-called proletarian barter. Special trains were sent to rural areas carrying goods desperately needed and desired by the peasants, such as salt, tobacco, agricultural tools, matches, boots, and textiles. These materials could be bought only for an exchange of lard, eggs, butter, flour, etc.[133] The plan seemed ideally suited to the problem; the cities would be fed and the country would be supplied with industrial goods, thus by-passing the stumbling block of money. In reality it was a failure, for only the well-to-do peasants had the necessary medium of exchange, agricultural produce. The embittered poor peasant faced the double frustration of finally realizing his long sought dream of possessing money only to discover that he was again at a disadvantage vis-à-vis his rich neighbor. His confidence and loyalty in the new regime, never really evident, disappeared completely.

Two overwhelming reasons compelled the leaders of the soviet republic to adopt agricultural producer cooperatives as the solution to their problem. First, both their economic and theoretical convictions led them to the inevitable conclusion that intensive production could be carried out only in a large plant, with the full utilization of machines and manpower. Therefore, they wanted to adapt the methods of industrial production to the farm. Second, they had to maintain production, and this could not be carried out by small farmers who lacked the necessary machines, know-how, and credit. Confirming the government in its convictions were the successful cooperatives established in Somogy County by the peasants themselves. Due to Communist

131. *Tanácsköztársaság*, 14 April 1919 (Order No. 38).

132. Vera Szemere, *Az agrárkérdés 1918–1919-ben* [The agrarian question in 1918–1919] (Budapest: Kossuth, 1963), p. 103.

133. Jenő Varga, *A Földkérdés a magyar proletárforradalomban* [The land question in the Hungarian proletarian revolution] (Berlin), p. 17 (in the Archives of the Party Institute, MM/21b/85/6).

agitation the landless peasants in Somogy (and Aszód, in the vicinity of Budapest) seized the land and voluntarily established cooperatives.[134] The government, encouraged by this action, proceeded to form cooperatives on the nearly 6.5 million holds it socialized.[135]

Commissar of Agriculture Hamburger offered still another reason, a political consideration, necessitating the formation of cooperatives. The parcelling out of land into middle and small landholdings would have created small peasant landowners hostile to communism. Hamburger also pointed to the mistakes of Russia, where, as a result of the seizure of land by the peasants, such a situation did arise, forcing the government into taking corrective action at a later date.[136] It was, thus, doubly difficult for Hamburger to justify the law allowing estates up to 100 holds to remain in private hands. His defense, at the National Congress of Councils, although rather specious, went unchallenged. According to Hamburger estates under 100 holds were noncontiguous, parcelled out in various sections, and thus impossible to absorb into large cooperatives, planned and formed by the government.[137]

Even if one accepts this argument, the obvious failure of the regime to gain the support of the peasants, as well as its inability to maintain production on the farms, and to get whatever was produced to the cities, needs an explanation. A thorough examination of this question forces one to divide the underlying causes into two categories: on the one hand, those caused directly by the ineptness and shortcomings of the regime, and on the other, those caused by inherent problems impossible of short-term solutions.

One of the worst errors committed by the government was its order to exempt from taxation and tax arrears all holdings up to 100 surveyed holds (10, if vineyards).[138] It was obvious that the law was passed to appease, and possibly to gain the loyalty of the small landowners, causing them to cooperate in supplying the cities with food. The results were just the opposite. The very class which benefited by this law became greatly alarmed, for it was convinced that the elimination of the taxes was a prelude to the socialization of their land.[139] The reaction of the poor peasants was resentment and the firm conviction that any government which disallowed taxation had to be a weak government. Thus, not only did animosity increase between the regime and the peasantry, but the government's prestige was irreparably damaged. No amount of counteraction (pamphlets, agitators, promises of a new land tax) could change the opinion of the peasants.

Another serious consequence of this order was the bankruptcy and the financial

134. Ibid., p. 9 (Varga claims 300,000 holds were thus formed into cooperatives). Also, "Eddig két és fél millió holdon alakultak termelőszövetkezetek" [Up to now agricultural cooperatives were formed on two and a half million holds), *Vörös Ujság*, 19 April 1919, pp. 2–3; this source claims 600,000 holds in Somogy County being formed into cooperatives.

135. *MMTVD*, 6/B:95; Vilmos Bőhm (*Két Forradalom Tüzében* [In the crossfire of two revolutions], [Vienna: Bécsi Magyar Kiado, 1923], p. 272) claims that 7 million holds were socialized with 6.3 million holds remaining in private hands.

136. "A magyar földműves-proletárság igazi megváltása" [The real redemption of the Hungarian agricultural proletariat], *Népszava*, 25 April 1919, p. 2.

137. *A Tanácsok*, p. 47.

138. *Tanácsköztársaság*, 13 May 1919, p. 1 (Order No. 88).

139. *A Tanácsok*, p. 32.

impotency of the village councils. Deprived of their revenues, these councils now had to turn to Budapest for funds to carry out their programs, meet their payrolls, and pay their bills. With existing chaotic conditions, this situation often meant a lack of funds and a loss of confidence in the government.[140]

A second failure directly attributed to the government was due to the personnel it employed to run the cooperatives and the production trustees and agitators it sent to the villages. On the county and district levels, the socialized land was to be administered by committees of three elected farmers and an agricultural expert, who, although voteless, could suspend, for the common good, all decisions of the committees.[141] Agricultural managers and experts of cooperatives were, in most cases, either the former owners or their overseers, since these men were the only ones capable of managing large agricultural units. The government did its utmost to protect these men and to pay them well in order to insure their needed cooperation. To the peasant, it seemed that nothing had changed; he still had to work for the same employer, just as before the revolution. These men still had their four-horse coaches, maids, and servants, and they still gave the orders.[142] Although the government was blameless for the general ignorance and lack of trained personnel, it was remiss in not transferring these experts to estates where they were unknown.

Much more serious, was the error in the selection of production trustees and agitators sent to the villages. A veritable deluge of words deal with the topic in the National Congress of Soviets. According to the peasant delegates, these men were young, inexperienced in the traditions and ways of the peasants; wore city clothes; demanded automobiles to conduct their business (while the peasants lacked gasoline for their farm machines); sat around offices; collected food for their relatives in Budapest; understood absolutely nothing of the problems of the peasants; issued contradictory orders; sent reports; lived well and did nothing.[143] Although in later debates anti-Semitism and a general hatred against these men is evident, it is still obvious that the choice of the men sent to the country by the government was extremely poor. The upper echelon of the Commissariat of Agriculture was chosen mostly from the former National Association of Farmers. That the wrong men were chosen, even among the commissars, was evident by the fact that in the third week of the dictatorship, Sándor Csizmadia had to be relieved of all his duties and placed under house arrest, for excesses committed while intoxicated.[144]

A third serious error committed by the government was its permission to allow Szamuely and others to use force and occasional terror to suppress counterrevolutionary activities in the country. Only a few peasants were hanged but, of even more serious consequence, was the indiscriminate collection of the so-called war indemnity,

140. Ibid.
141. Pongrácz, *A Forradalmi*, 1:58–59 (4 April 1919, Order No. 40).
142. Vilmos Lázár, "Az első magyar proletárdiktatura agrárpolitikai célkitűzései" [The agricultural goals of the first Hungarian dictatorship of the proletariat], *Közgazdasági Szemle*, 6, no. 3 (March 1961), p. 291.
143. *A Tanácsok*, pp. 57–106, especially in the debates following the reports of Varga, Lengyel, and Hamburger.
144. Jenő Varga, *Földosztás és földreform Magyarországon* [Land distribution and land reform in Hungary] (Budapest, 1919), p. 14.

or as Szamuely called it "booty," and the requisitioning of materials by different bands causing terror and fear among the peasants. Whenever an area showed any sign of opposition, the villages in such areas were forced to give up their livestock, grain, and other goods on threats of death. Telegrams sent by Szamuely list, with almost painful detail, every single head of livestock, poultry, and wagon of agricultural goods, taken from the peasants in reprisals and sent to Budapest to relieve the food shortage.[145]

Not all were as honest, disciplined, and dedicated as Szamuely. Telegrams, complaining to army headquarters, describe acts of intoxicated terrorist bands conducting "hanging rehearsals," requisitioning food and clothing, and keeping the villages in constant terror.[146] The government and the army tried to stop the activities of these terrorists, in vain. A number of telegrams from Kun, Böhm, and Landler, ordered them to keep within bounds and to return to Budapest, but the orders were either disobeyed or their execution delayed.[147] The results of these activities account for some of the hatred evidenced by the peasantry against the regime. Peasant delegates warned the leaders repeatedly not to threaten the peasants, the largest segment of the population, for "he'll give you the shirt off his back if you are friendly, but he will burn his fields if you use force."[148]

Not all of the hatred was caused by the actions or the mistakes of the government. The regime inherited the sins of four hundred years of enforced illiteracy, superstition, and ignorance, pressed upon the peasants of Hungary by their feudal, aristocratic system of government. In the spirit of the suppressions, accompanying the Dózsa peasant rebellion in 1516 (when György Dózsa was roasted alive and two of his starved followers were forced to devour his corpse), the Hungarian peasant had been brutalized, exploited, and kept in ignorance. The natural antipathy of the Roman Catholic church toward communism, compounded by the fact that all church land over 100 holds were socialized,[149] made it a powerful foe of the government which was most influential among the peasantry and encouraged further dissatisfaction and hatred.

The fact that some of the Communist agitators sent from Budapest threatened to turn churches into movie houses, helped to fan the flames of discontent. Even the most idealistic Communist failed to penetrate the suspicion, the fear, and the natural weariness of the country for the ways of the city. The peasant's mistrust of the city was a weapon in the arsenal of the counterrevolution, for communism was cosmopolitan and spoke principally for the industrial workers. The National Congress of Soviets reflects the mistrust of the country delegates for their urban counterparts. None of these delegates fails to point out his ignorance, his lack of education, but at

145. P. I. Archivum, Fol. Hung. 2191/III, telegram from Szamuely to Kun, 10 June 1919, pp. 66-68.

146. P. I. Archivum, Fol. Hung. 2191/IV, telegram to army headquarters, 15 June 1919, pp. 100-101.

147. P. I. Archivum, Fol. Hung. 2191/XI, telegram to Ferenc Rákosi from Sándor Krammer. (Krammer, a leader of one terrorist band, was ordered back to Budapest in mid-June.)

148. A Tanácsok, p. 68.

149. Pongrácz, A Forradalmi, 3:32 (17 May 1919; Order No. 95).

the same time he points out the indolence and the easy and corrupt life of the city dweller which makes his erudition possible.[150]

Permeating and undermining not only agriculture, but every domestic program of the government, was the growing paralysis caused by corruption. Starting in June, it became the recurring theme in speeches, official pronouncements, and newspaper articles. Throughout the month small deeds of corruption became widespread, and by July, this practice had proliferated beyond control. Reports of large payroll thefts and fiscal irregularities,[151] exposures of thefts of large depots of foodstuffs and cash[152] involving many persons were coupled with petty thefts of housewives who were called counterrevolutionaries. The problem of corruption was one of the main themes of the National Congress of Soviets. Charges of chicanery, reports of larceny, influence peddling, nepotism, favoritism, and plain thievery echoed and re-echoed from the halls of the Városi Szinház.[153] Nothing describes better the deterioration of public and private morality, the lack of scruples, the everlasting drive for a good life, than the lead article in *Népszava*, in mid-July. The article was written by Commissar Varga, and it painted an excellent picture of the public apathy and its resultant erosion of values, one of the main reasons for the collapse of the soviet republic:

Sadly one must confess that this loose moral attitude we find in every strata of society: the proletariat take as much advantage of their official power as the educated men; the former Communist as well as the former Social Democrat; the old as well as the new generation, the soldiers no less than the civilians. Conditions in the countryside are worse than in the capital. Trustees sent to the rural areas occupy themselves with hoarding of foodstuffs; the village executive committees issue orders against food deliveries. Today they declare the old [blue] money non-negotiable, tomorrow, the same authority demands payment in old money. The Red Guards, instead of strictly enforcing all orders, in many places participate in transgressions, themselves. The biggest worry of the office workers is how to find a new swindle to get into a higher pay category. The majority of the physicians are contributing to the sacking of the proletarian state in a most dastardly fashion, by declaring each office worker who comes to them, ill, and sending him to a spa for an eight week cure. In the public distribution of food the abuses are daily. The food supplies are robbed on their way to the capital. . . . While the decent and capable bourgeoisie keep themselves apart and refuse to participate in production and organization, the scum of this class is busily active in "comrading" everyone, loudly screaming [about] their loyalty and stealing everyone blind. . . . This situation is desperate and the decent man is incapable of producing anything due to the constant fear that no matter whom he entrusts with something, the result is always bribery and corruption. . . .[154]

150. *A Tanácsok*, p. 69.

151. *P. I. Archivum, Fol. Hung. 2191/II*, telegrams, p. 27; p. 34.

152. "Egy gazdasági repülőbiztos fosztogatásai" [The lootings of an economic "Flying Commissar"], *Vörös Ujság*, 31 July 1919, pp. 3–4.

153. *A Tanácsok*, especially pp. 27, 29, 39, 40, 58, 59, 67, 71, 72, 98, 99, 190, 197, 211.

154. Jenő Varga, "Korrupció" [Corruption], *Népszava*, 15 July 1919, p. 1.

Hundreds of years of exploitation, ignorance, and superstition could not be cured, even under ideal circumstances in 133 days. The leaders of the Hungarian Soviet Republic, blinded by Marxist dogma, failed to realize that internalized value systems could not be changed overnight. The humanitarian idealism which permeated so much of their social programs was doomed to failure due to the lack of funds, the lack of time, and errors in execution. Failure of its armed forces, political and economic quarantine by the Western powers, and the failure of the Russian Soviet Republic to link forces with its beleaguered ally, all contributed to the internal collapse of the Hungarian soviet government.

With dissolution of the regime obvious by July, no amount of effort on its part could save its domestic program. Inflation nullified the raises the workers and peasants received from the government. The lack of goods and widespread corruption destroyed their morale. The dreams of March ended on August 1, when the first soviet government outside of Russia collapsed. Its leaders fled into exile and the nation faced a return to the feudal and chauvinistic policies of her nineteenth-century masters.

Nationality Problems of the Hungarian Soviet Republic

Eva S. Balogh

For centuries the Danubian basin, surrounded by the Carpathian Mountains, has been a meeting place of the various nationalities of eastern Europe. Before the outburst of nationalist sentiments in the nineteenth century, people of diverse tongue and heritage lived rather amiably side by side under the protection of the Hungarian crown. By the beginning of the nineteenth century, however, as the idea of nationalism spread across Europe, the nationality question in this heterogeneous kingdom became a potential threat to the territorial integrity of the thousand-year-old Hungarian state. Rumanians in Transylvania could, by the second half of the nineteenth century, find in the newly emerged kingdom of Rumania a symbol of their national identity. Nor were the Serbs unaffected by Serbian nationalism and the expansionist ambitions of the ever-growing Serbian kingdom. The Hungarians, also fiercely nationalistic, answered the threat with oppression and a policy of Magyarization. The government's fear that the aspirations of the nationalities might not ultimately be checked by these methods proved to be well founded.

At the end of World War I, with the victorious neighbors of Hungary laying claim to territories inhabited by various nationality groups, Hungary's territorial integrity, indeed her very existence, was jeopardized. The magnitude of her potential loss can be seen in the fact that half of her population was of other than Hungarian nationality.

At this period of crisis there occurred, in 1918 and 1919, two revolutions: a bourgeois democratic revolution headed by Mihály Károlyi on October 31, 1918; and, when his government failed to prevent the foreign occupation of large parts of Hungary, on March 21, 1919, a bloodless Bolshevik revolution led by Béla Kun.

The Károlyi government, in its efforts to preserve the territorial integrity of Hungary, promoted a liberal nationality policy. Following the constructive federative plans of Oszkár Jászi, minister of nationalities, the government granted autonomy to several nationalities and was willing to negotiate with others. The regime based its hopes for keeping Hungary intact on the allegiance of its nationalities, trusting that the Paris Peace Conference would allow plebiscites in the disputed areas.

This article is based on a paper which was originally written as a master's thesis at Yale University in 1967 under the guidance of Professor Piotr S. Wandycz. I would like to thank Professor Wandycz for all his advice concerning the topic and Brenda Jubin, dean of Morse College, Yale University, for her wonderful help in editing the manuscript for publication.

The success of any government in Hungary at this time hinged on its ability to save as much of historical Hungary as possible. Thus, the development of a sound nationality policy was crucial. It is the purpose of this essay to examine the Hungarian Communists' attitudes and practices toward the nationalities living in still unoccupied Hungary. It will also concentrate on Communist designs toward the outlying areas formerly belonging to Hungary but already under foreign occupation.

The Communist party of Hungary at the time of the proclamation of the Hungarian Soviet Republic was not quite one year old. Originally established in Russia on March 24, 1918, as the Hungarian Group of the Russian Communist party (Bolshevik), the group changed its name to the Communist party of Hungary at a Moscow conference on November 4, 1918. The name of this group[1] as well as the presence of nationality representatives on its executive committee[2] underscore the fact that, as late as November, 1918, both Hungarian Communists and their Russian comrades counted on the survival of a multinational Hungary.

Béla Kun arrived in Hungary on November 17, 1918, joining about two hundred fellow Hungarian Communists who had been dispatched during that month from Russia for propaganda purposes.[3] After several days of negotiations with dissident factions of the Hungarian Social Democratic party, Kun was able to unite these elements; on November 24, 1918, the establishment of the Communist party of Hungary was announced.[4] At that time no party program as such was published.[5] Therefore there was no official party statement on the nationality question. Nor did the slogans which had been accepted by the members and used between November, 1918, and March, 1919, as guidelines contain any reference to the future of Hungary's nationalities.[6]

Although the Communist party of Hungary had no official program, some foundation for its activities can be found in Béla Kun's pamphlet *Mit akarnak a kommunisták?*

1. The Hungarian name of the party was *Kommunisták Magyarországi Pártja*. The implication of this name is that the party was to include all peoples of Hungary, not just those of Hungarian nationality.

2. György Milei et al., eds., *A magyar internacionalisták a Nagy Októberi Szocialista Forradalomban és a polgárháborúban (1917–1922): Dokumentumgyűjtemény* [Hungarian Internationalists in the great October revolution and in the civil war (1917–1922): a collection of documents], 2 vols. (Budapest: Kossuth, 1967–69), 1:251.

3. György Milei, "A Kommunisták Magyarországi Pártja megalakításának történetéhez" [To the history of the formation of the Communist party of Hungary], *Párttörténeti Közlemények* [Party historical notes] 4, no. 4 (November 1958):68–69.

4. Although these dissatisfied elements had formed independent circles, such as the Karl Marx Circle and the Ervin Szabó Circle, they did not intend to break away from the main body of the Social Democratic party. See Ferenc Tibor Zsuppán, "The Early Activities of the Hungarian Communist Party, 1918–19," *The Slavonic and East European Review* 43, no. 101 (June 1965):317. Therefore, they were reluctant to join with the newly arrived Communists from Russia to form an independent Communist party. See Milei, "A Kommunisták Magyarországi Pártja," p. 74.

5. Béla Kun, *Válogatott írások és beszédek* [Selected writings and speeches], ed. Henrik Vass, Mrs. István Friss, and Éva Szabó, 2 vols. (Budapest: Kossuth, 1966), 1:276. However, in this lecture given on May 15, 1919, Béla Kun requested that the Social Democratic party program of 1903 be adopted with Bolshevik modifications. Ibid., pp. 276–77.

6. Milei, "A Kommunisták Magyarországi Pártja," p. 80.

[What do the Communists want?], published in Moscow during May, 1918. In this pamphlet, which is considered by Communist party historians to be "the first program-like document of the Hungarian Communist movement,"[7] Kun dwelt on such immediate tasks of the Hungarian Communists as the seizure of power and the socialization of banks, factories, and land. The nationality question was not directly discussed. However, he did point out to the proletariat that, though they were being told to support their fatherland, "the borders of the fatherland are [really] the borders of the state,"[8] which will become a meaningless entity after the establishment of the proletarian dictatorship. Furthermore, he reasserted Marx's dictum that the "proletarian has no fatherland."[9]

Béla Kun's emphasis on international ideological ties led him to renounce, in a letter to Ignác Bogár (March 11, 1919),[10] the principle of territorial integrity.[11] By renouncing this principle, he did not exclude the possibility of a revolutionary war against the Czechs, Rumanians, and Yugoslavs. However, Kun claimed that he would consider such a war only if "there was every guarantee that the war would not create a new oppression of nationalities."[12]

Unlike the newly created Communist party of Hungary, the Social Democrats had not only a party program but also a long tradition.[13] The first socialist associations were formed in 1868 and, by 1880, the General Workers' party of Hungary held its first congress.[14] The party program which was adopted at that time was influenced by the Gotha program of 1875 of the German Social Democratic party. Although one of the important aims of the party was cooperation between workers of different nationalities, the nationality question was not specifically mentioned in the document.[15] The second party program, adopted in 1890 and based on the Hainfeld program of the Austrian Social Democratic party,[16] also failed to mention the nationalities.

The party program of 1903, which was still in effect in 1919, was based on the Erfurt program of the German Social Democratic party (1891). This document was the first party program to touch on the nationality question within Hungary. It demanded the equality of all nationalities and local administrative autonomy for nationality groups, but made no reference to regional autonomy.[17]

7. Ibid., p. 63.

8. Kun, *Válogatott írások*, 1:107.

9. Ibid., p. 104.

10. Ibid., pp. 190–97. This letter served as the basis for the platform of the merger of the Social Democrats and the Communists (March 21, 1919).

11. Ibid., p. 192.

12. Ibid.

13. For a brief but excellent study of the Hungarian Social Democratic movement see Rudolf L. Tőkés, *Béla Kun and the Hungarian Soviet Republic: The Origins and Role of the Communist Party of Hungary in the Revolutions of 1918–1919* (New York: Praeger, 1967), pp. 1–47.

14. Dezső Nemes et al., eds., *A magyar forradalmi munkásmozgalom története* [The history of the Hungarian revolutionary workers' movement], 3 vols. (Budapest: Kossuth, 1966–69), 1:25.

15. Ibid., p. 26.

16. At this time the name of the party was changed to the Hungarian Social Democratic party. Ibid., pp. 33–34.

17. Ibid., pp. 48–50.

The Austrian Social Democratic party, with which the Hungarian Socialists had strong ties, demanded, in its party program formulated at its congress in Brünn [Brno] in 1899, the establishment of autonomous national administrative units in the Austrian part of the monarchy. Karl Renner and Otto Bauer, on the basis of this program, worked out a comprehensive nationality plan known as the Austro-Marxist solution to the nationality question. According to their proposal, nationalities living in contiguous territories could form autonomous regions while all nationalities, even if they lived in scattered settlements, would enjoy cultural autonomy and national equality.[18]

Although the Hungarian Socialists were familiar with the Austrian solution to the nationality question, they failed to incorporate it into their own party program. Thus, in October, 1918, having no comprehensive plan of their own, they simply adopted Oszkár Jászi's solution. Jászi acknowledged the right of self-determination of nations but envisaged this development in such a way that the territorial integrity of Hungary would remain intact.[19]

In their proclamation of October 8, 1918, the Social Democrats declared:

> We believe that a Hungary based on the free federation of equal, free, and demo-cratic nations will be a better and surer safeguard of the society of nations, the prosperity of its people, and of human progress than a Hungary which is carved up, mutilated, and disjointed.[20]

The principle of territorial integrity was an organic part of the Social Democrats' program.

On October 13, 1918, the Social Democratic party held a special congress at which the questions of peace and the future of Hungary were discussed. Zsigmond Kunfi, the principal speaker, suggested that the party adopt a federal approach to the question of the territorial integrity of Hungary, but the Socialist leaders of the nationalities showed a distinct reluctance to endorse this program.[21] Later that month the Hungarian Social Democratic party formed a coalition with the Radical party and Károlyi's party within the National Council. In a joint proclamation of October 26, they accepted the self-determination of nations principle in the hope that, with such a move, they could place the territorial integrity of Hungary "on more secure foundations."[22]

When, on March 21, 1919, the Communists and the Social Democrats merged in

18. László Kővágó, "Államszövetségi tervek a Tanácsköztársaság idején" [Federative plans during the soviet republic], *Történelmi Szemle* [Historical review] 9, nos. 3–4 (1966):300.

19. Ibid., p. 303.

20. Mrs. Sándor Gábor et al., eds., *A magyar munkásmozgalom történetének válogatott dokumentumai* [Selected documents from the history of the Hungarian labor movement], 6 vols. (Budapest: Szikra, Kossuth, 1956–1969), 5:246 (hereafter cited as *MMTVD*).

21. János Kende, "Az MSzDP nemzetiségi szekcióinak állásfoglalása a párt 1918. október 13-i rendkívüli kongresszusán" [The attitude of the nationality sections of the H(ungarian) S(ocial) D(emocratic) P(arty) at the party's special congress of October 13, 1918], *Párttörténeti Közlemények* 9, no. 1 (February 1963):153–62.

22. Nemes et al., *A magyar forradalmi munkásmozgalom*, 1:165.

order to declare a soviet republic, neither party was deeply committed to a comprehensive nationality policy. If the Social Democratic program suffered from a lack of originality (by March, 1919, it was also infeasible), the Communists' solution hinged on expectations of an imminent European-wide socialist revolution.

The Communists were naturally not unaware of the explosive nature of the nationality conflict, for they had found it a useful weapon against the Károlyi regime in 1918. Béla Kun called pre-1918 Hungary "a classic example of nationality oppression,"[23] and in 1918 he saw the nationality conflict within Hungary as one of the disruptive forces which eventually were bound to bring down the Károlyi regime.[24]

However, after the declaration of the establishment of the Hungarian Soviet Republic, the optimism concerning the imminent outbreak of a large-scale proletarian revolution overshadowed any thoughts the Communists might have entertained about the nationality question. Although shortly after the installment of the new regime Béla Kun did, in a March 30 interview with a correspondent of the *Neue Freie Presse*, unofficially renounce the territorial integrity of Hungary,[25] this statement was neither elaborated upon nor followed by a clear-cut declaration of the new regime's intentions concerning the nationalities.[26] Moreover, although the new Communist regime, following the Károlyi government's initiative, declared Hungary to be a federal republic, this announcement was buried in the provisional constitution published on April 2, 1919, and received no publicity or further elaboration.

The first official declaration of the regime, written by Béla Kun and József Pogány, commissar of war at the time, was the March 22 message "To All," which, like its Russian example, was addressed to the proletariat of the world. It contains no mention of the nationality question per se.[27] It does, on the other hand,

call the workers and peasants of the Czech lands, Rumania, Serbia, and Croatia for an armed alliance against the bourgeoisie, the boyars, the landowners, and the

23. Kun, speech at the party Congress, June 12, 1919, in his *Válogatott írások*, 1:356.

24. *Pravda*, 31 October 1918, in Kun, *Válogatott írások*, 1:180–87. In this article Kun compares Károlyi to Kerensky and predicts that the regime's "collision with the oppressed nationalities, especially with the Southern Slavs, is inevitable." Ibid., pp. 181, 185.

25. Kun, *Válogatott írások*, 1:215.

26. Among Marxist historians the current opinion is that the Hungarian Soviet Republic's nationality policy lacked a sound ideological foundation, that is, the Leninist formula of self-determination of nations. See László Kővágó, *A magyarországi délszlávok 1918–1919-ben* [The Southern Slavs of Hungary in 1918–1919] (Budapest: Akadémiai Kiadó, 1964), pp. 168–69. For a contrary opinion see Tibor Hajdu, "A nemzeti kérdés és az 1918–1919-es forradalmak. A dualizmus nemzeti politikájának csődje és a monarchia felbomlása" [The nationality question and the revolutions of 1918–1919: The bankruptcy of the nationality policy of the dualism and the collapse of the monarchy], in *A magyar nacionalizmus kialakulása és története* [The emergence and history of Hungarian nationalism], ed. Erzsébet Andics (Budapest: Kossuth, 1964), p. 272.

27. "To All," March 22, 1919, in *MMTVD*, 6A:3–4; see also István Kovács, Introduction to "Államjog" [Political law], in *A Magyar Tanácsköztársaság jogalkotása* [The jurisprudence of the Hungarian Soviet Republic], ed. Pál Halász, István Kovács, and Vilmos Peschka (Budapest: Közgazdasági és Jogi Könyvkiadó, 1959), p. 44; and L'udovít Holotík, "O Slovenskej republike rád roku 1919" [On the Slovak republic of 1919], *Historický časopis* 7, no. 2 (1959):182.

dynasties. [The Soviet Republic] invites the workers of German Austria and Germany to follow the example of the Hungarian working class.[28]

This declaration gives a partial answer to the question of why the Hungarian Communists did not labor over the nationality question.[29] They were certain, as were their Russian colleagues,[30] that the declaration of the Hungarian Soviet Republic would be followed by a series of revolutions in eastern Europe and perhaps also in Germany.

Thus, when the first article on the nationality question appeared in the *Vörös Ujság* [Red newspaper], the author of the article came to the conclusion that "the nationality question can be solved completely and forever by an *international proletarian revolution*."[31] The same article categorically announced that "there are no such things as nations, only classes, and the proletarians speaking different languages do not care about the nationality of the bourgeoisie which oppresses them."[32]

The boundless belief in the outbreak of a world-wide proletarian revolution was an *idée fixe* of the international Communist movement and thus also of the Hungarian Communist leaders, especially those whom Oszkár Jászi calls the "Bolshevist experimentalists."[33] The attitude of these experimentalists was messianic, mystical, and nurtured by German idealism. Good examples of these elements in the leadership were József Pogány and his deputy, Tibor Szamuely.[34] On March 30, Szamuely bravely announced that "this fight will be the fight of heroic sacrifices. If we win, the reward of the revolutionary sacrifices will be the liberation of the proletariat of the whole world."[35] Pogány announced on April 6 that "this revolution must be carried beyond our borders because the social revolution is possible only in the form of a world revolution,"[36] According to these Communists, a revolutionary war would

28. An English translation of this document was published in an appendix to Albert Kaas and Fedor de Lazarovics, *Bolshevism in Hungary: The Béla Kun Period* (London: G. Richards, 1931), p. 326. However, their translation of *Czech lands* as "Czechoslovakia" is misleading.

29. The omission of the Slovaks from the document is curious. The generic Hungarian term for Slovak is *tót* which recently acquired a somewhat derogatory connotation. However, in 1919, this distinction between Slovak and *tót* did not exist. All through the documents of the period Czechs and Slovaks are referred to as *cseh-tót* proletariat or *cseh-tót* bourgeoisie. Whatever the reason for the omission, the next day in a new declaration entitled "To All," it was corrected. Béla Kun called on the Czechoslovak proletariat to rise against their oppressors. See "To All," March 23, 1919, in *MMTVD*, 6A:7.

30. For Lenin's belief in a world revolution see Kommunisticheskaia Partiia Sovetskogo Soiuza, *Vos'moi S'ezd Rossiiskoi Kommunisticheskoi Partii (Bol'shevikov)* [The Eighth Congress of the Russian Communist party (Bolshevik)], 2nd ed. (Saratov: Sougrafia, 1919), p. 6.

31. *Vörös Ujság*, 28 March 1919, in *MMTVD*, 6A:69.

32. Ibid.

33. Oscar [Oszkár] Jászi, *Revolution and Counter-revolution in Hungary*, trans. E. W. Dickes (London: P. S. King & Son, Ltd., 1924), p. 120.

34. The changes in the composition of the Council of Commissars were very frequent. Most of the commissars had several posts during the short period of the soviet republic.

35. *Vörös Katona* [Red soldier], in Ervin Liptai, *A Magyar Vörös Hadsereg harcai, 1919* [The battles of the Hungarian Red Army, 1919] (Budapest: Zrinyi, 1960), p. 52.

36. *Népszava* [People's Voice] (organ of the Social Democratic party), 6 April 1919, quoted in Kővágó, *A magyarországi délszlávok*, p. 173.

solve the nationality problem which had plagued the country for so long since, as Pogány put it, "where there is proletarian rule, the proletariat finds his fatherland immediately even if he speaks a different language."[37]

The left-wing and centralist Social Democrats adopted the Communist solution of a European-wide revolution in the wake of which a federated union of all nations in the Danubian area would be created. Sándor Garbai, president of the Revolutionary Governing Council, announced on March 21: "We are convinced that our significant decision [to proclaim a Soviet Republic] will have an influence not only on the Serbian, Rumanian, German, and Czech comrades but also on our comrades in Italy and France."[38] As far as actual plans for such a federal solution are concerned, we have little evidence. Béla Kun did mention on March 27, 1919, that negotiations were being conducted between Soviet Russia, the Soviet Ukraine, and Hungary "for the creation of a unified territory of the three countries."[39] However, this solution hinged on the successes of the Russian Red Army. On May 20, Kun announced in Sopron [Ödenburg] that "we are ready at any moment to create a federative state with the proletariat of German Austria," that is, if a soviet republic were to be declared there.[40] Antonín O. Janoušek, the president of the Czechoslovak Group of the International Socialist Federation of Hungary in Budapest and later head of the government of the Slovak Soviet Republic, envisaged a Czechoslovak Soviet Republic federated with Russia, the Ukraine, and Hungary.[41]

However, a European-wide revolution was not materializing, and the Hungarian Communist leaders became desperate. For they viewed this revolution as necessary to ensure the victory of their revolution at home. In explaining why he refused General Jan C. Smuts's offer of more advantageous Hungarian demarcation lines, Béla Kun pressed this theme:

> We do not stand on the principle of territorial integrity, but we want to live; that is why we were unwilling to agree to these demarcation lines. We were unwilling to drive under the capitalist yoke our proletarian brothers living in the neutral zone because this would have meant that we were taking away from the Hungarian proletariat the possibility of physical existence.... When we proclaimed the proletarian dictatorship in Hungary, we did not base our calculations on such illusions as that we would be able to fight against the Entente powers in an organized war.... We emphasized and we still emphasize that we entrusted the fate of the Hungarian proletariat and the Hungarian Soviet Republic to an international revolution.[42]

37. József Pogány, 1 April 1919, in *MMTVD*, 6A:80.

38. *Az egység okmányai* [Documents of unity] (Budapest, 1919), p. 3, quoted in Kővágó, "Államszövetségi tervek," p. 305.

39. *P. I. Archivum, A Forradalmi Kormányzótanács 1919. márc. 27-i jegyzőkönyve* [Minutes of the Revolutionary Governing Council, March 27, 1919], quoted in Kővágó, "Államszövetségi tervek," p. 310.

40. Kun, *Válogatott írások*, 1:315.

41. *Armáda proletářů* [Army of the proletariat], 15 June 1919, quoted in Kővágó, "Államszövetségi tervek," p. 311.

42. Kun, speech at the meeting of the Budapest Council, 19 April 1919, in *Válogatott írások*, 1:242.

In this statement the survival of the Hungarian Soviet Republic is seen as intertwined economically and politically with the outbreak of similar revolutions in neighboring countries. Béla Kun's reluctance toward General Smuts's offer was based on his belief in the immediacy of such revolutions.

After the fateful visit of Smuts, the left wing of the Communist party of Hungary,[43] headed by Szamuely and Pogány, started clamoring for revolutionary war.[44] On April 13, Pogány announced that "although we do not stand on the basis of territorial integrity, [revolutionary war] is the only possible way to liberate the Hungarian proletarian masses from the hated rule of foreign capitalists and boyars."[45] Indeed, with Kun's declining the offer of General Smuts, the die was already cast. The Rumanians attacked and soon reached the Tisza River, meeting little opposition from the disorganized Hungarian Red Army.

Béla Kun's reaction to the Smuts offer seems to have worried Lenin who, in the middle of April, warned Kun against the danger of leftist deviation with regard to revolutionary war. Characteristic of Béla Kun's peculiar logic and his cockiness was his reply that "I will never drift to the left; left-wing Communism is impossible in our country because we are so much to the left already that further drift to the left is impossible."[46]

Kun was indeed to the left of Lenin. Not only did they disagree about the nature of an international revolution, but they also disagreed on the nationality question.

At the time of the establishment of the Hungarian soviet regime, the Eighth Congress of the Russian Communist party (Bolshevik) was in session. At that conference there was an extensive debate[47] on the nationality issue after which Lenin's formula of self-determination of nations was accepted.[48] Béla Kun, however, followed the minority view of Bukharin[49] and adopted the principle of the self-determination of the proletariat. Thus Kun, unlike Lenin, found the "nationality question . . . unimportant."[50]

---

43. To avoid confusion in the text, we shall continue calling the unified party the Communist party of Hungary.

44. Indeed, conducting a revolutionary war was on the agenda from the very beginning. The question came up even before the proclamation of the soviet republic during the negotiations with the Social Democrats on March 11, 1919. By March 24, another announcement "To All" officially proclaimed that the Hungarian Soviet Republic was "organizing a huge proletarian army, and with its help will establish the proletarian dictatorship of the workers and peasants against the Hungarian capitalists and landlords as well as against the Rumanian boyars and the Czech bourgeoisie." Halász, Kovács, and Peschka, *A Magyar Tanácsköztársaság jogalkotása*, p. 54.

45. *MMTVD*, 6A: 203.

46. Kun to Lenin, 22 April 1919, in Kun, *Válogatott írások*, 1: 247.

47. For the debates between Lenin and Bukharin, and Lenin and Piatakov, see *Vos'moi S'ezd*, pp. 21–31, 44–47, and 60–65.

48. Mrs. Sándor Gábor, "A szovjet és a magyar pártprogram és alkotmány 1919-ben" [The Soviet and Hungarian party program and constitution in 1919], in *Ötven év. A Nagy Október és a magyarországi forradalmak* [Fifty years: the great October and the revolutions of Hungary], ed. Zsuzsa L. Nagy and András Zsilák (Budapest: Akadémiai Kiadó, 1967), p. 330; Mrs. Béla Kun, *Kun Béla (Emlékezések)* [Béla Kun (Memoirs)], 2nd ed. rev. (Budapest: Kossuth, 1969), pp. 246–49.

49. Árpád Szélpál, *Les 133 jours de Béla Kun* (Paris: Fayard, 1959), p. 169.

50. Kun, "Speech on the modification of the party program," 15 May 1919, in his *Válogatott írások*, 1: 289.

In his important series of speeches designed to introduce the modification of the old Social Democratic party program of 1903, he clearly defined his stand:

As you know, my comrades, in the nationality question there are in existence two viewpoints, one promulgating the right of national self-determination and the other the right of self-determination of the proletariat. Regardless of who thinks what, my viewpoint is—and this is strictly a Marxist viewpoint—the right of self-determination of the proletariat.[51]

He announced that "self-determination from our point of view is merely a fictitious principle because we want . . . proletarian union and not separation."[52] From the Leninist principle of self-determination of nations Kun learned only that "for us, Hungarian-speaking proletarians, it is especially important, just as Lenin emphasized, that we follow a conciliatory course toward those proletarians who speak a foreign tongue."[53]

Kun's position was certainly a far cry from the Leninist formula of self-determination of nations. His basic criticism of Lenin was echoed in the *Vörös Ujság*: "The self-determination of nations in capitalism—just as democracy—means the self-determination of the bourgeoisie."[54] A pamphlet published in the first half of April summarized the whole question in these terms:

The solution of the so-called nationality question is very simple. We no longer consider the non-Hungarian-speaking inhabitants nationalities, and the "question" does not exist.[55]

Gyula Hevesi, commissar of social production, later recalled:

In those days we did not understand the relation between proletarian internationalism and proletarian patriotism, and we did not see much difference between whether the country was occupied by an enemy who spoke Hungarian or a foreign tongue. We wanted an international Soviet Republic, or an international federation of Soviet Republics. . . .[56]

The question of class was crucial; that of nationality, nonexistent.

The Hungarian Communist leaders did not follow the Russian example. Instead of making peace they waged a revolutionary war and instead of accepting the Leninist

51. Ibid., pp. 289–90.
52. Ibid., p. 290.
53. Ibid.
54. *Vörös Ujság*, 17 May 1919, quoted in Gyula Hajdú, "A Magyar Tanácsköztársaság nemzetközi kapcsolatai" [The international relations of the Hungarian Soviet Republic], in *A Magyar Tanácsköztársaság állama és joga* [Government and jurisprudence of the Hungarian Soviet Republic], ed. Márton Sarlós (Budapest: Akadémiai Kiadó, 1959), p. 280.
55. *MMTVD*, 6A:174.
56. Gyula Hevesi, *Egy mérnök a forradalomban* [An engineer in the revolution] (Budapest: Kossuth 1959), p. 225.

formula of self-determination of nations they followed the principle of self-determination of the proletariat associated with the left wing of the Russian Communist party (Bolshevik).

Although in theory Béla Kun found the nationality question unimportant, in practice he could not ignore it. The soviet government inherited the fruits of Oszkár Jászi's efforts when he was minister of nationalities in the Károlyi regime. On March 21, the new government was confronted with a *fait accompli*: both the Ruthenians and the Germans of Hungary had been won over to the idea of autonomous status. By March, two separate ministries had been created: one for handling German affairs in the region of *Deutschwestungarn* and the other for looking after *Ruszka Krajna* [Ruthenian region], a newly created autonomous region within Hungary.

The Provisional Constitution of April 2, 1919, indicated that these regions had the right to autonomy:

> Every nation, if it lives on a continuous larger territory, may form a separate national council and executive committee. It will be the Congress of Hungarian Councils which will decide on the creation of these national councils, their relationship to each other, and on the final Constitution of the Federal Soviet Republic of Hungary.[57]

Moreover, the government assured the continuous existence of the two ministries established during the Károlyi period by appointing a commissar of German affairs and a commissar of Ruthenian affairs.

Nonetheless, the government did little to emphasize the federal structure of the state or officially to acknowledge the right of national self-determination. The lack of an official confirmation of the self-determination of nations principle, that is, the right of secession, seems to have caused considerable anxiety in Russia because, on April 6, G. V. Chicherin, Russian commissar of foreign affairs, sent a telegram to Béla Kun in which he inquired about the attitude of the Hungarian leaders toward the nationality question.

> What are the plans of the government regarding the nationality question, always a burning problem in Hungary? Please let us know whether you have worked out any program on this question and whether you are negotiating or plan to negotiate with the representatives of the various nationalities.[58]

This telegram, however, failed to inspire the Hungarian government to devise a master plan for dealing with the nationality problem. —

On April 7, Zoltán Rónai, commissar of justice, did suggest at a meeting of the Revolutionary Governing Council that the government should make an official

57. *MMTVD*, 6A:100–101.

58. Gábor, "Dokumentumok Szovjet-Oroszország és a Magyar Tanácsköztársaság kapcsolatairól" [Documents on the relations of Soviet Russia and the Hungarian Soviet Republic], *Párttörténeti Közlemények* 7, no. 1 (March 1961):215, quoted in T. Hajdu, "A nemzeti kérdés," p. 271.

declaration about the fact that soviet Hungary was a federal state. Such a declaration was never issued. In fact, in the first few days of soviet rule there was little sign, outside the appointment of the commissars for Ruthenian and German affairs, that the new government would extend autonomy to the smaller nationalities still living in unoccupied Hungary. For example, the idea of autonomy for the Croats of Burgenland, the Serbs of southeastern Hungary, and the Slovenes of southwestern Hungary was shelved by the government in spite of the fact that the former Károlyi regime had already negotiated with their leaders for autonomous status. Sándor Garbai, the president of the Revolutionary Governing Council who was responsible for the affairs of the nationalities, simply placed the whole question *ad acta* because, in his opinion, the nationality question ceased to exist as soon as there was a proletarian regime in power.[59] Negotiations with the representatives of the nationalities on the periphery of former Hungary were also ignored because of the current optimism concerning the imminent outbreak of a world revolution.

In spite of this disinclination to concern itself with the nationality question, the regime was compelled to make some legal provisions for the nationalities before the approval of the final constitution in June, 1919. Of the two pertinent declarations, the first, Order No. 41, announced on April 7 that "all authorities must accept any official request written in any of the languages used in Hungary and answer it in the language of the request."[60] This provision did not amount to more than cultural autonomy and, even as such, was vague.[61] On April 28, in Order No. 77 of the Revolutionary Governing Council, it was announced that

all national oppression will cease to exist in the Soviet Republic, which is based on the federation of the proletariats of equal nations speaking different languages, and the Soviet Republic does not recognize any nationality question in the old sense.... The Revolutionary Governing Council orders the elections for the German and Ruthenian councils even before the acceptance of the Constitution. It is the duty of the German and Ruthenian National Councils to represent the German and Ruthenian proletariat of Hungary at the meetings of the drafting committee of the final Constitution of the Hungarian Soviet Republic.[62]

Thus, by the end of April, the right of Germans and Ruthenians to form autonomous regions and to participate in the drawing up of the constitution was approved.

The legal foundation for the soviet government's nationality policy lay in the final Constitution of June 23, 1919, in which there are four significant clauses dealing with the nationalities. Clause 84 proclaimed that

in the Hungarian Socialist Federated Soviet Republic every nation may use its own language freely and cherish and develop its own national culture. Therefore every

59. Kővágó, *A magyarországi délszlávok*, p. 174.
60. Halász, Kovács, and Peschka, *A Magyar Tanácsköztársaság jogalkotása*, p. 86.
61. It is possible that this order was supposed to be the immediate reaction to Chicherin's telegram, but, if so, it was extremely unsatisfactory.
62. Halász, Kovács, and Peschka, *A Magyar Tanácsköztársaság jogalkotása*, p. 88.

nation, even if it does not live on a continuous territory, may form a national council for the development of its culture.

It added that such a national council "may not disrupt the structure of the hierarchy of councils which are organized on a territorial basis."[63] This clause reflects the influence of the Austro-Marxist nationality policy based on cultural autonomy.[64] However, this arrangement, side by side with the introduction of territorial autonomy, a Leninist principle, was confusing and overlapping in function.

Clause 85 stated that "the local administration is to be handled by the workers of the nationality which is in the majority in the given locality."[65]

Clause 86 elaborated on the status of the autonomous regions:

More than one *járás* [township or parish] can constitute an independent district and more than one district a national district. The district councils will send to the national council one representative per 10,000 inhabitants. . . . The Congress of Hungarian Councils will conduct its affairs with the national districts through the national councils of the national districts.[66]

Although this clause establishes a clear governmental hierarchy within the national districts, it does not specify the relationship between the districts comprising the autonomous region and the traditional units of government, the counties. In one case, that of Bereg [Beregovo] County and the Bereg District (in *Ruszka Krajna*), the district was the Ruthenian-inhabited part of Bereg County. Bereg County was governed by its County Council; Bereg District, by its District Council. Since the district was a part of the county, Bereg District was responsible to two councils which, to make things even more confusing, were supposed to have equal rights.[67] Under this arrangement, Bereg District, though granted the right of autonomy by belonging to *Ruszka Krajna*, could not have been completely autonomous.

Clause 88 of the constitution announced that

the Hungarian Soviet Republic is not opposed to an arrangement whereby those nationalities which inhabit territories which are in the process of liberation [that is, being reoccupied by the Hungarian Red Army] and whose numerical and economic strength warrants it, may form separate Soviet Republics allied [*szövetséges*] to the Hungarian Soviet Republic.[68]

This clause is thoroughly ambiguous since it leaves unclear to what extent, if any, these territories could determine their own fate; the Hungarian word *szövetség* may

63. Ibid., p. 71.
64. Kővágó, "Államszövetségi tervek," p. 319.
65. Halász, Kovács, and Peschka, *A Magyar Tanácsköztársaság jogalkotása*, p. 71.
66. Ibid., p. 72.
67. M. Troján, "Bereg vármegye dolgozóinak harca a tanácshatalomért az 1918–1919-es években" [The fight of the workers of Bereg County for the establishment of Soviet power in 1918–1919], *Századok* [Centuries] 98, nos. 1–2 (1964):139–40.
68. Halász, Kovács, and Peschka, *A Magyar Tanácsköztársaság jogalkotása*, p. 72.

mean either alliance or federation. The ambiguity of this formula became evident when Slovak independence was declared.

The clauses in the constitution dealing with the rights of nationalities were eclectic and ambiguous. Austro-Marxism, Leninism, traditional units of government, and new units were combined but not made consistent with one another. Provisions which, by themselves, seemed just became unworkable when juxtaposed with other clauses. And some statements were, from the very beginning, unclear. The difficulties within the constitution were disastrously magnified when the soviet government dealt on a practical level with its nationality groups.

The earliest beneficiaries of the liberal nationality policy of the Károlyi regime were the Ruthenians, a backward group of people closely related to the Ukrainians.[69] They were the first to receive their own autonomous region (*Ruszka Krajna*), which was proclaimed on December 25, 1918 (People's Law No. 10 of 1918).[70] The Károlyi government's speed was understandable: they were eager to demonstrate to the Entente powers their sincerity in dealing with the nationalities.

Yet when the Béla Kun government came into power, only three months after the establishment of *Ruszka Krajna*, this territory had seen enough chaos to make it seem an old state. This backward region with its uneducated, rural, Ruthenian population[71] saw the emergence of pro-Hungarian, pro-Ukrainian, pro-Czech, and pro-independence factions, both at home and among immigrant groups in the United States; it was invaded by Rumania and Czechoslovakia. Within a month of the proclamation of *Ruszka Krajna* only a part of the province was still in Hungarian hands.

Communist propaganda found fertile soil in Ruthenia, where the living standards were extremely low and where, during the war years, famine was not uncommon.[72] When, on the evening of March 21, the telegram announcing the establishment of the Hungarian Soviet Republic arrived in Munkács [Mukachevo], a meeting was held in which almost five thousand people participated.[73] According to the *Vörös Ujság*, "the

69. According to the official statistics of 1910 there were 472,587 persons of Ruthenian origin living in Hungary. Most of these resided in the counties of Bereg, Máramaros [Marmarosh], Ung [Uzh], Ugocsa [Ugocha], Sáros [Šariš], and Zemplén [Zemplín]. See Hungary. Központi Statisztikai Hivatal, *A Magyar Szent Korona országainak 1910. évi népszámlálása* [The 1910 census of the countries of the Hungarian Holy Crown] (Budapest, 1912), pp. 35–36 (hereafter cited as *Népszámlálás*). The languages spoken in the area are dialects of Ukrainian, called *lemko*, *boiko*, and *hutsul*. See Augustin Stefan, "Myths about Carpatho-Ukraine," *The Ukrainian Quarterly* 10, no. 3 (Summer 1954):223. The indigenous population calls itself *rus'in*, hence *rutén* or *ruszin*.

70. André Frey, "La Ruthénie," *Nouvelle Revue de Hongrie* 59 (November 1938):430.

71. According to the 1910 official statistics there were only 542 persons of Ruthenian mother tongue in all Hungary practicing "intellectual professions." See C. A. Macartney, *Hungary and Her Successors: The Treaty of Trianon and Its Consequences 1919–1937* (London: Oxford University Press, 1937), p. 211. Only 1,264 Ruthenians lived in towns, and in the six counties where the Ruthenian population was sizable only 50.8 percent of the people above the age of six were literate. See *Népszámlálás*, pp. 36 and 47–48.

72. For a description of life and the nationality conflict in Ruthenia before World War I see Béla Illés, *Carpathian Rhapsody*, trans. Grace Blair Gárdos, 2 vols. (Budapest: Corvina, 1963).

73. V. V. Usenko, *Vpliv Velikoi Zhovtnevoi sotsialistichnoi revoliutsii na rozvitok revoliutsiinogo rukhu v Zakarpatti v 1917–1919 rr.* [The influence of the great October Socialist revolution on the

declaration of the proletarian dictatorship . . . was received with universal enthusiasm" in *Ruszka Krajna*.[74]

Because of Russian interest in their Ruthenian brothers, the treatment accorded to *Ruszka Krajna* by the Hungarian Soviet government had international significance. The maintenance and strengthening of this region's autonomy was immediately regarded as a tangible sign of good will toward Soviet Russia.[75] The new regime thus had the task of developing a sound governmental structure for *Ruszka Krajna*.

The People's Law No. 10 of 1918 which proclaimed Ruthenia an autonomous region also provided for a Ruthenian diet or *seim* to be elected on the basis of universal suffrage, a governor in the person of Augustin Stefan residing in Munkács, the capital of *Ruszka Krajna*, and a Ruthenian ministry in Budapest headed by Dr. Oreszt Szabó. The region's *seim* was granted autonomy in matters of language, religion, education, and justice.[76] On March 4, elections were held for the Ruthenian *seim* in the county of Bereg, which was still unoccupied.[77]

Béla Kun's government recognized the whole Ruthenian region as part of Hungary (as had the Károlyi regime), despite the partial occupation of the territory.[78] Accordingly, the new government appointed a commissar of Ruthenian affairs. Whether through lack of concern for the nationality question or simply because of the scarcity of genuine Ruthenian Communists, the regime did not trouble to appoint a new man to this post but left in office the old minister, Oreszt Szabó. Szabó, however, immediately resigned and was replaced by Augustin Stefan, the former governor of *Ruszka Krajna*.

On April 7, Augustin Stefan urged the Revolutionary Governing Council to clarify the status of *Ruszka Krajna* in the shortest possible time. In response, the council appointed a committee of four men, including both the commissar of Ruthenian and the commissar of German affairs, to help the Constitutional Committee in its deliberations on the territorial questions of the autonomous regions.[79] It was also decided that the German and Ruthenian national councils should be formed as soon as possible, even if for the time being they would not be entrusted with the administration of the area but only granted the right to conduct negotiations with the central government.[80]

---

growth of the revolutionary movement in Ruthenia between 1917 and 1919] (Kiev [published in Ukrainian]: Vid-vo Akademii Nduk Ukr. RSR, 1955), pp. 128–29. The population of Munkács in 1910 was 17,275. See *Népszámlálás*, pp. 216–17.

74. *Vörös Ujság*, 28 March 1919, in *MMTVD*, 6A:69.

75. Ibid.

76. Frey, "La Ruthénie," p. 430.

77. Troján, "Bereg vármegye," p. 132.

78. The Ruthenian inhabited parts of Máramaros, Ugocsa, Bereg and Ung counties constituted the region of *Ruszka Krajna*. The fate of the Ruthenian areas of Zemplén, Sáros, Abaúj-Torna, and Szepes was to remain pending until the peace negotiations. László Domokos, *Ruszka-Krajna a népek ítélőszéke előtt*. [Ruszka-Krajna before the tribunal of mankind], (Budapest: Mór Ráth, 1919), p. 26.

79. *MMTVD*, 6A:155–56.

80. Ibid., p. 156.

The Ruthenian Commissariat decreed that elections must be held before April 12 for the local councils.[81] This announcement was in conformity with the scheduling of elections in the rest of the country. The elections duly took place on April 6 and 7, 1919, in the unoccupied parts of *Ruszka Krajna*.[82]

On April 2, a Ruthenian constitution appeared in *Rus'ka Pravda*, a Ruthenian newspaper published in Budapest.[83] This constitution seems to have been a reworked version of the Károlyi government's constitutional framework for the district. The only notable differences were the establishment of local and district councils and the appointment of political commissars to each district and to the autonomous region as a whole. These commissars were the local emissaries of the commissar of Ruthenian affairs in Budapest.[84] The highest political organ of the autonomous region was the Ruthenian Congress of Councils.[85]

Rus'ka Pravda hailed the constitution in a somewhat confusing manner. First of all, it announced that the Hungarian Soviet Republic recognized the Ruthenian people's independence, that is, presumably, their autonomy. It also made the observation that the Ruthenians need not worry about future borders because the Hungarian Soviet Republic does not recognize borders created by foreign occupation. Further, it assured the people that "each village and city will belong to whichever particular territorial federation it wishes."[86]

We know little of the implementation of Communist policy in *Ruszka Krajna*. Already in 1918 the official language of the region was declared to be Ruthenian. In April, 1919, the University of Budapest set up a Ruthenian language department, and some Ruthenian school texts were also published. A commission established during the soviet period defined the Ruthenian districts where the majority of inhabitants was Ruthenian and obliged the councils to conduct all their affairs with the population in Ruthenian.[87] The only Ruthenian newspaper, *Rus'ka Pravda*, was published in Budapest as the organ of the Ruthenian commissariat.[88]

One rather surprising feature of the political reorganization of *Ruszka Krajna* was that the *seim*, whose members had been elected on March 4, before the Communist

81. M. F. Lebov, *Vengerskaia Sovetskaia Respublika 1919 goda* [The Hungarian Soviet Republic of 1919] (Moscow: Izd.-vo sotsial'no ekom. Lit.-ry, 1959), p. 108 n. 1.
82. The elections in most of the rural districts were not secret. M. Troján, "Bereg vármegye," pp. 137–38; G. I. Turjanyica, "A magyarországi proletárforradalom és a tanácshatalom megteremtése Kárpátalján 1919-ben" [The proletarian revolution of Hungary and the creation of soviet power in Ruthenia in 1919], in *A Magyar Tanácsköztársaság történelmi jelentősége és nemzetközi hatása. Előadásgyűjtemény* [The historical significance of the Hungarian Soviet Republic and its international influence: a collection of lectures], ed. Mrs. Sándor Gábor (Budapest: Kossuth, 1960), p. 366.
83. Usenko, *Vpliv*, p. 131.
84. Troján, "Bereg vármegye," p. 143.
85. Usenko, *Vpliv*, p. 132.
86. *Rus'ka Pravda*, 12 April 1919, in *MMTVD*, 6A:193.
87. Usenko, *Vpliv*, pp. 150, 152.
88. *Rus'ka Pravda*, a weekly paper, was published between 12 April and 3 May 1919. Altogether four issues appeared. See Usenko, *Vpliv*, p. 151. All other newspapers published in the area were Hungarian-language papers: *Beregi Munkás* [Beregovo worker], *Ugocsai Munkás* [Ugocha worker], *Munkácsi Népszava* [Mukachevo people's voice], etc. See Turjanyica, "A magyarországi proletárforradalom," p. 375.

take over, was allowed to convene on April 17 in Munkács.[89] This body was not at all representative of the political aspirations of the Communist regime, and its membership had nothing to do with the elections for the councils.

Considering the imminent threat of total foreign occupation, a great deal of effort was spent in order to strengthen the military preparedness of the region. In addition to the Ruthenian Red Guard, which eventually formed a Ruthenian division of the Hungarian Red Army, there was a Ruthenian battalion in the Fifth Division of the Red Army stationed at Nyíregyháza.[90]

Another military group of the soviet regime, the Red Militia, was created on March 26, 1919, by the Revolutionary Governing Council. The Ruthenian commissariat followed suit, establishing a Ruthenian Red Militia in which the official language was Ruthenian.[91] The Red Militia's main task was to replace the police force and the gendarmery; it was the most important military organization in tracking down counterrevolutionaries. However, the Ruthenian Red Militia was, in fact, comprised mainly of former members of the police force, and therefore at the time of counterrevolutionary uprisings it proved to be quite useless.[92]

By the middle of April, *Ruszka Krajna* was the scene of several counterrevolutionary uprisings. The activities of these counterrevolutionaries were facilitated by the turn-coat commissar of Ruthenian affairs himself, Augustin Stefan. Stefan, the former governor of *Ruszka Krajna*, was no Communist; moreover, it is doubtful whether he was loyal to the cause of autonomy within Hungary. Information reached Béla Kun that the Ruthenian commissar was reputedly a supporter of the Ukrainian independence movement and had signed a secret declaration in December, 1917, for the incorporation of Ruthenia into the Great Ukraine.[93]

Being anything but a Bolshevik, Stefan placed his counterrevolutionary friends into important positions. For example, he appointed József Kaminszky, a lawyer, to serve as the political commissar for the whole district, and all councils were subordinated to Kaminszky. The executive committee of the Bereg County Council complained to the Hungarian Revolutionary Governing Council. The man who was sent to study the situation was Henrik Guttmann, the son of the owner of one of the local factories; Kaminszky, of course, was not removed from his post.[94] Stefan and his friends also managed to get permission from the Hungarian Revolutionary Governing Council to introduce legislation which was not in conformity with the wishes of the regime. For example, schools operating under the churches were not nationalized, and compulsory religion remained a part of the school curriculum.[95]

The center of the counterrevolution was in Munkács, headed by Kaminszky and Emil Roskovics, a military man. This organization was affiliated with others in such cities as Beregszász, Huszt [Khust], and Szolyva [Sveliava].[96] An underground White

89. Usenko, *Vpliv*, p. 135.
90. Ibid., p. 165.
91. Lebov, *Vengerskaia Sovetskaia Respublika*, pp. 120–21.
92. Usenko, *Vpliv*, p. 166.
93. Gyula Csehi, Ruthenian party secretary, to Béla Kun, 19 July 1919, in *MMTVD*, 6B:480.
94. Troján, "Bereg vármegye," p. 144.
95. Ibid.
96. Ibid., p. 149.

Guard was also organized which, on April 19, 1919, strove to occupy Beregszász. The executive committee of the Bereg County Council asked help from the district commander of the Hungarian Red Army in Nyíregyháza. Although the White Guard had to retreat temporarily, on April 21, a counterrevolutionary uprising occurred within the city and the old regime was re-established.97 At the same time, another uprising occurred in Munkács. On the evening of April 21, several hundred well-armed counterrevolutionaries attacked the local Red Guard who, a day later, had to abandon the city.98

In view of the state of affairs in Ruthenia, a special regiment was sent to Munkács and Beregszász. This regiment reoccupied Munkács on April 24, and martial law was put into effect; 130 persons were arrested and sent to Budapest, where 24 of them received sentences. Beregszász was also reoccupied on the same day, with 40 counter-revolutionaries being arrested and sent to Sátoraljaújhely to be tried at the revolutionary courts.99

The re-establishment of the soviet regime in Munkács and Beregszász proved to be short-lived. By April 25 and 26, the Red Army units stationed in the towns were threatened by Rumanian troops. The Rumanians succeeded in occupying Beregszász on April 26 and Munkács on April 27. On April 30, Czech troops also arrived in Munkács, and by May 5, the whole territory was under foreign occupation.100 Recognizing a *fait accompli*, a new *Tsentral'na rus'ka narodna rada* [Central Ruthenian National Council] voted in Ungvár [Uzhgorod] on May 8, 1919, for the unification of the Ruthenian autonomous region with Czechoslovakia.101 Thus, the soviet government of the Ruthenian region ceased to exist after less than forty days.

The other substantial minority living in unoccupied Hungary was the German.102 Unlike the Ruthenian settlements, however, the German areas were not contiguous; with the exception of the counties of Sopron, Moson, and Vas near the Austrian border,103 they were widely scattered throughout the western part of the country.

On November 22, 1918, the Provisional National Assembly of German Austria declared:

From a geographical, economical and ethnical point of view, the territory of the Pressburg [Pozsony], Wieselburg [Moson], Eisenburg [Vas] and Ödenburg [Sopron] "comitats" [counties], as far as inhabited by a coherent German population, belongs to German Austria. . . .104

97. Ibid., pp. 150–51.
98. Ibid., p. 151.
99. Ibid.
100. For a good discussion of the Czechoslovak occupation of Ruthenia, see the pertinent sections of L'udovít Holotík, "Úloha talianskej a francúzskej vojenskej misie na Slovensku r. 1919" [The role of the Italian and French military missions in Slovakia in 1919], *Historický časopis* 1, no. 4 (1953):561–94 and 2, no. 1 (1954):39–70.
101. Usenko, *Vpliv*, p. 178.
102. Their number in the trans-Danubian area was over 600,000. See *Népszámlálás*, pp. 2–97.
103. Today this area, known as Burgenland, is part of Austria.
104. Sarah Wambaugh, *Plebiscites since the World War*, 2 vols. (Washington: Carnegie Endowment for International Peace, 1933), 1:274.

The only bright spot in this declaration, as far as the Hungarian government was concerned, was that the Austrians called for a plebiscite, a policy to which the Hungarians themselves adhered.[105] The Hungarians, however, still notified the Austrian government that "Hungary would consider any annexation policy as an unfriendly act, likely to jeopardize the pending negotiations between the two countries."[106] Although most of the pro-Austrian agitation at the time came from outside the western Hungarian German region, the situation was serious and the Károlyi government recognized that any delay in the concrete implementation of a liberal nationality policy could have serious consequences.

Heading the German agitation for autonomy was Géza Zsombor who, in spite of his Hungarian-sounding name, was the editor-in-chief of *Grenzpost*, the leading German newspaper of the area, published in Sopron.[107] Zsombor played an ambiguous role: on the one hand, he was negotiating with the Károlyi government for the establishment of an autonomous German region and, on the other, he became the leader of those who desired to unite with Austria. However, in late 1918, Zsombor seemed to use the pro-Austrian agitation only as a weapon against the Hungarian government in order to achieve far-reaching autonomy. On December 27, 1918, he announced that the Germans "either get autonomy or they will proclaim an independent German Republic."[108]

First, because of their scattered settlements, only cultural autonomy was offered, but especially after the success of the Ruthenians and the bellicose behavior of Zsombor, the government decided to grant full autonomy. Thus, on January 27, 1919, an autonomous German province was proclaimed under the name of *Deutschwestungarn*. This new province was to contain all the German-speaking areas of western Hungary, including a number of enclaves of both Magyars and Croats.[109] János Junker became the minister of German affairs[110] and Zsombor, the governor of the region.[111]

However, dissension immediately broke out: the city council of Sopron, the capital of the new province, voted to exclude itself from the new area on the ground that Sopron was a Hungarian city.[112] Because of the shortness of time and the dispute over the actual extent of the province, the situation concerning the German province was still fluid at the end of March when the Communists took over the reins of government.

105. Vilmos Böhm, *Két forradalom tüzében* [In the cross fire of two revolutions], 2nd ed. rev. (Budapest: Nepszava, 1946), p. 87.

106. Elizabeth de Weiss, "Dispute for the Burgenland in 1919," *Journal of Central European Affairs* 3, no. 2 (July 1943):151.

107. László Koncsek, "A bécsi és Sopron megyei ellenforradalom kapcsolatai 1919-ben" [Relations between counterrevolutionaries in Vienna and Sopron County in 1919], *Soproni Szemle* [Sopron Review] 10, no. 2 (1956):107.

108. Ibid.

109. Andrew F. Burghardt, *Borderland: A Historical and Geographical Study of Burgenland, Austria* (Madison: University of Wisconsin Press, 1962), p. 171.

110. T. Hajdu, "A nemzeti kérdés," p. 258.

111. Koncsek, "A bécsi és Sopron megyei ellenforradalom," p. 107.

112. Burghardt, *Borderland*, p. 185. In fact, according to the 1910 census, the Hungarians were in the minority in Sopron, comprising 44 percent of the total population. See *Népszámlálás*, pp. 46–47. However, over half the Germans spoke Hungarian in addition to their own mother tongue. Ibid.

Communist strength in Sopron was very small in the pre-March days. Moreover, the few adherents to the Communist ideology were all Hungarian newcomers. Two young men, László Bors, a newspaperman who came to Sopron only a few months before the 1918 revolution, and Dezső Entzbruder, an elementary teacher and former prisoner of war who came to Sopron to be discharged from the army, became the spokesmen of the Communist cause in Sopron.[113] Bors, on March 27, 1919, brought from Budapest a close friend of Béla Kun and one of the co-founders of the Communist party of Hungary, Sándor Kellner, to take over the leadership of the provisionally established Workers' Council.[114] All three men—Bors, Entzbruder, and Kellner—were Hungarians.

With the new regime, Henrik Kalmár, a Social Democrat who had been one of the undersecretaries of the former ministry, became the commissar of German affairs.[115] Considering the explosive nature of the whole German question, this decision was anything but wise. Zsombor, the former governor, was dismissed,[116] and it is small wonder that his proannexationist propaganda, which previously had been used only as a lever against the Hungarian government, was continued in a much more serious manner.

At the beginning of April, the government was still not quite sure about its plan of action. The regime announced that in the near future the German territory would be divided into three districts: the Western Hungarian District (Burgenland), the Central District (presumably comprising some of the scattered settlements in the counties of Fejér and Veszprém), and the Sváb-Török District (in Tolna and Baranya counties).[117] Eventually, the Revolutionary Governing Council vetoed the establishment of the Central and Sváb-Török districts and agreed to the maintenance of only the Western Hungarian District.[118] This decision was again a bad one because it discouraged the German population which, after the announcement of the creation of three regions, maintained high hopes.

It took the Communist leadership more than a month to announce, on April 30, the formation of the *Gaurat für Deutschwestungarn*. Moreover, to add insult to injury, the *Gaurat* was headed by Sándor Kellner, who was neither a German nor came from the region.[119] His deputies were Adolf Berczeller and Miklós Lazarovits. It was

113. On the background of László Bors, see András Bors, "Emlékeim a soproni Kommünről" [My memories of the commune in Sopron], *Soproni Szemle* [Sopron Review] 9, nos. 1–2 (1955):33–48. On Dezső Entzbruder, see András Bors, "A szépség és szenvedély útján az emberi jogokért" [In the path of beauty and passion for human rights], *Vasi Szemle* [Vas Review] 1 (1961):50–63.

114. András Bors, "Kellner Sándor, az igaz bolsevik" [Sándor Kellner, the true Bolshevik], *Soproni Szemle* 14, no. 3 (1960):197.

115. *MMTVD*, 6A:5.

116. Koncsek, "A bécsi és Sopron megyei ellenforradalom," p. 107.

117. Called Swabian-Turkish because these German settlers, mostly Swabians, came to Hungary after the Turkish occupation.

118. Law No. 139 of the Revolutionary Governing Council, 17 July 1919. See Kővágó, "Államszövetségi tervek," p. 307.

119. Kellner was a typesetter who came to work in the Röttig Press in Sopron shortly before the outbreak of World War I. See Bors, "Kellner Sándor," p. 194.

announced that the *Gauratversammlung* [Congress of District Councils] would assemble on about May 15 in Sopron. The organization of a separate German Red Army was under way and school reform was going to be worked out. The surprising announcement was that the *Gaurat* would conduct its own international commerce; the directorate was beginning negotiations with Austria about possible commercial treaties.[120]

In spite of this wide autonomy, the movement for secession from Hungary and for unification with Austria intensified inside and outside of Hungary. At the *Gauratversammlung* on May 20, Béla Kun referred to this pro-Austrian agitation as a bourgeois phenomenon. "We do not believe that the German proletariat, which was always at the front of the working class movement, would want to unite with a capitalist country."[121] He added that "we are, at any moment, ready to create a unified, federated country together with the proletariat of German Austria."[122]

The question of autonomy, especially of *Deutschwestungarn*, is connected with another important issue, that of a centralized, unified, and homogeneous party. National autonomy, according to Leninist doctrine, cannot be extended to the party organization itself, which is supposed to be highly centralized. Béla Kun, however, was ready to yield on the principle of a centralized party, mostly on the insistence of the German group for national autonomy within the party organization. The draft proposal of June 13 for the party statutes stated that, for the organization of non-Hungarian nationalities, separate national party committees would be formed. Their duties would be propaganda work in the territory of the given nationality and the creation of new party organizations on a lower level. The representatives of these organizational committees would attend the meetings of the Central Committee, where they would have the power to negotiate. At the party congress they would be able not only to take part in the negotiations but also have the right to vote.[123]

Thus the paradoxical situation occurred: while the nationality question was underemphasized by the regime, in the case of the Germans the idea of national autonomy was carried so far that the Germans conducted commercial negotiations with Austria and pressed for a federal structure within the party organization. This is only another example of the lack of a firm ideological foundation which produced the confusion for which the Hungarian soviet regime has been criticized ever since.

The undefined nature of the German-inhabited areas, in the meantime, only added to the conservative German peasantry's dislike of the soviet regime. Géza Zsombor, the former governor, became the spokesman for unification with Austria as well as the head of counterrevolutionary sentiments. The first clash between the Red Army and the German peasantry came as early as April 3, 1919. This was perhaps the first of a whole chain of counterrevolutionary uprisings which culminated in June in the trans-Danubian area. The uprising was led by Zsombor. The peasants, who were

120. *MMTVD*, 6A:357.

121. Kun, *Válogatott írások*, 1:315.

122. Ibid. For Kun's efforts in Austria, see Alfred D. Low, "The First Austrian Republic and Soviet Hungary," *Journal of Central European Affairs* 20 (July 1960):175–92.

123. *MMTVD*, 6A:698–99; 6B:46–48.

vineyard owners, were distressed over the governmental decision of complete prohibition; their livelihood was threatened. They attacked the headquarters of the Communist party, where the members of the Red Army killed three and wounded eight.[124] Zsombor was arrested and taken to Budapest, from where he escaped. The situation intensified in the area until, on May 4, 1919, the *Gaurat* proclaimed a state of martial law.[125] However, nothing seemed to help and, by June, a series of uprisings took place throughout the whole region.

If, in 1918, only half of the German population of western Hungary was in favor of unification with Austria, by the middle of 1919 most of them would have been happy to leave the Hungarian Soviet Republic behind.[126] Not only were the territorial confines of *Deutschwestungarn* unsatisfactory from the German point of view, but the activities of the Sopron triumvirate of Bors, Kellner, and Entzbruder were repulsive to them. The extended prohibition law was economically injurious to the winegrowers of the region. And, finally, the terror which followed the counterrevolutionary uprisings turned the majority of Germans against the Hungarian regime.[127]

It is doubtful that Hungary would have been able to keep these territories in any case. The Paris Peace Conference readily granted the Austrian demand without a plebiscite because of the solid German population of the area and because of economic considerations which were so important in maintaining a moderate Social Democratic regime in Vienna. However, if a plebiscite had been granted, the activities of the Hungarian soviet regime would have been detrimental to the interest of Hungary. The Communist nationality policy in this area was close to disastrous.

The Slovenes living in the counties of Vas and Zala did not fare so well as the Germans.[128] Although the Károlyi government took the initial steps of recognizing a separate Slovene district cut out of these counties, appointing a governor, and granting the Slovenes a separate ministry in Budapest and a national assembly,[129] the Soviet regime did not follow through.

According to the *Vörös Ujság*, a few days after the proclamation of the soviet regime "the Workers' Council took over the power in Muraszombat [Murska Sobota]

124. Koncsek, "A bécsi és Sopron megyei ellenforradalom," p. 107.

125. Ibid., p. 105.

126. De Weiss, "Dispute," pp. 155–56.

127. Tibor Szamuely and his "Lenin boys" visited the cities and villages of the counties of Sopron and Vas, leaving behind twenty to twenty-two dead. See Zsuzsa L. Nagy, *Forradalom és ellenforradalom a Dunántúlon 1919* [Revolution and counterrevolution in trans-Danubia, 1919] (Budapest: Kossuth, 1961), p. 144.

128. The Slovenes were one of the numerically less important nationalities of Hungary. The 1910 census did not even have a separate category for them. The area they inhabited was small, 950 square kilometers, where they constituted 73.9 percent of the population. See L. Kevago [Kővágó], "Iugoslaviane v Vengrii i pravo natsii na samoopredelenie (1918–1919 gg.)" [The Southern Slavs of Hungary and the right of self-determination of nations (1918–1919)], *Acta Historica* 11 (1965):147.

129. The decision to establish a separate Slovene region was reached on December 6, 1918. However, it was only on January 14, 1919, that Béla Obál, the government representative and future governor, was able to obtain an agreement to this plan from the Slovene representatives. See Kevago [Kővágó], "Iugoslaviane v Vengrii," pp. 149, 152.

and extended its authority over the Slovene districts." Moreover, according to the news item, a Revolutionary Governing Council of the autonomous region was created.[130] All this was done without central approval, yet the Slovene Revolutionary Governing Council went on organizing. They declared Muraszombat the capital and laid claim to the administration of the Slovene parts of the counties of Vas and Zala.[131]

The situation in this area became chaotic. The executive committees of the Zala-egerszeg, Alsólendva, and Szentgotthárd district councils, for instance, flatly refused to recognize the claims of the Slovene Revolutionary Governing Council.[132] Until they became aware of the large-scale smuggling going on between the Slovene region and Austria, the Budapest government did not interfere, and even then their attempts to investigate the smuggling operation were futile.[133]

Counterrevolutionary elements took advantage of this chaotic state of affairs. Assured of help from Austrian groups in case of a counterrevolutionary uprising, the dissatisfied Vilmos Tkalecz, a twenty-five-year-old grammar school teacher who styled himself the political commissar of the region, and twelve members of the Muraszombat Council (which also styled itself the Slovene Revolutionary Council) proclaimed an independent Mura republic on May 29. Tkalecz became president of the newly formed state.[134]

On May 31, the government of the Mura republic sent a telegram to the Commissariat of Foreign Affairs of the Hungarian Soviet Republic announcing its existence, claiming the Slovene parts of the counties of Vas and Zala, declaring itself a socialist state, and asking for recognition by the Hungarian Soviet Republic. The Mura republic announced its willingness to live in peace with Hungary but added that, if Hungary were to attack, the Mura government would appeal to the Entente powers for protection. Finally, the Hungarian government was asked to withdraw the Hungarian Red Army from the territories of the independent Mura republic.[135]

The Hungarian Soviet Republic did not hesitate to send troops to Zalaegerszeg, where fighting continued until June 5.[136] Among Tkalecz's troops were a number of Slovene peasants who had been promised land by the Mura republic and fought valiantly against the Hungarian Red Army. Tkalecz himself escaped to

130. *Vörös Ujság*, 27 March 1919, in *1919 god v Vengrii. Sbornik materialov k 40-letiiu Vengerskoi Sovetskoi Respubliki* [The year 1919 in Hungary: a collection of documents for the fortieth anniversary of the Hungarian Soviet Republic], ed. B. Geiger (Moscow Gos. izd-vo polit. lit-ry, 1959), p. 73.

131. P[árttörténeti I[ntézet] Archivum, A. II/10/74, quoted in Kővágó, *A magyarországi délszlávok*, p. 216.

132. László Kővágó, "Az 1919. évi szlovén-vidéki ellenforradalomról" [On the Slovene counterrevolution of 1919], *Hadtörténelmi Közlemények* [Military history notes] 11, no. 2 (1964):207.

133. Ibid., pp. 210-11.

134. Kővágó, *A magyarországi délszlávok*, p. 231.

135. Zs. Nagy, *Forradalom és ellenforradalom*, p. 132. The counterrevolutionaries, who were standing on the basis of territorial integrity and who supplied Tkalecz with money, arms, and men from Austria, were, in fact, double-crossed by Tkalecz when he proclaimed an independent Slovene republic. See Kővágó, "Az 1919. évi szlovén-vidéki ellenforradalomról," p. 225.

136. Kővágó, *A magyarországi délszlávok*, p. 232.

Yugoslavia, where he was put in jail. However, he was released shortly thereafter and allowed to go to Szeged, where the counterrevolutionary government was organizing.[137]

After the insurrection was over, Jenő Landler, commissar of internal affairs, came to the region in order to clarify the whole Slovene situation. Béla Obál, who had been governor (as well as lord lieutenant of Vas County) from the time of the Károlyi period, was removed from his post on June 11 due to his "unclear role in the Slovene affairs."[138] On June 15, new elections were held for the local village councils, and serious efforts were made to win over the people. The village council of Muraszombat was to look after the affairs of the *járás* until elections for the *járás* council could take place.[139]

The autonomy of the Slovene region was so far from being defined that there was considerable division of opinion about the advisability of setting up such a region at all. The Vas County Council was of the opinion that among the Slovenes there was such strong sympathy toward Yugoslavia that the creation of an autonomous region would only add oil to the fire.[140] In the end, the Slovenes lost the autonomous rights promised to them by the Károlyi government.

While the Germans managed to gain very wide autonomy during the soviet republic, the Slovenes lost theirs. The discrepancy between these two cases further illustrates that the Hungarian Soviet Republic had neither effective central control nor a uniform nationality policy.

The Croats of Burgenland also fared rather poorly during the Soviet period. With the creation of an autonomous German region in western Hungary, the Croats were under the governance of Commissar of German Affairs Henrik Kalmár. The Croat answer to German autonomy was open hostility; Croat villagers, for instance, bodily attacked several of the speakers sent down from Sopron and Budapest.

The Croats had reason to complain, for the Sopron Council often acted in a chauvinistic manner toward them. The village of Cinkfalva, for example, claimed that the Sopron Council would not grant the village a Croat-language school.[141] And Géza Faragó, the man dealing with school reform for the region, made no mention of the problem of Croat schools.[142]

Since the Croat villages were scattered throughout the counties of Moson, Sopron, and Vas, no clear-cut geographic division between the Croats and the Germans was possible. Territorial autonomy for the Croats was thus out of the question. But the Budapest government, which professed adherence to the principle of cultural autonomy, failed to implement this principle in the case of the Croats. For its in-

137. Kővágó, "Az 1919. évi szlovén-vidéki ellenforradalomról," p. 213 n. 42.
138. Ibid., pp. 222–23.
139. Ibid., p. 223.
140. Kővágó, *A magyarországi délszlávok*, p. 241; and "Az 1919. évi szlovén-vidéki ellenforrada-lomról," p. 206.
141. *Crvena Zastava*, 7 June 1919, quoted in Kővágó, *A magyarországi délszlávok*, p. 213.
142. Ibid., p. 209.

difference to the Croats the government paid dearly; counterrevolutionary sentiments were greater among these people than in purely Hungarian territories.

The Slovaks, one of the most important nationalities living in prerevolutionary Hungary, presented an especially complex problem to the Hungarian Soviet Republic because of the birth of Czechoslovak nationalism. The Slovak question was made even more intricate by the fact that the Slovaks' numerical strength and the territory they inhabited were great enough for them to fall into the category stipulated in Clause 88 of the Hungarian Soviet Constitution; i.e., they could form, if they wished, a separate soviet republic. Another factor which created immense difficulties for the Hungarian soviet government was the fact that part of the Slovak-inhabited territories were reconquered by the Hungarian Red Army from the new republic of Czechoslovakia, and incorporation of these territories looked to many like an undisguised attempt to recover all the lost territories of former Hungary.

After the Károlyi regime came into power in October, 1918, the newly created Ministry of Nationalities under Oszkár Jászi immediately started negotiations with the representatives of different nationalities. The Slovaks, headed by Milan Hodža, turned down the Hungarian offer of wide autonomy and instead announced their desire to join the Czechs in a Czechoslovak republic. The Slovak Social Democrats also supported this decision.

This refusal did not deter the Hungarian government from working out a detailed plan for Slovak autonomy in preparation for the forthcoming peace conference. Although the Slovak region had been occupied by Czech troops since November, 1918, the Ministry of Nationalities issued the Slovak statute on March 12, 1919 (People's Law No. 30 of 1919).[143] This statute provided for a Slovak region, *Slovenska Krajina*, which would have a national assembly autonomous in internal affairs (justice, education, and religion). To deal with matters of concern to both the Slovak and Budapest governments, the Slovaks were assured representation in the Hungarian Parliament. This statute also promised a Slovak ministry, which would be responsible to both bodies. With the Czech occupation and the dominant pro-Czech feeling in Slovakia, however, this statute could not be implemented.

The new soviet regime was dedicated to the idea of an international revolution and viewed Slovakia as a prime target for propaganda. From the several thousand workers of Slovak origin who had migrated southward to Budapest during the previous twenty-five years,[144] the Communists organized a Slovak section of the Communist party of Hungary. This section was entrusted with propaganda and organizational work among the Slovaks both inside and outside of unoccupied Hungarian territories.[145] On March 27, 1919, these Slovaks began publishing a daily paper called

143. Macartney, *Hungary and Her Successors*, p. 23 n. 4.

144. Holotík, "O Slovenskej republike," p. 185.

145. Holotík, in "O Slovenskej republike," p. 185, claims that it was organized at the end of 1918. According to Kővágó, "Internacionalisták Tanácsmagyarországon" [Internationalists in the Hungarian Soviet Republic], in Zs. Nagy and A. Zsilák, eds., *Ötven év*, p. 382, there is no documentary evidence of its existence before the proclamation of the soviet republic in March, 1919. However, police reports prior to March refer to Slovak propagandists on the editorial board of *Vörös Ujság*.

Červené noviny [Red newspaper],[146] and on April 2, they announced their formal adherence to the Hungarian Soviet Republic.[147]

On April 5, the Slovak section organized a meeting at which at least two future members of the independent Slovak Soviet Republic, Jozef Varecha and Jozef Šluka, were present and made speeches. At this meeting it was declared that "even at the price of our lives we will bring the proletarian dictatorship to Upper Hungary."[148] Referring to Slovakia as Upper Hungary and neglecting to mention the Czech lands, the Slovak and Hungarian Communists apparently considered the Slovak territories as part of Hungary.

Although the Czech colony in Budapest was small, by late March, 1919, there was also a Czech Communist group attached to the International Socialist Federation of Hungary organized by Antonín O. Janoušek.[149] At a meeting of the Czech group on April 12, at least two thousand people gathered though only a few hundred had been expected. Two hundred Czech soldiers of the International Brigade of the Hungarian Red Army could not even get into the building.[150] It is safe to assume that not only members of the Czech colony but also some Slovaks attended the meeting. Beginning on May 18, the Czechs also published a weekly newspaper, *Armáda proletářů*. This paper was not an official organ of the International Socialist Federation of Hungary, to which the Czech group belonged, but was intended for distribution among the Czech troops occupying Slovakia.[151]

The leaders of both the Czech and Slovak groups were allegedly in constant and direct contact with Communists and Communist sympathizers in Czech and Slovak territories. Between Prague, Kladno, Košice, and Budapest a continuous, well-organized messenger route was established.[152]

The Czech and Slovak Communist groups united at the end of April. On April 25, the united body held a meeting at which the workers of the two nationalities announced their wish to fight for the proletarian dictatorship in Slovakia and the Czech lands.[153] However, the union of these two groups remained loose and, very often, even after the announcement of the creation of the Czechoslovak group, the Slovaks acted

146. The *Červené noviny* was published continuously until July 31, 1919. See Endre Arató, "Magyar, cseh és szlovák munkások együttműködése a Nagy Októbert követő forradalmi fellendülés időszakában (1917–1920)" [The cooperation of Hungarian, Czech, and, Slovak workers during the period of revolutionary ferment following the October revolution (1917–20)], *Századok* 93, no. 1 (1959):61.

147. Dezső Nemes, "A Magyar Tanácsköztársaság történelmi jelentősége" [The historical significance of the Hungarian Soviet Republic], *Századok* 93, no. 1 (1959):28–29.

148. *Vörös Ujság*, in *MMTVD*, 6A:110–11.

149. Kővágó, "Internacionalisták," p. 382.

150. According to *Népszava*, 13 April 1919, in *MMTVD*, 6A:194.

151. László Kővágó, "A Magyarországi Nemzetközi Szocialista Föderációról" [On the International Socialist Federation of Hungary], *Párttörténeti Közlemények* 12, no. 2 (June 1966):141.

152. Martin Vietor, "A proletárdiktatúra hatalomrajutásának kísérlete Csehszlovákiában és a Magyar Tanácsköztársaság" [The attempt of a Communist take-over in Czechoslovakia and the Hungarian Soviet Republic], in Gábor, ed., *A Magyar Tanácsköztársaság történelmi jelentősége*, p. 152.

153. *MMTVD*, 6A:313.

independently. For example, the *Červené noviny* continued to be published exclusively as the organ of the Slovak section.[154]

At the time that these two groups united, the Slovak question took on a new dimension. With Béla Kun's rejection of the Smuts offer, the very existence of the Hungarian Soviet Republic was in serious danger. By the beginning of May, Rumanian troops were pushing ahead. Fortunately for the Hungarian regime, these troops, for a variety of reasons, stopped at the Tisza River.

After some hesitation, the Communist government decided to launch a counteroffensive, not against the Rumanians but against the Czechs. This decision was based partly on military considerations, since the Czech army was estimated to be considerably weaker than the other Entente forces occupying Hungary. Another consideration was political. The Czech lands, being industrialized, had a sizable proletariat, so a proletarian revolution seemed more likely there than in any of the other neighboring countries.[155] A third consideration was that the industrial district of the counties of Nógrád and Borsod were essential to the economic survival of the country.[156] Finally, the Hungarians had legal grounds for this action: they could point to the Czech attack of April 29 when forces crossed the designated demarcation line and occupied Miskolc, Szerencs, and Sátoraljaújhely.[157] On May 4, Lieutenant Colonel Károly Szabó Papp was sent to negotiate with the Czechs for withdrawal of their troops, with no result. Thus, there was a legal excuse for the counteroffensive.[158]

The plan of launching a counterattack in the north was first devised by Aurél Stromfeld, the chief of staff of the reorganized Hungarian Red Army and a professional soldier of considerable military talent. Stromfeld was a new recruit to the Social Democratic party who, like most of his fellow officers, led the Red Army for patriotic reasons.[159] Stromfeld's plan was to separate the Czechoslovak from the Rumanian troops. The operation was very successful and, a week later, on June 6, the Hungarian Red Army entered Kassa [Košice]. On June 9, they occupied Eperjes [Prešov]; on June 10, Bártfa [Bardejov] and Rozsnyó [Rožňava]. Within two weeks the Hungarian Red Army occupied 2,835 square kilometers of Slovakia.[160]

154. Kővágó, "A Magyarországi Nemzetközi Szocialista Föderációról," p. 129.

155. The Czechoslovak group's major aim was to intensify any revolutionary ferment in Czechoslovakia. See Michal Dzvoník, "A Szlovák Tanácsköztársaság és a szlovák nemzet önrendelkezési joga" [The Slovak Soviet Republic and the self-determination of the Slovak nation], in Gábor, ed., *A Magyar Tanácsköztársaság történelmi jelentősége*, pp. 134–49. There was a certain amount of Slovak opposition to the Czechoslovak government which was "quickly exploited by Magyars and pro-Magyar elements." See Alfred D. Low, *The Soviet Hungarian Republic and the Paris Peace Conference*, Transactions of the American Philosophical Society, n.s., vol. 53, pt. 10 (Philadelphia, 1963), p. 25.

156. Tibor Hetés, Introduction to *Stromfeld Aurél válogatott írásai* [Selected writings of Aurél Stromfeld], ed. Tibor Hetés (Budapest: Zrinyi, 1959), p. 80.

157. Ibid.

158. Böhm, *Két forradalom tüzében*, p. 255.

159. After the failure of the soviet republic, Stromfeld was imprisoned by the counterrevolutionary government. His nationalism is revealed in the diary he wrote while in jail. Addressing his deceased sister, he wrote, "You, a fanatical lover of the Hungarian fatherland, you now lie in foreign soil [Slovakia]. Was I not right to have tried to prevent this?" Hetés, *Stromfeld Aurél*, p. 260.

160. Kálmán Nagy, "Stromfeld Aurél, a Magyar Vörös Hadsereg vezérkari főnöke" [Aurél Stromfeld, the chief of staff of the Hungarian Red Army], *Századok* 85, nos. 1–2 (1951):236–37.

The Communist hierarchy, as well as the population, was overjoyed. Béla Kun considered "the nórthern campaign . . . extremely significant."[161] Joyous articles appeared and speeches were made on the success of the Hungarian Red Army and its international significance. However, nothing definite was said about future plans for the reconquered territories.

G. V. Chicherin, the foreign commissar of Soviet Russia, felt it necessary to inquire from Kun about his plans and to give advice. He sent a telegram to Kun on June 9, saying,

> Entente radios announced that Hungarian Red troops occupied non-Hungarian territories. Would it not be advisable to announce the self-determination of the Slovaks in order to avoid the growth of Czech nationalism?[162]

To this Kun replied that "all preparations for the declaration of the Slovak Soviet Republic have been made. The proclamation will be made within the shortest possible time. Our nationality policy is Leninist."[163] However, none of the utterances of Kun, other government officials, or the members of the Czechoslovak group gives any indication that preparations had in fact been made prior to Kun's reply.[164]

There is no doubt that Janoušek, the leader of the Czechoslovak Communist group and later foreign commissar of the independent Slovak Soviet Republic, was a steadfast supporter of the idea of a Czechoslovak Soviet Republic and did not contemplate the creation of an independent Slovak state. All his statements prior to June 16, the day the Slovak Soviet Republic was proclaimed, show this clearly. The Czechoslovak group was certain that "the dictatorship of the proletariat is not possible in Slovakia without the support of the proletariat of the Czech lands, Moravia, and Silesia."[165]

On June 8, at a meeting of the Czechoslovak Communist group, neither Janoušek nor Štefan Mokráň,[166] the future commissar of agricultural affairs of Slovakia, made any reference to an independent Slovak republic.[167] As a matter of fact, on June 9, Janoušek welcomed the military occupation of Slovakia, stressing the fact that proletarian power would be established in the territory of Czechoslovakia.[168] The first congress of the Communist party of Hungary met in Budapest on June 12 and 13. At this meeting, Janoušek and Mokráň again gave no indication that they were aware of any preparations for the establishment of an independent Slovak Soviet Republic.[169]

161. Mrs. Béla Kun, *Kun Béla*, p. 197.

162. *MMTVD*, 6A:697.

163. Ibid.

164. It is impossible to ascertain the exact date of Kun's reply to Chicherin's telegram.

165. V. V. Mar'ina, "Velikaia Oktiabr'skaia sotsialisticheskaia revoliutsiia i razvitie revoliutsionnogo dvizheniia v Slovakii v 1918–1920 gg." [The great October Socialist Revolution and the growth of the revolutionary movement in Slovakia between 1918 and 1920], in *Iz istorii revoliutsionnogo dvizheniia narodov Chekhoslovakii* [From the history of the revolutionary movement of the peoples of Czechoslovakia], ed. A. Kh. Klebanskii and I. N. Mel'nikova (Moscow: Izd-vo Akademii SSR, 1959), p. 351.

166. The representative of the Slovak proletariat had Magyarized his name earlier and was also known as Mokrássy. See *MMTVD*, 6B:674.

167. *MMTVD*, 6A:695.

168. Dzvoník, "A Szlovák Tanácsköztársaság," p. 141.

169. *MMTVD*, 6B:10–11.

Janoušek's wife, Maria Janoušková, together with Václav Gruber, another Czech Communist, even crossed the Austrian-Czechoslovak border on June 13 in order to transmit a letter to Dr. Alice Masaryková, the daughter of the Czechoslovak president. Janoušek's letter, somewhat naïvely, tried to convince Tomáš G. Masaryk not to resist "the socialist revolution which will not stop at the borders of the republic."[170] In the letter Janoušek emphasized that "the Hungarian proletariat is not an enemy of the Czechoslovak Republic" and that "the Hungarian Soviet Republic recognizes the borders of the Czechoslovak state."[171]

On June 14, at the Congress of Hungarian Councils, Janoušek elaborated on the notion of a confederative proletarian state which would include both Hungary and Czechoslovakia. On June 15, only a day before the proclamation of the Slovak Soviet Republic, his article in *Armáda proletářů* further developed this theme, envisaging a Czechoslovak Soviet Republic federated with Hungary, Russia, and the Ukraine.[172]

If the Czech and Slovak Communists did not plan to proclaim an independent Slovak Soviet Republic prior to June 16, the Hungarians were equally reluctant to do so. Béla Kun, who appeared at the meeting of the German section of the Communist party of Hungary on June 9, the date of Chicherin's telegram, made no reference to any plans for the establishment of a new republic in the near future.[173] On the following day, Kun was in Kassa making a fiery speech at the celebration of the city's liberation.

> We liberated you, proletarians of Kassa. It was the Red Proletarian Army which liberated you.... The Red Army did not come here to create new oppression as did the Czech imperialists' army but to liberate the workers without any national distinction.... We shall implement with peace and love in the territory of the [Hungarian] Soviet Republic the slogan "Workers of the world, unite!"[174]

Again, no hint of the establishment of the Slovak Soviet Republic nor even a specific promise of self-determination. Moreover, the appointment of János Hirossik, one of the original founders of the Communist party of Hungary, as commissar of the occupied territories does not suggest an independent Slovakia.[175]

On June 11, the *Vörös Ujság*, in a joyous article hailing the victories of the Hungarian Red Army, was quite specific about Slovakia's status.

> This occupation is no conquest.... The international revolution unites the Slovak and Hungarian proletariats. We do not unite under the slogan of territorial integrity nor because the schools of intellectual oppression taught us to love our

170. Kővágó, "Internacionalisták," p. 399.

171. Ibid.

172. Kővágó, "Államszövetségi tervek," p. 311.

173. In fact, Kun mentioned only "national and complete cultural autonomy." See *MMTVD*, 6A:697-98.

174. Kun, *Válogatott írások*, 1:344.

175. Holotík, "O Slovenskej republike," p. 189.

thousand-year-old Hungary . . . but because we have to take up the class warfare in unison simply for reasons of compelling economic necessity.[176]

Béla Kun's speech at the party congress (June 12), though it avoided any explicit reference to the Slovak situation, implicitly admitted that Slovakia was considered to be part of the Hungarian Soviet Republic.[177]

Due to the lack of a clear-cut policy, the proclamation of the Slovak Soviet Republic came out a week after the Hungarian Red Army occupied Eperjes, the most northernly Slovak city of the area. In the presence of the military leaders of the Red Army, the new republic was proclaimed on June 16 in this city.

As far as one can ascertain from the scarce documentary evidence, after the occupation of Eperjes on June 9, a provisional workers' council was established in the city. On June 15, elections took place and, on the same day, posters appeared announcing an important public meeting the next day. Here, in the presence of Vilmos Böhm, commander in chief of the Hungarian Red Army, and of some members of the Czechoslovak group in Budapest, the proclamation was made.[178] The *Kassai Vörös Ujság*, reflecting the general confusion, reported the event under the headline: "Yesterday the proclamation of *Slovenska Krajna* [*sic*] took place in Eperjes."[179]

At this public meeting a provisional revolutionary council was elected which transferred its activities to Kassa, closer to the Hungarian border.[180] The decision to proclaim the Slovak Soviet Republic in Eperjes and then to designate Kassa the capital was based on several considerations. Eperjes, although it had a sizable Hungarian population, was more of a Slovak city than Kassa, where the majority of the population was Hungarian. Therefore, the proclamation seemed more "genuine" if it took place in Eperjes.[181] However, Kassa, close to the Hungarian border, seemed a much safer place for the headquarters of the Slovak Revolutionary Governing Council.[182] The permanent council was not announced until June 20.[183] Among the commissariats of the republic was one for foreign affairs.[184]

176. *MMTVD*, 6A:657–58.

177. Kun, *Válogatott írások*, 1:356.

178. Mar'ina, "Velikaia Oktiabr'skaia revoliutsiia," pp. 352–53.

179. *Kassai Vörös Ujság* [Red Journal of Kassa], 17 June 1919, in: Tibor Hetés, ed., *A Magyar Vörös Hadsereg*, (Válogatott dokumentumok) [The Hungarian Red Army, 1919 (selected documents)] (Budapest, 1959), pp. 376–77.

180. Mar'ina, "Velikaia Oktiabr'skaia revoliutsiia," p. 353.

181. Martin Vietor, *Slovenská sovietska republika v r. 1919* [The Slovak Soviet Republic in 1919] (Bratislava: Slovenské vydavateľstvo politickej literatúry, 1955), p. 193.

182. Because of this transfer there is some confusion in the literature concerning the place the Slovak Soviet Republic was declared. Even Dr. Ferenc Münnich, the commander in chief of the Slovak Red Army at the time and prime minister of Hungary between 1958 and 1960, remembered that there had been two Slovak governments in Slovakia, one in Eperjes and another in Kassa. According to Dr. Münnich, the "Eperjes government had no financial basis. Even for the Kassa government I brought arms and ammunition for 5,000 men from Budapest." Münnich to the author, 24 November 1967.

183. *Vörös Ujság*, 21 June 1919, in Hetés, *A Magyar Vörös Hadsereg*, p. 378.

184. List of commissars of the Slovak Soviet Republic: President, Antonín Janoušek; Foreign Affairs, Antonín Janoušek and Ernő Pór; Military Affairs, Ján Vavrica and Gyula Kovács; Financial

Chicherin's telegram of June 9 obviously found the Hungarian government unprepared and the Czechoslovak group, headed by Janoušek, opposed to the idea of an independent Slovakia. However, since the Czechoslovak group was a loose association, some Slovak members of the editorial board of *Červené noviny*, as the Hungarian Red Army began to occupy Slovakia, started a campaign for an independent Slovakia.[185] Kun, pressed by Chicherin's questions concerning the self-determination of Slovakia, found supporters of his newly formulated idea of Slovak independence among these dissident Slovaks. The delay in proclaiming the new republic most likely stemmed from the fact that it took time to win over the leadership of the Czechoslovak group for this new solution.[186]

At the time of the declaration of the new independent Slovak republic on June 16, the Congress of Hungarian Councils was in session. The next day, Dezső Bokányi, the president of the congress, told his audience that the government had received a telegram from the members of the Slovak Soviet Republic greeting the Hungarian Soviet Republic and expressing their "hope that they would soon be able to conduct the affairs of the two republics" together with the Hungarians.[187] The verbal confusion regarding the status of Slovakia was increasing by the day. Two republics whose leaders conduct their affairs together: did this mean a federation? The Hungarians seemed to act under this impression.

Moreover, the officials of the Slovak Soviet Republic seemed to be confused on the status of their own country. At a meeting in Kassa on June 22, János Hirossik, the commissar of commerce and railways of the Slovak government, felt compelled to announce that

> I can assure you that in those territories which will be designated [as the Slovak republic] there will not be any national discrimination. It will be decided on the basis of plebiscite which *part* of the country [*országrész*] you will belong to.[188]

At the same meeting, Zoltán Farkas, a member of the Kassa Council, added:

Affairs, Jozef Hanzík and Vilmos Baján; Internal Affairs, Ferenc Fehér and Jozef Šluka; Agriculture, Štefan Mokráň and József Czápai; Commerce and Railways, János Hirossik and Jozef Varecha; Justice, Mikuláš Ungár and Vladimír Czereny; Socialization, Gusztáv Fleischer and Samu Csapó; Education, Vince Suk and Edvard Krompašský; Health and Welfare, Lajos Jakab; Food, Štefan Stehlík. *MMTVD*, 6B:289.

185. Holotík, "O Slovenskej republike," pp. 190-91.

186. L'udovít Holotík suggests that one reason for delaying the proclamation of an independent Slovakia might be that it had been decided to wait until the party congress laid down some specific principle on foreign policy. See Holotík, "O Slovenskej republike," p. 191. The discussion at the congress does not support this hypothesis. Holotík also suggests that there might have been serious opposition to an independent Slovakia within the Revolutionary Governing Council. The confused statements of government officials even after the declaration in Eperjes suggest that the creation of the Slovak Soviet Republic had been privately arranged between Béla Kun and some of the members of the Slovak section. Kun was in the habit of not informing his closest co-workers about important matters. *Egy mérnök a farradalomban*, p. 310.

187. *MMTVD*, 6B:119.

188. *Kassai Magyar Munkás* [Košice Hungarian worker], 24 June 1919, in *MMTVD*, 6B:302. Italics are mine.

Let us express our trust in the independent Slovak Soviet Republic, especially since the Commissar of Internal Affairs [*sic*] officially announced in front of you that the question of which territories will belong to which *country* [*ország*] will be decided by plebiscite.[189]

Two speakers were talking about two different things: Hirossik referred to different parts, meaning Slovak and Hungarian parts, of the same country, whereas Farkas explicitly mentioned two separate countries. Furthermore, the Hungarian-language paper in Kassa, the *Kassai Vörös Ujság*, kept referring to the Slovak Communist party as the Slovak section of the Communist party of Hungary, even after the declaration of independence.[190] The status of the new Slovak regime was extremely ambiguous.

The commissariat of the Slovak Soviet Republic was structured according to the Hungarian system of having two commissars for every post. The two commissars of foreign affairs were the president, Janoušek, and Ernő Pór, a close friend of Kun who had been one of the founding members not only of the Communist party of Hungary but also of the Hungarian Group of the Russian Communist party (Bolshevik).

The presence of Pór in the important post of commissar of foreign affairs indicates that he was supposed to be the official watchdog over the new state's affairs. One wonders whether Pór was informed of the contents of a telegram sent by Janoušek on June 20 to Prague in which he assured the Czechoslovak government that "the majority of the commissars is Slovak. . . . Some commissariats are headed by Czechs. . . . Comradely and brotherly solidarity ties us to the Czech proletariat, and we wish to live with them in an indivisible federal state."[191] The Hungarian collection of documents quotes *Pravda* instead of their own files for this telegram.

The Slovak question took on international significance with Clemenceau's ultimatum to the Hungarian government to cease its military aggression in Slovakia. In his speech to the Congress of Hungarian Councils on June 19, Béla Kun pleaded with the congress to agree to the withdrawal and accept the terms confronting Hungary. The opposition to Kun's proposals was sizable. József Pogány, a left-wing member of the Revolutionary Governing Council, argued:

If we were to accept these borders we would condemn the Soviet Republic of Hungary to death. . . . We would condemn it to death because . . . within these borders this country cannot survive. It would be impossible to live here in any social or state form, whether it is a feudal, capitalist, or socialist state.[192]

Other opponents considered it foolish to withdraw while the Hungarian Red Army was victorious. It was also openly admitted during this debate that without the military occupation of Slovakia by the Hungarian Red Army the Slovak revolutionary movement would be too weak to ignite the necessary spark for the outbreak of a genuine proletarian revolution.

189. Ibid., p. 303. Italics are mine.
190. Holotík, "O Slovenskej republike," p. 196.
191. *Pravda*, 20 June 1919, in *MMTVD*, 6B:279.
192. *MMTVD*, 6B:158.

At the end, Béla Kun came out of the debate victorious. He claimed that "the withdrawal [from Slovakia] does not mean stabbing the international revolution in the back."[193] He also acknowledged that the unfortunate result of the Hungarian penetration into Czechoslovakia had been that

> the class warfare decreased, decreased to the degree that the Czechoslovak chauvinists could gather the working class into their ranks and could ensure class cooperation with the bourgeoisie. . . . Now [by withdrawing] we pull out the ground under the feet of Němec and the other chauvinists, for we take out of their hands their last winning card, namely [their claim] that we created a Bolshevist imperialism when we took away territories legally theirs from the point of view of national self-determination.[194]

The decision came too late. In spite of the withdrawal of the Hungarian Red troops from Slovak territories, the Hungarian Soviet Republic was unable to survive, partly because of lack of popular support and partly because of the Rumanian offensive. On August 1, 1919, the Rumanian army drove the soviet government out of Budapest; the 133 days of the Hungarian Soviet Republic were over.

Janoušek and the other members of the Slovak government fled from the Czech army into Hungary, but Janoušek had to stand trial after the establishment of the counterrevolutionary government. Ironically, he was accused of organizing a new state in Slovak territories, thereby violating the territorial integrity of the kingdom of Hungary.[195]

The establishment of the Slovak Soviet Republic was but a brief episode; it ceased to exist after less than three weeks. Nevertheless, it provides the only example of a Hungarian proletarian revolutionary war and its aftermath. Béla Kun admitted that the creation of the Slovak Soviet Republic was disastrous, that class struggle decreased with the establishment of the new republic. Thus the Marxist claim that "the greatest victory of the Leninist nationality policy of the Hungarian Soviet Republic was . . . the proclamation of the establishment of the Slovak Soviet Republic"[196] cannot be taken seriously. The Hungarian government not only had no clear policy toward Slovakia but also lost effective control over Slovak affairs after the formation of the new republic. Revolutionary sentiments waned while the attitude of the Entente powers toward Hungary became increasingly hostile. The establishment of the Slovak Soviet Republic was probably the greatest defeat of the nationality policy of the Hungarian Communists.

193. Kun, *Válogatott írások*, 1:406.
194. Ibid., p. 407.
195. Holotík, "O Slovenskej republike," p. 194 n. 62a.
196. T. Hajdu, "A nemzeti kérdés," p. 263.

Problems of Foreign Policy before the Revolutionary Governing Council

Zsuzsa L. Nagy

The Subject and the Sources

Today there already is a sufficient amount of literature available to discuss the international situation and foreign policy of the Hungarian Soviet Republic of 1919. The materials on which this essay is to be based are the minutes of the sessions of the Revolutionary Governing Council and its various committees including the United Central Executive Committee. To date only parts of these minutes have been published, although Hungarian studies of the soviet republic have utilized these sources adequately.

The Revolutionary Governing Council was established on March 21, 1919, replacing the previous government. Its president was Sándor Garbai; its membership consisted of twenty-nine people's commissars or deputy peoples' commissars who fulfilled ministerial or deputy ministerial functions. On the third of April the council changed its form, raising the number of commissars to thirty-four and the deputy peoples' commissars were elevated to the rank of commissar. While on March 21 there were only two Communist peoples' commissars and nine deputy peoples' commissars as members of the governing council, the following April their number was increased to thirteen and their position was strengthened by adequate representation of Left Social Democrats.[1]

The Revolutionary Governing Council was the real decision-making body, the responsibilities of which included all aspects of public and private life. It had to operate without a legal popular mandate for a significant period because the elections were not held until April 7–10, and, thus, the National Congress of Soviets (which fulfilled the functions of a parliament) was not convened until the middle of June.

The governing council, at least in the beginning, held daily sessions and had to take care of a tremendous number of problems. There also were a great number of political problems which required quick decisions and not every case was brought to the *full* sessions of the governing council. In order to facilitate decision-making, on April 12 a five-member Political Committee was established which held its first

---

1. Tibor Hajdu, *A Magyarországi Tanácsköztársaság* [The Soviet Republic of Hungary] (Budapest: Kossuth, 1969), pp. 45–46, 98 ff.

meeting on April 17.[2] The importance of the Political Committee need not be emphasized; in reality it had responsibility for every important internal and external problem. However, there were only a very few notes taken during its sessions and details of the discussions were not included in its minutes. The same can be said of the decisions made at the governing council's general sessions.

On June 23, the National Congress of Soviets elected a 150-member United Central Executive Committee. According to the constitution, the National Congress of Soviets was supposed to meet only twice a year, and this committee was supposed to supervise the decisions of the Revolutionary Governing Council between the biannual sessions. The executive committee established several subcommittees. They included the committees of defense, education, foreign affairs, health and welfare, and control. The membership of the Foreign Affairs Subcommittee consisted of Péter Ágoston, Elek Bolgár, Illés Brandstein, Samu Jászai, Albert Mihály, Zsigmond Kunfi, Béla Nagy, Ernő Pór, László Rudas, and Árpád Szakasits. Its president was Béla Kun, and Gyula Alpári served as his deputy.[3]

The Fundamental Principles of the Soviet Republic's Foreign Policy

The creation of the soviet republic brought about an ideological and foreign policy orientation quite different from that of the bourgeois democratic republic's foreign policies. Mihály Károlyi's governing principles and his foreign policy were pro-Entente, Wilsonian, and were based on the search for ties with the West. Károlyi himself stated his policy thusly: "I base our foreign policy on the ideals of Wilson. We only have one ideal: Wilson, Wilson and thirdly Wilson."[4] He expected that, as a result of these ideals, the sympathies and good will of the Entente could be turned to favor Hungary, that at the peace conference Hungary would be treated with respect, and that, when the final boundaries were to be set, Hungary could fit in the new European order established by the Great Powers.

Paris, however, did not respect either the democratic internal policies of Hungary or the pro-Entente foreign policies of the government. The negotiators treated Hungary as a vanquished state and did not recognize the Károlyi regime. With their indifferent and unsympathetic behavior they contributed a great deal to the decline of Károlyi's popularity and to the disappearance of illusions about the western Great Powers. These policies also were to blame for the internal dissatisfaction which pressed for a new foreign policy orientation.[5]

Another cause for the failure of the foreign policy of the bourgeois democratic regime was its nationality policy. The Hungarian bourgeois democratic system in 1918–19 could not completely abandon a foreign policy based on the principle of

2. Archives of the Institute of Party History, Budapest, file 601, group 1, minutes of 12 April 1919; hereafter cited as *P.I. Archivum.*

3. Ibid., 600, 2.

4. *Pesti Hirlap,* 31 Dec. 1918.

5. Zsuzsa L. Nagy, *A párizsi békekonferencia és Magyarország, 1918–1919* [The Paris Peace Conference and Hungary, 1918–1919] (Budapest: Kossuth, 1965); Tibor Hajdu, *Az 1918-as magyarországi polgári demokratikus forradalom* [The bourgeois democratic revolution in Hungary, 1918] (Budapest: Kossuth, 1968).

territorial integrity. It attempted to fulfill the unrealistic program of keeping historial Hungary intact. As a result of this policy, the regime's moral and political authority was compromised at the international forums, and it became virtually impossible for the Károlyi government to continue meaningful discussions with its neighbors. Furthermore, these policies made it possible for the Czechoslovak and Rumanian governments to identify Károlyi's policies in their propaganda with those of the monarchy.

The direction of the foreign policy adopted by the soviet republic was fundamentally different. There were, however, two very important foreign policy limitations and these two factors remained the same even under the soviet rule: (1) Hungary was a vanquished country which had been on the losing side in the war and therefore its territory and its borders remained uncertain; (2) the international situation of the government was not at all clear for it had practically no diplomatic relations.

The revolutionary foreign policy of the soviet republic was based on an alliance with Soviet Russia and on a union with the world revolutionary Communist groups. On March 22 the new government stated that it

declares its complete theoretical and spiritual union with the Russian Soviet government and welcomes an armed alliance with the proletariat of Russia. It sends its brotherly greetings to the workers of England, France, Italy and the United States. It calls on them not to tolerate, even for a minute, the horrid gangster war of their capitalist governments against the Hungarian Soviet Republic. It calls the workers and peasants of the Czechoslovak state, Rumania, Serbia and Croatia to join in an armed alliance against the bourgeoisie, against the great landlords, and against the great dynasties. It calls on the workers of German-Austria, and Germany to follow the example of the Hungarian working class, to completely break their ties with Paris, to join in an alliance with Moscow, to establish soviet republics and to oppose the conquering imperialists with weapons in their hands.[6]

This declaration and program was an echo of the telegram to the people of the Austro-Hungarian monarchy sent by Lenin, Iakov M. Sverdlov, and Lev B. Kamenev on November 3, 1918. This telegram, as well as the declaration of the Communist International, sent a few months later, emphasized that "only the proletarian dictatorship can assure possibilities for free existence to the small nations," and that only a proletarian revolution can "liberate the world's productive forces from the narrow shackles of nation states."[7] In short, it meant that the workers of these states should establish dictatorships of the proletariat and should join in an alliance and solve the common social and national contradictions which existed in the Danube basin.[8]

6. "Mindenkihez" [To Everyone], *Vörös Ujság*, 22 Mar. 1919.

7. *Manifest, Richtlinien, Beschlüsse des Ersten Kongresses*, in Mrs. Sándor Gábor, et al., eds., *A magyar munkásmozgalom történetének valogatott dokumentumai* [Selected documents from the history of the Hungarian labor movement] 6 vols. (Budapest: Szikra, Kossuth, 1956–64) hereafter cited as *MMTVD*, 5:618.

8. *Lenin Magyarországról* [Lenin on Hungary] (Budapest: Kossuth, 1965), pp. 45–49.

The internal and external policies of the Hungarian Soviet Republic were delineated by the then generally accepted theory of the development of the international proletarian revolution and by the hopes for a vast, world-wide victory of that revolution. The entire international Communist movement expected that there would be Central European and western proletarian revolutions which would be fostered by the 1917 revolution in Russia, by the fundamentally changed situation at the end of the war, and by the deep social class and national contradictions existing in these states.

The fundamental characteristics of the foreign policy of the proletarian dictatorship were summed up by Béla Kun:

> Our foreign policy does not consist of secret diplomacy or of playing at diplomacy. It is the foreign policy of the class struggle and it consists of policies which will foster solidarity with the international revolution and support the international revolution fighting against international imperialism.[9]

Some of the most important lines of this foreign policy based on the class struggle are self-evident. They included union with Soviet Russia and the desire to cooperate with the workers of all states, especially those neighboring on Hungary. At the same time the leaders attempted to establish peaceful ties with the western Great Powers because they needed time to build a new Hungarian social, economic, and political system.

The Revolutionary Governing Council openly and decisively broke with the Hungarian political tradition of territorial integrity. This was a fact of historical importance because even the most liberal Hungarian spokesmen for bourgeois democracy did not advocate this policy prior to March, 1919. Those circumstances in which the governing council attempted to implement its policies also made its new orientation of historical importance. After the war in Europe, the waves of debates over nationalist desires and the creation of new boundaries reached enormous heights. Discarding the theory of territorial integrity conflicted sharply with the interests of the Hungarian landed and large capitalist classes, with the desires of the middle classes, and even with the feelings of a substantial portion of the workers and the peasants. This proletarian national policy was an entirely new phenomenon among the states of the Danube. This policy could have been the basis for the normalization of the relationship between Hungary and its neighbors.[10] Unfortunately, it was rejected by the neighbors of revolutionary Hungary.

Questions of Foreign Policy before the Beginning of Intervention

It was natural that at the meetings of the governing council, discussions of the international situation and the spread of the world revolution, as well as the possibilities of such a revolution, were placed high on the agenda.

9. *P.I. Archivum*, 600, 2 (Minutes of the United Central Executive Committee), 15-16 July 1919.
10. Hajdu, *A Magyarországi*, p. 61; *MMTVD*, 6:259.

For Béla Kun and the other peoples' commissars there was never any doubt that the future of the Hungarian Soviet Republic would be closely tied to the development of the international revolution. "If the revolution is not spread further we are isolated. It [the survival of the Hungarian Soviet Republic] depends on the international revolution,"[11] stated Béla Kun in the session of March 27. At other times he had characterized the situation of the state thusly:

> when we established the dictatorship of the proletariat in Hungary we did not base our policies on opposing the armies of the Entente with military strength. . . . We emphasized that we based the fate of the Hungarian Soviet Republic on the international proletarian revolution.[12]

The Hungarian leaders felt that it was absolutely necessary for the revolution to spread to these Central European states in which the international possibilities for such revolutions were already present. This belief explains the reason for the frequent and serious discussions of the Austrian situation at the meetings of the Revolutionary Governing Council, and it also explains why the council, which believed that its Communist duty was to support the forces of revolution, on an international scale, attempted to help the Austrian Communist movement.

At the March 25 meeting of the council, Varga, Kunfi, and Ágoston emphasized the importance of maintaining good relations with the Austrians and Germans for the future of Hungary and for the future of revolution.[13] On March 27 the council discussed in detail the Austrian situation and the possibilities that could be exploited. Béla Kun called attention to the political unrest which was caused by the news circulating in Vienna concerning the possibility of Entente occupation of Austria. Kun characterized the situation by saying that among the Austrian "workers there was a great movement for a Soviet Republic." Also mentioned in the meeting, however, was the fact that while the Social Democratic members of the Austrian government remained friendly and even wanted to establish diplomatic relations with the Hungarian Soviet Republic, they did not desire to take further steps toward revolution and they did not want an Austrian proletarian dictatorship. In this same council meeting, the leaders explained the enormously difficult economic situation which would deprive Austria of food, placing it in a position to simply be starved into submission by the Entente.

In this connection, the governing council discussed what kind of food products could be sent to Austria, but the distribution of food was closely tied with political questions and with the cause of the revolution. Kun, in the heat of the argument, stated: "For me the most important thing is not the bread but the spread of the revolution in the West. . . . If there is revolution in Austria there will be one in the Czechoslovak state, and then we can carry the revolution to the French borders."[14]

11. *P.I. Archivum*, 601, 1.
12. *MMTVD*, 6A:259.
13. *P.I. Archivum*, 601, 1.
14. Ibid., and *MMTVD*, 6A:47.

At this time there was hope for revolution in Germany, because, in the first half of April, the Bavarian Soviet Republic was established. Thus, Kun was not talking about unreal illusions when he outlined the possibilities of an alliance between the German, Austrian, and Hungarian proletarian dictatorships and referred to the Bavarian Soviet Republic as the natural ally of the Hungarian dictatorship of the proletariat.[15]

The Austrian developments and the possibilities of a revolution were discussed again at other sessions of the governing council. Kun emphasized the importance of good relations between Austria and Hungary and mentioned the possibility of a food agreement between the two countries. He said:

Our relationship to German-Austria is especially friendly and we are going to prove this with deeds. As soon as we conquer our own shortage in food, we are going to supply Austria with food and, indeed we believe that the Hungarian proletariat, in order to prove its solidarity with the Austrian proletariat, will be willing to suffer various shortages.[16]

The existence of the soviet republic, the isolation of the Hungarian revolution, and the spread of the world revolution were all closely connected with the behavior of the Great Powers and their Central European allies. It is almost certain that the governing council was not completely informed of the activities of the Rumanian and Czecho-slovak governments taking place in Paris, but the council knew that plans were being drawn up to invade Hungary. Anxiety over an expected attack caused the council to attribute greater importance to the establishment of a proletarian dictatorship in Austria, because the existence of an Austrian Soviet Republic would have greatly limited the possibilities of a military intervention against soviet Hungary. While the governing council hoped to avert an attack, it was ready for the fight if it was pro-voked.[17]

The session of the governing council held on April 6 discussed the mission of General Smuts to Budapest and made a somewhat mistaken evaluation of the general's visit. The decision makers at the Paris Peace Conference, by sending Smuts to Hungary, temporarily strengthened the position of the governing council, and by dispatching this mission forced the French and Rumanian military leaders to alter an already agreed-on date of attack.[18] The council (Garbai, Böhm, and others), for this reason, therefore, were correct in their interpretation of the importance of Smuts's mission in Budapest. However, Böhm was incorrect when he stated that "the appear-ance of Smuts and his note shows that this is the last warning. If they do not attack now they have simply stated that they don't have enough strength to attack us. This

15. *MMTVD*, 6A:176.

16. *Vörös Ujság*, 30 March 1919.

17. *P.I. Archivum*, 601, 1.

18. Cf. Zsuzsa L. Nagy, "The Mission of General Smuts to Budapest, April, 1919," *Acta Historica*, 1965, no. 11.

is a very great victory for us."[19] In the end, the majority of the council accepted this unrealistic evaluation, and thus, they too are responsible for the interventionist attack catching Hungary without adequate preparation.

As is well known, the governing council did not accept Smuts's conditions and note. According to Garbai, one of the reasons for the rejection of Smuts's note was that the Szeklers (*székely*), a portion of the population of Transylvania, would not have accepted the method recommended by Smuts for altering the demarcation lines. It also would have been nearly impossible to convince the population to accept a settlement which offered only slightly better conditions and only slightly more favorable demarcation lines than those which on March 20, 1919, led to the fall of the bourgeois democratic government and the Károlyi regime. In addition, the governing council was certain that the negotiations were not completely cut off.[20]

The possibility of an attack on Hungary and the methods of defense against the invaders remained on the agenda for the future sessions of the governing council. Since close ties had been established between the Hungarian and Russian governments, the governing council informed Moscow of the developing situation and of the dangers facing the Hungarian republic. Béla Kun announced the purpose of this new exchange of information at a session on April 11: "We made contact with Chicherin and Lenin in order to unify our military forces." Kun requested that in case of an attack on the Hungarian republic, the Soviet Red Army should attempt to break through from the area of Máramaros. With this action, the military pressure on the Hungarian soviet republic would be lessened and it would be possible to establish direct ties between the two soviet powers.[21]

During the following deliberations the debates centered on the possible direction from which the military attack might be expected. From the minutes it is clear that the governing council least expected Czechoslovak action because of the sympathies of the Czechoslovak socialist workers. Emphasizing this position, Böhm declared on April 12, that "according to all our reports the Czechs do not want to attack."[22] The members of the council thought that the attack would be coming from the south because of the initial role of the French military leaders. Böhm was convinced that "if the Entente wants to attack then they can only invade us from the South and they would only want the Czechs to attack in order to prevent Russian help reaching us."[23]

Throughout these four weeks, from March 21 to April 16, the positions taken by a certain strata of the population caused significant problems for the leaders of revolutions; unlike the leaders who thought in terms of world revolution, a significant portion of Hungarians could only think about politics on the basis of territorial integrity and on the basis of keeping Hungary intact. This conflict was especially

19. *P.I. Archivum*, 601, 2, minutes of 6 April 1919. There is no trace of detailed discussion in the minutes. There is no evidence to support the thesis that the governing council debated the reply.
20. Ibid.
21. *P.I. Archivum*, 601, 1, minutes of 11 April 1919.
22. Ibid., minutes of 12 April 1919.
23. Ibid.

noticeable in the Hungarians of Transylvania, the Szeklers, who at that time comprised a significant part of the organized Red Army. These Szekler soldiers criticized the governing council even for the reply note which they gave to General Smuts in which the council did not unconditionally demand the return of the Transylvanian areas where they lived. The patriotic feeling of the Szekler soldiers was influenced by their own attitudes and by the political opinions of their officers who were greatly disappointed when the governing council did not demand the return of their land.[24]

It is clear from the minutes of the governing council that even the few weeks of peace between March 21 and April 16, 1919, were shadowed by the possibilities and dangers of an armed attack.

The Situation after the Intervention

On April 16 and 26, 1919, the armies of the Rumanian monarchy and the Czechoslovak republic, respectively, crossed the military demarcation lines and began an armed attack against Hungary. Yugoslavia at this time did not participate in the attack even though General Franchet d'Esperey had tried to convince the Yugoslav government to follow suit. It is needless to mention the seriousness of the situation; in Hungary a cease fire had been in effect only since the beginning of November, 1918. The people still remembered very vividly the suffering and trials of four years of war. The country's economic strength and productivity became minimal as a result of the war and of the collapse of the Austro-Hungarian monarchy. The new political regime had been in power only for four weeks, a tremendously short time for the establishment and strengthening of a new government. While the organization of the Red Army continued, it certainly was not at all developed and its fighting power had not reached the level needed to defend the country.

On April 18, at the first meeting of the governing council following the Rumanian attack, a discussion of the invasion was placed on the agenda. It was clear to each peoples' commissar that the only possible course of action was to repel the attack. At the meeting there was no dissenting opinion. Béla Kun summed up the most important tasks in the following manner:

> We cannot keep the dangerous situation secret because, by making it public knowledge, we will be able to raise the desire of the proletariat to sacrifice themselves. We must send a declaration to the workers that the revolution is in danger and we need effective, strong methods to deal with the counterrevolution. I do not trust anyone except the proletariat.[25]

This trust in the workers characterized the entire discussion and also the final decisions. The governing council made the public aware of the gravity of the situation.

There were two ways in which the council tried to solve the external problem: (1)

24. Ibid. Vilmos Böhm's speech.
25. Ibid., minutes of 18 April 1919.

by military counteractivities and (2) by taking diplomatic steps or organizing international activities which would place the soviet republic in a more favorable position.

The question of the type of military response to the attack by the Entente was debated at length. Landler recommended that an offensive be started toward the south in order to demonstrate the strength of the Red Army. The governing council, however, rejected the proposition. The general counteropinion was stated by Kun: "There is no reason for us to provoke the Entente. Now we have to prove that we can stop the Rumanian offensive. As long as we have no need for desperate steps, we should not take them. We cannot prepare a successful offensive toward the south." This decision was correct because the opening of a new front, especially one resulting from a Hungarian attack, could only have worsened the military and political situation of the soviet republic.

As a result of the new situation after the military intervention, even greater attention was placed on Austria. According to Landler, "In regard to our foreign policy, the most important thing is to force Vienna to side with us" and in this respect the members of the governing council accepted his judgment. When these discussions took place, the members of the governing council still expected that the large-scale workers movement of April 17 in Vienna could bring about such a change. But it was clearly visible that the Austrian revolution had faced enormous difficulties and it was reiterated that Austria had to be supplied with large quantities of food. This help was viewed as a necessity in order to encourage Austrian independence from Entente pressures and was thought of as a measure which would convince the Austrian Social Democratic leaders to accept the dictatorship of the proletariat and establish closer connections with the soviet republic.[26]

The soviet republic, however, while expecting military help from Soviet Russia and hoping for a possible turning point in Austria, did not remain passive. "We must rely primarily on our own strength," Kun stated, "because we have to hold out until the active help of the international proletarian revolution can arrive." The picture that Kun painted to the Budapest Workers' and Soldiers' Soviet and to the soldiers who were starting for the front must have given them hope. "The proletariat is revolting in Vienna where they are fighting with arms to establish their dictatorship. The armies of the brotherly Russian Republic have crossed the boundaries of East Galicia."[27]

By the end of April the military situation became catastrophic. As a result of the overwhelming strength of the invaders, their organization, and the desertion of the Szekler division of the Red Army, it seemed that it would be impossible to stop the interventionist army from moving toward Budapest. The revolution and the national existence was endangered. In these circumstances Béla Kun and Elek Bolgár, the Hungarian ambassador to Vienna, attempted to stop the Rumanian advance through diplomatic maneuvers and negotiations. They attempted to offer certain concessions to the Entente in order to save the proletarian dictatorship.[28]

26. Ibid.
27. *MMTVD*, 6A:260. Minutes of 19 April 1919.
28. The background and details of the conference in Nagy, *A párizsi*, p. 121 ff.

These negotiations were first mentioned at the meeting of the Political Committee of the governing council on April 23. It was here that Kun discussed the conversations undertaken with Professor Philip M. Brown and Thomas Cuninghame. Kun reported on the positions taken by Brown and Cuninghame and requested clearance to continue the negotiations. But concessions to the Entente created problems and debates within the governing council, where Rezső Fiedler, peoples' commissar of defense, rejected the negotiations on the basis that concessions to the Allies could mean possible conflict between the council and the workers.[29]

The progress of negotiations and the demands of Philip M. Brown (removing the far-left members of the governing council, and stopping the Communist propaganda outside the Hungarian boundaries) indeed sharpened the debates in the council. On April 26, Antal Dovcsák, who represented the positions of the Social Democratic functionaries and the right-wing trade-unionists, queried whether it would not be better for the governing council to resign because—as he saw it—the workers did not want to fight. In the debates, the polemics were mostly concerned with the evaluation of the attitudes of the workers, and criticisms were raised against the defeatists. Dovcsák's position was rejected by the left and center Social Democratic peoples' commissars as well as by the Communists. Fiedler complained that "a portion of the Governing Council is beginning to waiver. This waivering must be ended because if it becomes generally accepted we have lost."

The question of whether the negotiations and concessions would render the maintenance of socialist conditions in Hungary impossible was also discussed. Garbai and Kun thought that the concessions did not fundamentally limit the soviet system and that the negotiations resembled those at Brest where the most important consideration was gaining time for the revolution. In Kun's opinion, through the negotiations a temporary peace could be concluded which would give time to the soviet republic to deal with its own internal problems. Kunfi held the opinion that "without a bloody civil war, capitalism could not be restored in Hungary. There has never been a more clear class struggle in the world than the one that exists here." He was convinced that under the existing conditions and after all that had happened it was impossible to return to a "reformist socialist position." Kun expected that the negotiations could stop the Rumanian armies, that the Rumanians would withdraw to the boundaries stated in Vyx's note, and that Debrecen, an ethnically Hungarian city, would be governed by Hungarians again. In this case he would have been willing to stop the international propaganda and make some personnel changes in the governing council. These personnel changes were accepted by those concerned (for example Tibor Szamuely).[30] The governing council supported the idea of continuing negotiations. It also accepted the conditions laid down by Brown and considered them possible to fulfill. However, as a result of the critical military situation the governing council, at the same time called on Woodrow Wilson to stop the military advance. They also sent the president the texts of the notes suing for peace which were dispatched by

29. *P.I. Archivum*, 601, 1, 23 April 1919 (meeting of the Political Committee). The negotiations with Brown also were placed on the agenda of the 26 April 1919, meeting of the governing council.

30. Ibid., minutes of 26 April 1919, and *MMTVD*, 6A:327 ff.

Béla Kun to the Czechoslovak, Yugoslav, and Rumanian governments. The requests sent to Wilson characterized the situation of the country following the interventionist attack dramatically but truthfully. The message stated:

Sir: Blood and smoke—practically the last drop of blood of the proletariat and the smoke of villages destroyed in wars—mark the road of your allies. [Their activities were committed] in the name of higher civilization and in the name of love for peace advocated by you. We do not believe that their actions correspond to your ideals because your ideals demand that every state must be allowed to determine its own fate.[31]

The governing council could rightly state that it took over the power under peaceful circumstances without the least opposition, that until the interventionist attack it worked peacefully within its own borders. It also emphasized that the politics of the Entente did not support the entire population but rather that small strata of the exploiters and the owners of large wealth which supported Germany during the war.

Kun's terms for peace stated clearly and unequivocally that "Hungary does not stand on the idea of territorial integrity" and, therefore, future bloodshed was foolish and needless. He also stated decisively, however, that "we consider our internal institutions our own problem" in which no one has a right to interfere. He placed the responsibility for the future on the interventionists troops and their governments.

From this moment on, no national interest justifies the continuation of the present state of war. There can be no doubt that from now on the continuation of war on the part of the governments mentioned serves only their national interests, it is carried on in the interests of external imperialism and in the interest of the Hungarian ruling classes.[32]

On May 1 and 2, the governing council held almost round-the-clock sessions. The Political Committee of the governing council at an impromptu session debated the critical military situation. The Rumanian troops were at the Tisza River and the Hungarian government did not know at that time that the forward movement had already stopped. In addition, nothing had resulted from the negotiations with Brown. At this session the representatives of the right-wing socialist, trade-union leaders appeared and again called for the resignation of the governing council. They also recommended that the power be transferred to a twelve-man directorium. This recommendation meant that a temporary government was to come to power with which, it was thought, the Entente powers would be willing to negotiate.

A substitute motion proposed that the representatives of the Red Army should be invited to the meeting of the Political Committee. There the situation would be made clear to them and they would be asked to take a stand. This motion implied the rejection of the trade-union leaders' demands and meant that the governing council

31. *Vörös Ujság*, 28 April 1919.
32. Ibid., 30 April 1919.

desired to stay in power. On the morning of May 2, Kun informed the full governing council of the session held during the previous night and stated both positions. He did not, however, take a position himself holding his own opinions until the end of the debate for, as he stated, he did not want to influence the decision.[33]

This meeting of the governing council lasted until the early hours of May 3. The peoples' commissars who represented the right wing of the Social Democrats would have been glad to accept the resignation of the government and the creation of a temporary directorium. There were many who felt that the governing council had no alternative but to resign. Károly Peyer and Ferenc Miákits, who most vehemently advocated this view, were surprised to find that Kun, Szamuely, Szántó, Landler, and others decisively rejected this course of action and insisted on keeping power and organizing the defense. There was no final decision made. While the council members decided to defend the city and take the necessary steps in order to prevent robbery and bloodshed, they did not decide on the fate of the government and the soviet republic. Béla Kun announced that there would be a meeting with the workers' trustees, with the ironworkers, and with the Budapest Workers' and Soldiers' Soviet. Following these meetings, another session of the governing council would be held. Since there was no previous announcement of these meetings, this statement carried a great weight, especially with those who had previously expected that the governing council was ready to submit its resignation.[34]

During the evening of May 2 the governing council was informed of the results of these discussions. Landler, who participated in the meeting of the ironworkers, maintained that the ironworkers uniformly and enthusiastically wished to fight; that they were willing to defend Budapest; and that they opposed the resignation of the government.[35] The statement made by Pogány was less encouraging. He had met with representatives from various factories in the capital city, and their opinions were divided. Pogány, however, thought "that the workers of the more important factories were willing to defend the city." As a result of these discussions the governing council decided not to resign and began taking control of the situation.[36] The military commandants received the following order: "the Governing Council orders the strongest possible defense of the entire front. All the workers of Budapest will be sent to the front to strengthen the troops."[37]

The fact that the Rumanian and Czechoslovak troops stopped their offensive by the first of May meant that the council was given time to reorganize and renew the army. This work continued with great speed, and in two weeks the first counteroffensive of the Red Army began. The success of the intervention, however, encouraged the various groups of the Hungarian counterrevolution in Vienna as well as in Szeged, which was under French occupation. They organized counterrevolutionary committees and they even formed a government, in addition to establishing contacts with the counterrevolutionary groups operating on the territory of the soviet republic. In

33. *P.I. Archivum*, 601, 1 (Minutes of the governing council), 2 May 1919. Cf. Hajdu, *A Magyarországi*, pp. 178–79, 182.

34. *P.I. Archivum*, 601, 1. *MMTVD*, 6A:389.

35. *MMTVD*, 6A:389, 392.

36. Ibid., p. 389; *P.I. Archivum*, 601, 1.

37. *MMTVD*, 6A:405.

order to combat these activities the governing council expropriated the property of the counterrevolutionaries.[38]

At the May 30 session of the governing council, Kun informed the council of the unauthorized negotiations taking place between Peyer, Miákits, and the English mission concerning the termination of the dictatorship of the proletariat. According to the brief mention of the subject in the minutes, there was lively debate over the issue, but the governing council decided to take no action. This decision seems surprising because Peyer and his supporters were actively working to bring down the government.[39]

The governing council, and the army leadership, succeeded (even under the very difficult economic and political circumstances) in their efforts to resupply the army.[40] In the second half of May the Red Army began a counteroffensive on the northern front, and it was successful in throwing back the Czechoslovak troops. The leaders of the governing council interpreted the military victory as a chance to expedite the international revolution. When the status of the liberated portions of Slovakia was discussed on June 4, it was primarily emphasized that a dictatorship of the proletariat must be established there. It is true that at that time it was not quite clear what the relations of the two soviet republics would be, but the intent of the council was to form a union between two independent soviet republics.

By the middle of June the soviet republic had reached its maximum successes militarily, politically, and economically. It had thrown back one wing of the Czechoslovak armies and, on June 16, had helped to establish the Slovak Soviet Republic. It still seemed possible at this time to link the territories of Soviet Russia and Soviet Hungary.[41] These military successes, however, forced the Prague government and the Allied command leading the Czechoslovak armies to demand the quick and effective intervention of the Great Powers, but Paris at that time could not offer military aid. Diplomatic means, however, were available to the Allies. Shortly after the Hungarian victory, the Allies dispatched an ultimatum to the soviet republic demanding that the Hungarian troops withdraw to a location near the border delineated by the Vyx note and promising that the Rumanian troops would also retreat. The debate over the note was concentrated among the ranks of the party leadership and in the Political Committee rather than in the governing council. The most important questions were dealt with by these organs and later by the United Central Executive Committee which had been founded at the end of June.[42] The minutes of the sessions of these bodies, however, have not survived, but from other sources we can reconstruct the different points of view expressed there.[43]

38. Zsuzsa L. Nagy, *Forradalom és ellenforradalom a Dunántúlon 1919* [Revolution and counterrevolution in trans-Danubia, 1919] (Budapest: Kossuth, 1961), chaps. 5 ff.; also *P.I. Archivum*, 601, 1. Minutes of 17 May 1919.

39. *P.I. Archivum*, 601, 1, minutes of 30 May 1919.

40. One aspect of the economic crisis is treated in Zsuzsa L. Nagy, "Az antant gazdasági segélyprogramja és Magyarország, 1918–1919" [The economic aid program of the Entente and Hungary, 1918–1919], *Párttörténeti Közlemények* [Party historical notes], 1963, no. 3.

41. Ibid. and *Vörös Ujság*, 7 June 1919.

42. The material is very spotty. Agoston's diary, however, fills some of the gaps. *P.I. Archivum*, Ágoston diary, Ágoston collection.

43. *MMTVD*, 6B:146 ff.

It was the party leadership which discussed the withdrawal of Red Army troops from the northern territories. On June 28 the party leaders "recommended withdrawal from the Czechoslovak territories to the demarcation lines based on the reasoning that the war cannot be continued. [This fact was confirmed] by reports coming from the army." The members of the governing council accepted this reasoning. They thought that the military balance, "the [need for] internal strengthening of the dictatorship and the need to organize the economic life"[44] demanded withdrawal. During these days the leaders' attention was completely occupied by the military situation and they were unable to spend time with other problems. These problems included the dissatisfaction of the peasants and the industrial workers who felt that they must carry an inappropriately heavy burden. There was a great need to concentrate on the internal situation because during the month of June there were new counterrevolutionary activities including a strike of the railroadmen and a military uprising.

These concerns were mentioned in the June 30 session of the United Central Executive Committee where Kun explained the withdrawal of the Red Army on the basis of internal difficulties. The soviet republic was forced to withdraw "because of internal disorganization" and not as a result of the strength of the Czech and Rumanian military. Szamuely and Pór supported Kun's opinions.[45] Kun said that withdrawal was needed because by consolidating its power in Hungary the soviet republic prevented a return of "the most severe reaction and monarchism" and was able to preserve "the dictatorship of the proletariat."[46] Kun, Kunfi, and others recognized that the withdrawal gave the government a chance to consolidate power in Hungary, and they interpreted the acceptance of the Allied ultimatum as similar to Russia's acceptance of the Peace of Brest Litovsk.

The leaders of the Hungarian soviet realized that while the Red Army occupied Slovakia "the Czechoslovak social chauvinists could rally the working class to the side of the bourgeoisie." With the withdrawal, however, the argument of "Bolshevik imperialism" would no longer be valid. But Kun emphasized that, in spite of the retreat, the strength and organization of the army must be kept intact "because the army is a very important foreign policy factor."[47]

The debates did not end with the withdrawal. Szamuely, who opposed the acceptance of the ultimatum, again wondered whether the retreat would mean peace for the soviet republic. He thought that the analogy to Brest Litovsk was fallacious. He demanded the obtaining of guarantees from the Great Powers. Without such guarantees he thought it would be impossible to consolidate the power of the dictatorship.[48] Varga threw new light on the acceptance of these conditions. According to him, only one-third of the territory and 45 percent of the population would remain within the

44. *P.I. Archivum*, 601, 1, minutes of 29 June 1919.

45. Ibid., 600, 2 (Minutes of the United Central Executive Committee), 30 June 1919. Some of the material was discussed at closed sessions as requested by Zoltán Rónai.

46. Ibid.

47. Ibid.

48. Ibid.

new boundaries. Yet, he was convinced that the territories thus occupied would be able to produce an adequate food surplus. With a fundamental reorganization of society and with the end to the blockade, the standard of living in Hungary could equal that of Holland or even Denmark.[49]

Kun's closing speech accepted the majority opinion that the withdrawal was necessary and correct because, from the standpoint of the international proletarian revolution, the continued existence of the Soviet Republic of Hungary was the most significant point. Kun expected that the Hungarian Soviet Republic would not remain isolated. These hopes also were supported by the world-wide strike planned for July 21 and the various new items reporting the solidarity of the workers of the world with the Hungarian and Soviet revolutions.[50]

At the end of June it seemed that the behavior of the Great Powers supported the opinions of those who advocated the rejection of the ultimatum of the peace conference and who opposed the withdrawal from the northern territories. The Rumanian government failed to abide by the Allied demands and categorically refused to withdraw their troops to the new borders.[51] While the Great Powers criticized the Rumanian government, they failed to apply any kind of sanctions against it. It was under such circumstances that, on July 10, the governing council debated the recommendation of the army leaders to force the Rumanian army to abide by the decisions of the peace conference. It was envisioned that by an attack across the Tisza River, the Rumanian army would be forced to withdraw. In spite of the unfavorable circumstances and the critical situation, the governing council accepted the recommendation to attack, for they trusted the judgment of the military leadership.[52]

On July 15 and 16, prior to the attack, the United Central Executive Committee discussed the problems of the soviet republic. Kun indicated that the foreign situation was more favorable than Hungary's internal situation. He was convinced that the note of the peace conference sent in July[53] was a preliminary to actual negotiations, and hence, recognition.[54] The reality, however, was that by the middle of July, the soviet republic was in a hopeless situation because the international revolution had not spread to other countries. The peace conference was not willing to negotiate with the soviet republic, and there were lively debates in Paris concerning a new and final intervention against Hungary.

Kun stated that the Entente would not use its own troops to squelch the revolution for that would lead to internal problems in the Entente countries. He opposed those who lost faith because the world revolution had not advanced and who thought the demands of the Entente had to be accepted at any price. Both Kun and Gyula Hajdu criticized those who were already maintaining close contact with the Western powers, those who were willing to accept any and all conditions, those who advocated the

49. Ibid.
50. Ibid.
51. *Documents on British Foreign Policy, First Series* (London, 1956), 6:120–21.
52. *P.I. Archivum*, 601, 1.
53. U.S. Department of State, *Papers Relating to the Foreign Relations of the United States. The Paris Peace Conference*, 13 vols. (Washington: Government Printing Office, 1946), 7:120–21.
54. *P.I. Archivum*, 600, 2 (Minutes of the United Central Executive Committee), 15–16 July 1919.

resignation of the governing council, and those who favored the creation of a government made up of the "uncompromised" Social Democratic politicians.[55]

The governing council also had to deal with the Austrian peace treaty which transferred contested or ethnically Hungarian territories in west Hungary to Austria. They felt that the transfer of such territories from the proletarian dictatorship to capitalist exploitation was unacceptable from ideological and political points of view. Kun did not want to give up a single inch of territory to Austria. Varga considered this an illogical position to take and he advocated delayed action, neither accepting nor rejecting the demands. Kun somewhat modified his position and thought that the control of the territories concerned should be settled by a plebescite. Finally, the council accepted Kun's recommendation and empowered Kun to discuss this problem with Otto Bauer.[56]

The last minutes of the governing council are dated July 29. At this meeting Landler reviewed the military situation, and decisions were made concerning raising the morale of the troops and other governmental problems. The few lines of the minutes which remain do not discuss the catastrophic situation, yet they make it clear that the Social Democratic leaders thought of the failure of the soviet republic as a *fait accompli*.

There are no minutes from the last meeting of the governing council which was held August 1. This session was held when it became clear that the Great Powers would not negotiate with Hungary if the soviet government stayed in power. Consequently, at this session the discussions were concerned with the resignation of the council. By that time there was no possibility for diplomatic maneuvering or for the resumption of military action. The governing council could not accept the responsibility for agreeing to the demands of the Entente. Hoping that they could stop the Rumanian army and save Budapest from Rumanian occupation, they resigned. In a dramatic meeting, the Budapest Workers' and Soldiers' Soviet accepted the resignation and requested Gyula Peidl to form a new government.[57]

Translated by Iván Völgyes

55. Ibid. The appointment of Böhm on July 17 to become the Hungarian ambassador to Vienna made it possible for the Entente to discuss the problems of Hungary with an acceptable negotiating partner.

56. *P.I. Archivum*, 601, 1, minutes of 21 July 1919.

57. Ibid., Diary, Ágoston Collection, and 600, 3.

Soviet Hungary and the Paris Peace Conference

Alfred D. Low

On March 21, 1919, at a moment of national crisis, a soviet government came into existence in Budapest. The new Communist-dominated government was considered a serious threat both by the neighboring countries and the Western powers because of its revolutionary and sociopolitical character as well as its territorial claims and national aspirations.

The proletarian revolution in Hungary had peculiar characteristics. It was, as the Vienna Social Democratic daily, the *Arbeiterzeitung*, quickly pointed out, not so much a revolution against her own *bourgeoisie* as one against the Entente *bourgeoisie*. The Hungarian *bourgeoisie* had made "the desperate decision to abdicate temporarily, to leave the state power to workers and peasants without a struggle. . . . Thus, the proletariat, without meeting resistance, seized power. The social revolution served the defense of the country against the external enemy."[1] *Izvestiia*'s evaluation of the political turnover in Hungary and of the soviet government serving the purposes of national defense, followed virtually the same lines.[2]

The first impact of the news of the birth of the soviet republic in Hungary upon the Allied representatives gathered in Paris and the peace conference was tremendous. The British delegate Harold Nicolson considered it a "very serious" event, though it had been "foreseen," and anticipated correctly that due to their quick demobilization during the past months the Allies were in no position to enforce their terms.[3] And the American General Tasker H. Bliss, a member of the American delegation in Paris, wondered whether the "whole world" was not "going Bolshevik."[4]

The Hungarian *coup d'état* which shocked the West and the Paris Peace Conference, in turn delighted Soviet Russia and gave great encouragement to the Communist International, which at that very moment was holding its founding congress in Moscow. Lenin, though soon warning that Hungary was only a small country, and that it could be easily strangled, stressed, on the other hand, the great revolutionary significance of the Hungarian turn of events and extolled its stirring example.[5]

The author is indebted to the American Philosophical Society for the permission given to make use of portions of his study *The Soviet Hungarian Republic and the Paris Peace Conference, Transactions of the American Philosophical Society* (Philadelphia, 1963).

1. "Ungarn und wir," *Arbeiterzeitung* (Vienna), 23 March 1919.

2. *Izvestiia*, 25 March 1919; similarly *Pravda* of the same day.

3. Harold Nicolson, *Peacemaking, 1919* (London: Constable & Co., 1933), p. 287.

4. Frederick Palmer, *Bliss, Peacemaker* (New York: Dodd, Mead and Co., 1934), p. 379.

5. V. I. Lenin, *Sochineniia*, 3rd ed., 35 vols. (Moscow: Institut Marksa-Engelsa-Lenina, 1941–50), 24:261, also 178.

The proclamation of the dictatorship of the proletariat in Hungary was quickly followed by the withdrawal from Budapest of all Entente missions. The Western powers thus gave clear expression to their disapproval and mistrust. Official diplomatic relations between Soviet Hungary and the Entente thus were virtually nonexistent during the critical soviet period. A few remaining contacts were provided by the presence of various individual Allied officials, though these were not authorized to act as Allied spokesmen and make any binding agreements. Among the most prominent agents of the Western powers in Hungary were the Italian Lieutenant Colonel Guido Romanelli and Prince Livio Borghese. The British Colonel Sir Thomas Cuninghame and the American Professor A. C. Coolidge used neighboring Vienna as a base for their operation, visiting Budapest rather frequently. These men and their assistants served as the eyes and ears of the Allied powers, and their reports to Paris were given close and careful attention. Though the new government was a challenge to the West, it never went so far as formally to cancel the armistice agreements. After the soviet regime had been set up, Hungarian troops remained at the line of demarcation and did not attack the opposing troops of the neighboring states. Yet the army was quickly strengthened beyond the limits permitted in the armistice.

Since Soviet Hungary from its beginnings was evidently an outpost of Russian bolshevism in the very heart of Europe and seemed to defy the Western powers and the peace conference, it was unlikely that the emerging Western policy *vis-à-vis* the new regime would be marked by a show of friendliness and toleration.

The Hungarian Soviet Republic was hardly set up when it turned toward the East. In a radio dispatch to Soviet Russia, the new rulers dutifully reported to Lenin that a proletarian dictatorship had been established in Hungary and simultaneously saluted him as the leader of the international proletariat, thus clearly subordinating themselves to Moscow's authority. The Hungarian government then asked for a treaty of alliance with Russia and requested pertinent instructions.[6]

From its first days Hungarian communism, however, not only looked eastward, but also turned to her immediate neighbors, to Germany, and to the West. In an appeal "To All," the Hungarian Socialist party extended its greetings to the working classes of Great Britain, France, Italy, and America and called on them not to tolerate the infamous campaign of their regimes against the Hungarian soviet government.[7] It also appealed to the workers and peasants of the adjoining victorious countries, of Bohemia, Rumania, Serbia, and Croatia, to form "an armed alliance against the boyars, estate-owners, and dynasties." Finally, it called upon the workers of the vanquished states, Germany and German-Austria, to follow the example of the Hungarian proletariat, to make a final break with Paris and to join Moscow. The Hungarian soviet regime appealed to the European proletariat to prevent an attack of their *bourgeoisies* upon Soviet Hungary and to extend the base of social revolution throughout Europe.

From its very birth the Hungarian soviet government perceived the paramount

6. *Pravda*, 24 March 1919; see also Alfred D. Low, "The First Austrian Republic and Soviet Hungary," *Journal of Central European Affairs* 20 (1960):179.
7. *Soziale Revolution* (Vienna), 26 March 1919.

importance of extending bolshevism into neighboring countries, especially into Austria and southern Germany and engaged in feverish propaganda to further its goals. The Austrian envoy in Budapest, von Cnobloch, wrote to the Austrian foreign secretary: "Propaganda abroad is [the soviet government's] only activity in foreign policy."[8] It is true that Kun once remarked: "Our example is propaganda in itself; our mere existence is a danger to the capitalists of the world, a pattern which will be followed by the proletarians of the entire globe."[9] Yet, the soviet government in its daily activities went much beyond a propaganda which rests its case on its mere existence and patiently waits for the European proletariat to follow its example. Driven by its messianic faith, it worked feverishly to extend bolshevism beyond its borders. The Hungarian Communist party, even before the seizure of power, tried its best to spread communist propaganda among Rumanians, Czechs, Serbs, and Croats, as Béla Kun informed Lenin in a message of January 5, 1919.[10] It was such activism which Lenin had in mind for the Hungarian Communist party when in a "Letter to Comrades" he exhorted them to be an example for Central Europe.[11] Yet not only Central Europe, but all of Europe, he prophesied, would soon follow the Hungarian example. "The victory of communism will not stop at the borders of Hungary, it will be worldwide."[12] "Our aim," Kun had written soon after the seizure of power, "an aim in which we are in no small measure assisted by our geographical position," is "to promote the internationalization of the world. We are doubly predestined to constitute ourselves a bridge for ideas coming from the East. It is conceivable that by reason of our central position, we may become a nucleus for Internationalism."[13]

Though pointing here to Soviet Hungary's predestination and staking out extensive claims as to her proletarian mission, her importance as springboard for further expansion of the proletarian revolution, Kun and the soviet government stressed frequently that Soviet Hungary could be secured and saved only through international proletarian solidarity. As the Austrian envoy in Hungary put it, the soviet government "considered the spreading of Bolshevism into neighboring countries the best means to attain its own salvation."[14] In looking upon the victory of communism in adjoining states as a guarantee for its own survival, the revolutionary government in Budapest merely followed the example of Russian bolshevism at the time.

In 1919 both Moscow and Budapest tended to exaggerate the revolutionary potentialities of the rest of Europe, and especially of the proletariat in the victorious countries. Yet the Hungarian soviet government was utterly unrealistic in assessing the opportunities for the spread of bolshevism into neighboring countries and the rest of

8. *Österreichisches Staatsarchiv*, Vienna, 881, Liasse Ungarn I, 3; April 4, 1919.

9. Kun's speech of June 19 is printed in full translation by Baron A. Kaas and Fedor de Lazarovics, *Bolshevism in Hungary: The Béla Kun Period* (London: Richards, 1931), app. 16, pp. 346–62.

10. *Kun Béla a Magyar Tanácsköztársaságról* [Béla Kun on the Hungarian Soviet Republic] (Budapest: Kossuth, 1958), pp. 137–38.

11. *Népszava*, 27 March 1919, in *Kun Béla*, pp. 154–57.

12. *Pravda*, 12 April 1919.

13. Quoted by Kaas and Lazarovics, *Bolshevism in Hungary*, pp. 196–97.

14. Low, "The First Austrian Republic," p. 183.

Europe. Soviet Russia's error at least was balanced by an underestimation of her own considerable resources which made it possible for her to survive in the struggle against a hostile world. The Hungarian soviet government, in an incomparably more difficult position, tended to overlook its smaller resources and greater geographic and military vulnerability.

When on March 27 Marshal Ferdinand Foch made his report to the Council of Four, it soon became evident that he was bent on taking advantage of the Hungarian soviet coup and its apparent threat to Rumania to lay his grandiose anti-Bolshevik scheme before the council. In presenting his new military plan concerning Soviet Hungary, he took care to camouflage his ulterior purposes. Yet President Wilson, Lloyd George, and Clemenceau were alert to the wider implications of Foch's project and wary of being caught in the carefully laid net.

Foch pointed out that to halt the Bolshevik infiltration it was necessary to erect "a barrier in Poland and Rumania, closing the breach at Lemberg" and cleaning out "infected areas in the rear, such as Hungary, by assuring the maintenance of communications via Vienna."[15] Vienna ought to be occupied by Allied troops under an American commander. As far as Rumania was concerned, he recommended dispatch of supplies and equipment which the Rumanian army was lacking, and also advised that the equipment should be placed under the command of a French general.

President Wilson immediately countered with the observation that what was proposed here was the beginning of a march eastward. The Allies had examined more than once the problem of military intervention against Soviet Russia, "and we always have arrived at the conclusion that we cannot consider military intervention." He insisted that the Great Powers limit themselves to the immediate object, namely to taking all necessary measures to strengthen Rumania, without taking offensive action against anyone. The president, however, did not speculate about the question of whether a militarily bolstered Rumania would refrain from engaging in military action against Soviet Hungary.

In the eyes of Marshal Foch and other Allied military and political leaders, the occupation of the Hungarian and Austrian capitals was necessary for the stabilization of Central Europe. In reality, the occupation was part of a wider interventionist scheme against Soviet Russia. Though the British General Sir Henry Wilson conceded that the question of military action against bolshevism was basically a political decision, he seemed to side with his French and Italian military colleagues. "The longer we procrastinate, the more difficult will the solution of the problem be," he warned. "The invasion of Bolshevism in Hungary has already strengthened the frontier which must be guarded by several hundreds of kilometers." Of all the military representatives, only the American General Bliss held out against militarily crushing Hungarian bolshevism in late March, 1919. It was necessary, he insisted, to distinguish between "revolutionary" and "Bolshevik." If one could be certain that the revolutionary movement originated in Russia, then obviously it was there that it ought to be killed, but the problem was actually more difficult. A *cordon sanitaire* might halt the Bolsheviks but not bolshevism.

15. Paul Mantoux, *Les délibérations du conseil des quatre: 24 Mars–28 Juin, 1919*, 2 vols. (Paris, 1955); for the following see 1: 52–57.

This view was then the very view of President Wilson himself. An intervention, according to the president, raised the question of whether the Western powers possessed the necessary troops and sufficient material means for military action and whether public sentiment supported such policy. Troops, at least the use of American troops, could not be depended upon, and public opinion in the West would definitely be opposed to any aggressive Allied move. There was doubt in the president's mind whether the revolutionary movement could be arrested with the help of the army. The latter might actually be infected, especially since an element of sympathy existed toward the forces which the men would oppose. Once more the president reiterated his opposition to "the reconstitution of an eastern front, and this is what is proposed here once again,"

> . . . a plan which aims at the formation of a line stretching from the Baltic to the Black Sea. One talks about saving Hungary, which means crushing of Hungarian Bolshevism. *If this Bolshevism remains within its frontiers, it does not concern us.* [Italics added.] The only problem which we had intended to solve today was that of aid to furnish to Rumania.

Clemenceau and Lloyd George strongly supported the position of President Wilson. While Clemenceau stressed the need for the council to limit itself to aiding the Rumanian army with sufficient equipment to make it an effective fighting force, Lloyd George in particular also echoed President Wilson's view that a Hungarian revolution remaining within its frontiers ought not to be of concern to the Allies.

On April 1 the young British diplomat Harold Nicolson, a close observer of the fateful Allied decisions and moves at the time, entered in his diary: "It seems that the Supreme Council have given up the idea of sending General Mangin to reduce Hungary with the help of the Rumanian army."[16]

Thus the Allies, with the exception of the French military, were opposed to an intervention against Hungary either by their own forces or those of Hungary's neighbors, especially the Rumanians and Czechoslovaks; however, they made their position contingent on the nonaggressive character of Hungarian bolshevism. Only the Italian government came out in support of the occupation of Budapest and Vienna, since Austria in its view seemed to drift into the Communist camp. In the end, however, Italy endorsed the decision of the majority.

The final Allied decision was the result of numerous factors and considerations. Direct military intervention at that time did not seem to be feasible to the Entente. Demobilization had already proceeded at too fast a pace, and public opinion was averse to intervention. For these reasons the Great Powers had already decided against a major military undertaking in opposition to the obviously greater Bolshevik menace of Soviet Russia. The Great Powers actually were concealing the advanced stage of their demobilization even from their allies.

There was also the belief among many in the West that a political and even a social revolution was needed in Hungary, and President Wilson himself expressed sympathy for the Hungarian people who, it was believed, were merely striving to

16. Nicolson, *Peacemaking, 1919,* p. 292.

improve their living conditions. A noble humanitarianism combined with ignorance of the true character of the messianic revolutionary drive of bolshevism and the naïve hope that Hungarian communism might stay within its frontiers shaped Allied policy. Finally, concern for public opinion, the concept of self-determination, and international law, also influenced the Allies. If in the following weeks and months the Western powers were to swerve from the charted course, and at times seemed on the point of encouraging an intervention especially by Rumanian and Czechoslovakian troops, it was because of the accumulating evidence and their growing conviction that Magyar bolshevism was resolved to spread beyond the lines of demarcation, even beyond ethnic and historic lines, into the neighboring countries.

Only a few days after the Council of Four of the Paris Peace Conference had first considered the new situation in Hungary, a communication of the new Hungarian government reached the Great Powers. Béla Kun had transmitted an *aide-mémoire*, dated March 24, to the Italian Prince Borghese in Budapest. The note had been brought to Vittorio Orlando in Paris and was given by him to Lloyd George on March 29.[17] The first communication of the new Hungarian government to the Great Powers was significant and revealing for its assertions, denials, and challenges. "The new Government of Hungary," the note asserted, "recognizes the validity of the Treaty of Armistice signed by the former government and does not think that the non-acceptance of the note presented by Colonel Vyx has infringed it." Though the recognition of the armistice by the soviet government was of interest, the statement was highly ambiguous. It refrained from declaring positively that the soviet government was willing to accept the Allied demand for withdrawal of the Red Army behind the new line of demarcation, a demand which the Western powers maintained was in accord with the armistice. While the new Hungarian government, the note asserted, had asked Russia to enter in an alliance with the Hungarian Soviet Republic, it "has not thought that this might be interpreted as an expression of its desire to break all diplomatic intercourse with the Powers of the Entente." The alliance with Russia was not a formal diplomatic alliance, but was at the most an *entente cordiale*, a natural friendship justified by the identical construction of their respective constitutions, and had no aggressive purpose. "The new Hungarian Republic, on the contrary, has a firm desire to live in peace with all the other Nations and to devote its activities to the peaceful social reorganization of its country." The new social state to be constructed would not be hostile to other nations. The soviet government was ready to "negotiate territorial questions on the basis of the principle of self-determination of the people and [it] views territorial integrity solely as in conformity with that principle."

The purpose of the Hungarian soviet government's note was rather obvious. It was to soft-pedal Soviet Hungary's relations with Soviet Russia and to allay the fears of her neighbors and the Great Powers. While it assured them that the new government was not wedded to the idea of territorial integrity, it wished to negotiate territorial

17. U.S., Department of State, *Papers Relating to the Foreign Relations of the United States: The Paris Peace Conference*, 13 vols. (Washington: Government Printing Office, 1946), 5:18 (hereafter cited as *PPC*).

questions—a right which was not acceded to its predecessor. The government wished to negotiate specifically on the basis of self-determination—a principle as important to President Wilson as to Lenin. Negotiation on this basis might enable the soviets to retain control of Magyar-inhabited disputed regions. The note was designed to open channels of communication to the West. Engaging in talks and negotiations with Budapest would make it more difficult for the Western powers to undertake a military intervention against Soviet Hungary and might perhaps lead to a recognition of the soviet regime. The communication ended with the assurance that the soviet government would "gladly welcome a civil and diplomatic mission of the Entente in Budapest," would "guarantee to it the right of extra-territoriality," and would provide for its absolute safety. This note was designed not only to give needed legal assurances, but also to wipe out the bad impression which the arrest of members of the Western diplomatic missions immediately after the Soviet coup in Budapest had made in Paris.

The *aide-mémoire* found the Allies in a receptive mood and contributed to their early restraint in their dealings with Soviet Hungary. If Magyar bolshevism was reasonable and moderate, Allied policy had to be similarly marked by reasonableness and moderation. Consequently on March 31 the Allies decided to send a delegation headed by General Smuts to Budapest. This mission, without recognizing the new government on behalf of the Allies, was to enter into discussions with it concerning matters of Allied concern.

A feeling of guilt for having contributed to the emergence of the Hungarian soviet government by pursuing a faulty policy lay heavily upon the Allied statesmen gathered in Paris. Error had been piled upon error. The Austro-Hungarian armistice, the source of many Allied-Hungarian difficulties, had been drawn up, as Lloyd George admitted, somewhat hastily. The Allies had given little encouragement to the pro-Allied, democratic government of Mihály Károlyi, and their ultimatum of March 19, 1919, had finally triggered the chain of events climaxing in the establishment of a soviet regime in Budapest. Discussing matters with the new government seemed to be a less risky course than refusing to talk with it. Besides, as President Wilson stressed, "the Budapest government had not yet been charged with crimes,"[18] and it was probably only a nationalistic government.

It could be argued that the Allies' accord on sending the mission signified not an agreement on policy but rather the postponement of a decision. Yet by sending Smuts to Budapest and having him talk and possibly negotiate with Béla Kun and his government, the Allies risked lending prestige to a shaky regime, strengthening it, and prolonging its life. Smuts, to avert this peril, carefully tried to avoid giving Kun and the soviet government even the semblance of Allied recognition or approval. During his stay in Budapest, Smuts did not even leave the railway station![19]

Béla Kun, nevertheless, made the most of General Smuts's visit to Budapest. The Hungarian press maintained silence about the odd circumstances surrounding his stay in Budapest and later also about his abrupt departure. And *Népszava*, commenting on the talks between General Smuts and the soviet government, observed that until

18. Mantoux, *Déliberations*, 1:98–99.
19. Nicolson, *Peacemaking, 1919*, pp. 300, 302.

recently the Entente had refused to engage in any negotiations and had merely sent ultimatums; now, however, "the same Entente which had not deigned to have any dealings with the half-bourgeois Government of the People's Republic except through the medium of ultimatums" had entered into negotiations with the soviet republic![20]

In two telegrams to Balfour dated April 4 and 6, 1919, General Smuts reported about his meeting with Béla Kun and two important members of the government, President Garbai and Commissar for Education Kunfi. In a long conversation with Kun on his arrival, he had explained that the line of demarcation of which Colonel Vyx had notified the Hungarian government was not intended to be a permanent political frontier and that the withdrawal of the Hungarian troops behind it and the creation of a neutral zone occupied by Allied troops was necessary for the maintenance of peace and order and would in no way prejudice the Hungarian case at the peace table.[21]

Kun, however, remained adamant on the question of the military withdrawal, and not even the hope of Allied lifting of the blockade would make him change his stand. While the Hungarian government recognized the principles of nationality laid down by President Wilson, accepted self-determination, and "renounced the ideals of territorial integrity formerly prevalent," it made clear that the definitive settlement of the boundary questions ought not to be reached by the Great Powers at the Paris Peace Conference. Rather it should be agreed upon at meetings between representatives of the Hungarian, German, Austrian, Bohemian, Serbian, and Rumanian governments, at which the Entente powers were not represented!

Smuts's account of his meeting with Kun reveals the extent of the Allies' willingness to meet the Hungarian soviet government. The Allies, as the General's first message to Balfour showed, were unwilling to go back on their earlier ultimatum to Károlyi and insisted on Magyar compliance with Colonel Vyx's line of demarcation, though assuring Kun, as stated, that the line would not be the permanent political frontier. From conversations with General Smuts the Hungarian soviet government must have had the impression that the Allies were willing to establish peaceful relations with it. In return for Hungarian withdrawal behind the Vyx line, they would lift the blockade and make it possible for the soviet regime to restore prosperity.

In his second telegram to Balfour dated April 6, 1919, Smuts revealed that he had made further concessions to the soviet government. He had proposed to the soviets a "new armistice line, running further east than Colonel Vyx's line, but nevertheless well to the west of the territory which the Rumanian Committee of the Conference assigned to Rumania in its report."[22] According to Smuts, the Hungarian ministers, apparently Garbai and Kunfi, had been ready to sign the draft of an agreement which had already been drawn up, when, after consultation with their colleagues, they refused to do so, "saying that if they did so, civil war would break out in the neutral zone and the Government would fall at once." In their counterproposal they suggested

20. *Népszava*, 5 April 1919.
21. *PPC*, 5:41–43; for the following also pp. 61–62.
22. Ibid., pp. 61–62.

that the Rumanians withdraw their forces behind the Maros River, the line laid down by General Franchet d'Esperey on November 13 in Belgrade. Smuts, realizing that this would cause trouble with Rumania, rejected this proposal.

What General Smuts asked for was basically the acceptance by the soviet government of the occupation of all of Transylvania by the Rumanian army and of the establishment of a neutral zone between Hungarian and Rumanian troops. Yet Smuts's offer constituted an improvement over the terms of the Vyx ultimatum. The entire eastern line of demarcation was to be shifted in Hungary's favor to an extent of between 8 and 10 kilometers and at some places 20 kilometers. It was asserted that the new line would have no influence upon the final peace terms. The new line left Debrecen in Hungary, and the cities of Arad, Nagyvárad, and Szatmár, which according to the Vyx ultimatum were to be occupied by Rumania, were now placed inside the neutral zone. The latter was to be established immediately. Smuts also promised to propose to the Great Powers in Paris that the blockade be raised at once. Hungary, on the other hand, had to observe the armistice agreement and cease rearming.

Kun's counterproposals, approved by the entire cabinet, were presented to General Smuts on the evening of the same day that Smuts had made his demands. In his reply to Kun, Smuts was very frank, and left little doubt that the peace conference would not issue any order to the Rumanians to withdraw behind the Maros River.

In a mood compounded of revolutionary overconfidence, underestimation of western determination, and nationalist intransigence, the Hungarian Communist leaders had turned down Smuts's proposals. An acceptance of the proposals of General Smuts would have signified abandonment of Transylvania—a heavy political liability —since the promise that the line of demarcation would have no bearing upon the final determination of the political boundaries was, by its very nature, a doubtful one. But a neutral zone would have offered a measure of guarantee to Soviet Hungary against further Rumanian encroachments and would have given international recognition and prestige to the new regime. On the other hand, it would have imposed upon Soviet Hungary the obligation of carrying on peaceful relations with her neighbors, as well as refraining from spreading revolutionary propaganda abroad, from engaging in nationalist activities in the disputed regions, and from offering indirect military assistance to the struggling Soviet Russian regime. It may perhaps be argued that in early April, 1919, the Hungarian government and nation, owing partly to revolutionary desires and partly to territorial ambitions, were unable to make a rational choice. The new government had been swept to power on a tremendous wave of national resentment and continued to be supported by Hungarian nationalists, critical though they were of the economic and social program of the Bolsheviks. Under these circumstances, the Kun government was in no position to accept Smuts's proposals. Kun had to reject territorial losses not markedly less grievous than those imposed by the Vyx ultimatum which had proved unacceptable to his predecessor. As a consequence, the soviet government might not have survived the acceptance of the Smuts proposals.

From his visit to Budapest, Smuts, as Harold Nicolson reported, had gained the conviction that Béla Kun and Hungarian bolshevism were not a serious menace and could not last.[23] Since the soviet government had rejected Smuts's propositions, he held that his mission had failed. His recommendations to the council in Paris were in accordance with his view that the soviet regime was a transitory phenomenon.[24] Although public opinion in the western countries coupled with their lack of military and psychological preparedness were largely responsible for the emerging Allied policy, Smuts's low opinion of the soviet government's chances for longevity also helped to shape Allied policy. His conclusions lent themselves to a justification of a policy short of direct military intervention on the part of the Great Powers.

Only a few days after General Smuts's propositions had been turned down, the military offensive of the Rumanian troops, to whom the Allies had just promised new material support, began in earnest and was soon in full swing. There is no evidence, however, that the Big Four in Paris gave any direct order or indirect encouragement to the Rumanian army to take the offensive against the Hungarian lines, though there were widespread rumors that French army leaders favored the Rumanian move. Rumania, anxious to occupy all of Transylvania and even areas beyond it, needed little encouragement from the West. In a few days the Rumanian forces advanced not merely to the new line of demarcation, but pushed further to the Tisza River and at Szolnok some Rumanian units even crossed the Tisza. When the Rumanian forces prepared to march on Budapest, Allied policy toward Soviet Hungary and Rumania became most puzzling.[25] At this critical juncture the Allies abruptly interposed the authority of the peace conference and vetoed any further Rumanian advance toward the Hungarian capital. In a personal meeting with Ionel Bratianu in Paris, Clemenceau peremptorily prohibited Rumanian troops from crossing the Tisza.[26] Had the Allies not intervened, Budapest might have fallen and the Bolshevik experiment might have ended right then owing to Rumania's intervention.

In view of the basic hostility of the Allied powers and of the peace conference to Hungarian bolshevism and due to their desire to eliminate this advanced base of Russian bolshevism in Central Europe, the Allied order to Rumanian troops and Allied policy in general appear enigmatic. Most likely, the Allies preferred an over-throw of the soviet regime by the Hungarian people itself to one from the outside by foreign troops. They may have feared that world public opinion would have made them responsible for the Rumanian intervention and for the ousting of the Kun government by foreign troops. The aggressiveness of the Soviet Hungarian regime was to reach its climax later and had not yet become fully apparent at that moment. The rise and quick fall of another soviet regime in Munich in early April may have

23. Nicolson, *Peacemaking, 1919*, p. 307; see also Steven Bonsal, *Unfinished Business* (New York: Doubleday, 1944), chap. 4.

24. Mantoux, *Délibérations*, 1:166–67.

25. Diary I, 11 April 1919, Box 65, T. H. Bliss Papers, Library of Congress, Washington, D.C.; Ray Stannard Baker, *Woodrow Wilson and World Settlement*, 3 vols. (New York: Doubleday, Page, and Co., 1922), 3:239–41.

26. Clark, V., *Greater Rumania*, p. 191.

unjustifiedly strengthened the West's belief in the basic stability of all of Central Europe.

Most important, however, the peacemakers, while opposed to bolshevism in Hungary and elsewhere, were concerned with the excessive territorial demands of some of the succession states, particularly Rumania. The Allies were fearful of whetting Rumania's appetite by permitting her troops to occupy Budapest. Such occupation was likely to aggravate their difficulties in drafting a peace treaty acceptable to both Hungary and Rumania. This task seemed difficult enough while the Rumanian troops were entrenched along the Tisza River, west of the line promised to them in August, 1916, while the Hungarians were still bent on preserving the historic integrity of their country.

When during the month of May Hungarian troops invaded Slovakia, the Czechs anxiously anticipated relief from Rumania. Owing, however, to the continuing Allied prohibition concerning the crossing of the Tisza, Rumanian help was not forthcoming. It was Allied diplomatic assistance to Czechoslovakia, in addition to French military leadership for Czechoslovakian troops, which finally turned the tables. The Allied ultimatum of June 13 categorically demanded Hungarian withdrawal from the occupied areas of Slovakia, promising in return Rumanian withdrawal from the Tisza to the new border. This promise, however, was made without prior consultation either with the Rumanian government in Bucharest or its chief, Bratianu, who was still in Paris.

The Allied statesmen in Paris were most concerned with the restoration of the social, economic, and political order in Central Europe and bent on the elimination of bolshevism. Yet imperative as this matter appeared to them, the main objective of the peace conference was the making of peace, delineating the new frontiers and having them accepted by the opposing states, their own friends and allies as well as by Soviet Hungary. If the Allies disregarded their pledges to their allies in Central and Southeast Europe, they would weaken their bonds with them and only strengthen Soviet Hungary, without necessarily winning her friendship. If, on the other hand, they permitted their opposition to bolshevism to dictate or greatly influence the tracing of Hungary's frontiers, they ran the risk of consolidating social radicalism in Hungary, strengthening her alliance with Soviet Russia, and of alienating the Magyars permanently.

When the Allies had called upon the Hungarian Bolshevik regime to withdraw from all of Slovakia, which in December, 1918, had been definitely assigned to the new Czechoslovakian state, it was both the desire to assist their hard-pressed Czech ally and the wish to have the new frontiers respected and peace secured which had moved them. The latter consideration had also prompted the Allies when they simultaneously called upon the Rumanians to withdraw to the new frontier.

Had the Allies merely faced the task of exterminating bolshevism or teaching a "lesson" to a recalcitrant enemy nation which was seething with chauvinism and unwilling to accept the verdict of the war, the continuing prohibition to the Rumanians to cross the Tisza River would clearly have been illogical and inconsistent. Yet the peace conference was, after all, concerned with writing what was hoped would be an enduring peace. It was therefore unwilling to pursue a course likely to lead to the imposition of intolerable losses on Hungary.

What may partly serve as an explanation of Allied policy, does not necessarily amount to its justification. The risks which the Allies ran were rather considerable. Allied policy was based upon several unproven assumptions: namely, that Hungarian bolshevism would surely fail because of its internal contradictions; that revolutionary forces elsewhere in Central Europe would be easily defeated and order everywhere restored; and finally that Russia would prove unable to assist Soviet Hungary.

The Allied demand for Rumanian withdrawal from the Tisza River met with resolute opposition,[27] and the Great Powers suffered an embarrassing defeat. They had earlier succeeded in halting the Rumanian troops at the Tisza. Now, however, they failed in making them withdraw from this line. In late May, when President Wilson came closer than at any previous or later time to favoring French occupation of Budapest, Clemenceau opposed it. He also was not enthusiastic about a Rumanian move against Budapest, though the Rumanian army was already anxious to march on the Hungarian capital. At the meeting of the Council of Four on March 30, at the initiative of Clemenceau, the Allies vetoed the Rumanian proposal that their army march against Budapest.[28] This time Bucharest bowed to Paris. While the Western powers were unable to persuade Rumania to withdraw her troops from the Tisza River, they were successful in pinning them down at the river line and in dissuading Rumania from marching against Budapest and crushing the Hungarian soviet regime. Paris also succeeded in stopping the Serbian armies on the southern Hungarian front.

Although the Allied Powers had terminated their work relating to Hungary's frontiers in early May, it was not before early June that the Paris Peace Conference was to inform all Central and Southeast European states of the new frontiers as laid down in the peace treaties.

By early June the military situation of Czechoslovakia had worsened. More than one third of Slovakia had been lost to the Magyar troops and the Czechs were still retreating along the entire front. As Eduard Beneš later revealed, Kun's success "affected our prestige and position in Paris for a while very considerably."[29] It was Allied diplomacy which saved Czechoslovakia. In response to three desperate appeals of Beneš for help, Clemenceau on June 8 and again on June 13 sent sharply worded ultimatums to Béla Kun. In the second note he informed the soviet government of the new Hungarian frontiers and demanded the immediate withdrawal of the Red Army to the new lines.

In a telegram dated June 7, but apparently dispatched to the Hungarian government on the following day, the Secretariat of the Conference of the Allied and Associated Governments reminded the Hungarian government that the Allies had already shown their

firm determination to put an end to all useless hostilities by twice stopping the Rumanian armies which had crossed the armistice lines and then those of the

27. *PPC*, 7:24, July 5.
28. Ibid., p. 133.
29. Quoted by Clark, *Rumania*, p. 110.

neutral zone, and by preventing them from continuing their march on Budapest; and also by stopping the Serbian and French armies on the Southern Hungarian front.

In these circumstances the Government of Budapest is formally requested to put an end without delay to its attacks on the Czecho-Slovaks, otherwise the Allied and Associated Governments are absolutely decided to have immediate recourse to extreme measures to oblige Hungary to cease hostilities and to bow to the un-shakeable will of the Allies to make their injunctions respected.—A reply to the present telegram should be made within 48 hours.[30]

This ultimatum left little doubt of the Entente's new determination which, in the past, had not always been evident. It reminded Soviet Hungary that it owed its very existence to the interposition of the Great Powers against an intervention by Hungary's neighbors and French troops. The note was meant to be a last warning to the Hungarian soviet government to take better cognizance of the new situation. This sharp communication was merely the forerunner of the Allied ultimatum of June 13.

On that day Clemenceau sent another telegram to Hungary, addressed to Béla Kun, in which the latter was informed of the new permanent Hungarian boundaries, and he and his government were called upon immediately to withdraw the Hungarian army now fighting in Czechoslovakia behind

the assigned frontier of Hungary, within which all other Hungarian troops are required to remain. If the Allies and Associated Governments are not informed by their representatives on the spot within four days from midday on June 14, 1919, that this operation is being effectively carried out, they will hold themselves free to advance on Budapest and to take such other steps as may seem desirable to secure a just and speedy peace. The Rumanian troops will be withdrawn from Hungarian territory as soon as the Hungarian troops have evacuated Czechoslovakia.[31]

In spite of the warnings by Hungarian military leaders and against the urgings of die-hard Communists, the government, recognizing the superiority of Allied power and its own weakness, ordered withdrawal from the occupied regions of Slovakia. Nothing revealed more clearly Soviet Hungary's utter weakness than the ready abandonment of the territories which she had just regained.

On the nineteenth of June, the Hungarian papers revealed that Kun had sent a telegram to Clemenceau informing him that hostilities continued due to alleged attacks by Czechoslovakian troops. "This telegram," Böhm conceded, "was based on previous agreement. We still hesitated to order withdrawal."[32] Finally, however, the withdrawal of Hungarian troops began in earnest and was completed by the end of

30. *PPC*, 6:246–47.

31. *Népszava*, 19 June 1919; also *PPC*, 6:412.

32. Wilhelm Böhm, *Im Kreuzfeuer zweier Revolutionen* (Munich: Verlag für Kulturpolitik, 1924), p. 472; see also Zsuzsa L. Nagy, *A párizsi békekonferencia és Magyarország, 1918–1919* [The Paris Peace Conference and Hungary, 1918–1919] (Budapest: Kossuth, 1965), pp. 153 ff.

June. The publication of the foregoing diplomatic notes, especially the disclosure that the frontiers had been definitely drawn, speeded the process of disintegration, since further bloodshed seemed now in vain. The masses of the Hungarian people saw no further purpose in prolonging the war except the questionable one of keeping in power a harsh, unrepresentative, and now discredited regime.

Kun and the soviet government felt the need for justifying their readiness to accept the Entente's offer which they had rejected in March. "Many may ask why we did not accept the terms offered us by Smuts?" asked Kun. He replied that what then would have been a mistake, was now the correct policy.[33] Kun voiced the hope that the proletariat of Czechoslovakia, Rumania, and Yugoslavia would seize power and annul the peace terms dictated to Hungary.[34] Actually, the revolutionary situation had been more promising in late March and early April than it was in June, as Béla Kun must have been aware. Yet the argument evidently served as a rationalization for his retreat.

The decision of the Kun government to accept Clemenceau's ultimatum was prompted not only by its consideration of the military balance of power in Central and Southeast Europe, but also by the increasingly desperate internal situation of Hungary. The Hungarian people, as Lenin put it, needed a breathing space. In the background there was the hope that, owing to the impending revolution in Hungary's neighboring states and the rest of Europe, any territorial arrangement would prove to be merely a provisional one. Kun wanted peace in June, 1919, since it would enable him to turn against the Hungarian counterrevolution and also to wait for an improvement in the military situation of Russia.[35] His Social Democratic minister of war, Vilmos Böhm, wrote later: "Kun wanted the peace in order to stir up a new war."[36]

In accepting Clemenceau's ultimatum, the soviet government also consented to the new frontiers. While the boundaries laid down at the Paris Peace Conference were far from favorable, Hungary's recent military efforts had not been quite in vain. The new frontiers were an improvement over the Allied line insisted upon in March, 1919.

The acceptance of Clemenceau's ultimatum of June 13 by the Hungarian soviet government and the retreat of the Red Army from the conquered regions of Slovakia did not remove the Hungarian problem from the agenda of the Paris Peace Conference. Soviet Hungary was ideologically expansive, nationally and territorially dissatisfied, and economically and socially stirred up. The threat which she continued to present to her neighbors was felt to be serious. It reached its climax in the resumption of hostilities against Rumania on July 21. Rumania's determination to prevent Hungarian reconquest of Transylvania, as well as the Allies' mounting interest in the definitive removal of the Hungarian soviet menace, made the Hungarian question the

33. *Kun Béla*, p. 270.

34. Böhm, *Im Kreuzfeuer*, p. 472; Rudolf L. Tőkés, *Béla Kun and the Hungarian Soviet Republic* (New York: Praeger, 1967).

35. F. Münnich, "The October Revolution and the Hungarian Red Army," *Voprosy istorii*, March 1959, p. 46 f.

36. Böhm, *Im Kreuzfeuer*, p. 274.

focus of attention of the peace conference in the month of July and led to a reassessment of Allied policies among the Great Powers.

It was the need for economic recovery of Central and Southeast Europe to which Herbert Hoover, director general of relief, had drawn attention in a letter of July 1, 1919, addressed to Secretary of State Robert Lansing, then also in Paris.[37] In the session of the heads of delegations of the five powers on July 5, Hoover likewise pointed out that the situation in Hungary was by no means merely an internal Hungarian question, but was tied up with the economic rehabilitation of Central Europe. Hoover thus offered a justification for Allied moves against the economically disruptive Hungarian soviet regime.

Balfour, complimenting Hoover for his extremely lucid statement, pointed out that the latter had approached a very complex question from the economic side alone. Yet an equitable distribution of the means of subsistence in southeastern Europe could not be brought about without a radical change of the Hungarian situation. He held therefore that the case must be approached from the military side.[38] "Prompt military action . . . would be justified by Hungary's flagrant breach of the armistice."[39]

It was then Clemenceau's turn. He seemed to pour cold water on Balfour's recommendations:

> France was demobilizing and could not stop the process. . . . At the end of October the French army . . . would be on a peace footing. The French Chamber was resolutely opposed to intervention in Russia . . . . If Parliament declines to fight Bolshevism in Russia, it would equally refuse to fight it in Hungary.[40]

Balfour had mentioned Czech, Rumanian, Serb, and French troops. Yet this would require money, and he, for one, could not supply any. Clemenceau ruled out the blockade as an effective means of unseating the Kun government, doubted the military capacity of the Czechs as compared with the Hungarians and the willingness of the Rumanians to fight, and noted pointedly the unavailability of British and American troops.

Clemenceau had made his points which, with slight variation only, he was to repeat until the Hungarian soviet regime succumbed. At the moment he was only willing to threaten Hungary with intervention. He wanted to wait, to temporize, hoping that "Providence might furnish some means of escape." He was fully aware that this was not a noble policy and also aware of the danger of the Hungarian soviet challenge being followed by Germany. Germany so far had behaved well, but might change her attitude. Though critical, almost derisive, of the Napoleonic ambitions of Generals Foch and Franchet d'Esperey, he did not definitely abandon the notion of applying military force against Soviet Hungary, but he made it clear that military

37. *PPC*, 7:29–30.
38. Ibid., p. 23.
39. Ibid., p. 24.
40. Ibid., pp. 24–26.

intervention would have to be a truly cooperative effort. For the moment Hungary might be surrounded by a *cordon sanitaire*. Hoping for the best, he voiced his conviction that communism would not last long in that country.

While now Great Britain and also the United States (neither of which had any troops in Central Europe, as Clemenceau was quick to point out) seemed eager to have Hungary's neighbors, in combination with two French divisions in the area, militarily intervene in Hungary, the French government was clearly reluctant to engage in any military adventure. The French reluctance was mainly due to the unwillingness of Britain and the United States to go beyond giving moral and diplomatic support to such a project. In the debate of the council on Allied policy toward Soviet Hungary on July 5 and July 9, 1919, each of the Great Powers more than once came close to approving intervention against Soviet Hungary, though only France offered its own troops contingent upon support by other Great Powers. The possibility, however, of applying military force against Soviet Hungary at some future time had not been excluded. In spite of the fact that at the moment the supporters of the case for military intervention against Hungary faced overwhelming obstacles, the intervention was to remain on the agenda of the Paris council until the overthrow of the Hungarian soviet regime a few weeks later.

On July 11 the Hungarian soviet regime began a determined diplomatic offensive. Béla Kun sent a telegram to Clemenceau, reminding him of the dispatch of June 13,[41] wherein he had assured Kun that the Rumanian troops would, as soon as the Hungarian army had evacuated territory ceded to the Czechoslovakian republic, make similar movement of evacuation. In spite of Clemenceau's assurances, however, the Rumanians failed to withdraw and Rumanian troops continued their attacks against the Hungarian units. The council, however, held that Soviet Hungary had violated the armistice, having rebuilt her armed forces beyond the six divisions permitted to her.[42]

Consequently the council intended to take no action against Rumania. On the other hand, the possibility of a military move against Hungary was seriously examined. The Allied powers had declined to enforce their previous order to Rumania to withdraw from the Tisza, but in July they considered the military threat emanating from Soviet Hungary as the main and immediate problem of Central Europe. The military experts advised them that, as long as military intervention against Soviet Hungary was considered, Rumanian troops ought not to abandon the line of the Tisza River. Furthermore, the Hungarian evacuation of all of Slovakia, in response to Clemenceau's ultimatum, while seemingly giving proof of Hungarian acquiescence to the Western powers, actually reduced the length of the Czechoslovak-Hungarian border and thus did not diminish, but rather increased the danger to Rumania. It was the Hungarian soviet military threat which had become a primary source of anxiety to the Allied and associated powers in mid-July, and they were therefore in no mood to weigh the unquestionable merits of Hungary's case relating to the Tisza line.

On July 17, the council considered the opinion of Allied military experts on a "plan of operations against Hungary," which Foch submitted to it. This plan had

41. Ibid., 6:411–12, 416.
42. Ibid., 7:121.

been drawn up in accordance with the order of the Supreme Council of the Allied and Associated Powers of July 11 and was based on information provided by General Maurice Pellé for the Czechoslovak army, General Nicola Pašič for the Serbian army, and General Constantin Prezan for the Rumanian army; further information also was furnished by the Czechoslovakian, Serbian, and Rumanian governments as well as by General Franchet d'Esperey, commander of the French army in Hungary. The Allies, the report concluded, would be able to dispose of 100,000 to 120,000 combatants. The forces available to the Entente would "appear to be adequate to undertake, within a short time and with chances of success, a military operation against Hungary," but only under the following conditions: (1) a single supreme command for operations must be organized; (2) the supreme command must be authorized to establish a new government in agreeing with the views of the Entente; and (3) the Austrian government must accede to furnish munitions to the Czechoslovaks.[43]

When in March, 1919, the Hungarian soviet regime had been set up, the Allies had briefly contemplated military intervention, but had quickly vetoed it. Almost four months had elapsed. During this time, the soviet regime had taken the offensive, propagandistically and militarily, had frequently challenged the Allied powers in Paris, and, last but not least, had imposed a harsh and brutal regime on its own people. Many foreign diplomatic and military observers in Hungary, in adjoining Austria, and also in faraway Paris, in spite of the liberal inclinations of some of them, had reluctantly come to acknowledge the Hungarian peril and the unsettled character of the political and social order of Central Europe, and now favored military intervention.

In early May, both the liberal American Professor A. C. Coolidge, who held a key quasi-diplomatic post in Vienna, and Lieutenant W. H. Osborn favored a military intervention. By July, Henry James also favored intervention in his "Memorandum Concerning Possible Action at Budapest" before the American Commissioners Plenipotentiary. Lieutenants Emory Pottle and Dr. E. Dana Durand of the American Relief Administration in their "Memorandum regarding Conditions in Hungary" also voiced this opinion.[44] General Bliss, however, who had opposed military intervention against Budapest in March, 1919, continued to direct scorching criticism against Foch's plan for military involvement. In any case, though many American experts had come to look more favorably on intervention, it was to be an intervention by the other Great Powers or by Hungary's neighbors which was contemplated, not one by American troops. In spite of a general agreement that Soviet Hungary was a menace, however, not even the immediate neighbors of Hungary who felt especially threatened were elated about the prospect of becoming involved in hostilities with a militant Soviet Hungary.

Foch was clearly disappointed with the outcome of the debate. He had expected more than Balfour's spirited defense of the legal and moral position of the Allies; he apparently had hoped for concrete and substantial offers of military contribution from Great Britain and other great and small powers. He seemed convinced of the peril

43. Ibid., 187–90; App. B to HD-9.
44. Ibid., 456, 459, and 11:188, 312, 320.

which Hungary, especially Soviet Hungary, represented not only to her immediate neighbors, but also to the Great Powers gathered at Paris. He still favored decisive military methods in quickly bringing peace and stability to Central Europe.

While the debates continued in Paris the increasing scarcity of food, the lack of the most urgent necessities throughout the country, the breakdown in administration and the growing anarchy contributed to undermining the morale of the entire Hungarian people. Yet it was the regime's reckless military aggressiveness which dug its own grave. The Hungarian soviet government keenly felt the need for bolstering the tottering regime by military success. The increasingly desperate internal situation merely increased the soviet government's willingness to take risks. News from Paris in early July of the Allies' indecision toward Soviet Hungary and, after the middle of the month, of the growing firmness and hostility of the Allied and associated powers, may have convinced the soviet government that it could only gain from an offensive and had little to lose.

The Hungarian military offensive against the Rumanians was undertaken for the immediate purpose of dislodging them from the Tisza River, but, if successful, might not have been confined to this objective. It came about ten days after diplomatic representation concerning the line had been made to Paris;[45] the Allies had then ignored the Hungarian note. Though in a way forewarned, the offensive, nevertheless, came as a startling surprise to the Allies. For when the Béla Kun government had yielded earlier to Clemenceau's order to evacuate all territories in Slovakia which Hungarian troops had formerly wrested from Czechoslovakia, it had most strikingly displayed subservience toward the Paris Peace Conference.

On July 21, the day the Hungarian Red Army began its attack against the Rumanians, Béla Kun sent the following radio message to Clemenceau: "In the face of the attitude of the Rumanians who have been aggressive in defiance of the will of the Entente, we were forced to cross the Tisza and try to make the will of the Entente respected by the Rumanians."[46] Under this spurious pretense the soviet government again not only threatened the peace and stability of Central and Southeast Europe, but also threw down a gauntlet to the Allies and the Paris Peace Conference.

The Hungarian situation called for clear decisions and energetic moves on the part of the peace conference, but no such decision and action was forthcoming. The call for some definite policy concerning Hungary, issued by Herbert Hoover in his letter to Secretary of State Robert Lansing on July 1, warning of the danger of the economic collapse of the countries surrounding Hungary, remained unanswered even after the new turn of events.[47] The council in Paris clearly exhibited an inability to make prompt and firm decisions.[48] The lack of consensus among men who widely differed in their attitudes toward Soviet Hungary (for instance Herbert Hoover, General Bliss, and the French General Pellé) was evident.[49] The Allied powers, beset by

45. Ibid., 7:125–27.
46. Ibid., 248–49, App. B to HD-12.
47. Ibid., 30.
48. J. Dillon, *The Inside Story of the Peace Conference* (New York: Harper, 1920), p. 79.
49. *PPC*, 7:29–30; Diary I, 17 July 1919, Box 65, *Bliss Papers*, and Pelle in *PPC*, 7:115.

numerous difficulties, were weakened by demobilization and by the unwillingness of public opinion in their respective countries to support what actually seemed to be a new war, a war of intervention to stamp out a radical socialist regime. The Entente, therefore, adopted the policy of waiting partly for the outcome of the Hungarian military offensive, partly for the realization of plans of Hungarian opposition leaders on the democratic Left to overthrow the Bolshevik government. Such a policy, based on mere hopes and procrastination, was a policy of weakness. As the debates of the peace conference had revealed, it was not one heartily endorsed either by Balfour or by Clemenceau or any of the other statesmen assembled in Paris; none of them was "proud" of it.[50]

The possibility of achieving the overthrow of the soviet government and its compliance with the armistice by troop reduction without direct military intervention intrigued the Entente. Action by social democratic commissar for war, Vilmos Böhm and his friends, combined with the threat to the soviet regime posed by the armies of Hungary's neighbors and the Entente, might produce the desired political and military change in Hungary. Even Foch held that a mere ultimatum, backed by military force, might bring about some Hungarian acquiescence to Allied demands, and result in effective disarmament without actual occupation of her territory.[51]

At times Clemenceau seemed hopeful that a policy short of military intervention might succeed. What he had in mind was an economic blockade of Hungary by her neighbors and the Western powers. He conceded that this was an "inglorious" weapon. Balfour's hope that the past prestige and economic power of the Allies— "half of the policy" he had earlier suggested—might bring about the overthrow of the soviet government was rather similar to Clemenceau's expectations. The economic weapon was, in his opinion, still available to the Allies.[52] Herbert Hoover, according to Clemenceau, held the key to the solution of the Hungarian question.[53] Clemenceau seemed to be well aware that the policy of prudence which he suggested for the time being involved some elements of risk, because, as Balfour had pointed out, Kun might possibly score military success with his new offensive, "but there was a greater risk in giving an ultimatum which, if rejected, would lead to war."[54]

On July 26 the Allied and associated governments proclaimed that they were anxious to sign a peace treaty with the Hungarian people and help to make possible the economic revival of Central Europe. This aim could not

even be attempted until there is in Hungary a Government which represents its people, and carries out in letter and the spirit the engagements into which it has entered with the Associated Governments. None of these conditions are fulfilled by the administration of Béla Kun.[55]

50. *PPC*, 7:24–26.
51. Diary I, 12 Dec. 1918–17 Aug. 1919, Bliss Papers.
52. *PPC*, 7:321.
53. Ibid., 319–20.
54. Ibid., 321.
55. Ibid., 321–22.

In this appeal of the Great Powers to the Hungarian nation over the head of their government, the Hungarian people were told that the soviet government was guilty of violation of the armistice; it was accused of engaging in aggression at that very moment and of using terrorism against its own people. The Hungarian nation was urged to overthrow this government. In return, major economic gains and the end of the occupation of Hungarian territory were promised. But no military move against Soviet Hungary either by the Entente or by Czechoslovakia and Yugoslavia was planned. The only tangible help extended to Rumania was, in Clemenceau's words, to encircle "Hungary with a ring of hostile states and rely on her to rid herself of a minority in her own way."[56]

This was not the first time that Clemenceau had suggested surrounding Hungary with hostile states and waiting for the Hungarian people to overthrow the soviet government. The initiative in ridding Hungary of bolshevism was, the Allies hoped, to come from within, not from without. This was no bold aggressive policy on the part of the Entente and her friends. Hungary was to be besieged, but the besiegers, unprepared to make sacrifices, were to wait for a revolt in the beleaguered fortress. This policy of weakness ignored the fact that the besieged opponent was just then making a desperate attempt to breach a segment of the surrounding wall held by Rumania, and her friends and allies made no determined move to come to her assistance.

The major powers, it was evident, had embarked on a course compounded of pious hopes, indecision, and procrastination. The recent Hungarian attack on the Rumanians might fail, which, in Balfour's words, would make a great difference. "Should Béla Kun fall of his own weight, it would certainly be better than if he were overthrown by the Allies." Furthermore, General Böhm's attempt to overthrow Kun might be successful; this was another hope of the conference and of Clemenceau.[57] Yet it was clear that the Allied powers had not reached any decision on alternate policies to be pursued, if either of these eventualities should fail to materialize and Béla Kun's regime weather all storms. Balfour warned that if, after issuing the declaration in the hope of encouraging General Böhm and other Hungarian groups to overthrow the soviet regime, "it was intended to do nothing . . . this was hardly desirable." Clemenceau, who after the council's approval of the foregoing declaration, suggested that in the meantime conversations might be undertaken with the smaller powers immediately concerned with the Hungarian situation, countered Balfour by pointing out that he had not meant to convey the impression "that he would never act: on some favorable occasion he might."[58]

The Allies had reached an impasse. They hoped for the best to extricate themselves from a precarious situation; they waited eagerly for the success of Böhm's undertakings and for the impact of Hoover's and the Allies' threats and promises aimed at the Hungarian nation. At that very moment they had neither reached the decision to intervene militarily, nor had they definitely come to the conclusion to wash their

56. Ibid., 319.
57. Ibid., 322.
58. Ibid.

hands of the Hungarian affair. In spite of the fact, however, that the Hungarian situation, owing to the Magyar aggression against Rumania, had grown more acute during the month of July, the debates in Paris, while revealing a stiffening of the Entente, a determination to deal no longer in any way with the soviet government, still did not attain the real climax: the decision to intervene. The advisability of military intervention in Hungary had long and seriously been considered. When for the time being at least it was abandoned, it was done so mainly for practical reasons—the relative military weakness and the psychological unpreparedness of the West.

The breakdown of Soviet Hungary on August 1 came in consequence of the failure of the Hungarian soviet offensive against Rumania. Bolshevism in Hungary, which had drawn much of its strength from Hungarian nationalism, crumbled when unable to fulfill the hopes and ambitions of the nationalists. Its fall saved the Western powers from having to make hard and fast decisions. The military intervention in Central Europe which the Entente had long discussed, but on which it had never agreed and not definitely approved, was no longer necessary. The "inglorious" policy of "holding the issues and waiting" had paid dividends.

Soviet Russia and Soviet Hungary

Iván Völgyes

The Hungarian Soviet Republic is portrayed in many of the scholarly works as an integral part of "Lenin's attempts in 1919–1920 to organize a revolution in Europe."[1] Béla Kun is referred to as "a sinister Comintern agent and revolutionary mastermind"[2] who created the Hungarian Soviet Republic as a part of Lenin's "blueprint for world conquest." It has been widely accepted that Kun merely followed the policies dictated to him by Lenin. Until recently the Hungarian dictatorship has been regarded by scholars as a simple duplication of the Russian dictatorship and the leaders of the Hungarian Soviet Republic were believed to be obedient tools of Soviet Russian policies. A careful examination of the relationship between Soviet Russia and Soviet Hungary, between Kun and Lenin, or between the Communist Internationals and the Communists of Hungary, however, reveals a startlingly different picture. Indeed, it appears that Soviet Hungary was not created according to Lenin's blueprint for world conquest, that the Hungarian regime did not function as a satellite of Soviet Russia, and that neither Béla Kun nor the Hungarian Communists were obedient tools of the Russian leadership.

The history of the 133 days of the Hungarian Soviet Republic shows that Béla Kun and the Hungarian soviet government acted independently, and, in many instances, quite contrary to Bolshevik policies in Russia. The Hungarian dictatorship of the proletariat was not directed by men who were willing to accept the guidance of Moscow, but by leaders of communist and socialist persuasions who followed an independent, if disastrous, policy during the brief existence of the Hungarian Soviet Republic.

Part of the historical confusion relating to the relationship between Moscow and Budapest is due to the fact that although Kun was a Socialist in Hungary prior to World War I, he did not become a Bolshevik until he was interned in a prisoner of war camp in Russia. Many scholars used this fact to justify a view of Kun as a servant of Moscow.

During the first week of January, 1918, a thirty-one-year-old Hungarian, named Béla Kun, arrived in the city of Petrograd from the prisoner of war camp at Tomsk,[3] and contacted the Department of International Propaganda of the Commissariat of

---

1. Arthur Rosenberg, *A History of Bolshevism* (New York: Doubleday, 1967), p. 160.

2. Andrew György, *Communism in Perspective* (Boston: Allyn and Bacon, 1965), p. 193.

3. "Negyven éves az első magyar kommunista ujság" [The first Hungarian Communist newspaper is forty years old], *Népszabadság* [People's Freedom], 1 Jan. 1958, p. 4.

Foreign Affairs. As a former journalist, and as a member of the Bolshevik section of the Russian Social Democratic Labor party, he offered his services to *Nemzetközi Szocialista*,4 a pro-Bolshevik journal printed in Hungarian and intended for Hungarian prisoners of war in Russia. Soon, he became the leading spokesman for the Bolshevik Hungarian prisoners of war in Russia. From January, 1918, until the beginning of the Hungarian revolution in October of the same year, he worked faithfully for the Russian Bolsheviks filling many important offices. On January 22, 1918, he was appointed the leading organizer of the Hungarian prisoners of war.5 During the German attack on Russia following the breakdown of the Brest Litovsk negotiations, Kun led one of the large groups of prisoners of war, who had been enlisted in the International Brigades of the Red Army, in an attempt to stop the German advance at Narva.6 He also was one of the founding members of the Hungarian section of the Russian Communist party7 and became the president of the section.8 In addition, Kun also served as the president of the Federation of Foreign Groups9 and led the pro-Bolshevik Latvian and Hungarian troops against the Social Revolutionaries in July, 1918.10 It was under his guidance and direction that the Union of Communists of Hungary was established on October 25, 1918, and again it was under his leadership that in Moscow this union was transformed into the Communist party of Hungary

4. *Vos'moi S'ezd R.K.P.(B)* [Eighth Congress of the R.C.P.(B)] 2nd ed. (Moscow, 1933), p. 434; *Boevoe Sodruzhestvo Trudiashchikhsia Zarubezhnykh Stran s Narodami Sovetskoi Rossii* [Military collaboration of the workers of foreign lands with the peoples of Soviet Russia] (Moscow, 1957), p. 157.

5. György Milei, "A magyar hadifoglyok a Nagy Októberi Szocialista Forradalomban" [Hungarian prisoners of war in the great socialist revolution of October], *Élet és Tudomány* [Life and Science], 1957, no. 45, p. 1412.

6. *Kun Béla a Magyar Tanácsköztársaságról* [Béla Kun on the Hungarian Soviet Republic] (Budapest: Kossuth, 1958), p. 540; Jenő Györkei and Antal Józsa, comps., *Magyar Internacionalisták a Nagy Októberi Szocialista Forradalomban* [Hungarian Internationalists in the great socialist revolution of October] (Budapest: Kossuth, 1957), p. 27; Milei, "A magyar,"; Antal Józsa, "Adalékok az oroszországi magyar hadifoglyok történetéhez" [Additions to the history of the Hungarian prisoners of war in Russia], pt. 2, in *Hadtörténelmi Közlemények* 10, no. 2, pp. 105-44; Tibor Szamuely, *Riadó* [Alarm] (Budapest: Kossuth, 1957), p. 18.

7. M. F. Lebov, *Vengerskaia Sovetskaia Respublika 1919 goda* [The Hungarian Soviet Republic of 1919] (Moscow: Izd.-vo Sots. ek. Lit.-ry, 1959), p. 35; György Szamuely, "A Kommunisták Magyarországi Pártjának előkészítése" [The preparation of the Communist party of Hungary], *Sarló és Kalapács* [Sickle and Hammer], 1932, no. 4, pp. 49-53; Endre Gerelyes, *Lenin Üzent* [Lenin sent a message] (Budapest: Legujabbkori Történeti Muzeum, 1961), p. 7; Milei, "A magyar," p. 1413; Györkei and Józsa, *Magyar Internacionalisták*, p. 28; *Kun Béla*, p. 540; Endre Zsilák, "Az Orosz Kommunisták (bolsevik) Pártja Magyar Csoportjának szerepe a Vörös Hadsereg internacinalista egységének szervezésében 1918-1919-ben" [The role of the Hungarian group of the Russian Communist party in the organization of the international units of the Red Army], *Történelmi Szemle* 4, no. 3 (1961):350.

8. *Kun Béla*, p. 541.

9. *Vos'moi S'ezd*, p. 435.

10. Pál Gisztl, "A moszkvai eszer lázadás leverése és a főposta visszafoglalása" [The defeat of the SR mutiny and the reconquest of the main Post Office in Moscow], *Hadtörténelmi Közlemények*, 1957, nos. 3-4, p. 182; István Pintér, "Riadó Moszkvában" [Alarm in Moscow], *Népszabadság*, 23 Oct. 1957, p. 3.

on November 4, 1918.[11] In short, during the time Béla Kun spent in Russia he was regarded as an able Communist organizer and entrusted with important positions. Available evidence indicates that he was well liked by the Bolshevik leaders especially Grigorii Zinoviev, Bukharin, Lenin, and Lenin's immediate family.[12]

The Communist party of Hungary at its inception in Moscow adopted a platform advocating action similar to that followed by the Bolsheviks in Russia. As Kun stated: "The one-year existence of the Russian dictatorship of the proletariat leaves no doubt that we must duplicate its course in Hungary."[13] Hence, alliance or collaboration with the Social Democratic party was impossible.[14] Like the demands of the Bolshevik party of Russia, the Hungarian Communists' "demands cannot even be satisfied by the most radical democracy, or by any kind of bourgeois power . . . the attainment of power (by Communists) is the only way to liberate the proletariat."[15]

The Hungarian willingness to adhere to the Bolshevik policies was further reinforced by the decision of the founders of the Hungarian Communist party in Moscow. The decision stated:

The [Communist Party of Hungary] accepts as its fundamental rules those of the Russian Communist Party. The [founding] meeting declares that until the Third International and the International Soviet Republic are constructed, the party recognizes as the representative of the international working class the Central Committee of the Russian Communist Party and subjugates itself in general political respects to the decisions and judgments of this body.[16]

11. Mrs. Sándor Gábor et al., eds., *A magyar munkásmozgalom történetének válogatott dokumentumai* [Selected documents from the history of the Hungarian labor movement] 6 vols. (Budapest: Szikra, Kossuth, 1956–64), 5:350 (hereafter cited as *MMTVD*); "A Kommunisták Magyarországi Pártjának előkészítése" [The preparation of the Communist party of Hungary], *Sarló és Kalapács*, 1932, no. 4, pp. 52–53; Rózsa Csonka and Ágnes Szabó, comps., *A magyar és a nemzetközi munkásmozgalom története* [The history of the Hungarian and international labor movements] (Budapest: Kossuth, 1963), p. 231.

12. At least this is the inference one may draw from the various recollections of Clara Zetkin and from Kun's letter of January 5, 1919, sent to Lenin in which Kun sends his warmest personal regard "to Nadezhda Konstantinovna and Maria Ilyichnina" (Lenin's wife and sister). *Kun Béla*, p. 132 and elsewhere. Also: Rudolf Tőkés, *Béla Kun and the Hungarian Soviet Republic* (New York: Praeger, 1967), p. 67.

13. *Kun Béla*, p. 133.

14. *MMTVD*, 5:35.

15. *Kun Béla*, p. 133. A few days earlier Kun had clearly denied the possibility of collaboration with the Social Democrats: "We Communist Bolsheviks are finished completely (eternally) with social democracy . . . that party is the party of democratic reaction today. . . ." *MMTVD*, 5:350. It is interesting to note that Lenin must have been worried about the possibility of cooperation between Communists and Socialists. In the middle of May, 1919, he asked Szamuely whether such a collaboration was possible. Szamuely assured Lenin that it was impossible, but Lenin was not very satisfied. "A KMP előkészítése," pp. 49–50. On Szamuely's trip see György Tamás, "Repülőgép a Kárpátok felett" [An airplane above the Carpathians], *Néphadsereg* [People's Army], 1958, no. 681, p. 3; Ervin Liptai, *A Magyar Tanácsköztársaság* [The Hungarian Soviet Republic] (Budapest: Kossuth, 1965), pp. 311–12.

16. *MMTVD*, 5:351.

In short, Béla Kun and the Hungarian Communist party members expected to go home and duplicate the course of the Russian Revolution. In Russia, Béla Kun assumed the role of a pedestrian Lenin, accepted the Bolshevik example, and promised to follow it upon his return to Hungary.

The proposition has often been advanced that Lenin's revolutionary strategy envisioned the Hungarian Bolshevik revolution as the next step in the crumbling of imperialism. Rudolf Tőkés correctly stated that Hungary was perhaps the "best potential host for the virus of social revolution."[17] While it is true that there were a great many similarities between prewar Hungary and prewar Russia,[18] and that these similarities did not go unnoticed by Lenin,[19] Lenin understood clearly that significant differences between Hungary and Russia also existed.[20]

Lenin and most of the Bolshevik leaders expected the revolution to break out in Germany, not in Hungary. Reading the pages of Russian Bolshevik papers gives one a feeling that, in comparison to Russian concern for Germany, other countries seemed secondary considerations. Until the establishment of the Kun regime, Hungarian events were given scant coverage and very little was said about non-German revolutionary movements. Further, the Bolsheviks dispatched Karl Radek to Germany to help with the establishment of a strong German Communist party while no Russian leader of comparable stature was sent to Hungary. Thus, it can be concluded, that the Russian Bolshevik leadership attempted to inject the "bacilli of Bolshevism" into the Hungarian political life through the return of pro-Bolshevik Hungarians held in Russia as prisoners of war. But it is unwarranted to say that the Russian leadership expected Hungary to be the second weak link in the chain of imperialism. They did not expect it to be the first country after Russia where a proletarian revolution would occur. Therefore, they merely sent advice and provided some limited financial support to the Hungarian Communists. In short, Béla Kun and the Hungarian Communists were not sent home with the expectation that they would be the next Communist group "to make a revolution."[21] The Bolsheviks envisioned Kun's task as establishing a strong Communist party organization which would be able to capture power *after* a successful German revolution.

The bulk of the Hungarian Communists (approximately 200 to 500 men) arrived in Hungary from Russia during the second and third weeks of November, 1918, and on November 20 or 24[22] after long, drawn out discussions and several compromises,

17. Tőkés, *Béla Kun*, p. 73.

18. Franz Borkenau, *The Communist International* (London: Faber and Faber, 1938), p. 108.

19. V. I. Lenin, *Polnoe Sobranie Sochinenii* [Complete Collection of Works], 55 vols. (Moscow: Izd. vo Pol. Lit.-ry, 1963), "Zhelezo v krestianskom koziaistve" [The iron in the peasant economy] (21 August 1913), 23:377–79.

20. Ibid. (16 July 1913), 23:339–45.

21. Herbert Hoover, *The Ordeal of Woodrow Wilson* (New York: McGraw-Hill, 1958), p. 135; Angelica Balabanoff, *My Life as a Rebel* (New York: Harper and Bros., 1958), p. 224; Borkenau, *The Communist International*, p. 114.

22. Irén Kun (Mrs. Béla Kun), *Kun Béla* [Béla Kun] (Budapest: Magvető, 1966), p. 102; Béla Kun, "Összehívjuk az alakuló gyűlést" [The convocation of the founding meeting], *Társadalmi Szemle* [Societal Review], 4, no. 11 (1958):96; Csonka and Szabó, *A Magyar*, pp. 99–100; Rezső Szaton, "A történelmi pillanat" [The historical moment], *Népszabadság*, 20 Nov. 1958, p. 6; Béla

the Communist party of Hungary was re-established in Budapest. In the beginning, membership in the party was very small. The central committee of the new party was composed⁻ of four different dissatisfied elements: (1) the former pro-Bolshevik prisoners of war, many of whom were members of the various Communist groups in Russia; (2) the Revolutionary Socialists who actively opposed the war and the bourgeois liberal government; (3) the left Social Democrats who opposed the coalition policy of the Social Democratic party; and (4) a group of engineers[23] who originally attempted to form their own party.

The Communist party of Hungary accepted a platform that basically followed that of the Russian Bolsheviks. But the situation facing the Hungarian Communists was vastly different from that confronting the Russian Bolsheviks. While in Russia Lenin was able to enforce the principle of democratic centralism within a tightly knit party that obeyed the orders of the central committee, Kun had to make compromises with the members of the party. The very composition of the central committee reveals that various views were represented on it. Only six of the eighteen-member central committee had been Communists in Russian captivity, the others were recent converts to communism from various opposition groups. It is true that in the beginning Kun succeeded in uniting the revolutionary groups which were opposed to the democratic coalition government, but it must also be noted that by joining them in a group Kun relaxed the iron discipline he learned from Lenin. Kun further compromised the principles of the Communist party by his recruitment policies. While Lenin and the Russian Communists were able to trust the rank and file of the party, the Hungarian Communists had to embark on a hasty recruitment policy which resulted in the acceptance of practically all comers, syndicalists and anarchists alike. As a result of this loose recruitment policy the Hungarian Communist party cannot be considered an effective centralized elite group or a vanguard, in any sense of the word. Unfortunately for Kun, discipline—a key ingredient of the Russian Bolshevik success—was weak, and often it was entirely missing.

The Hungarian Communists received some support from Moscow. The most notable form of this support was money which apparently was supplied relatively freely through the Russian Red Cross representatives in Budapest and Vienna.[24] Kun

---

Szántó, "Hogyan alakult meg a Kommunisták Magyarországi Pártja" [How was the Communist party of Hungary established], *Uj Március* [New March], March 1928, p. 160; Béla Fogarasi, "Viszszaemlékezések a Párt megalakulásának harcaira" [Recollections concerning the battle to establish the party], *Magyar Tudomány* [Hungarian Science], 1959, no. 1, p. 9; Jolán Kelen, "A Kommunisták Magyarországi Pártjának megalakulása" [The founding of the Communist party of Hungary], *Pártélet* [Party Life], Nov. 1958, p. 11; Aladár Mód, *400 Év Küzdelem az Önálló Magyarországért* [400 years of struggle for an independent Hungary] (Budapest: Szikra, 1954), p. 478; György Milei, "Mikor alakult meg a KMP?" [When was the CPH established?], *Párttörténeti Közlemények*, 1965, no. 2, pp. 121–41.

23. This small group originally followed the theories of Ernst Mach and believed itself to be superior to the proletariat; Gyula Hevesi, *Egy mérnök a forradalomban* [An engineer in the revolution] (Budapest: Európa, 1959; Kossuth, 1965), pp. 159–66; József Lengyel, *Visegrádi Utca* [Visegrádi Street] (Budapest: Kossuth, 1957), pp. 33–39.

24. The amount of financial support has never been determined. Vivian states that it was 120,000 pounds in dollars and bank notes or 40 million rubles: Charles Vivian, *Emperor Charles of Austria*

himself often asked Lenin to send him money.[25] He also established direct communication with Moscow through a secret telegraph, and it is presumed that practically daily he reported to Moscow.[26] This financial dependence, however, did not mean that Kun also was dependent on Moscow for advice.

It is clear that Kun sent a number of couriers to Lenin and that he asked for Sverdlov and Zinoviev to come to Hungary in January, 1919.[27] But it is improbable to believe that Lenin would take time out to give *daily* instructions to Kun. It is more reasonable to presume that in the early phases of the party's activities, Kun essentially operated within the framework of an agreed upon general policy. Thus, his goals were to attempt to split the Social Democratic party, as well as to infiltrate and control the trade-unions and the militia. In accomplishing these aims he probably was advised to follow the Bolshevik example, but in February, 1919, he clearly deviated from these policies and acted contrary to the advice of Lenin. In fact, he even received a letter from Lenin in which Lenin must have warned Kun against the idea of a premature *Putsch*. On January 5, 1919, in reply to this advice Kun wrote: "Please rest assured, I am taking care of the business . . . on a Marxist basis: there is no possibility of any sort of *putsch* . . . ."[28] Yet on February 5, 1919, exactly one month later, disregarding Lenin's admonition, the Hungarian Communist leadership began planning a coup.[29] They planned to follow the Spartacist example to topple the government, but hoped to do it "in a much better organized fashion."[30] As a probable result of this plan, a premature clash occurred a fortnight later between the Communists and the government. This example as well as others seem to prove that Béla Kun was not a particularly obedient servant of Moscow; even when he was advised not to attempt a coup he disregarded that advice and independently embarked on a course that was disastrous for his new party. His financial dependence on Moscow apparently did not require him to give up independent action.

(London: Grayson and Grayson, 1932), p. 199. The Tharaud brothers maintained that Kun had only 200,000 rubles: Jerome Tharaud and Jean Tharaud, *When Israel is King* (New York: McBride, 1924), p. 152. The *Current History Magazine* stated that Kun operated with 30 million rubles; see "Second Revolution in Hungary," *Current History Magazine* 10, pt. 2 (May 1919):288. Varying figures are quoted in David Cattell, "Soviet Russia and the Hungarian Revolution of 1919" (Master's thesis, Columbia University, 1949), p. 6; Pavel Miliukov, *Bolshevism* (London: Allen and Unwin, 1920); Hoover, *The Ordeal of Woodrow Wilson*, p. 135.

25. *Kun Béla*, p. 138.

26. Gerelyes, *Lenin*, p. 7. The Csepel telegraph office handled messages for the entire soviet government. It maintained contact not only with Moscow but also with the Ukrainian government in Kiev. The volume containing all the telegraphs sent to Moscow has been secured by László Réti and is now located in the Hungarian Party History Archives. Tibor Hajdu, *A Magyarországi Tanácsköztársaság* [The soviet republic of Hungary] (Budapest: Kossuth, 1969).

27. *Kun Béla*, p. 138, and Irén Kun, *Kun Béla*, p. 101, identify two of the couriers: Vladimir Urasov and Lajos Németi but there were at least two others. Tibor Szamuely flew to Kiev and Moscow on May 23, 1919, and tried to convince the Russian leaders to attack Rumania or Galicia. All these missions were quite spectacular but not successful. Soviet Russia was fighting for its own survival and could not be expected to give armed support to Soviet Hungary. Liptai, *A Magyar*, pp. 311–12.

28. *Kun Béla*, p. 138.

29. *MMTVD*, 5:500.

30. Ibid. For a discussion of the actual coup see *Pesti Hirlap*, 22 Feb. 1919.

As a result of the disastrous coup attempt the Communists suffered serious reverses and most of the Communist leaders, including Kun, were imprisoned, but by this time the Károlyi government was in serious difficulties. In March the Allied and associated powers presented increasing territorial demands which the government found itself unable to meet and remain in power. Hunger and dissatisfaction were widespread. The liberal government collapsed and the Socialists were given a chance to try to govern Hungary alone. The Social Democratic party, however, felt that it could not govern without the support of the Communist party. Hence, they approached Kun and the Communist leaders (who, incidentally, were still in prison as a result of the attempted coup in February) about the possibility of forming a coalition government. Béla Kun acted against the advice of many members of the central committee and on March 21, 1919, agreed to the establishment of the "dictatorship of the proletariat" in Hungary; thus, another "communist regime" came to power much to the discomfort of the Allies in Paris.[31]

The establishment of the Hungarian Soviet Republic was viewed by the negotiators in Paris as having been engineered by the Russian Bolsheviks. The Bolsheviks themselves did little to discourage this view. Lenin in discussing the creation of the Hungarian Soviet Republic alluded to the role played by Russia:

> Old people used to say: "Our children have grown up and become adults, we can die now." We are not preparing to die, we are moving toward victory, but when we see children, such as Hungary, where there is already Soviet power, then we [can] say, that we have done our share [of the work], not only in Russia but also in other nations. . . .[32]

However, one must not confuse Bolshevik rhetoric with Bolshevik activities. Besides training a small core of prisoners of war in Bolshevik agitator-schools, and supplying the Hungarian Communists with money and occasional advice which, as we have seen, frequently went unheeded, the role of the Russian Bolsheviks in the creation of the Hungarian Soviet Republic was minimal. The fact that the Russian Soviet armies were near the Carpathians, around Tarnopol, posed a threat to the Allies and to Count Károlyi's foreign policy, but the collapse of the Károlyi regime was not due to Russian machinations.[33]

A vast difference existed between the Bolshevik revolution of 1917 and the March revolution of 1919 in Hungary. In the first instance a determined party captured power without help from the Socialists, without support from any other major party, and without sharing its power with any major party; but the Hungarian Communist party, from the outset, was weakened by compromise and factionalism. In Russia, the Bolsheviks took power as a result of an armed uprising but the Hungarian Soviet

31. Harold Nicolson, *Peacemaking, 1919* (New York: Grosset and Dunlap, 1965), p. 287.

32. Lenin, *Polnoe Sobranie*, 23:262.

33. The dismal outlook on the joining of the two Soviet armies is faithfully recorded by Vilmos Böhm, in *Két forradalom tüzében* [In the cross fire of two revolutions] (Vienna: Bécsi Magyar Kiadó, 1923), pp. 346-47.

Republic was established as a peaceful coalition between the Socialists and the Communists. The Hungarian regime imitated Soviet Russia by calling itself a soviet republic, but it was different from the Russian regime in many respects. In Hungary the Communists did not even have a majority in the government![34] Furthermore, the existence of the government was based on the possibility of cooperation between the Social Democratic and Communist parties. The hated enemies of the Communists overnight became comrades, and the two parties were unified into one. While Lenin insisted on completely separating the Socialists from the Communists even in name, Kun agreed to the exact opposite: he agreed to the unification of the two parties and accepted the name, Socialist party of Hungary. Instead of keeping his party intact, Kun dissolved his party, accepted power and became the leading exponent of the new government as the commissar for foreign affairs. Kun, the opportunist, defied Lenin's example and became a part of a Socialist-Communist government.

Needless to say, after the establishment of the Hungarian Soviet Republic, Lenin was extremely skeptical about such an easy acquisition of power.[35] At first he did not even believe that Kun succeeded in gaining power and Kun had to prove his identity to Lenin on the telegraph.[36] On March 23 he asked Kun to explain what "concrete guarantees" Kun had that the "new Hungarian government is really Communist and not simply Socialist, i.e., social-traitor."[37] He agreed that "under the special circumstances of the Hungarian revolution it would be a mistake to merely follow the Russian tactics in every respect."[38] But he wanted to know whether the Communists had a majority in the government and wished to find out what was meant by Kun when he said that the Socialists accepted the dictatorship of the proletariat.[39] Kun apparently succeeded in dispelling all of Lenin's doubts by April 2, 1919;[40] nonetheless, it was clear that the Hungarian government at best could be labelled socialist. Therefore, the traditional view of the Hungarian Soviet Republic as a communist government is not essentially correct.

If Kun was Lenin's obedient servant, Lenin's foreign and domestic policies ought to have served him as a model. In the area of foreign affairs Kun was present in Russia during the first year of Soviet rule, where he had ample chance to observe Lenin's policies from an excellent vantage point. It seems, however, that Kun's own position of power blinded him and he was unable to realize that he needed to duplicate Lenin's successful foreign policy. When the Allies sent the mission headed by General Jan. C.

34. Of the thirty-three peoples' commissars and deputy peoples' commissars only fourteen were Communists, while the rest were mostly Social Democrats and a few were from former liberal parties. The Communists composed of 42.4 percent of the total number of peoples' commissars, but only two of them (16.6 percent of the total) were full rather than deputy peoples' commissars.

35. Irén Kun, *Kun Béla*, p. 145: Kun himself expressed some misgivings, but he was unable to see where he went wrong.

36. Lengyel, *Visegrádi utca*, pp. 151–52.

37. Lenin, *Polnoe Sobranie*, 38:217.

38. Ibid.

39. Ibid.

40. *MMTVD*, 6A:63; Lenin, *Polnoe Sobranie*, 38:260; *Vos'moi S'ezd*, p. 434.

Smuts to Budapest to negotiate a possible peace with the Hungarian Communists, Kun rejected the proposals advanced by the mission.[41]

This rejection amounted to a refusal to accept a Hungarian version of the Brest Litovsk treaty and insured that Allied hostility would continue unmollified.[42] According to both Harold Nicolson and Vilmos Böhm, Kun was the strongest opponent of the Smuts proposals, for he thought that after only a few days existence "the young Soviet Republic could not afford a treaty of Brest-Litovsk." Further, Kun indicated that an acceptance of the Smuts recommendation would also "mean a break with Russia and a serious crises for the revolution."[43] It seems that Kun utilized his personal position and his weight with Moscow as a threat to convert his colleagues to his position, but there is no evidence that Moscow had any direct role in these negotiations.

In another instance Kun again acted contrary to Lenin's advice concerning foreign policy. On June 18, 1919, Lenin sent an admonition to Kun urging him to negotiate with the Allies, asking him to

> make the fullest possible use of every opportunity to obtain a temporary armistice or peace, in order to give the people a breathing spell. But do not trust the Entente powers for a moment. They are deceiving you, and are only attempting to gain time in order to be able to crush you and us.[44]

Kun's reply emphasized that he considered himself to be "more aware" than Lenin concerning the "*mala fides*" of the Allies,[45] yet Kun did *not* attempt to make every possible move to negotiate even for a breathing spell. His colleagues charged him with inconclusiveness and accused him of withholding, even from his own central committee,[46] information and advice from Lenin. Kun apparently felt that he was better equipped to deal with the situation in Hungary than Lenin would have

41. Nicolson, *Peacemaking, 1919*, pp. 295-305. It is difficult to realize to the full extent the haughty attitude expressed by the behavior of the Smuts mission. From a fifty-year perspective Kun's position seems to have been justified perhaps, for there is very little doubt about the insincerity of the offer. For Communist interpretations of the Smuts mission cf: Zsuzsa L. Nagy, "A párizsi békekonferencia és az 1918-1919 évi magyarországi forradalmak" [The Paris Peace Conference and the revolutions of 1918-1919 in Hungary], *Élet és Tudomány*, 1964, no. 26, pp. 1235-39; Nagy, *A párizsi békekonferencia és Magyarország, 1918-1919* [The Paris Peace Conference and Hungary, 1918-1919] (Budapest: Kossuth, 1965). The best English language work to date is Alfred D. Low's *The Soviet Hungarian Republic and the Paris Peace Conference, Transactions of the American Philosophical Society*, n.s., Vol. 53, pt. 10 (Philadelphia, 1963).

42. *Vörös Ujság*, 7 April 1919.

43. Böhm, *Két forradalom tüzében*, pp. 284-85.

44. U.S., Department of State, *Papers Relating to the Foreign Relations of the United States: The Paris Peace Conference*, 13 vols. (Washington: Government Printing Office, 1946), 7:22.

45. *Kun Béla*, p. 280.

46. On specific charges and official denial of their validity cf: *Taktik der Kommunistischen Internationale gegen die Offensive des Kapitals: Bericht über die Konferenz der Erweiterten Exekutive der K. I., Moskau vom 24 Februar bis 4 Marz. 1922* (Hamburg: C. Hoym, 1922); *Bericht über die Tätigkeit der Präsidiums und der Exekutive der Kommunistischen Internationale durch die Zeit vom 6 Marz bis 11 Juni, 1922* (Hamburg: Kommunistischen Internationale, 1922). For the factional charges see the works of Henrik Ungár, Ernő Bettelheim, László Rudas, and others published in Vienna in 1921 and 1922.

been. He refused to follow a course which was more conciliatory toward the Allies and might have resulted in an armistice.[47] Once more, although Kun paid lip service to Lenin's advice, he acted contrary to it.

In domestic affairs Kun followed policies even more clearly contrary to those of Lenin than were his foreign policies. It has been noted earlier that the very creation of the soviet republic, through the formation of a coalition government with the Socialists, had been viewed by Lenin with misgivings. Unlike the Communists in Russia the Communists of Hungary comprised a minority in the new "soviet" government. Although Kun's position was dominant in the government as far as foreign affairs was concerned, almost all the domestic policies were dictated by Socialists rather than Communists.

The unification of the two parties was certainly the greatest difference between the Russian and Hungarian circumstances in matters of strategy and it insured a watering down of the Hungarian Communist party structure, party principles, and party discipline. The misgivings expressed by the Communist International on the truly Communist nature of the newly founded Socialist party of Hungary were explicit. They strongly recommended that the party adopt the name Communist party, for it was "necessary that the name of your party should correspond in everything to your program and fight."[48]

The matter of the name of the party came up once more and signified little change from the previous situation. During the first party congress on June 12 and 13, 1919, the name of the party was slightly altered as a compromise measure, and it became Socialist-Communist Workers' party of Hungary. But this concession was not what the executive committee of the Communist International demanded. The Comintern executive committee wanted to have the party renamed the United Communist party of Hungary.[49] Yet, the leaders of the Communists in Hungary were not even sufficiently strong to carry through this requested change, and Kun accepted rather willingly a compromise measure, much to the disgust of the left-wing faction of Communists.[50]

Another area in which the Hungarian regime significantly differed from the Russian was in matters of enforcing the power of the government. In Hungary the Socialists theoretically accepted the need for the dictatorship, but it became evident very soon that the interpretation of the term depended upon whether Socialists or Communists did the interpreting.

The Socialists, led by Zsigmond Kunfi, objected vigorously to the indiscriminate use of coercion especially as it was supposed to be applied in the sphere of art, litera-

47. There is considerable doubt whether any conciliatory attempts would have been of value in view of the Allied extremists' determined efforts to topple Kun. Notably Balfour and the right wing of the French military planners wanted to overthrow Kun at any price. Hoover and many of his associates joined this group. Hoover, *The Ordeal of Woodrow Wilson*, p. 135, and Thomas C. Gregory, "Overthrowing a Red Regime," *World's Work*, June 1921, pp. 152–64.

48. *MMTVD*, 6A:16, 17.

49. Ibid., 6B:8.

50. László Rudas, "Lényeg és forma" [Essence and form], *Internacionálé* [International], 15 June 1919, pp. 1–6.

ture, and cultural freedom in general.[51] The Communist left wing insisted on undertaking what they considered necessarily stringent measures needed against the *bourgeoisie*. Tibor Szamuely, Mátyás Rákosi, and even József Pogány complained about the restrictions placed on them in enforcing the rule of the proletariat.[52] But the question of the methods used to enforce the proletarian dictatorship was settled amicably.

Although the party congress in theory insisted on the greater use of terror to combat opponents of the government, realistically speaking no organization comparable to the Cheka operated in Hungary. Indeed, perhaps one may attribute the two well-organized internal rebellions against the soviet republic during the last fifty days of the existence of the soviet regime to the the lack of such an extraordinary commission. In this case, too, Kun failed to follow the Leninist example and, as György Lukács bitterly remarked, was "forced to accept continuous compromises in the interest of the great goal [of socialism]."[53]

In the issue of land reform Kun also deviated from the Bolshevik example and from Lenin's advice. Lenin realized that the peasants had to be won over to the Bolshevik side and hence ordered agrarian reform, giving lands to the peasants. He realized that it was a necessity and, inefficient as that measure was for the state, he did it for political reasons. Kun was not satisfied with a Leninist land policy. In the first proclamation of the regime it was clearly stated that the peasant's lands would be socialized and cooperatives would be established.[54] This policy doomed the relationship between the new workers' regime and the countryside. The peasantry's hopes for land reform vanished and the farmers refused to sell food to the slowly starving cities. Outbreaks of violence were daily occurrences in the countryside, and the Hungarian peasantry contributed greatly to the fall of the soviet regime.

Kun and other Hungarian Communists vigorously implemented the measures of "war-communism" which Lenin so despised. Unlike Lenin, Kun went beyond the possible in enforcing these measures. Mátyás Rákosi, Kun's deputy peoples' commissar for commerce, expropriated all the small private businesses, abolished all private property from bathtubs to water-tank factories, and nationalized all the means of production. An order was published closing all stores and factories with the exception of grocery stores, apothecary shops, and tobacconists. Anyone who disobeyed the order was threatened with the death penalty.[55] Although this decree was revoked soon after its publication, the damage was done. As Franz Borkenau concluded,

> Private commerce had been frightened away and never returned: the more so as persecution continued. The new rulers seemed to think that it was an important task of socialism to nationalize children's sweetmeats and barbers' perfumes.[56]

51. *MMTVD*, 6B:22-27.
52. Ibid., p. 35.
53. Ibid., p. 227.
54. Ibid., 6A:3.
55. Ibid., pp. 28-29.
56. Borkenau, *The Communist International*, p. 120.

Although there are a multitude of instances in which Kun failed to follow Lenin's policies and examples, the cases cited make it amply evident that Kun's policies during the 133 days of the Hungarian Soviet Republic were independent of Lenin and the Russian Bolsheviks. The reasons for which Kun ignored Lenin's direction were manifold. The realities of the Hungarian situation—it seemed to Kun—did not allow a blind following of Russian theories. Perhaps he also felt that for Hungary his policies were superior to those of Lenin. But whatever the reasons, it is sufficiently clear that Kun was not the so-called obedient servant of Lenin and that the Hungarian dictatorship was not an extension of the Russian Bolshevik revolution. In fact, in retrospect it may be clear that Kun's regime was the first to apply the principles of national socialism, or national communism. The Hungarian Soviet Republic was a Hungarian experiment with much needed social and political reform.

In the past, historians of both pro- and anti-Communist persuasion probably have made a basic misappraisal of the Hungarian Soviet Republic. One group emphasized the progressive nature of the republic and attributed it to the progressive rule of the Communists. The other view emphasized the terroristic aspects of the dictatorship and its connection with an alleged Communist "blueprint for world conquest." It now seems that both of these schools were wrong in their appraisal of the Hungarian Soviet Republic. The Hungarian soviet was, first, a national revolt against the difficulties and the hopelessness of Hungary's situation in March, 1919. Secondly, it was a long-overdue experiment in social reform in a country where reform was badly needed. Thirdly, it was an experiment in coalition politics between the Communists and the Socialists. It is a tragedy for the Hungarian labor movement that neither the national revolt, the reforms, nor the coalition attempts succeeded.

Béla Kun: The Man and the Revolutionary

Rudolf L. Tőkés

According to his application for readmission to membership in the Russian Communist party, Béla Kun was born in 1886 of a bourgeois family. He was a lawyer by profession, who spoke and wrote Russian and German. He had been a member of the Hungarian Social Democratic party since 1902. He had previously served in the Austro-Hungarian army, in the Red Guard and in the Red Army in the Urals, and in the Ukraine in 1918 and 1920. As he stated, he had originally joined the Russian Communist party in Tomsk "before June 1916." Since 1917 as a member of the Tomsk city party committee, Kun had worked as a propagandist and journalist (March–October, 1917), and after the October revolution as a correspondent of *Pravda* and editor of *Szociális Forradalom*. In 1918 he was the founder and chairman of the Communist party of Hungary, later a member of the Communist parties of Austria and Germany and of the Presidium and the executive committee of the Communist International, and (most recently), a special emissary of the Communist International in Germany.[1]

By any contemporary standard, these were impressive credentials worthy of an accomplished professional Communist revolutionary with considerable experience on the various battlefields of international class struggle. In 1921, at any rate, Béla Kun certainly seemed like a man who had earned his place on the "general staff" of the world revolution. The same man was arrested sixteen years later, in early June, 1937, on charges of subversive deviationist activities, Trotskyism, and an alleged record of treasonable conduct in the Communist International.[2] He was executed in November, 1939.[3] In February, 1956, during the Twentieth Congress of the CPSU [Communist Party of the Soviet Union], Kun was declared to be a victim of Stalin's cult of per-

Research on which this study is based has been supported by an American Council of Learned Societies–Social Science Research Council Faculty Research Grant. The staff of the Department of Government, Wesleyan University, and of the Research Institute on Government Affairs, Columbia University, contributed clerical and research assistance. Also, I wish to thank Professors István Deák (Columbia University), Nathanael Greene, and Fred I. Greenstein (Wesleyan University) for their comments on an earlier version of this study.

1. Irén Kun (Mrs. Béla Kun), *Kun Béla* (*Emlékezések*) [Béla Kun (Memoirs)] (Budapest: Magvető, 1966), pp. 53–54 (hereafter cited as *Kun Memoirs*).

2. Cf., "Tizenkilenc év távlatából. . . . A magyar kommün tanulságai" [From a distance of nineteen years. . . . The lessons of the Hungarian commune] *Szabad Szó* [Free Word] (Paris) 3, no. 13 (26 March 1938):5–8; and Sándor Poll, "Fasizmus és demokrácia harca Magyarországon" [Struggle of fascism and democracy in Hungary] *Szabad Szó* (Paris) 2, no. 45 (6 Nov. 1937):1, 5.

3. Ferenc Münnich "Előszó" [Foreword] to *Kun Béla a Magyar Tanácsköztársaságról* [Béla Kun on the Hungarian Soviet Republic] (Budapest: Kossuth, 1958), p. 31. The fourth Russian edition of

sonality and an unjustly maligned hero of the international working-class movement.[4]

Since this belated act of political rehabilitation, Kun's widow and surviving friends have attempted to rescue Kun from political oblivion and establish him as the greatest figure in Hungarian Communist history.[5] In this process, efforts have been made to picture Kun as a Hungarian Lenin and a counterpart of the exiled patriot Lajos Kossuth. As the embodiment of such revolutionary and patriotic traditions, Kun has been called an ideological forerunner of the Hungarian party's post-1956 policies of de-Stalinization, internal consolidation, and democratization of public life.

Notwithstanding—and perhaps because of—these claims, the rescue operation is still far from complete. Kun's surviving factional opponents, their children and families, and the native wing of the party have been successful thus far in preventing the publication of classified party documents which might exonerate him from past accusations of political ineptitude as the leader of the underground Communist party and a major figure in the Communist International.

On the other hand, Kun's friends have seen to it that no additional information is published that could tarnish Kun's painstakingly restored political credentials. As a result, this study will be based on incomplete documentary evidence of uneven quality on the career of Béla Kun; hence the tentative nature of some of our arguments and conclusions about Béla Kun's personality and politics, especially after 1921.

The purpose of this study is fivefold. It seeks: (1) to contribute to the growing literature of Communist revolutionary elites by presenting a documented biographical profile of Béla Kun, the man and the revolutionary; (2) to challenge and modify traditional interpretations concerning the personality and intellectual motivations of Béla Kun in selected periods of his career; (3) to offer new evidence and partial reinterpretation on the Comintern background and Béla Kun's role in the German "March action" of 1921; (4) to suggest, through the example of Béla Kun, a tentative analytic framework for the study of the behavior of non-Russian Comintern elites in Moscow in the 1920s and during the Great Purges; (5) to evaluate on the basis of biographic data thus presented, the nature, especially the psychological motivating factors of Béla Kun's revolutionary personality and politics.

For the purposes of this reassessment Kun's career will be divided into five periods each corresponding to a distinct stage of his political and intellectual development. In order to avoid duplicating any material presented in the preceding essays, this study will not consider Kun's activities in the period between October, 1918 and August, 1919.

The Provincial Radical: Adolescence and Political Action (1902–17)

Béla Kun was born in the small Transylvanian village of Lele (population 750) in the Szilágycsehi District, Szilágy County on February 20, 1886. As the oldest of three

Lenin's *Works* (Moscow: Progress Publishers, 1950–1966) 40 vols., identified Kun as "a traitor to the cause of communism"; see 29:537.

4. E. Varga, "The Seventieth Anniversary of the Birthday of Béla Kun," *Pravda*, 21 Feb. 1956.
5. It took eight years for the Russians to completely rehabilitate Kun. Cf., *New York Times*, 21 March and 6 May 1967.

children (his sister, Irén, later became a seamstress and his brother, Sándor, a farm manager in the Soviet Union),[6] it was the young boy's responsibility to accompany his father to the nearest town to sell a few sacks of cereal to supplement the old Kun's meager salary as village notary. Although the Kuns (at least the father) were Jewish, there is no evidence that the family actually observed any Judaic laws or customs. At the age of thirteen Kun was said to have participated in the traditional *bar mitzvah* ceremony[7] but later never followed the cultural or philosophical traditions of the Jewish faith. Several factors militated against the development of the young Kun's sense of Jewishness and Jewish intellectual identity: his Kossuth-idolizing father's coarse radicalism; the nonconformist traditions of Transylvania; his partly Calvinistic schooling, and the predominantly freethinker provincial intelligentsia among whom Kun received his first lessons in politics and philosophy; and especially the obsessive assimilationist urge of lower-middle-class Jews at the turn of the century.

The elder Kun was a drunkard who mercilessly beat his children and a trouble-maker who got into all kinds of difficulties with the law and its local representatives, the village landlord and the gendarmerie.[8] The memoirs of Béla Kun's wife suggest that these childhood memories of cruel beatings by his alcoholic, boorish peasant father later compelled Kun to foreswear alcohol beyond the social necessities and to oppose punishment of children.[9]

After graduating from the one-room village grade school Kun entered the famous Calvinist *kollégium* (boarding school) in Zilah. Because of the boy's inadequate academic background, an older student by the name of Endre Ady was hired to tutor him.[10] Throughout his school years, the Kun family continued to live in poverty: the father proved to be a luckless dilettante both in his get-rich-quick schemes and in holding down a better paying job, while the mother, anxious to contribute her last penny to her favorite son's education, stayed in the family's rented flat for want of warm clothing during the winter months.

Kun, as his widow delicately puts it, was a "problem child" in school. He tended to rebel against any kind of discipline and had great difficulties with his science and German language courses. On the other hand, literature, particularly patriotic poetry and folk ballads, greatly interested the young boy. One is impressed by the romantic Populist imagery of the seventeen-year-old Kun's essay on the spirit of his native Transylvania and its people:

the tiny Székely nation, surrounded by mountains and isolated from, though not behind the outside world lives by . . . [and is] . . . devoted to its traditions . . . yet it is sensitive to the new ideas and incorporates them into its spiritual world. [These

6. *Kun Memoirs*, p. 91 n.

7. Géza Herczeg, *Béla Kun, eine Historische Grimasse* (Berlin: Verlag für Kulturpolitik, 1928), p. 8.

8. *Kun Memoirs*, pp. 7–8.

9. Ibid., p. 9.

10. Ady was the greatest twentieth-century Hungarian poet. Later on Kun was aware of and possibly influenced by Ady's political journalism rather than by his poetry which must have appeared too cosmopolitan for Kun's patriotic and rustic literary tastes. Cf. *Kun Memoirs*, p. 9, and László Gellért, "Kun Béla diákkorából" [Béla Kun: The student years] *Köznevelés*, 7 March 1961.

two tendencies are] like a placid lake . . . capable of producing giant waves in a storm and a gaily flowing clear river which mirrors the constant changes of the passing scenery.[11]

The transition from a schoolboy's local patriotism to a more universal concept of nationalism was facilitated by his discovery of Sándor Petőfi's lyric and patriotic poetry.[12] Petőfi, the impulsive literary genius who died by a Cossack dagger, like Lord Byron for a Victorian schoolboy, or Pushkin or Lermontov for Russian students in the 1880s, became Kun's lifetime hero and his most lasting intellectual and emotional tie to his native country. He seemed to have been greatly influenced by Petőfi's personal dynamism and political activism. The conclusions of Kun's prize-winning essay (written as a graduating senior in Gymnasium) on Petőfi's patriotic poetry tend to reinforce this impression:

The storming rage of Petőfi's soul . . . turned against the privileged classes, against the people's oppressor . . . and confronted them with revolutionary abandon. Petőfi felt that the country would not be saved through moderation but through the use of the most extreme means available. He detested even the thought of cowardice. . . .
    Petőfi's vision was correct. There is no room for prudence in revolutions whose fate and eventual success is always decided by boldness and raw courage . . . this is why Petőfi condemned his compatriots for the sin of opportunism and hesitation [when] faced with the great problems of their age. . . . Petőfi's works must be regarded as the law of the Hungarian soul . . . [and of the] . . . love of country.[13]

In pre-World War I Hungary a Gymnasium degree invariably entitled its holder to some kind of white-collar position, most often in the state or county bureaucracy. For Jews, however, there were relatively few openings in government administration and political appointments were difficult to come by. Commerce, the "free professions," medicine, law, journalism, and the arts, while lacking the security of a civil service sinecure, were quite open to all, including Jews and Magyarized nationalities.[14] The Kun family, therefore, acted most reasonably when sending the promising young man to the law school of the University of Kolozsvár to obtain his *doctor utriusque juris* degree and, with it, economic security and established middle-class status. For reasons still not explained by Kun's biographers, he left the school after a semester and apparently drifted for a year. In 1905 he found part-time employment as a clerk at the local Workers' Insurance Bureau and an unpaid position as an apprentice

11. *Kun Memoirs*, p. 14.
12. Sándor Petőfi (1823–49).
13. *Kun Memoirs*, p. 13–16.
14. Zoltán Horváth, *Magyar századforduló. A második reformnemzedék története, 1896–1914 [Fin de siècle in Hungary: The history of the second reform generation, 1896–1914]* (Budapest: Gondolat, 1961).

reporter at a newspaper.[15] In 1906 Kun left for Nagyvárad, where he joined the radical daily *Szabadság* as a full-time reporter.

When not engaged in news gathering in the city hall, in coffeehouses or in the courtroom, Kun enjoyed visiting trade-union halls and meeting socialist workers and organizers there. As a professed freethinker and possibly a member of the local Masonic lodge he considered it his duty to contribute to the organized worker's educational programs and to aid their political and strike activities to the best of his abilities.[16]

While it seems quite improbable that Kun actually joined the Hungarian Social Democratic party in 1902 at the age of sixteen,[17] as Kun asserted in 1921, we may assume that by 1906 he was acquainted with some of the city's labor leaders and socialist organizers, both as a former part-time employee of the insurance bureau and as a journalist sympathetic to the aspirations of the much harassed socialist trade-unionists.

The available record on Kun's political journalism during the years of 1905-7 offers several clues to his intellectual development and the range and direction of his political activism. In these years Kun successfully mastered his craft and became a competent journalist. He developed a lively written style, a sharp eye for detail and journalistic "angles" and an immediate grasp of the social and political implications of the story involved.[18] In retrospect his political writings appear as unduly exaggerated efforts to promote his employers' party preferences which in the case of the *Kolozsvári Friss Ujság*, meant the opposition "Forty-eight" or Independence party. This party gave up many of its radical nationalist slogans when it took power in 1906 and Kun was compelled to shift to other targets such as the People's (Catholic) party, the local clergy, and the inefficient city bureaucracy. This reorientation from national to local issues won him a certain amount of notoriety as an *enfant terrible* who walked where his less audacious and more experienced colleagues feared to tread. The young reporter's general appearance and dashing attire (he sported a wide-brimmed black hat, red silk scarf, and a fresh flower in the buttonhole) marked him as a habitué of the mirror-lined New York coffeehouse where the intelligentsia rubbed elbows with card-playing local merchants, drinking politicians, and swaggering Hussar officers.

Although Kun's journalistic reputation opened many doors for the ambitious young man, he never gained full acceptance as one of Kolozsvár's and later Nagyvárad's public figures. The causes of Kun's subsequent estrangement from the con-

---

15. Tamás Dersi, "Kun Béla mint szinikritikus" [Béla Kun as a theatre critic], *Napjaink* [Our Days], 1 Sept. 1966.

16. Active involvement in workers' evening seminars and study groups by radical intellectuals in the provinces became quite fashionable after the Free School of Social Sciences was launched by the radical philosopher Oszkár Jászi and his twentieth-century group in the fall of 1906. Cf. my *Béla Kun and the Hungarian Soviet Republic* (New York: Praeger, 1967), pp. 18-21.

17. According to his daughter, Kun "joined the workers' movement in 1912." István Regős, "Nyolcvan éve született Kun Béla. Beszélgetes Kun Ágnessel" [Béla Kun was born eighty years ago. A conversation with Ágnes Kun], *Dolgozók Lapja* [Workers Paper], 20 Feb. 1966.

18. Cf. Tamás Dersi, *A publicista Kun Béla* [Béla Kun the journalist] (Budapest: Magvető, 1969). See also, Nándor Hegedüs, "Kun Béla mint fiatal ujságiró" [Béla Kun as young journalist], *Magyar Nemzet* [Hungarian Nation], 19 March 1961.

temporary Hungarian society and politics, however, went beyond his occupation, and his somewhat left-of-center politics. By virtue of being a Transylvanian intellectual —deeply attached to the values of the land of his birth—Kun, like Endre Ady, remained alienated from the mainstream of Hungary's intellectual life; but unlike Ady, Kun did not have the opportunity before the war to transcend his provincial horizons and establish his own intellectual identity beyond that of a provincial radical. Contemporaries describe Kun as a headstrong, intensely vain, aggressive young man-about-town bent on seeking out and demolishing the reputation of authority figures, while at the same time hoping and practically demanding to be accepted as one of the local notables. In view of these conflicting ambitions, Kun's fragile ego and frequent outbursts of violent temper became distinct liabilities in the larger-than-life, semitheatrical world of provincial journalism. He was addicted to extreme epithets in his political columns and to violent language as a regularly featured speaker for Socialist and trade-union groups.[19] Whether posing as a chivalrous defender of a young Socialist woman agitator and reporter, whose honor had been impugned by a yellow journalist, or "obtaining satisfaction" by physically assaulting the editor of a competing newspaper for a malicious remark, Kun was always on the alert for all would-be personal or political adversaries.[20]

Lacking a professional degree, family connections, and money, Kun was forced to start his career on the lowest rung of the middle-class social ladder. Therefore his rise at the age of eighteen from cub reporter to editor of an afternoon tabloid at twenty is all the more remarkable and attests to Kun's singleminded determination to take full advantage of all opportunities society offered to an ambitious and hard-working young man.

From the conflicting evidence offered by Kun's enemies and official biographers it is difficult to determine exactly what he did between 1907 and 1912.[21] Some sources suggest that he was imprisoned once or twice for militant socialist agitation and inciting to riot during this period. On the other hand, his widow's memoirs and recent Communist literature, including the 700-page documentary history of the Hungarian working-class movement between 1907 and 1914, are strangely reticent on this matter and offer no hints concerning Kun's activities in these formative years. We do know, however, that Kun attempted to join the staff of the Social Democratic daily *Népszava* but his application was turned down by the editor, Ernő Garami.[22]

19. Dersi, *A publicista*, passim.
20. Hegedüs, "Kun Béla."
21. According to Iván Völgyes, after a brief stay in Budapest, Kun returned to Transylvania first to Nagyvárad, then to Kolozsvár where he again took up journalism and joined a small literary society. Cf. Iván Völgyes "Communism Comes to Hungary: An Examination of Some Causes Leading to the Establishment of the Hungarian Soviet Republic" (Ph.D. diss., American University, 1968), pp. 375–76. Dersi, however, maintains that Kun's journalistic career in Hungary came to an end in 1907. Dersi, *A publicista*, p. 168.
22. Ernő Garami, *Forrongó Magyarország* [Revolutionary Hungary] (Leipzig-Vienna: Pegazus, 1922), p. 122. See also, Vántus, "A Népszava szerkesztőségében" [In the editorial offices of *Népszava*], in Borbála Szerémi, ed., *Nagy idők tanui emlékeznek* [Heroic times remembered] (Budapest: Kossuth, 1959), pp. 82–86.

Sometime in early 1910 Kun found employment as a clerk in the Kolozsvár office of the Workers' Insurance Bureau. It was about this time that Kun met his future wife, Irén Gál. Judging from a photograph taken a few years later, she was an attractive young woman—well worth the obstacles Kun had to overcome to marry her. When the suitor approached Irén's father for his permission to marry her, the father refused him on grounds of his apparent inability to provide for his wife and future family from the meager salary of a junior clerk at some socialist organization. To make matters worse, the girl was shipped to her parents' home to "forget Béla Kun." Kun chose to abide by Gál's petty bourgeois standards and set out to establish himself as a financially sound, respectable middle-class citizen worthy of Irén Gál's hand.

Within three years, Kun rose from a lowly clerk to the deputy managing director of the Workers' Insurance Bureau and also became a founder and board member of the Kolozsvár Workers' Building Cooperative Society—a distinctly reformist organization even by standards of the reformist Hungarian Socialist party. As a member of the city's Socialist hierarchy, Kun was elected as a delegate to the 1913 congress of the Hungarian Social Democratic party. There he delivered two short speeches, one critical of the party daily's alleged neglect of rural propaganda, the other mildly disapproving of the party leadership's conduct during a recent political crisis.[23]

Following his marriage in 1913, Kun was promoted to managing director of the insurance bureau and was well on his way to becoming a pillar of his community and a respectable supporter of his political party. Indeed, it seemed that Kun was ready to settle down to a tranquil routine of a trade-union bureaucrat: work in his office, lectures in trade-union halls, campaign speeches on behalf of Socialist candidates, and occasional articles for the Socialist press.[24]

In his spare time Kun became familiar with the writings of Franz Mehring, Ferdinand Lassalle, Marx, Engels, August Bebel, and perhaps those of Eduard Bernstein and Karl Kautsky as well. It seems almost certain that Kun was unaware of the activities and the literature of the Russian social democracy and that he had never heard of Lenin during these years.

By temperament and inclination, Kun was an activist who, then and certainly later, was unable to perceive and act on ideologies more esoteric than some of the more explicit tactical prescriptions contained in Marx's writings. *The Communist Manifesto, Civil War in France, Introduction to the Critique of Political Economy, Critique of the Gotha Program*, and a few popular tracts by Engels and Bebel were about all that the future leader of the Hungarian Soviet Republic could absorb and utilize in the course of his daily activities as a provincial Socialist bureaucrat and occasional political orator.[25]

23. Erényi Tibor et al., eds., *A magyar munkásmozgalom történetének válogatott dokumentumai* [Selected documents on the history of Hungarian labor movements] 6 vols. (Budapest: Kossuth, 1966), 4A:651–52.

24. It was alleged that Kun embezzled 300 crowns, and as a result, was demoted from his high post to that of a clerk in the bureau. Cf. Völgyes, "Communism comes to Hungary," p. 379.

25. This is not to suggest that Kun's ideological preparedness was in any way inferior to that of a middle echelon socialist organizer or of an average provincial journalist. Rather it is to emphasize that Kun was a "doer" and not a "thinker" on a level that clearly disqualified him from contributing to any of the debates on matters of Marxist theory and contemporary socialist philosophy.

Adventurer-Revolutionary: From Tomsk to Budapest (1916–18)

When the war broke out, Kun enlisted in the army and joined a reserve officers' training school for Gymnasium graduates. First as a cadet sergeant, and later as a reserve lieutenant, Kun served for fifteen months on the Russian front. In early 1916, he was taken prisoner during the Russian breakthrough in Galicia and was shipped to a prisoner-of-war camp in Tomsk in May or June of that year. To overcome the enforced idleness and boredom of camp life, Kun and several other junior officers formed a Marxist reading and discussion group essentially on the pattern of self-improvement study circles that flourished in such prisoner-of-war compounds in the fall of 1916. By early the next year Kun and his colleagues, many of whom were to become leaders of Bolshevik-sponsored prisoner-of-war movements in Russia and key Communist participants in the soviet republic in Hungary, established contacts with both (Bolshevik and Menshevik) factions of the Russian socialists.[26] It was at this point that Béla Kun's Russian revolutionary career began.

Rather than retracing Kun's activities prior to his return to Hungary, described elsewhere in some detail,[27] it seems more profitable at this juncture to explore the impact of the Russian Revolution on the development of Kun's political ideas, with special reference to his prediction of the impact of the Russian events on the proletariat and impoverished petty *bougeoisie* of Europe.

Between April, 1917, and November, 1918, Kun published over twenty articles and news commentaries in *Sibirskii Rabochii* (Tomsk) and later in *Pravda*.[28] On rereading these articles one has the impression that they were written in a state of breathless euphoria and unbounded optimism. The turmoil of rapid and violent revolutionary changes virtually electrified Kun and suddenly liberated his yearnings for involvement in meaningful action that enabled him to lead large masses of people to overthrow and destroy the old order. Béla Kun's hitherto latent ambitions for leadership and a romantic storming of the fortress of capitalism were to be fully realized and his damaged self-esteem restored.

While in Russia, Kun was not concerned with the domestic aspects of the Russian Revolution, but concentrated on the international implications of the Russian events. Although lacking the necessary background to make valid judgments about the leadership, actual strength, and political determination of the West European and especially the German socialist movement, he boldly prophesied the impending rise of the

26. There is no evidence that Kun had joined the local Bolshevik organization "before June, 1916" as he stated in his Russian Communist (Bolshevik) party membership application in 1921. In fact, it is doubtful that Kun had had an opportunity to meet anyone from Tomsk before the winter of that year when he spent two months in the city hospital with a severe lung and asthma condition. Cf. my *Béla Kun*, pp. 55 ff. According to an old Bolshevik who served as Kun's sponsor to membership in the Bolshevik party, Kun first appeared at the Tomsk district committee "in the middle of 1917." János Nemes, "Kun Béla ajánlói" [Béla Kun's sponsors], *Népszabadság*, 3 May 1966.

27. See my *Béla Kun*, chap. 3.

28. These were later republished in Béla Kun, *Válogatott irások és beszédek* [Selected writings and speeches], 2 vols. (Budapest: Kossuth, 1966), 1:39–96 and in Béla Kun, *Revolutionary Essays* (London: [B]ritish [S]ocialist [P]arty, 1919).

war-weary starving masses of Europe and the inevitable doom of their reactionary governments.[29] Kun might have been a poor prophet insofar as the immediate impact of the Russian October on Germany was concerned, but he certainly was a good "visceral Marxist" in placing implicit faith in the revolutionary potential of the Spartacist "active minority" committed—in Engels's phrase—to "make their own history." Will to power and determined leadership were crucial variables in Kun's blueprint for a permanent revolution in Europe.

Overemphasis on the subjective factors of a revolution[30] and neglect of the underlying historical, socioeconomic, and political realities was characteristic of Kun's political style and subsequently became his greatest political asset and liability. This attitude, though proving immensely helpful in his and his party's struggle prior to seizing the "commanding heights of power" in Hungary, turned into the worst kind of handicap when Kun attempted to consolidate the achievements of the Communists and the left Socialists after the successful coup in March, 1919, in Hungary. For Kun the entire phenomenon of revolution was either an end in itself or simply an incremental development within the cataclysmic whole of the permanent revolution.

The pains Kun took to elaborate on a scenario for the seizure of power were in sharp contrast with his virtual neglect of contingency planning for the postrevolutionary period. This dichotomy was reminiscent of an anarchosyndicalist's blind faith in the inherent ability of the victorious proletariat to overcome all difficulties upon overthrowing the capitalist state. As *Pravda*'s resident expert on German and Central European affairs in the spring and summer of 1918, and as the leader of the newly established Hungarian Section of the Russian Communist (Bolshevik) party, Kun's revolutionary optimism ultimately led him to a simplistic blueprint for a social revolution in Europe. His plans may be reconstructed as follows: first, the proletariat, driven by starvation would resort to general strikes to protest its condition and to advance its economic and political demands; second, the government would be compelled to suppress organized dissent with the help of the military. This, in turn, would lead to a "disintegration of the discipline of the army, which is made up of masses of urban and rural workers," hence to mutinies and an armed uprising. Third, rebellious soldiers would join forces with the armed proletariat, overthrow the government, destroy its bureaucracy, and launch a social revolution. This process when completed would climax in the fourth stage, that is, in the establishment of the dictatorship of the proletariat.[31]

When applied to Hungary, this fit into a two-stage scheme of revolution. The first stage was to be "nationalistic and anti-German" in character (involving, no doubt, Hungary's secession from the Dual Monarchy without, however, abandoning the

29. "Will There Be a Revolution in Germany?" *Sibirskii Rabochii* (Tomsk), Dec. 1917. Also in Kun, *Válogatott írások*, 1:47–50.

30. This phrase is used here in a "Leninist sense" and it implies a historical turning point when the "people are no longer *willing* to abide by the rule of the old order" and the ruling classes "are no longer *able* to uphold their power in the old way" (objective condition). Emphasis added.

31. Béla Kun, *Mit akarnak a kommunisták?* [What do the Communists want?], 3rd Hungarian ed. (Budapest: A Kommunisták Magyarországi Pártja, 1919).

chauvinistic petty *bourgeoisie*'s claim for the continued Magyar control over the nationalities), while the second stage would combine elements of nationalism and the revolutionary *élan* of the proletariat. At the end both would culminate in a social revolution.[32]

Although one may fault Kun's neglect of vastly complex social problems in favor of a sweeping action program, his suggestion regarding the combination of nationalism and revolutionary spirit was a brilliant insight into the dynamics of the current Russian and future Central European revolutions. Kun was also correct in sensing the crucial importance of the lower middle classes for the launching and eventual stabilization of a revolution led by the proletarian minority. Yet, when it came to drawing tactical conclusions from his essentially sound formula of nationalism *cum* revolutionary fervor he proved to be a dogmatic Marxist (and surely a poor Leninist): "The proletarian dictatorship that betrays a readiness to make concessions to the lower middle class is threatened with destruction."[33]

Kun's intellectual transformation from orthodox social democracy to revolutionary bolshevism was an uneven and contradictory process. He did not know enough Russian to appreciate the subtleties of Lenin's arguments and was also removed from the Bolsheviks' day-to-day policy dilemmas. Therefore, Kun's understanding of the post-October situation in Russia was, of necessity, quite superficial and was moreover limited to the external implications of the Russian Revolution. Compared to the leading Bolsheviks, Kun's grasp of Marxist theory, especially its economic aspects, was quite rudimentary; hence, after his return to Hungary, he was unable to conceptualize and apply the lessons of the momentous changes that he had witnessed in Russia. Apart from his well-known failure to imitate Lenin's policy of distributing the land to the peasants in Hungary, Kun also ignored the record of the Bolsheviks' prudently gradualist economic policies in the early transition period. That is, instead of selective socialization of the means of production, involving only large scale enterprises, Kun unhesitatingly advocated a program of full-scale nationalization to "control production" and the introduction of rationing to "eliminate commerce" and to "control consumption." Obviously, this maximalist program bore little resemblance to the realities of Russia, and, a year later, even less to the economic problems of Hungary.

The contrast between Kun's inflexible revolutionary prescriptions and what even a casual observer of the Russian scene could infer from the experiences of the first year of Bolshevik rule defies conventional explanations. Kun, however, was a special kind of observer as were the motivations that compelled him to opt for the most extreme solutions both in a personal and ideological sense. When the February revolution liberated him from the rigors of the prisoner-of-war camp, Kun decided to make the most of his newly gained freedom. Socioeconomic turmoil and a vacuum of legitimate political authority in Russia provided him with a unique opportunity to obtain that which had been denied to him in Hungary: virtually unlimited opportunities for personal initiative, for political leadership, power over men and public

32. Béla Kun, "A School for Social Revolution," *Pravda*, 15 May 1918.
33. Béla Kun, "Marx and the Middle Class," *Pravda*, 4 May 1918.

recognition—in short, a chance of becoming somebody of consequence. Kun's hitherto constrained and underutilized talents for agitation, propaganda, and organization suddenly burst forth and propelled him to the general staff of the Russian revolutionary leadership.

Paradoxically, Russia and the Russian people meant very little to Kun. He considered the country backward and its people primitive and barbarian compared to Central Europeans in general and Hungarians in particular. Lacking any emotional attachment to the scene of his first revolutionary exploits, Kun regarded the entire affair as a dress rehearsal to the real "textbook" revolutions that were to come in Europe.

Although party historians tell us that Kun spent many hours with Lenin discussing future revolutions, judging from Kun's activist disposition and personal style, it is more likely that Kun perceived his relationship to Lenin as perhaps that of a father and son—at least in his mind. Later events tend to bear out this hypothesis: whenever the need arose in Hungary, Kun freely used Lenin's authority to enhance his leadership in the Communist party and to justify his policies in debates in the soviet republic's Revolutionary Governing Council. On the other hand, he did not hesitate to ignore many ironclad rules of Leninism (such as caveats against premature insurrections, alliance with the Socialists, inflexible foreign policy, etc.), and, at times, going as far as to misinform his mentor about the actual state of affairs in Hungary. When some of his schemes backfired, he was anxious to justify himself before Lenin by blaming the Socialists for the Hungarian Soviet Republic's internal failures, Entente imperialism for the military defeats, and Christian Rakovsky's "intrigues" for the frustrated Russian breakthrough to Soviet Hungary. At the end he pronounced the entire Hungarian working class guilty of abandoning him and his revolution. It is doubtful that Lenin really accepted these lame excuses of his flamboyant Hungarian disciple. However, in these years actions and results rather than impeccably orthodox phraseology and painstakingly prepared political blueprints mattered for the leader of the world revolution.

Béla Kun and the March Action of 1921

The next stage of Kun's political career began with his arrival as a political exile in Austria in August, 1919. He left Hungary bitterly disappointed with the working class which had failed to fulfill its historical mission of collective political and spiritual emancipation. In Kun's mind, the Hungarian Communists had been cheated out of the well-deserved fruits of their victory by an insufficiently class-conscious proletariat, a wavering middle class, a hostile peasantry, treacherous trade-union bureaucrats, vengeful Czechs, Serbs, and Rumanians and, in a way, by the Russians themselves, who through suspected military mismanagement, if not outright sabotage, had failed to do their share to link up with the besieged revolutionaries in Hungary.[34]

34. George A. Brinkley, *Allied Intervention in South Russia, 1917–1921* (Notre Dame, Ind.: University of Notre Dame, 1966), p. 365 n, quotes V. Vynnychenko, *Vidrozennia natsii*, 2 vols. (Vienna: Dzvin, 1920), 3:321 ff.

Having identified these mitigating circumstances for the defeat in Hungary, Kun sought to establish himself as the authoritative interpreter of the "lessons of Hungary" for the benefit of the Russian and Central European, especially German, proletariat. In view of Kun's discreet silence about his own errors of leadership during the Hungarian Soviet Republic, the advice and political guidance he was about to dispense were helpful and relevant for other countries only to a very limited extent. That is, while the agitation, propaganda, recruitment, and mobilization techniques that Kun developed and employed with stunning success before the March take over might have had wider applicability beyond Hungary, his internal policies and reckless disregard for the country's actual revolutionary preparedness (a major error that he never repudiated) remained, with disastrous results in the March action, a crucial aspect of Kun's political style.

Following a year of confinement in various Austrian internment camps, prisons, and hospital security wards, Kun was granted passage to Russia and arrived in Petrograd on August 12, 1920.[35] As the exiled leader of the second soviet republic in history, Kun now had an air of authority about him, as well as a curious sense of defensiveness concerning his and his party's real and alleged mistakes committed in the process of attempting to translate the Russian revolutionary blueprint to the conditions of another country. He was confident that only a battle had been lost in Hungary and that the war of the world revolution was still being fought on many fronts, providing further opportunities for his personal and political redemption. The latter aspect is worth emphasizing because, in the fall of 1920, Béla Kun was in serious political trouble and was under attack from three different directions.

Former Hungarian prisoners of war who had fought on the Bolshevik side in the civil war—mostly in Siberia and Turkestan—had gained control over the Central Bureau of the Hungarian groups (at the central committee of the Russian party) and had declared the bureau the legitimate successor to the government of the defeated Hungarian Soviet Republic. They were extremely critical of Kun's insufficiently energetic leadership of the Hungarian cause, and demanded in connection with the current Russo-Polish war, that slogans of a "second soviet republic" and "return to Hungary with arms in hand" be issued.[36]

The second group attempting to undermine Kun's political credentials consisted of the Vienna- and Berlin-based Landler faction, which included Lukács, József

35. Cf. "Greetings from the Petrograd Workers to Béla Kun," *Izvestiia Petrogradskogo soveta rabochikh i krasnoarmeiskikh deputatov Aug. 12, 1920*, reproduced in G. D. Obichkin, Henrik Vass, et al., eds., *A magyar internacionalisták a Nagy Októberi Szocialista Forradalomban és a polgárháboruban* [Hungarian internationalists in the great October socialist revolution and in the civil war] 2 vols. (Budapest: Kossuth, 1967), 1:421–22.

36. Personal from Mr. Sándor Kőrösi-Krizsán, a leading member of the "Siberian" faction of Hungarian prisoner-of-war activists in Soviet Russia. See also, "Resolution of the Hungarian Group at the Central Committee of the Russian Communist (Bolshevik) Party concerning the formation of the Revolutionary Committee of Hungary" (dated August 6, 1919), and "Resolutions of the Second National Conference of the Hungarian agitation and propaganda departments at the Central Committee of the Russian Communist (Bolshevik) Party" (Sept. 26–29, 1920) in Obichkin et al., eds., *A magyar Internacionalisák*, 2:315–16 and 439–50.

Révai, Rudas, Lengyel, János Hirossik, and many others. This group had been recruited from members of the right and left opposition to the Kun-led center during the soviet republic. They maintained that to a considerable extent, Kun and his methods of leadership had been responsible for the defeat, and he was therefore unworthy of remaining as the party's leader and sole spokesman in Moscow.[37]

Thirdly, by virtue of his close association with Zinoviev and Bukharin, Kun was vulnerable to the exigencies of internal Bolshevik struggle for power and factional rivalry for Lenin's and the central committee's support. Subsequent developments suggest that as early as 1920, at least, Trotsky, Rakovsky, and perhaps even Stalin were unimpressed with Kun's exaggerated personality and political style; hence it may be assumed that it was in Kun's best interests to do his utmost not to incur the wrath of these formidable Bolsheviks.

Anxious to silence his critics, Kun plunged into frenzied activity immediately after his return to Russia. Within a period of six weeks, he launched a project to revolutionize the Hungarian-speaking workers of America,[38] called an all-Russian conference of former Hungarian prisoners of war for the purpose of reorganization and reindoctrination, delivered a long speech at the First Congress of the Peoples of the East,[39] spoke to the Petrograd soviet reporting on that congress,[40] wrote several articles for *Pravda*, *Vörös Ujság*, and *Proletár*[41] and an introduction to a volume on the lessons of the Hungarian Soviet Republic.[42]

"Idle tongue wagging," Kun's favorite phrase when attempting to evade serious discussion, did not satisfy him while there was a civil war in progress a few hundred miles from Moscow. He requested and received an assignment on the southern front, and on October 1 obtained a commission as a member of that front's Revolutionary Military Council (*revvoensovet*) under the famous civil war hero M. V. Frunze.[43] Whether it was the irresistible lure of excitement, adventure, and opportunity for personal heroism that only the battlefield could offer, or a practical way of escaping

37. The specifics of the Landler group's case may be found in various issues of *Proletár* (Vienna) and *Vörös Ujság* (Vienna and Berlin) between the fall of 1920 and the spring of 1922.

38. Béla Kun, "Egységes Kommunista Pártot az Únióban!" [For a united Communist party in the United States. Letter to Hungarian workers in America], *Proletár* [Proletar] (Vienna) 1, no. 15 (1 Oct. 1920) [letter dated 19 Aug. 1920].

39. Text in *Kommunisticheskii Internatsional, Pervy S"ezd Naradov Vostoka. Stenograficheski Otchet.* [First Congress after the Peoples of the East. Stenographic minutes] (Moscow: Izdatel'stvo Kommunisticheskogo Internatsionala, 1920), pp. 174–86.

40. *Kun Memoirs*, p. 292.

41. Including "Protivniki Sovetskoi Rossii" [The enemies of Soviet Russia], *Pravda*, 15 Aug. 1920, and "Miről mesél a lengyel front a magyar katonáknak" [Message of the Polish front for Hungarian soldiers], *Vörös Ujság* (Moscow), 26 Sept. 1920.

42. Béla Kun Introduction and Epilogue, in *Mit mond a III. Internacionálé a magyarországi proletárforradalomról* [The Third International on the Hungarian proletarian revolution] (Moscow: OKP Magyar Agitációs Osztályai Központi Irodája, 1920). This volume represented the first of the several rescue missions undertaken by Béla Kun's Comintern patrons to defend him from his factional enemies in the Hungarian party.

43. For the text of the Supreme Revolutionary Military Council's order concerning Kun's appointment, see Obichkin, Vass, et al., *A magyar internacionalisták*, 2:483.

Comintern and Hungarian party intrigues, Kun's dispatches suggest that he thoroughly enjoyed the experience and was exhilarated by his martial activities.44

Kun's participation in Frunze's campaign to overcome Peter N. Wrangel's forces in the southern Ukraine and Crimea became notorious on the strength of two exploits. The first involved a one-man mission through White lines to arrange for a temporary truce with anarchist leader Nestor I. Makhno whose troops could have jeopardized the security of Frunze's and Semën M. Budenny's cavalry units then engaged in mop-up operations behind the southern front. The fearless and resourceful Kun succeeded not only in securing Makhno's neutrality but actually obtained the Anarchists' active cooperation to the planned anti-Wrangel drive.45

Because of this agreement and at the cost of some appalling bloodletting on both sides, Frunze's army occupied the Crimea by mid-November, 1920.46 Frunze then was reassigned to another front, and Béla Kun was named chairman of the Crimean soviet in charge of both civilian and military forces on the peninsula. At that point, in violation of the general amnesty Frunze had promised to all White officers who voluntarily surrendered, Kun rounded up ten to twenty thousand officers and men and a great number of Makhnovites and ordered their execution by firing squad or drowning in the sea.47 All reliable informants agree that this atrocity was the greatest blunder of Kun's soviet political career. Hardened Bolsheviks, who did not hesitate to send thousands of men to certain death on the battlefield or in the service of the world revolution, were appalled to hear that Béla Kun (a foreigner and a Jew) had had the temerity to order the execution of Russian soldiers, many, if not most of whom could have been persuaded to join the Red Army, fight in the civil war, and ultimately become useful citizens of Soviet Russia. In the minds of many Bolsheviks, including Trotsky, Stalin, and Lenin,48 Kun was a bloodthirsty maniac, a coward, and a fool who tried to make up for the Hungarian Red Army's poor showing in 1919 by a senseless massacre a year later in Crimea.49

44. *Kun Memoirs*, pp. 293–96.

45. Cf. G. P. Maximoff, *The Guillotine at Work. Twenty Years of Terror in Russia* (Chicago: The Chicago Section of the Alexander Berkman Fund, 1940), pp. 124–26.

46. For the text of Kun's draft report for *Pravda* and *Izvestiia TsiK* on the impending occupation of Crimea, see Obichkin, Vass, et al., *A magyar internacionalisták*, 2:490–92 and *Kun Memoirs*, p. 296.

47. "Béla Kun in the Role of Super-Executioner," *Sotsialisticheskii Vestnik* (Berlin), 1921, no. 2 (26 Feb. 1921), quoted in Maximoff, *Guillotine at Work*, pp. 124 ff.

48. According to Borkenau, "Lenin was notoriously beside himself, as he rarely was, when he heard of the massacre." Franz Borkenau, *The Communist International* (London: Faber & Faber, 1938), p. 115.

49. I am indebted to Dr. Tibor Szamuely of the University of Reading for information concerning the Soviet leaders' reaction to the Crimean events and their subsequent evaluation of Béla Kun as a man and a revolutionary. Additional evidence of the official disapproval of Kun's actions in Crimea may be gleaned from a 1930 edition of a documentary collection that failed to mention Kun's name in connection with the southern campaign in the fall of 1920. Cf., A. Gubovski, et al., eds., *Razgrom Vrangelia. Sbornik Statei* [The routing of Wrangel. A documentary collection] (Moscow: Gosudarstvennoe Izdatel'stvo, 1930). Kun's own version was uncharacteristically reticent on the details of his Crimean activities. Cf., "Az ellenforradalom végzete" [The fate of the counterrevolution], *Proletár* Vienna) 2, no. 5(32), (3 Feb. 1921).

Zinoviev, Bukharin, and Karl Radek, Kun's political patrons and factional confederates in the Comintern Presidium, apparently were not adversely impressed by the hotheaded Hungarian's latest blunder. On the contrary, Kun was exactly the man they needed to carry out the Left's plan for the bolshevization of the Communist party of Germany (KPD) and the engineering of a proletarian uprising in Germany.[50] The planned action was a part of the Communist International's concerted drive to enforce compliance with the "Twenty-One Conditions of Admission to the Communist International" by leaders of major European left socialist and communist parties. These parties were to undergo a dialectical, and indeed organizational, split into a reformist and revolutionary segment before the proletariat could reunite and lead the inevitable social revolution throughout Europe.

The Bolshevik left's "theory of the revolutionary offensive" (which incidentally was fully endorsed by Kun's Hungarian factional opponents) was designed to facilitate this process through direct intervention by special emissaries into the internal affairs of foreign socialist and communist parties.[51] Zinoviev's famous speech before the German Independent Socialist (USDP) conference in Halle that led to that party's breakup was one example of this kind of Comintern interference. Mátyás Rákosi's and Christo Kabakchiev's mission at the Italian socialist's Leghorn conference was similar: they were to promote a split between the Geacinto Serrati-led majority and Amadeo Bordiga's extreme left minority in order to create a Moscow-controlled, revolutionary avant-garde in Italy.

Paul Levi, the German Communist (KPD) representative at the Leghorn conference, was shocked by the Comintern's ruthless behind-the-scenes intrigues, and upon his return to Germany he denounced in the party press both the "notorious Hungarian and Bulgarian exiles" and their masters in Moscow as well.[52] Levi's public opposition to Comintern-sponsored artificial splits and reckless slogans climaxed in a confrontation in the KPD central committee between the supporters (Heinrich Brandler, Paul Froelich, August Thalheimer, etc.) and the opponents (Paul Levi, Klara Zetkin, Ernst Dàumig, et al.) of the Comintern executive's extreme strategy. After considerable debate, the central committee approved, with a vote of twenty-eight to twenty-three, of Rákosi's and Kabakchiev's conduct at Leghorn and endorsed the Comintern's theory of the revolutionary offensive. The subsequent resignation of Levi, Zetkin, and several others, though leaving Zinoviev's men at the helm, threw the KPD into disarray and rendered it unable to perform normal operations let alone the launching of a revolutionary offensive.

50. On the background of the March action, see Werner T. Angress, *Stillborn Revolution* (Princeton, N.J.: Princeton University Press, 1963); Richard Lowenthal, "The Bolshevization of the Spartacus League" in David Footman, ed., *International Communism, St. Anthony's Papers*, no. 9 (Carbondale, Ill.: Southern Illinois Press, 1960); Helmut Gruber, "Paul Levi and the Comintern," *Survey* (London), Oct. 1964, no. 53; Ruth Fischer, *Stalin and German Communism* (Cambridge: Harvard University Press, 1948), and Bernard Reichenbach, "Moscow 1921. Meetings in the Kremlin," *Survey* (London), Oct. 1964, no. 53.

51. Cf. Branko Lazitch, "Two Instruments of Control by the Comintern: The Emissaries of the ECCI and the Party Representatives in Moscow," in Milorad M. Drachkovitch and Branko Lazitch, eds., *The Comintern: Historical Highlights* (New York: Praeger, 1966), pp. 45-65.

52. Ibid., pp. 275-82.

Under these circumstances, the Comintern faithfuls in Germany were understandably in dire need of experienced leadership of the kind that only the seasoned Russian comrades could provide. Since Zinoviev and Bukharin were needed in Moscow and, because of his recent visit in Berlin, Germany did not seem to be a safe place for Radek, Kun appeared to be the logical choice as the Comintern representative to guide the embattled KPD *Zentrale* in Berlin. The choice of Kun as described here may tend to oversimplify the matter into a process of elimination or into a Zinoviev-led conspiracy to effect a revolutionary breakthrough in Germany.[53] Yet Kun's credentials seemed impeccable at that time. Lenin himself, in commenting on the first issues of *Kommunismus* (edited by Lukács, Rudas, and Kun in Vienna in 1920), although critical of Kun's leftist tendencies, had endorsed his evaluation of the German situation adding that "I could not have written a better criticism [of the German leadership]."[54] Therefore, it must be assumed that Lenin had been fully consulted and approved of Zinoviev's candidate for the delicate mission. Actually, in view of the obvious similarities between some aspects of the German situation in the spring of 1921 and that of Hungary in the months preceding the March coup, and Kun's brilliantly successful strategy in exploiting the latter, the Communist International really had no better man for this task.

Although Richard Löwenthal suggests that Kun's selection, on the eve of his departure for Germany, for membership in the Small Bureau of the Comintern executive was a "programme,"[55] it seems more likely that Kun's mandate, beyond the strategic task of the German party's bolshevization, was open-ended, permitting him to use whatever tactics he considered appropriate to produce the desired results. While it is doubtful that Kun was expressly authorized to launch an armed insurrection, the logic of Kun's tested formula—in fact, the *only one* he was capable of producing—to escalate the "subjective conditions for a revolution" into an open confrontation and attempt to overthrow the bourgeois government, must have been obvious to Zinoviev and Lenin even before they dispatched him to Germany.[56]

Béla Kun's team of Comintern instructors consisted of one Pole, August Guralski, and ten German-speaking Hungarian Communists. The Hungarians had been recruited from among Kun's personal friends, former prisoner-of-war activists from Siberia, and Kun's factional allies from Vienna. They were József Pogány, Ferenc

---

53. Ruth Fischer argues that the Kun mission had been "concocted by Zinoviev and Béla Kun" who had obtained "a secret mandate from a caucus and probably was not endorsed by the Politburo," Ruth Fischer, *Stalin and German Communism*, pp. 174–75.

54. V. I. Lenin, " 'Kommunismus'—Journal of the Communist International for the Countries of South-Eastern Europe," *Works*, 4th ed., 40 vols. (Moscow: Progress Publishers, 1950–1966), 31:165–67.

55. Lowenthal, "Bolshevization of the Spartacus League," p. 58.

56. That Kun was not about to stop halfway in Germany was made clear in an article written for the second anniversary of the death of Karl Liebknecht and Rosa Luxemburg: "Where this anniversary is still the time of torment and of grasping for a revolution, the next one will be that of victory and revenge over the murderers of Liebknecht and Luxemburg," *Vörös Ujság* (Moscow) 3, no. 2 (16 Jan. 1921). Kun's fellow delegate to Germany, József Pogány, was even more explicit in his article "Let us be Prepared for a Civil War" that he had written about two months before the March action; see *Proletár* (Vienna) 2, no. 7(34) (17 Feb. 1921).

Münnich, Ernő Lipschitz, Dezső Szilágyi, László Pollacsek, Ottó Steinbruck, Richárd Dornbusch, Sándor Krizsán, Ernő Müller, and Nándor Weisz.[57] Divided into three groups and traveling clandestinely, these men left Moscow for Germany in late February, 1921, to save the KPD from the dangers of parliamentarism and petty bourgeois opportunism and to lead it to a proletarian revolution.

Berlin in March, 1921 must have seemed to Kun as a stage set for a replay of the revolutionary drama of Budapest in early 1919. All the props for the successful repetition of the previous performance were there: the country had been defeated in the war; inflation, growing unemployment, and demands for staggering reparation payments crippled the nation's economy; the majority socialists were losing working-class support to the Independent Socialists and Communists; and, above all, the now predominant activist majority of the KPD *Zentrale* began to develop the "will to power."[58] Thus, in Kun's estimate Germany was ripe for a revolution. The next task was to persuade the still hesitant German Communist leaders to act on Kun's blue-print for a revolution.

These apparent similarities between Berlin and Budapest could be extended as far as Kun's political techniques were concerned. As in November, 1918, in Hungary, when Kun had succeeded in uniting scattered leftists groups into a Communist party after ten days of negotiations, promises, persuasion, and bribery, Kun now approached every incumbent of the central committee and certain former members like Klara Zetkin with approximately the following argument: the German working class, betrayed by the majority socialists and misled by the remaining Independents, was ready and expected, nay demanded, that under the flag of Karl Liebknecht and Rosa Luxemburg the KPD lead them out of the current economic, political, and military chaos; this would be accomplished by a radical sharpening of class struggle to which the army would respond by triggering an armed uprising, climaxing in a proletarian revolution. The German initiative would be inevitably followed by similar events in France, Italy, Central Europe, and the Balkans. The impending Silesian plebiscite, which might result in the loss of German territories to Poland, would precipitate a wave of nationalist resentment and probably lead to a war with Poland, and thereby to the necessity of a military and political alliance with Soviet Russia. In addition to the above line of reasoning, Kun probably also appealed to the German Communists' sense of proletarian internationalism in demanding immediate action to relieve the Russian party of capitalist pressures while in the midst of suppressing the Kronstadt uprising that threatened the very existence of Soviet rule in Russia.[59]

---

57. *Kun Memoirs*, p. 297, and personal from Mr. Sándor Kőrösi-Krizsán to whom I am indebted for a great deal of first-hand information on the background and the Berlin story of Béla Kun's revolutionary team.

58. On Kun's strategy and tactics under comparable circumstances in early 1919 in Budapest, see my *Béla Kun*, chaps. 5-6.

59. Julius Braunthal, *History of the International*, vol. 2, *1914-1943* (New York: Praeger, 1967), 226-28; Angress, *Stillborn Revolution*, p. 120 ff; Stanley Page, *Lenin and the World Revolution* (New York: New York University Press, 1959), p. 189, and Lowenthal, "Bolshevization of the Spartacus League," pp. 58-59.

The Comintern plenipotentiary's message was received by Zetkin and Levi with a mixture of disbelief and outright hostility. To them Kun appeared to be either mad or, worse still, an irresponsible adventurer, and an advocate of a senseless *Putsch* to conjure up a revolutionary situation in a country whose proletariat was tired of revolutions, especially the kind directed from abroad.[60] According to Boris Nicolaevsky, Kun also tried to win over the prominent Polish Communists, Adolf Warski and Paul Lapinski, who happened to be in Berlin at that time. When both categorically rejected his proposed strategy, Kun accused them of cowardice ("Sie haben Ihr Herz in den Hosen") and of inability to analyze the situation "in the Bolshevik way."[61]

Unlike these skeptical Communist veterans, members of the recently bolshevized KPD *Zentrale*

were primarily concerned that the KPD, under new management, would no longer be a do-nothing party, but a party of action, and that it would daringly lead the lethargic German workers out of the bondage of capitalist exploitation.[62]

There must have been an immediate rapport between the *Turkestaner*, as Levi labelled Kun, and his newly found activist friends in the German party. Although he was not known to have attended the KPD central committee's conference of March 16–17, the project of a nationwide general strike and armed insurrection finally adopted by this meeting bore the unmistakable Kun trademarks of haphazard planning, wishful thinking, and a blind urge to bring the simmering conflict to an immediate climax regardless of the cost.[63]

The Prussian government's last minute decision to occupy Saxony to prevent further lawlessness in that area was all that Kun needed to issue ringing denunciations of a "counterrevolutionary plot" and "police provocation"; and, in the party daily *Rote Fahne*, he called on the proletariat to arm themselves in self-defense. The German workers, however, were not impressed and failed to heed the left Communists' instructions. The inventive Kun and his friends were at first considering mock abductions or public assassination of Communist officials to break the ice of working-class apathy. In the end, neither isolated acts of terrorism nor even pitched battles between the Communist-led strikers and the police in Prussian Saxony brought

60. For Levi's version of these events, see his subsequently published polemical pamphlets: *Unser Weg wider den Putschimus* (Berlin: Seehof, 1921), and *Was ist das Verbrechen? Die Märzaktion oder die Kritik daran?* (Berlin: Seehof, 1921). Klara Zetkin's recollections are less clear on this point; cf. Klara Zetkin, *Reminiscences of Lenin* (London: Modern Books, 1929), pp. 25–26.

61. Boris Nicolaevsky, "Les premieres années de l'Internationale Communiste, d'après le recit du 'camarade Thomas,'" in Jacques Freymond, ed., *Contributions à l'Histoire du Comintern* (Geneva: Librarie Droz, 1965), p. 25; Victor Meric, *Coulisses et Treteaux, À travers la jungle politique et littéraire*, ser. 2 (Paris: Librarie Valois, 1931), pp. 69–77, republished in *Est & Ouest* (Paris), 16–31 Oct. 1957, no. 18, pp. 13–15.

62. Angress, *Stillborn Revolution*, p. 115.

63. Both the slogans and the attempts to create an artificial crisis were similar to the last detail to Kun's tactics in Hungary in the weeks preceding the central committee's detainment on February 21, 1919.

Kun and his confederates closer to a violent, hence presumably more revolutionary version of the bloodless seizure of power two years earlier in Hungary.[64]

Thus, spurned by rank-and-file Communists, the powerful trade-unions, the majority socialists, the Independents, the "greatest *Bakunist* Putsch in history,"[65] as Paul Levi put it, collapsed after ten days of frenzied attempts to revolutionize Germany.[66]

The human toll of the ill-fated *Putsch* included 3,470 imprisoned, 145 dead, and an undetermined number of wounded workers. The mastermind behind the fiasco took refuge in the Reichstag office of one of the Socialist deputies (where the premises were protected by parliamentary immunity) and fled Germany thereafter. The rest of Kun's revolutionary advisory team was left to its fate (there are haunting similarities between Kun's abandonment of his comrades in August, 1919, and April, 1921), and its members were picked up one by one from various coffeehouses, nightclubs, and brothels by the Prussian police which had kept them under surveillance from the day of their arrival.[67]

In early April, Lenin requested Kun's immediate return to Moscow. Shortly after what must have been a trying air trip from Germany or Latvia, Kun reported to Lenin. A former Comintern insider reports that "Lenin breathed fire and flames" at the hapless Hungarian. Upon leaving Lenin's office, Kun had a heart attack and collapsed on the street.[68]

On the General Staff of the World Revolution: Béla Kun in the Comintern (1921–34)

Béla Kun's career as a leading *apparatchik* of the Communist International could not have begun under less auspicious circumstances than the Third Comintern Congress of June–July, 1921. Despite its lengthy agenda, the congress was preoccupied with the evaluation of the March action and the Zinoviev-Bukharin-Radek-Kun-Thalheimer, et al., "theory of revolutionary offensive" that had laid the ideological groundwork for the German fiasco. For the second time in two years Kun was expected to provide an explanation for the failure of a revolution that he had instigated.

However, at this time, unlike in 1919, Kun was able to share the blame with his senior Comintern colleagues, including Lenin. It appears that on further reflection the latter must have decided that Kun had been an unwitting tool of the Bolshevik left and also was in no physical condition to stand up to public criticism at the forthcoming congress; hence the entire matter was to be resolved first within the Russian party, and only later between the united Comintern leadership and the sorely divided German Communists.

64. Cf. *Die Internationale* 2, no. 24 (24 June 1920).

65. A pun on the name of Béla Kun?

66. For an excellent description of the events of the short-lived March action, see Angress, *Stillborn Revolution*, pp. 137–66.

67. Thanks to the intervention and legal counsel of Dr. Kurt Rosenfeld, an attorney and an Independent Socialist Reichstag deputy, the lesser members of the Kun team were released and expelled from Germany after six to eight weeks of detention. (Personal from Mr. Sándor Kőrösi-Krizsán.)

68. Nicolaevsky, "Les premiers années," p. 26.

In his letter to Klara Zetkin and Paul Levi, Lenin readily conceded that "the representative of the Executive Committee defended a very leftist stupid tactic by immediately claiming: 'so as to help the Russians'—this representative often used to be too leftist,"[69] but later he generously defended his impulsive disciple's revolutionary credentials:

[the theory of the revolutionary offensive] . . . is an illusion, it is nothing but romanticism. It is for this reason that it was fabricated in the "land of poets and dreamers" with the aid of my dear Béla, who also belongs to a poetically gifted nation and who considers himself more left than the left. . . . For the time being we will listen more to Marx than to Thalheimer and Béla, although Thalheimer is a good, well-trained theoretician and Béla is an excellent and faithful revolutionary. The Russian Revolution continues, after all, to teach more than the German "March Action."[70]

These charitable words notwithstanding, Lenin went to great lengths to prevent Kun from being heard at the congress and actually ordered Zinoviev to give the task of delivering an unspecified report not to Kun but to Otto V. Kuusinen.[71]

Kun's public silence, however, did not inhibit several delegates from closely scrutinizing the "lessons" and the perpetrators of the March events and drawing uncomplimentary conclusions about Putsches in general and about hotheaded leftists in particular.[72] György Lukács, the spokesman for Kun's factional opponents in the Hungarian party, although refraining from directly attacking Kun and actually endorsing Lenin's overall evaluation of the matter,[73] proved rather conclusively that the March action had been masterminded by ideological illiterates who could not differentiate between theory and practice, and had not understood the Communist party's proper role in a revolutionary situation.[74]

69. V. I. Lenin, "Letter to Klara Zetkin and Paul Levi," in Leninskii Sbornik [Lenin Miscellany], 36 vols. (Moscow: Gosizdat, 1959), 36: 222.

70. Klara Zetkin, Reminiscences of Lenin, quoted in Helmut Gruber, International Communism in the Era of Lenin (Greenwich, Conn.: Fawcett Publications, 1967), p. 351.

71. V. I. Lenin, "Letter to Zinoviev," in Leninskii Sbornik, 36: 259. Published proceedings of the Third Congress of the Communist International do not include any report by Kuusinen either. Cf. Protokoll des III. Kongresses der Kommunistischen Internationale (Moskau 22. Juni bis 12 Juli 1921) (Hamburg: Hoym, 1921).

72. Cf. the proceedings of the second, third, fourth, seventh, eighth, eleventh, and thirteenth session in Protokoll des III. Kongresses, pp. 47–220, 301–34, 485–526, and 568–622. Lenin quite explicitly disowned Kun's "leftist stupidities" and counseled against the "illness" of nervousness and impulsiveness in situations comparable to those preceding the March action in Germany. See Leninskii Sbornik, 36: 278–80.

73. ". . . the March Action was a great step forward, in spite of the mistakes of its leaders." V. I. Lenin, "Speech in Defense of the Tactics of the Communist International," Works, 32: 473.

74. Cf. Protokoll des III. Kongresses, pp. 591–94. Trotsky, speaking before the Moscow party organization during the Third Congress, placed the matter in a more specific perspective: "Only a traitor could deny the need for a revolutionary offensive; but only a simpleton would reduce all revolutionary strategy to an offensive." Leon Trotsky, The First Five Years of the Communist International, 2 vols. (New York: Pioneer Publishers, 1945), 2: 28–29.

Thanks to Zinoviev's and Radek's repeated intercessions on his behalf and also to Lenin's willingness to write off the case as one resulting from the Comintern's collective failure to adjust to the receding of the postwar revolutionary tide, Béla Kun rode out the storm with little apparent loss of power in the Comintern and in the Hungarian party. As a member of the Comintern's powerful Small Bureau, he was in a position to silence his critics in the German party[75] and also to prevent the increasingly bitter Landler faction from obtaining a fair hearing before the executive committee.[76]

His adversaries in the Hungarian party, however, stubbornly refused to abide by the spirit of the Third Congress and immediately after returning to Vienna renewed their anti-Kun campaign on a considerably expanded scale.[77] Landler, Lukács, Rudas, Hirossik, Albert Király, Lengyel, Révai, Hamburger, and Bettelheim controlled the central committee, had contacts with the underground movement in Hungary, and, with much justification, considered themselves more in touch with the real problems of the party than the two-time loser Kun under Zinoviev's wings in Moscow. Members of this group were particularly incensed when they were told to stop their "Hegelian rubbish" and return to Hungary for illegal work.[78] Since previous attempts to revive the party had ended with the apprehension of the central committee's liaison men and usually led to mass arrests, Kun's opponents were understandably suspicious of the real motives behind such instructions.[79]

As Kun's luck would have it, some of the Berlin-based members of the Landler faction were alleged to have established contacts with an improbable group of Communist outcasts including Levi, Dr. Heinrich Laufenberg, Fritz Wolffheim, Herman Gorter, Pannekoek, and Seratti and began repeating some of *their* criticisms of the Russian-dominated Communist International.[80] To make matters worse, the Landlerites, in protest against the Comintern-appointed interim central committee that had been weighted in Kun's favor, resigned from the executive committee, issued an

75. Cf. Béla Kun, "Ot Sektanstva k Kontr-Revolutsii (K voprosu o Kommunisticheskoi Rabochei Partii Germanii) [From sectarianism to counterrevolution; concerning the problem of the KAPD], *Kommunisticheskii Internatsional*, 3, no. 18 (1921):4621–42.

76. Immediately after the Third Congress Kun succeeded in silencing the theoretical journal *Kommunismus* (Vienna), controlled by the Landler faction and, a month later, in persuading the "impartial" (Bukharin, Thalheimer, Radek) Comintern commission to adjudicate the Hungarian dispute in Kun's favor. Cf. *Die Tätigkeit der Exekutive und des Präsidiums des E.K. der Kommunistischen Internationale vom 13 Juli 1921 bis 1 Februar 1922* (Petrograd: Verlag der Kommunistischen Internationale, 1933), pp. 51, 104–5; "To the Communist Party of Hungary," *Bulletin of the Executive Committee of the Communist International* (Petrograd), 2 Sept. 1921, no. 2, pp. 47–49.

77. Cf. Jenő Landler, "A világkongresszus legfontosabb tanulságai" [The most important lessons of the world congress] *Proletár* (Vienna) 2, no. 39(66) (30 Sept. 1921). See also, "A magyar kommunisták gyászos szereplése a moszkvai kongresszuson" [The Hungarian Communists' sorry performance at the Moscow congress], *Az Ember* [The Man] (Vienna) 4, no. 33 (14 Aug. 1921):7–8.

78. Béla Kun "A pártszervezés kérdései" [Questions of party organization], *Vörös Ujság* (Moscow), no. 23 (15 Jan. 1921).

79. These misgivings were made public in "Pártügyek" [Party business], *Proletár*, 2, no. 8(35) (24 Feb. 1921), and *Az Ember*, 27 Feb. 1921, p. 16.

80. "Leszámolás az ellenzékkel! Beszámoló a munkásságnak!" [Squaring accounts with the opposition. A report to the working class], *Proletár* 2, no. 48(75) (1 Dec. 1921).

oppositionist newspaper *Vörös Ujság*, and led the entire full-time party *apparat* (about seventy men and women) on a political strike.[81] Under these circumstances, Kun could not have found it difficult to persuade members of the Small Bureau to reaffirm his position as the Hungarian party's rightful representative in Moscow and to initiate disciplinary measures against his "unprincipled" foes in Vienna.[82]

Kun's position was further strengthened by the arrival of about four hundred Communists who had been in Hungarian prisons and were sent to Russia in exchange for several hundred prisoner-of-war officers who had been held as hostages for this purpose. Kun saw to it that these wretched men were properly appreciative of his contributions to their release and immediately employed some of them (Dezső Bokányi and György Nyisztor) as his character witnesses in the Communist press. Later on he dispatched them to serve as lay judges at a political show trial designed to liquidate the remaining Social Revolutionaries in Russia.[83]

Though no match for Kun's newly gained constituency in Moscow, the Landlerites still persisted and again questioned the wisdom of Kun's and the Comintern executive's unwarranted meddling in the Hungarian party's internal affairs. All this could have been ignored had it not been for Ernst Reuter (Friesland), the oppositionists' newly found ally in the German party, who publicly reminded the KPD *Zentrale* of the March fiasco, and, by implication, of the man who had been responsible for it.[84] Friesland's involvement in the affair, the unfavorable publicity generated by the defection (or disappearance) of Endre Rudnyánszky, Kun's confidant and Bukharin's brother-in-law, with a considerable sum of Comintern money, the opposition's public appeal to the Comintern to reconsider its earlier judgment, and the publication of two books by members of the Landler faction highly critical of Kun, finally forced Zinoviev to reopen the case.[85]

A three man subcommittee consisting of Bukharin, Anatol' Lunacharskii, and Grigorii Sokolnikov was appointed to study the Landlerites' allegations and to make appropriate recommendations to the Presidium of the Comintern. The committee's final report found that "the charges concerning political irresponsibility ... betrayal

81. "Ifjumunkás-csoportalakitás Bécsben" [Formation of a young workers' group in Vienna], *Proletár*, 1 Dec. 1921.

82. Cf. *Die Tätigkeit der Exekutive*, pp. 255, 289, and 389.

83. Cf. György Nyisztor, "Miért lettem kommunista?" [Why I became a Communist], *Proletár*, 1 Dec. 1921; "A fegyházból kiszabaditottak és a kommunista párt" [The liberated men and the Communist party], *Proletár* 2, no. 52(79) (29 Dec. 1921).

87. Elemér Mályusz, *The Fugitive Bolsheviks* (London: Grant Richards, 1931), pp. 155–156; Béla Kun, "Emigrációs Mocskolódás" [Emigration mudslinging], *Proletár* 3, no. 4(83) (26 Jan. 1922). See also, Angress, *Stillborn Revolution*, pp. 207–16.

85. The books in question were: Henrik Ungar [Henrik Guttman], *Die Magyarische Pest in Moskau* (Leipzig-Zürich-Vienna: Pegasus, 1921), and Ernst Bettelheim, *Zur Krise der Kommunistischen Partei Ungarns* (Vienna: n.p., 1922). The third book by László Rudas, *Abenteuer und Liquidatorentum: Die Politik Béla Kuns und die Krise der K.P.U.* (Vienna: n.p., 1922), appeared too late for purposes of the requested Comintern investigation. According to Sándor Kőrösi-Krizsán, Rudnyánszky was then a Comintern courier sent to Vienna with gold coins and jewelry earmarked either for the Austrian or for the Hungarian party. The Landler faction's public appeal to the Comintern Presidium was published in *Vörös Ujság* (Vienna), 25 Jan. 1922, and an investigation commission was appointed in late January; cf. *Die Tätigkeit der Exekutive*, p. 389.

...allegedly too hasty departure after the fall of the soviet government...[and]... mismanagement of public funds...collapsed after the first probing...[and]... proved untenable in every respect."[86] Although these conclusions were seconded by five other members of the executive committee (Kuusinen, Boris Reinstein, Zetkin, Henryk Walecki, and Jakob Fries), Kun must not have been fully exonerated because four days later when he was proposed for membership in the Presidium, he requested to have the nomination withdrawn and someone else appointed in his stead.[87] But shortly thereafter the executive committee expelled two of the anti-Kun pamphleteers from the party, transferred Rudas to "other work," stopped subsidies to all Hungarian Communist newspapers in Vienna and ordered the disbanding of the entire Landler faction.[88]

From the aforementioned and generally from the record of foreign Communist leaders at the Communist International, several conclusions may be drawn that could explain Béla Kun's rather unique predicament in Moscow in these and subsequent years. It may be argued at the outset that a foreign Communist's standing and political influence in the Comintern hierarchy depended on several factors, many of which were unrelated to his native ability, ideological sophistication, and knowledge of the international scene. Some of these extraneous, but in Moscow, critically important factors were:

1. The nature of the foreign Communist's access to leaders of the Soviet party and to key members of the Comintern *apparat*;
2. The ability to stay out of internal Soviet power struggles and to judge correctly and early enough the outcome of such disputes;
3. The military, economic, or political importance of a country whose Communist party the foreigner represented to the Soviet Union;
4. The strength and effectiveness of such parties in carrying out Comintern directives and satisfying Soviet expectations associated with that country;
5. The foreign Communist's ability to prevent factional activities in his own party from impairing the party's operational effectiveness at home and/or his rivals from gaining private access to the CPSU leadership over the incumbent representative's head.

Béla Kun's Soviet political career began under the sponsorship of Bukharin, Radek, and Zinoviev in early 1918. These men, more so than Lenin, taught him almost

86. *Die Taktik der Kommunistischen Internationale gegen die Offensive des Kapitals* (Hamburg: Hoym, 1922), pp. 96-97.

87. Ibid., p. 143. Rumor had it that Landler had circulated copies of the opposition memorandum among all members of the executive committee and that the ECCI's unfavorable reaction forced Kun to withdraw his candidacy. Mályusz, *The Fugitive Bolsheviks*, p. 163.

88. *Bericht über die Tätigkeit des Präsidiums und der Exekutive der Kommunistischen für die Zeit vom 6. März bis 11 Juni 1922* (Hamburg: Hoym, 1922), pp. 5-7. According to one source, members of the Landler faction were not allowed to leave Russia for six months to prevent their possible sabotage of these measures. Mályusz, *The Fugitive Bolsheviks*, p. 164. This is corroborated by the reappearance of the Landler opposition in the form of a shortlived newspaper *Vörös Ujság* (Berlin) that was first published in October, 1922—exactly six months and ten days after the March ECCI decision.

everything he was to know about Bolshevik strategy and tactics. The Kun-engineered soviet republic in Hungary, despite its failure, represented a major propaganda contribution to the Bolsheviks' cause and it was this service that became Béla Kun's moral and political capital in the years to come. His relationship with Zinoviev and Bukharin was based on a mixture of personal compatibility, similar political temperament, and mutual political advantage insofar as certain Comintern projects were concerned. While it was these Bolsheviks and some left German Communists who should be credited with devising the "strategy of the revolutionary offensive," the execution of the first test case, i.e., the March action, was destined to fall to Kun—a man well qualified for the task and also in dire need of a political comeback after the Crimean events. Due in equal measure to Zinoviev's continued support and Lenin's willingness to write off the March fiasco as an unfortunate accident in the ideologically sound campaign of bolshevization of the Communist International, in the fall of 1921, Kun still seemed to wield a great deal of power in Moscow.

As political and economic instability (or revolutionary conditions) gradually receded in Europe, the Comintern was obliged to reassess its hitherto extreme leftist strategy and tactics which had proved singularly unproductive in the previous two years. In early 1922, therefore, the slogan of the "united front from below" was issued, calling for a broad nonrevolutionary alliance between the Communist parties and workers' parties affiliated with the Second and Two-and-One-Half Internationals.[89] From this it clearly followed that the successful implementation of this new directive required the kind of Comintern leadership that had not been directly compromised by recent leftist adventures, such as the March action. Thus, apart from the Landler faction's determined efforts to discredit Kun before his Russian political allies, his very presence on the highest Comintern councils in charge of the new tactical line and his well-known activist disposition could have jeopardized the entire operation; hence, he suddenly became a political liability as far as the Soviet leaders were concerned.[90]

According to Irén Kun, "in April 1922, Lenin asked Kun whether he would be interested in party work in the Urals." She adds that "Lenin's decision had been prompted by the unwillingness of certain Hungarian emigrant groups to cease their campaign of slander against Béla Kun. In fact, this [campaign] had assumed greater and greater dimensions. Lenin wisely thought that responsible work in the Russian party would occupy Kun's attention . . . [and] would be the best weapon against factional slander."[91]

This explanation, however, failed to mention that Kun's Siberian assignment came about after the Soviet government had attempted to send the entire Kun family to Stockholm, ostensibly for reasons of health—a plan that had run aground on the

89. Text of appeal in Gruber, "Paul Levi," pp. 362–71. See also, Jane Degras, "United Front Tactics in the Comintern 1921–1928," in Footman, *International Communism*, and Milorad M. Drachkovitch and Branko Lazitch, "The Communist International," in Milorad M. Drachkovitch, ed., *The Revolutionary International* (Palo Alto, Calif.: Stanford University Press, 1966), pp. 159–202.

90. Béla Kun, "Die Kommunisten und die Gewerkschaften," *Jugend Internationale*, 1921, no. 4, pp. 90–92.

91. *Kun Memoirs*, p. 335.

Swedish government's refusal to issue visas for the notorious revolutionary.[92] One can only guess why the Soviet government chose to send Kun to Stockholm and not to the Black Sea or some other health resort for treatment of his chronic asthma and more recent heart condition. The choice of Ekaterinburg in the Urals indicates other motives. We may surmise that perhaps it was not only Béla Kun's physical, but political health that required a cure.

Béla Kun's appointment as the head of the agitprop department of the Ural Bureau of the Russian Communist (Bolshevik) party suggested that the exciting days of stage-managing revolutions were over for him; it also marked the beginning of a new career of a special kind in the Comintern and in the Russian party.[93] That is, while most foreign Communist leaders functioned solely as representatives of their parties in Moscow, others such as the Finnish Kuusinen, Hungarian Varga, Ukrainian Dimitrii Z. Manuilskii, German Walter Ulbricht, Italian Palmiro Togliatti, Bulgarian Georgi Dimitrov, and, for a time, Louis Oscar Frossard, Jules Humbert-Droz, Willi Münzenberg, Kun and many less well-known Communists served, in effect, as the Russian party's representatives on various Comintern councils with occasional interruptions for assignments in the Soviet party and government.[94]

It was these assimilated and more-or-less Russified international-revolutionary bureaucrats who saw to it that Soviet interests were protected in the Comintern and that Soviet foreign policy objectives were fully supported by all foreign Communist parties. The required qualifications for this kind of work included absolute loyalty to the Russian party's current leadership, lack of an independent power base in one's "native" party (or its lack of power potential, often as a result of being outlawed), versatile skills in carrying out a wide range of assignments from bureaucratic house-keeping chores to personal involvement in dangerous missions abroad, an enormous capacity for sustained work, and the ability to make politically correct decisions in the intrigue-ridden, psychologically taxing atmosphere of the Comintern headquarters in Moscow.

92. *Leninskii Sbornik*, 36:473.

93. For more of Kun's activities in Ekaterinburg, see *Kun Memoirs*, pp. 337 ff.

94. For a comparative analysis of the career patterns of these prominent Comintern activists, the following works seem helpful: Carola Stern, *Ulbricht: A Political Biography* (New York: Praeger, 1965), esp. pp. 19–48; Giuglio Serriga, *Togliatti e Stalin: Contributio alla biografia del segretario del PCI* (Milan: Sugar editore, 1961); Renato Mieli, *Togliatti, 1937* (Milan: Rizzoli editore, 1964); László Tikos, *E. Vargas Tätigkeit Als Wirtschaftanalitiker und Publizist* (Tübingen: Bohlau Verlag, 1965); Angelica Balabanova, *My Life as a Rebel* (New York: Harper, 1938); A. Balabanoff, *Impressions of Lenin* (Ann Arbor: University of Michigan Press, 1964); Branko Lazitch, *Lénine et la IIIe Internationale* (Neuchâtel and Paris: Editions de la Baçoniere, 1951); Eudocio Ravines, *The Yenan Way* (New York: Scribners, 1951); E. Castro Delgado, *J'ai perdu la foi a Moscoú* (Paris: Gallimard, 1950); Arvo Tuominen, *Kremls Klockor* (Helsinfors: Söderstrom, 1958); Ypsilon [Karl Volk and J. Humbert-Droz], *Pattern for World Revolution* (Chicago: Ziff-Davis, 1947); Louis-Oscar Frossard, *De Jaurés à Lenine* (Paris: Bibliotheque de Documentation Sociale, 1930); Babette Gross, *Willi Münzenberg: Eine politische Biographie* (Stuttgart: Deutsche Verlags Anstalt, 1967); Margaret Buber-Neumann, *Kriegsschauplatze der Weltrevolution* (Stuttgart: Seewald Verlag, 1967); John H. Hodgson, *Communism in Finland* (Princeton, N.J.: Princeton University Press, 1967), esp. chap. 5. Also, "Comintern Reminiscences," *Survey* (London), April–June 1960, no. 32, pp. 109–15; "Remembrance of Things Past," *Survey*, Oct. 1964, no. 53, pp. 3–164.

Proceeding from this admittedly sketchy typology of Comintern elites,[95] we may now focus on the situation of Béla Kun as a special kind of Comintern *apparatchik*. The relevant memoir literature is unanimous in suggesting that Kun always seemed to be zealously loyal to his immediate political patrons, and, when they faded into the background at the end of the succession struggle of 1924–28, to the Russian party's Secretary General, Stalin. After a false start of siding with Bukharin against Lenin in the Brest Litovsk debate,[96] he went along with the Leninist majority at the Third Congress, attacked Trotsky on Stalin's and Zinoviev's behalf after 1924,[97] was one of the first foreign Communists to disown Zinoviev in 1926, and demanded Trotsky's punishment in 1927.[98] Although he failed to publicly criticize Bukharin in 1928–29, he was an early champion of Stalin after the Fourteenth Russian Party Congress in 1925. In fact, Kun's servile obeisance to Stalin and ruthless zeal in implementing the Russian party's decisions earned him in Comintern circles the unenviable notoriety of being considered one of the most unscrupulous political hatchet men in Moscow.[99]

Viewing the matter from a different perspective, it seems clear that Kun's constant display of unswerving loyalty to his superiors was—apart from specific personality factors about which more will be said later—the logical outcome of the Hungarian party's remarkably unsuccessful performance while under his nominal leadership between 1919 and 1935. While it did not help matters that the Communist party of

95. There is a dearth of systematic information in the available literature of the Communist International on the sociology and the psychology of the international Communist revolutionary elites as unique groups of versatile ideologues, development theorists, revolutionary strategists, and propagandists in the period between the two world wars. The following studies seem appropriate for purposes of constructing a composite picture of Comintern elite behavior and identifying the ingredients of a "personality-and-politics"-type model applicable for individual Comintern activists: Harold D. Lasswell and Daniel Lerner, *World Revolutionary Elites* (Cambridge, Mass.: The MIT Press, 1965), especially Lasswell's introductory essay (pp. 3–28) and George K. Schueller on the Soviet Politburo (pp. 97–178); Nathan C. Leites, *A Study of Bolshevism* (Glencoe, Ill.: The Free Press, 1953); Philip Selznick, *The Organizational Weapon* (New York: McGraw Hill, 1952); Harold D. Lasswell, Nathan C. Leites, et al., *The Language of Politics* (New York: George Steward, 1949); Jules Monnerot, *Sociology and Psychology of Communism* (Boston: Beacon, 1953); Robert C. Tucker, *The Soviet Political Mind* (New York: Praeger, 1963), especially pp. 145–65; Frank S. Meyer, *The Moulding of Communists* (New York: Harcourt, Brace and World, 1961), especially pp. 9–26; Alexander Dallin, "The Use of International Movements," in Ivo J. Lederer, ed., *Russian Foreign Policy* (New Haven: Yale University Press), pp. 311–50; E. Victor Wolfenstein, *The Revolutionary Personality: Lenin, Trotsky, Gandhi* (Princeton, N.J.: Princeton University Press, 1967).

96. Michael Károlyi, *Memoirs* (New York: Dutton, 1957), p. 159.

97. Cf., Béla Kun, "Die Ideologischen Grundlagen des Trotzkismus," *Die Kommunistische Internationale*, 1962, no. 1, pp. 9–33.

98. On the Hungarian party being the first to come to the aid of the threatened Stalinists in Russia, see "A Zinovjev-Trotzki blokk és a Komintern" [The Zinoviev-Trotsky bloc and the Comintern], *Uj Március* (Vienna) 2, no. 10 (Oct. 1926): 597, and Kun's statement before the Presidium of the Communist International in *International Press Correspondence* 7, no. 68 (1 Nov. 1927): 1531–32.

99. Fischer, *Stalin and German Communism*, p. 493; Ivan Karaivanov, *Les Hommes et les pigmées* (Belgrad, 1963), p. 56, cited in Branko Lazitch, "Les écoles de cadres du Comintern," in Freymond, *Contributions à l'Histoire du Comintern*, p. 251. Boris Souvarine, "Comments on the Massacre," in Milorad M. Drachkovitch and Branko Lazitch, *The Comintern*, p. 182, further elaborated on in M. Souvarine's letter of March 14, 1968, to the author.

Hungary was unable to fulfill Moscow's expectations concerning its underground activities (and compelling Kun to begin practically every plenary and congressional speech with an abject apology for his party's failures), it was the Landler faction's political and personal vendetta (whose intensity and longevity must have been unique in the history of a European Communist party)[100] that rendered Kun politically vulnerable to hostile criticism and left him, in effect, entirely at the mercy of his whimsical Russian masters.

Probably more in self-defense than for any other reason, Kun attempted to build up a constituency for himself both in Russia and abroad. Since the Landler faction controlled the underground party and Kun's personal emissaries were invariably apprehended by the disturbingly well-informed Hungarian police, after 1928 Kun lost touch with the new generation of native activists[101] whose actual leadership gradually slipped into the hands of several groups of non-Muscovite intellectuals and extreme left sects of industrial workers. Inside Russia, Kun's potential constituency included two or three thousand "old Bolshevik" Hungarians (i.e., former prisoner-of-war veterans of the civil war who chose to remain in Russia), a few score of Hungarian émigré writers, government bureaucrats, personal protégés in the Comintern, and a few prominent Russian and foreign communists—Iosif A. Piatnitskii, Waldemar Knorin, Grigorii K. Ordzhonikidze, Sergei I. Gusev, Nadezhda K. Krupskaia, Klara Zetkin, Walecki, Lapinski, and perhaps Palmiro Togliatti.[102] However, even in Russia he was regarded with enmity by the three Szántó brothers, defectors from the Landler camp, and, for various personal reasons, by two prominent individuals, Jenő Varga and György Lukács.[103]

Unlike many of his contemporaries in the Hungarian party, Béla Kun was a remarkably prolific journalist, an energetic organizer, a tireless and talented administrator, and an extremely effective public speaker who always threw himself into the

100. As late as 1934 Kun felt compelled to slander the former Landlerite György Lukács. Béla Kun, "The International Importance of Stalin's 'Foundations of Leninism,'" *International Press Correspondence* 14, no. 37 (29 June 1934):960-61; Ervin Sinkó, *Egy regény regénye* [Novel of a novel] 2 vols. (Novisad: Forum, 1961), 1:199.

101. This much was clear to the Russians by 1929. Cf. "Otkrytoe pis'mo k chlenam Kommunisticheskoi Partii Vengrii" [Open letter to members of the Communist party of Hungary], *Kommunisticheskii Internatsional* 11, no. 46-47(224-25) (1929):66-73. This is further corroborated in "A KMP Központi Bizottságának levele a párt tagjaihoz" [Letter of the central committee of the HCP to all party members], György Borsányi and Friss, eds., *Dokumentumok a Magyar Forradalmi Munkásmozgalom Történetéből, 1929-1935* [Documents from the history of the Hungarian revolutionary working class movement] (Budapest: Kossuth, 1964), pp. 82-89.

102. On Béla Kun's Hungarian and Comintern constituency in Russia, see Kun *Memoirs*, passim; Sinkó, *Egy regény regénye*, especially vol. 2; Ferenc Münnich's introduction to *Kun Béla a Magyar Tanácsköztársaságról* [Béla Kun on the Hungarian Soviet Republic] (Budapest: Kossuth, 1958), pp. 7-33; Béla Illés, "Emlékezés Kun Bélára" [Reminiscing of Béla Kun], *Élet és Irodalom* [Life and Literature], 17 Feb. 1961; Béla Illés, "Kun Béla és a szépirodalom" [Béla Kun and the belles lettres], *Kortárs* [Peer], March 1960, pp. 357-63; László Pollacsek, "Emlékezés Kun Bélára," *Magyar Nemzet*, 16, 17 Feb. 1966, and issues of *Sarló és Kalapács* (Moscow) for 1930-36.

103. Personal from Tibor Szamuely (London) and Gyula Háy (Brissago, Switzerland). Detailed documentation on this point will be provided in my forthcoming study, "The Communist Party and the Hungarian Left, 1920-1944."

thick of work both in the Comintern and in the Hungarian party. Although most of his writings—about 18 monographs, 250 articles, and 120 interviews and recorded speeches—originating from this period may be dismissed as shallow journalism designed to serve petty factionalist ends or to promote the "cult of Stalin's personality," one is impressed by the rapid broadening of his intellectual horizons and the wide range of his political, literary, and scientific interests. After a few attempts to engage his intellectual betters (Trotsky, Bukharin, Varga, and Lukács) in arguments on Marxist theory and Leninist practice, Kun chose to follow Radek's footsteps in attempting to establish himself as a kind of "mailed fist" of Comintern orthodoxy vis-à-vis the European (especially German and Austro-Marxist) socialist critics of Russia, the Socialist International, suspected deviationists in Central European Communist parties and the enemies of Soviet Russia at home and abroad.[104] Since he lacked Radek's stylistic brilliance, devastating wit, and theoretical profundity, Kun as a theorist was not taken seriously and was regarded as Stalin's tool both by his friends and enemies. Towards the end, he was given routine editorial chores, the writing of introductions to propaganda tracts and to nostalgic memoirs on the Hungarian Soviet Republic.

Between 1921 and 1934 Béla Kun, as a senior Comintern bureaucrat, was entrusted with diverse responsibilities: he served as an editor of *Inprekorr* and *Kommunisticheskii Internatsional* (1921–2?), as the Russian party's representative at the Komsomol Central Committee (1923–24), head of the Comintern's AgitProp Department (1924–26), head of the project to translate Lenin's *Works* into foreign languages (1925–27?), founder of the Comintern's Lenin School (1925), a lecturer there and at the Communist Academy (1926–34), head of the Balkan Secretariat (1930?–36?), leading spokesman on "problems of social fascism," and a member of the International Control Commission at various times.[105]

Between 1926 and the summer of 1928, Kun was on leave for full-time work in the Hungarian party. This necessitated clandestine trips to Vienna, Prague, and Berlin that lasted from three to four months each time. Although the Hungarian party failed to show noticeable improvement while under Kun's personal stewardship, we may surmise that he was more successful in his behind-the-scenes activities in helping to usher the Czechoslovak and Austrian parties into the Stalinist fold. Due to a conspiratorial mishap, Béla Kun and György Lukács (who voluntarily tried to intercede with the authorities on his behalf) were arrested by the Austrian police in late April, 1928, on charges of traveling under assumed names and illegally entering

104. For a rather incomplete bibliography of Kun's writings, see Béla Kun, *Válogatott írások*, 2:467–512.

105. Cf. *Kun Memoirs*, pp. 349–53, 365; Günther Nollau, *International Communism and World Revolution* (New York: Praeger, 1961), pp. 75, 133–35, 190. Béla Kun's involvement in the affairs of various European Communist parties has been determined from a content analysis of his speeches and published writings between the sixth and the thirteenth plena of the Comintern Executive (Feb. 1926–Nov. 1933) as published in the form of stenographic records and/or in *Imprecorr*, one of the four editions of *The Communist International*, and in the Hungarian party's theoretical journals, *Uj Március* and *Sarló és Kalapács*. See also, Jane Degras, ed., *The Communist International, 1919–1943*, vol. 3, 1929–1943 (New York: Oxford University Press, 1965), pp. 264, 276, 287, 292, and 371.

Austria.[106] After several weeks of much publicized legal proceedings, Kun was released and arrived in Moscow in time to be present at the Sixth Congress of the Communist International. To prevent the recurrence of an anti-Soviet propaganda campaign, similar to the one generated by Kun's adventures in Vienna, it was decided that in the future he would not be permitted to participate in any foreign missions involving clandestine activities.[107]

Years in the Death Row (1934–39)

The gradual erosion of Béla Kun's influence in the Communist International began in 1929 with a Stalinist historian's re-evaluation of the ideological significance of the Hungarian Soviet Republic of 1919.[108] The study in question maintained that the leaders of that revolution had failed to observe several elementary rules concerning correct Leninist tactics of alliances (thus, the Communist-Socialist merger was a "right opportunist" step) and economic policies (refusal to implement a land reform as an example of "ultra-leftism").[109] According to the author, there was "a clear parallel between the practical mistakes of the Hungarian Communists and the theoretical errors of Rosa Luxemburg." Consequently, citing Stalin's definition of the requirements for a "genuine dictatorship" ("the class alliance of the proletariat and the masses of working peasants"),[110] the Soviet historian concluded that in the absence of any such alliance one "cannot talk about the dictatorship of the proletariat in Hungary in 1919."[111]

Although Kun attempted to counter this argument in various commemorative articles and also through semipopular booklets written by junior members of his entourage,[112] this essentially negative evaluation became a part of the Stalinist version of Comintern history as well as a major political and psychological liability as far as the revolutionary credentials of Béla Kun and his fellow exiles were concerned.

In view of these menacing developments, Kun was compelled to make a choice between continuing to defend his and his party's record—an exercise that had proven futile in the German party for such diverse leaders as Levi, Brandler, and Heinz Neumann—and irrevocably committing himself to Stalin and his policies in the Comintern. For at least two reasons Kun chose the latter alternative. First, by simply

106. Willi Schlamm, "The Spectre of Communism is Haunting Europe! The Arrest of Béla Kun in Vienna," *International Press Correspondence* 8, no. 25 (3 May 1928): 479.

107. Mrs. Kun hinted that her husband considered this ban as undeserved political punishment rather than a measure to protect his personal safety.

108. V. Miroshevskii, "Vengerskaia Sovetskaia Respublika" [The Hungarian Soviet Republic], *Proletarskaia Revolutsiia*, 1929, no. 11(94).

109. Ibid., p. 74.

110. Cf. J. V. Stalin, *Voprosy Leninizma* [Problems of Leninism] (Moscow: Gosizdat, 1928), p. 173.

111. Miroshevskii, 'Vengerskaia," p. 82.

112. Pavel Hajdu, *Kak Borolas' i Pala Sovetskaia Vengriia* [How Soviet Hungary fought and fell] (Moscow: Moskovskii Rabochi, 1931); Iosif Lengyel, *Istoricheskii Reportazh* [Historical report] (Moscow: Sovlit, 1933); Mózes Kahana, *Taktika* [Tactics] (Moscow: Molodaia Gvardiia, 1933); E. Andich, "Vengerskaia Sovetskaia Respublika" [Hungarian Soviet Republic], *Istorik Márksist*, 1932, no. 4–5; and the special fourteenth anniversary issue of *Uj Március* (Vienna), 1933.

staying on his job, as did many of Stalin's defeated but live rightist opponents in 1930–31, he could have been biding his time in the hopes that the disastrous collectivization drive and the widespread famine would arouse the Russian central committee into openly opposing and eventually replacing Stalin.[113] Other than not wishing to share the fate of the disgraced Zinoviev, Bukharin, et al., the second somewhat paradoxical, but intellectually plausible reason for Kun's decision was his basic sympathy with Stalin's extreme leftist approach toward the European, particularly the German, social democracy after 1928. The re-emergence of the so-called objective conditions for a revolution in Europe during the Great Depression promised, if nothing else, a revival of the Comintern's early activist strategy and tactics and new opportunities for leadership and power for the hitherto sidelined veterans of earlier Comintern revolutionary attempts abroad.

If the above hypotheses are correct, then we can see why Kun must have been bitterly disappointed at Stalin's easy accommodation with Nazi Germany at the cost of abandoning the Germany Communist party and quashing the hope of a proletarian revolution in that country. After his emotionally charged attacks on nazism, fascism, and the "social fascist" European Socialist parties,[114] Kun found it impossible to adjust quickly enough to the Comintern's new popular front strategy when it was first discussed in the summer of 1934.[115]

By this time Kun was too deeply committed to and, in effect, became a captive of the logic of his notoriously extremist oratory, the momentum of which drove him along with Piatnitskii, Knorin, and a few other old Bolsheviks into resisting Stalin's sacrifice of revolutions abroad on the altar of collective security and rapprochement with fascist dictators. One wonders, therefore, whether these defiant words, written

113. Robert Conquest, *The Great Terror* (New York: Macmillan, 1968), pp. 27–38.

114. *Mezhdunarodnoe Polozhenie i Zadachi Kommunisticheskogo Internatsionala* [The international situation and the tasks of the Communist International], *X. Plenum Ispolkoma Kominterna* [Proceedings of the Tenth Plenum of the executive committee of the Comintern], 2 vols. (Moscow: Gosudarstvennoe Izdatel'stvo, 1929), 1:84–93, and 2:76, 102–3, 158–95, and 206; *Kompartii i Krizis Kapitalizma, XI. Plenum IKKI Stenograficheskii Otchët* [Communist parties and the crisis of capitalism. Stenographic minutes of the Eleventh Plenum of the executive committee of the Communist International], 2 vols. (Moscow: Partiinoe Izdatel'stvo, 1932), 1:329–31, 338–39, 574–79, and 2:117–23; *XII. Plenum IKKI. Stenograficheskii Otchët* [Twelfth Plenum of the executive committee of the Communist International. Stenographic minutes], 3 vols. (Moscow: Partizdat, 1933), 2:117–28, and 3:30–38; *XIII. Plenum IKKI. Stenograficheski Otchët* [Thirteenth Plenum of the executive committee of the Communist International. Stenographic minutes] (Moscow: Partizdat, 1934), pp. 341–55. See also, Béla Kun, "Razvitie Sotsial-Reformizma v Storonu Sotsial-Fashizma" [The development of social-reformism into social-fascism], *Kommunisticheskii Internatsional* 12, no. 29–30(207–8) (1929): 28–33; Béla Kun, "The Second Collapse of the Second International," *The Communist International* 8, no. 17 (1 Oct. 1931):482–92; Béla Kun, *Der Kommunismus im Kämpfe gegen die Sozialdemokratie* (Berlin: "Unsere Zeit," 1933); Béla Kun, "The Second Collapse of the Second International," *The Communist International* 10, no. 10 (1 June 1933):343–50.

115. "Dokumenty G. M. Dimitrova k VII. Kogressu Kommunisticheskogo Internatsionala" [Dimitrov documents concerning the Seventh Congress of the Communist International], *Voprosy Istorii KPSS* 9, no. 7 (July 1956): 88, and "VII Kongress Kommunisticheskogo Internatsionala" [The Seventh Congress of the Communist International], *Voprosy Istorii KPSS* 9, no. 8 (Aug. 1965): 49–31.

a month *after* a nineteen-man Comintern commission had convened to outline a new strategy, were addressed to the German Socialists or to Stalin:

> We Communists will never abandon our principles and tactics—at any price. We shall never approve or give our consent to collaboration between the working class and its class enemy, the bourgeois. We have advocated, we still advocate and always will advocate the revolutionary overthrow of the power of the bourgeoisie, whatever its form, whether it is in the form of fascist power or in the form of capitalist democracy. We stand for the unlimited power of the working class, for the dictatorship of the proletariat, for Soviet power, which can only be established by the application of proletarian violence as an offset to the violence of the bourgeoisie, only by revolution.[116]

The last years (1934–39) of Béla Kun's life in Moscow may be compared to time spent in "death row" awaiting arrest and execution. In elaborating on this statement we might consider some of the reasons that made him eminently vulnerable to the Great Purges.

A recent study of the fate of the Comintern elites in the thirties suggests that of the three groups of foreign Communists—Poles and the Zimmerwald Left; leaders of outlawed Central European, Baltic, and Finnish parties; and thirdly, those of the legal West European and Scandinavian Communist parties—the first two were doomed at the outset.[117] Robert Conquest's major work on the purges, although offering a similar classification, attempts to place the "foreign elements" into a broader framework of Soviet domestic and foreign policy priorities, suggesting that apart from Stalin's viciously xenophobic attitudes toward foreigners, the Comintern had outlived its usefulness as an instrument of Soviet foreign policy and therefore its leaders were eminently expendable.[118]

Proceeding from this argument, we could readily identify several equally plausible reasons that might have led Stalin to liquidate Kun and his fellow Hungarian exiles in Moscow. Some of these—not necessarily in order of importance—included: (1) Béla Kun's past association with Bukharin, Zinoviev, Radek, and several old Bolsheviks who, for reasons of intraparty politics, were also slated to be murdered between 1936 and 1939; (2) Stalin's pronounced dislike of Jews—especially the visceral revolutionary, intelligentsia-types, who could not be depended on to accept unquestioningly Soviet *raison d'état* against that of their native countries; (3) Kun's failure to impress Stalin as a political disciple as loyal, ruthless, effective, and Russified as Dimitrov or Manuilskii, with whom Kun had unsuccessfully competed for Stalin's favors in the late twenties; (4) Kun's inability to coerce the left sectarian activists of his party into genuinely accepting and willingly implementing the Comintern's directives for a

116. Béla Kun, "The Struggle for Unity of Action," *The Communist International* 11, no. 13 (5 July 1934):512.

117. Branko Lazitch, "Stalin's Massacre of the Foreign Communist Leaders" in Drachkovitch-Lazitch, *The Comintern*, p. 141.

118. Conquest, *The Great Terror*, pp. 3–18, 427 passim.

popular front in Hungary;[119] (5) the availability of the Hungarian party opposition as an alternative and perhaps more subservient replacement for the tottering Kun leadership; and (6) Kun's alleged refusal to Nikolai Yezhov's request to denounce Zinoviev and his co-defendants as "enemies of the people" following their trial in 1936.[120]

His widow's memoirs clearly indicate that from the Seventeenth Russian Party Congress on, and certainly after Sergei Kirov's assassination in December, 1934, Béla Kun knew that his days on the staff of the Comintern were numbered.[121]

The narrowing circle of foreign visitors who met Kun in these years found him in a depressed, melancholy, yet strangely defiant mood. László Pollacsek, Kun's former secretary and personal friend, relates that Kun developed interests in modern music, clinical psychology (he was fascinated by Freud), experimental physiology, and foreign languages—especially English, which he started studying shortly after his fiftieth birthday.[122] During his vacations not spent in the Kremlin hospital or in a Black Sea sanatorium, the Kun *dacha* became a haven where homesick Hungarian Communists gathered around a campfire swapping stories about their native land, singing folk songs, and reciting from memory verses of nineteenth-century Hungarian patriotic poets.[123] On another occasion Count Mihály Károlyi, who became a sort of aristocratic fellow-traveler in the thirties, condescendingly describes Kun as "listening for hours to gypsy music from Budapest and recalling with moist eyes the various cafes of the Hungarian capital, for which he had an intense longing."[124]

Béla Kun's gradual transformation from an impulsive revolutionary into an elder statesman in exile had certain poignant aspects, such as the return to his childhood literary hero Sándor Petőfi and his quite explicit self-identification with Lajos Kossuth, the exiled leader of the defeated revolution of 1848–49.[125] Kun's return to Hungary's

119. For a more detailed analysis of the Communist party's difficulties in implementing the popular front policy in Hungary, see my "Popular Front in Hungary," *Journal of Contemporary History*, Special Popular Front Issue (Spring 1970).

120. *Kun Memoirs*, p. 417.

121. Eudocio Ravines, a leader of the Communist party of Peru and a Comintern staff member in the thirties, describes the case of the Hungarian Lajos Magyar (member of the Eastern secretariat and well-known expert on Chinese agriculture and rural sociology) who was one of the first victims of the purge in the Comintern. In response to Manuilskii's accusations of having had contacts with Zinoviev, Bukharin and Kirov's murderer, the deeply shaken and strange-acting Magyar "did not specifically accuse, but . . . made terrible insinuations against the closest friends of Zinoviev Béla Kun . . . two of Bukharin's secretaries . . . the Fin, who called himself 'Martens' . . . who was one of Kuusinen's rivals . . . Chemodanov, president of the Communist Youth International—for whom Manuilsky bore a grudge . . . the old Piatnitsky, and several of the men protected in the Comintern by Zinoviev," see Eudocio Ravines, *The Yenan Way*, pp. 131–32. If Magyar had been put up to this speech by Manuilskii, in exchange for a more lenient treatment when his "case"—stemming from the alleged complicity of some of Magyar's students at the Communist Academy in Kirov's assassination—was considered, then Béla Kun was obviously a marked man as early as December, 1934.

122. Pollacsek, "Emlékezés Kun Bélára."

123. Illés, "Emlékezés Kun Bélára."

124. Károlyi, *Memoirs*, p. 267.

125. Béla Kun, *Irodalmi Tanulmányok* [Literary studies] (Budapest: Magvető, 1960), especially pp. 122–27.

radical revolutionary heritage and the democratic statesmanship of Kossuth might well have been the result of his intellectual reaction to Stalinism[126] or that of a sense of romantic nationalism—a kind of rediscovered intellectual umbilical cord to the radical, nonconformist traditions of his native Transylvania.

A few months after Béla Kun's last public appearance before the Seventh Congress of the Communist International,[127] the executive committee severely censored the Hungarian party for alleged sabotage in failing to implement the popular front policy in Hungary.[128] On May 8, 1936, the Comintern executive dismissed the old central committee and appointed a provisional party executive under Zoltán Szántó. A month later the party's organizations in Hungary were disbanded and were not revived until 1938.[129]

Having lost his nominal leadership over the Hungarian party, Kun then requested Stalin to reassign him from the Comintern, where he had found it "impossible to work with Manuilskii." After turning down Stalin's suggestion to take a year's leave and draft a new program for the Communist International, Kun asked to be appointed as the head of the Red Army's Main Political Administration: "Hitler is going to attack us sooner or later. To prepare the Red Army for an anti-fascist war—that would be my kind of work." "Excellent," said Stalin, but Vlacheslav Molotov objected because "the bearer of such an explosive name cannot be the head of the Red Army's Main Political Administration." Before parting, Stalin offered Kun a staff position in the Russian party's central committee, but left the implementation of the proposition to Yezhov, who, in turn, refused to deal with Kun for several months after this interview. Some time in 1936 Kun was named director of a publishing house, the last official position he was to hold in Russia.[130]

In May, 1937, at the meeting of the executive committee of the Comintern, Manuilskii denounced "citizen Kun" for his disrespectful and subversive attitudes toward Stalin on the basis of a grossly misquoted Comintern circular to the Hungarian party and accused him of having established secret contacts with the Rumanian secret police. According to Arvo Tuominen, the former secretary general of the

126. When Ervin Sinkó visited Kun in 1936, the latter began reminiscing about the events of the Hungarian Soviet Republic and ended the interview with a quotation from Rosa Luxemburg: "The proletarian revolution does not need terror for the attainment of its goals, for it loathes and disdains murder," Sinkó, *Egy regény regénye*, 2:130.

127. For the abbreviated text of Kun's speech before the Seventh Congress of the Communist International, see *International Press Correspondence* 15, no. 36 (17 Aug. 1936): 932–33.

128. Cf. István Pintér and László Svéd, eds., *Dokumentumok a Magyar Forradalmi Munkásmozgalom Történetéböl, 1935–1945* [Documents from the history of the Hungarian revolutionary working class movement, 1935–45] (Budapest: Kossuth, 1964), pp. 35–51.

129. Cf. "Open Letter of the Provisional Central Committee of the Communist Party of Hungary on the Application of the Resolutions of the Seventh Comintern Congress in Hungary," in ibid., pp. 61–64. A recent study on organizational developments in the Hungarian party states that "in the fall of 1936 the Communist International discussed the case of Béla Kun and . . . contrary to its May [1936] decision recalled him from the ECCI and directed him to refrain from maintaining any kind of contact with the Communist Party of Hungary." István Pintér, "A KMP az 1936–1944 es években" [The CPH between the years 1936 and 1944], in Tibor Erényi and Sándor Rákosi, eds., *Legyőzhetetlen Erő* [Invincible power] (Budapest: Kossuth, 1968), p. 108 n.

130. *Kun Memoirs*, p. 417.

Finnish Communist party, Kun went pale and "roared like a mortally wounded lion: This is a terrible provocation, a conspiracy to get me murdered. But I swear I never wanted to insult Comrade Stalin. I want to explain everything to Comrade Stalin himself." Then two NKVD men escorted him out of the room. As far as is known, this was the last time that Béla Kun's "comrades-in-arms"—Wilhelm Pieck, Kuusinen, Togliatti, Klement Gottwald, and Wang Ming—saw him alive.[131]

Béla Kun was arrested in early June—a few days after Stalin's telephone call requesting him to issue a denial of his rumored arrest.[132] As for the rest of the Kun family, Antal Hidas, Kun's son-in-law, a poet and a member of the Soviet Writers' Union, was arrested on January 9, 1938; his wife was arrested on February 23—on the twentieth anniversary of the birth of the Red Army, whose first foreign volunteers had served under her husband at Narva; and his daughter, Ágnes Kun, was detained n 1941 for a shorter period of time.[133]

Béla Kun spent twenty-nine months at the Lefortovo and later in the Butyrka prison. For several months he was brutally tortured but he apparently refused to confess to charges of espionage and Trotskyite conspiracy—charges to which Manuilskii cryptically alluded in his speech at the Eighteenth Russian Party Congress.[134] According to a more recent, unconfirmed bit of evidence, Kun went insane in prison believing his captors to be German Gestapo agents who had infiltrated the NKVD and the Comintern *apparat*.[135] The fifty-three year old founder of the Communist party of Hungary and leader of the first proletarian revolution outside Russia was executed in the Butyrka prison in Moscow, on November 30, 1939.[136]

Conclusions

The preceding consideration of five stages of Béla Kun's career that we might label as "provincial-radical," "adventurer-revolutionary," "revolutionary Putschmaker," "Comintern *apparatchik*," and "elder statesman" sought to establish the basic data with which to analyze the relationship between the man and the circumstances and ideas that made him a revolutionary.

Harold Lasswell suggests that "in a political man, private motives are displaced on public objects and rationalized in terms of the public interest."[137] In searching for "private motives" that might have had a subsequent politicizing effect on Kun the first part of the narrative focused on his family life, school years, and his journalistic

131. Cf. *Est & Ouest* (Paris) 15, no. 293 (1–15 Feb. 1963): 8–9; and Conquest, *The Great Terror*, p. 431.

132. *Kun Memoirs*, p. 418.

133. Cf. Antal Hidas, *A Városligettől a Csendes Oceánig* [From Budapest to the Pacific Ocean] (Budapest: Szépirodalmi Kiadó, 1968).

134. *World News and Views*, 6 Apr. 1939, p. 382.

135. The author has not been able to locate the issue of *Irodalmi Ujság* (Paris) which contains the reminiscences of a Hungarian Loyalist volunteer in the Spanish civil war who heard this story from a drunken NKVD colonel who had been one of Kun's interrogators in prison.

136. Münnich, "Előszó," in *Kun Béla*, p. 31.

137. Harold D. Lasswell, *Psychopathology and Politics* (New York: The Viking Press, 1960), p. 262.

career—that is, on circumstances that might have made a "political man" out of the young Kun.

Among the several *possible* reasons causing his estrangement from the values of his family and political environment, Béla Kun's Jewishness, his intellectual insecurity, and certain of his personality traits seem to be relevant as possible private motives.

Concerning the situation of Jews in Transylvania, it should be noted that it was a region with uniquely well-established traditions of religious tolerance; hence, the isolated and intellectually self-contained *shtetl* settlements of the kind that one could find in Russia, the Ukraine, Lithuania, and Poland simply did not exist in that part of historic Hungary.[138] Thus, in terms of discrimination and status insecurity, the situation of Jews was no worse than that of the Christian Armenians, Lutheran Saxons, and probably better than the Orthodox Rumanians who migrated from the old kingdom to live in Transylvania. In the absence of appreciable external constraints on the Transylvanian Jews' religious freedoms, mobility, and educational opportunities in public and certain Calvinist schools, the conditions that led Julius Martov, Pavel B. Axelrod, and many other Jewish intellectuals in Russia[139] to become professional revolutionaries did not prevail in this eastern hinterland of Habsburg Hungary.

Unlike his Russian contemporaries and future corevolutionists, Kun apparently did not benefit from any kind of systematic religious training. Background of this type would have been imparted through rabbinical interpretation of the great books including the rationalization of the "accepted body of doctrine and ritualistic practices"[140] and the mastering of the dialectical mode of reasoning in applying Talmudic maxims to daily practice. Without these formative spiritual and intellectual influences the young Kun was quite vulnerable to assimilationist pressures from his family and schools. Since the attainment of full-fledged membership in the Hungarian "political nation" required little beyond the mastering of the Hungarian language and superficial endorsement of the country's functional political myths ("thousand-year-old constitution," the romanticized traditions of 1848–49, and the "illegitimacy" of the Compromise of 1867, etc.), Kun's political socialization did not include traumatic experiences of political and religious persecution.

His essay on the "spirit of Transylvania" is clear proof of his enthusiastic identification with the values of his environment. When young Kun entered the Zilah *kollégium*, the political beliefs of anti-Habsburg radicalism and romantic local patriotism of his childhood actually reinforced and were reinforced by the school's nationalistic and rugged nonconformist spirit vis-à-vis Hungary's foreign rulers and the politically conservative Catholic church.

The next step in our analysis would require us to establish some kind of causality between the schoolboy Kun's adolescent romantic patriotism and the antiestablish-

138. One could, however, find such communities in the most backward northeastern counties (e.g., County Szatmár) of Hungary perhaps as late as the turn of the century.

139. Leopold H. Haimson, *The Russian Marxists and the Origins of Bolshevism* (Boston: Beacon Press, 1966), chaps. 1 and 4.

140. Ibid., p. 61.

ment writings and oratory of the nineteen-year-old cub reporter and volunteer trade-union organizer and activist. In the absence of biographic information on these politically crucial years we are unable to produce these missing links and account for the reasons for his break with the accepted pattern of social mobility dramatized by dropping out of the law school after one semester and drifting about for a year.

Since we do not know whether Kun's journalistic career was the result of a pre-meditated choice or of an impulsive decision by a former honors student in literature, we cannot attribute any political significance to this step other than suggesting that it was one of the several career options available to a Jewish Gymnasium graduate at the turn of the century. Having thus eliminated the possibility of insuperable obstacles to social mobility as a possible alienating or politicizing factor, let us turn to the problem of intellectual adequacy confronting Kun as a young journalist.

For a reader of Kun's journalistic output it seems painfully obvious that when he transgressed the reportorial boundaries of local politics, he was on unfamiliar grounds and became vulnerable to charges of dilettantism and distortion of facts. When Kun posed as an *ad hoc* drama critic, economic analyst, or commentator on world affairs (i.e., Budapest and Vienna) and his facts and interpretations were challenged by fellow journalists and conservative editors, his reaction was characterized by readiness to resort to abusive language and physical violence. After his spectacular rise to the editorship of an afternoon tabloid whose owner dismissed him after six months, subsequent efforts to restore his self-esteem as a journalist ended in failure. In the end he settled for full-time work in the local trade-union bureaucracy, the only arena of his native province where his particular talents for radical oratory and political pen-manship were appreciated though never adequately rewarded.

Kun's recurring escapes from conventional modes of problem-solving into frenzied activism represent the third, and, for purposes of this analysis, the most important aspect of his personality make-up as a "political man." Our narrative related several instances of this kind of behavior beginning with a duel with a hostile Kolozsvár editor to Kun's request to be named the chief propagandist of the Soviet Red Army. Whether the displacement of Kun's "private motives" (i.e., anxieties concerning his intellectual competence and general adequacy when confronting complex problems) on "public objects" through intense and emotionally exhilarating involvement in political acts and its "rationalization" in terms of communism, world revolution, and proletarian dictatorship do in fact add up to a psychological profile of a professional revolutionary is difficult to determine on the basis of the incomplete evidence that is presently available to us.

What seems almost certain, however, is that Kun's experiences as a child and a young adult alone did *not* predestine him to become a revolutionary, at least not in the "inevitable" manner that characterized the Russian intellectual-professional revolu-tionaries' road from membership in conspiratorial societies through exile and other forms of political punishment to leading the revolutions of 1905 and 1917. In Kun's case, insofar as it can be determined, neither his early experiences, nor profoundly internalized revolutionary ideologies, but the unique set of circumstances (the peculiar psychological climate of the prisoner-of-war camp in Siberia, the vacuum of recognized political authority in revolutionary Russia, and the virtually unlimited opportunities for self-realization as a leader) that served as catalytic agents transforming Kun's "private motives" into overt revolutionary behavior.

Judging from his articles in the Tomsk press and in *Pravda*, the Russian revolutionary events caught Kun intellectually unprepared yet receptive to the activist implications of the Bolsheviks' revolutionary appeal. Kun sought to overcome the burden of his limited understanding of the full meaning of the Russian internal developments by intense activism—which was a psychologically gratifying but an ideologically meaningless way of "displacing his private motives on public objects." In so doing, however, Kun invariably "overreached" himself. That is, there gradually developed a gap between the level of his activism and his ability to foresee and control the outcome and the implications of his conduct. Kun undoubtedly sensed this and, in an attempt to alleviate his subconscious doubts, he willingly subordinated himself to the leadership of those not beset by such uncertainties. Bukharin, Radek, and Lenin certainly seemed to know *what* they were doing and *why* they were doing it, and these were qualifications that Kun could not claim to possess either in Russia or in Hungary.

Thus, it was this sort of intellectual authority from which Kun derived his political leadership. After his return to Hungary this "residual charisma" was quite sufficient to impress the disorganized forces of the politically homeless Left into forming the Communist party of Hungary. He was also successful in leading the party to power, or rather accepting it when the country's leadership was presented to the Communists, as it were, on a silver platter. When the internal difficulties became overwhelming, the fortunes of the war deserted the soviet republic, and his SOS messages to Moscow failed to produce results, Kun's borrowed authority and his regime collapsed in a matter of days. Other than in certain lucid moments such as the May crisis, his foreign policy speech at the June Congress of Soviets, and his farewell address, it is doubtful that Kun succeeded in "catching up with himself" before his Siberian assignment or temporary exile in 1922–23.

From the foregoing it may be argued that Kun's revolutionary leadership was the product of his self-committing behavior[141] and also that the dichotomy between his activism and consciousness was sufficiently great to disqualify him as a professional revolutionary of the "ideal"—for our purposes—Russian intelligentsia-type.

If not a "true" revolutionary, then what or who was Béla Kun? Our evidence suggests that he was a radical socialist activist with the obvious psychological propensities of a "political man" who, under the cataclysmic influence of the Russian revolutionary events, became a highly visible, supporting actor, cast in a historical drama of world revolution whose dynamics he could neither comprehend nor influence for more than a fleeting moment of the 133-day long Hungarian Soviet Republic. In this

141. "... self-committing behavior may have effects in turn upon a person's attitudes. ... A political actor who adopts a position for expedient reasons may be convinced by his own rhetoric, or ... he may shift his attitudes to accord with his actions in order to reduce feelings of 'dissonance.' " M. Bewster Smith, "A Map for the Analysis of Personality and Politics," *Journal of Social Issues* 24, no. 3 (July 1968):19.

sense and in *this* sense only, Kun was a "hero in history" to whom "we can justifiably attribute preponderant influence in determining an issue or event whose consequences would have been profoundly different if he had not acted as he did."[142] The "elder statesman" Béla Kun, on further reflection, might have agreed with this epitaph.

142. Sidney Hook, *The Hero in History* (New York, 1943), p. 153, quoted in Wolfenstein, *The Revolutionary Personality*, p. 25 n.

List of Contributors

Eva S. Balogh, Department of History, Yale University.

István Deák, Director, Institute on East Central Europe, and Associate Professor of History, Columbia University.

Frank Eckelt, Superintendent of Schools, Putnam Valley, New York.

Joseph Held, Associate Professor, Department of History, Rutgers University.

Alfred D. Low, Professor, Department of History, Marquette University, Milwaukee, Wisconsin.

Zsuzsa L. Nagy, Institute of Historical Sciences, the Hungarian Academy of Sciences, Budapest, Hungary.

Rudolf L. Tőkés, Associate Professor of Political Science, University of Connecticut, Storrs, Connecticut, and Senior Fellow, Research Institute on Communist Affairs, Columbia University.

Gábor Vermes, Assistant Professor of History, University of California at Los Angeles.

Iván Völgyes, Associate Professor of Political Science and Coordinator of Slavic and Eastern European Area Studies, University of Nebraska.

Index

Hadik, János, 30, 32
Hainfeld program, 91
Hajdu, Gyula, 135
Halle, 184
Hamburger, Jenő, 53, 55, 84, 190
Hatvany, Lajos, 49
"Hero in history," 207
Hevesi, Gyula, 97
Hidas, Antal, 203
Hirossik, János, 116, 118, 119, 182, 190
Hitler, 202
Hoarding, 82, 83, 87
Hodža, Milan, 112
Honvéd army, 19
Hoover, Herbert, 151, 154, 155, 156
Hospitals, 73
House of Representatives, 23, 29, 30
House inspectors, 73
Housing conditions, 73
Housing laws, 75
Housing Office, 74
Humanitarian, 61, 72, 142
Humbert-Droz, Jules, 194
Hungarian Bank, 81
Hungarian Communists, 91, 97, 139, 145, 160, 162, 163, 164, 166, 167, 180, 185, 192, 197, 201
Hungarian democracy, 60
Hungarian dictatorship, 158
Hungarian emigrant groups, 193
Hungarian Group of the Russian Communist Party, 90, 119, 159, 178
Hungarian prisons, 191
Hungarian proletariat, 116
Hungarian Red Army, 100, 110, 111, 112, 113, 114, 115, 116, 118, 119, 120
Hungarian republic, 51, 127, 142
Hungarian Revolutionary Governing Council, 104
Hungarian Socialist party, 138, 176
Hungarian Soviet Constitution, 112
Hungarian Soviet regime, 92, 99, 102, 109, 111, 112, 140, 142, 150, 153
Hungarian Soviet Republic, 61, 72, 89, 90, 93, 94, 95, 96, 100, 102, 103, 109, 111, 112, 113, 114, 116, 117, 120, 121, 123, 124, 125, 138, 158, 164, 165, 169, 176, 180, 181, 182, 190, 197, 198, 206
Hungarian Teachers' Union, 65
Huszadik Század, 34, 64
Huszt [Khust], 104

Illegitimacy, 64
Illiteracy, 86
Imperialism, 67, 124, 131, 161, 180
Imprekorr, 192
Income tax, 23, 46, 79
Inflation, 23, 64, 71, 75, 76, 78, 82, 88, 186
Influence peddling, 87

Independence party, 174
Independent Socialists, 186, 188
Industrial districts, 114
Industrial laborers, 78
Industrial production, 83
Industrial proletariat, 82
Industrial society, 72
Industrial workers, 86, 134, 196
Industrialization, 13
Industry, 5, 14, 15, 16, 72, 80
Intellectuals, 7, 23, 27, 34, 35, 49, 55, 175, 196
Internal, 182, 192, 206; affairs, 2, 184, 191; consolidation, 171; policies, 122; rebellion, 168; situation, 134, 135, 150
Internalized value system, 61
Internalized revolutionary ideologies, 205
Internment camps, 13, 181
International, 52, 121, 124, 171, 177
International Brigades, 113, 159
International Control Commission, 197
International proletariat, 138
International revolution, 96, 112, 120, 125, 133, 135
International Socialist Federation, 95, 113
International Soviet Republic, 160
Internationalism, 139
Internationalization, 139
Intervention, 71, 132, 135, 141, 151, 152, 155, 157
Interventionist, 127, 131
Introduction to the Critique of Political Economy, 176
Istria, 18
Italian, 17, 18, 26, 140, 141, 184
Italy, 95, 123, 138, 184, 186
Izvestiia, 137

James, Henry, 153
Janoušek, O. Antonin, 113, 115, 116, 118, 119, 120
Janoušková, Maria, 116
Járás [township], 100, 111
Jászi, Oszkár, 8, 30, 33, 34, 37, 41, 42, 43, 44, 45, 46, 49, 89, 92, 94, 98, 112
Jászai, Samu, 122
Jewelry, 80
Jewish, 172; *Gymnasium* graduates, 205; intellectuals, 204; merchants, 4
Jewishness, 204
Jews, 13, 21, 22, 25, 27, 29, 48, 69, 172, 173, 183, 200, 204
Journalism, 70, 173, 175
Joseph II, 3
Józsefváros, 37
Judaic laws, 172
Junker, János, 106
Justh, Gyula, 33

Kabakchiev, Christo, 184